CAPITALISM AND CLASS POWER

Studies in Critical Social Sciences Book Series

Haymarket Books is proud to be working with Brill Academic Publishers (www.brill.nl) to republish the *Studies in Critical Social Sciences* book series in paperback editions. This peer-reviewed book series offers insights into our current reality by exploring the content and consequences of power relationships under capitalism, and by considering the spaces of opposition and resistance to these changes that have been defining our new age. Our full catalog of *SCSS* volumes can be viewed at https://www.haymarketbooks.org/series_collections/4-studies-in-critical-social-sciences.

Series Editor
David Fasenfest (York University, Canada)

Editorial Board
Eduardo Bonilla-Silva (Duke University)
Chris Chase-Dunn (University of California–Riverside)
William Carroll (University of Victoria)
Raewyn Connell (University of Sydney)
Kimberlé W. Crenshaw (University of California–LA and Columbia University)
Heidi Gottfried (Wayne State University)
Alfredo Saad-Filho (Queen's University, Belfast)
Chizuko Ueno (University of Tokyo)
Sylvia Walby (Lancaster University)
Raju Das (York University)

Capitalism and Class Power

Edited by
Ronald W. Cox

Haymarket Books
Chicago, IL

First published in 2023 by Brill Academic Publishers, The Netherlands
© 2023 Koninklijke Brill NV, Leiden, The Netherlands

Published in paperback in 2024 by
Haymarket Books
P.O. Box 180165
Chicago, IL 60618
773-583-7884
www.haymarketbooks.org

ISBN: 979-8-88890-344-5

Distributed to the trade in the US through Consortium Book Sales and Distribution (www.cbsd.com) and internationally through Ingram Publisher Services International (www.ingramcontent.com).

This book was published with the generous support of Lannan Foundation, Wallace Action Fund, and the Marguerite Casey Foundation.

Special discounts are available for bulk purchases by organizations and institutions. Please call 773-583-7884 or email info@haymarketbooks.org for more information.

Cover design by Jamie Kerry and Ragina Johnson.

Printed in the United States.

Library of Congress Cataloging-in-Publication data is available.

Contents

Acknowledgements VII
List of Figures and Tables IX
Notes on Contributors X

1   Introduction   1
    Ronald W. Cox

2   Class Power and the Military-Industrial Complex in the United States   11
    Ronald W. Cox

3   The Billionaire Dimension of Class Power within Economic Sectors   43
    Rob Piper

4   The Transnational Investment Bloc in the U.S. and Persian Gulf   78
    Mazaher Koruzhde and Ronald W. Cox

5   Fake News and Social Media: Neoliberalism and the Case of Bell Pottinger   108
    Adam D. Hernandez

6   Canadian Imperialism in Caribbean Structural Adjustment, 1980–2000   133
    Tamanisha J. John

7   Corporate Power and the Transition from Lomé to the CARIFORUM-EU EPA   177
    Melissa Boissiere

8   The Necessity of Poverty in the High-Income Countries   207
    Jamie A. Gough and Aram Eisenschitz

9   The Limits of the Concept of Neoliberalism in Action   236
    Bryant William Sculos

10 Corporate Power and Praxis in Critical Scholarship   266
    Ronald W. Cox

    Index   277

Acknowledgements

As editor of this volume, I would like to extend my deepest thanks and appreciation to the contributing authors, who have made this project possible with their dedication and hard work. I have a special relationship with many of the contributors—most of whom I have supervised in their dissertation work at Florida International University, while others I have worked with as editor of the journal *Class, Race and Corporate Power*, which provided the original source material for all chapters included here. The journal represents a collaboration over the past decade between me and the editorial board, specifically managing editor Nelson Bass, politics of culture editor Bryant Sculos, associate editor David Gibbs, and Ransford Edwards, who have each provided me with invaluable work for the journal, ideas for this edited volume, and provocative conversations about the politics informing our work. Editorial board member Raju Das deserves special thanks for making this relationship with Brill and Haymarket possible, and for his valuable contributions in helping us decide what themes and materials to include in our edited book series. I am also extremely grateful to the series editor at Brill, David Fasenfest, who helped guide us through the steps necessary to get this book to publication.

I have had the pleasure of decades-long conversations and collaborations with the following scholars, whose friendship and support have been a great source of inspiration over the years: Daniel Skidmore-Hess, David Gibbs, Jim Nolt, Bruce Cumings, Rick Tardanico, Paul Warren and Tom Ferguson. My work with graduate students at FIU has provided a steady stream of insights and suggestions, especially my recent conversations with Political Science PhD student Joshua Gold. I have also benefited from working with Tamanisha John, Mazaher Koruzhde, Sylvan Lee, Clarence Dodge, Michael Wartenbe, Melissa Boissiere, Rob Piper and Adam Hernandez, several of whom have chapters in this volume.

My colleagues in the Department of Politics and International Relations have been a steady source of support, encouragement, and inspiration, including Mohiaddin Mesbahi, Susanne Zwingel, Tom Breslin, Julie Zeng, John Clark, Kevin Evans, Joaquin Pedroso, Naisy Sarduy, and Clem Fatovic, among others, which includes support from our wonderful Department secretary, Maria Wilkinson-Diaz and Department Chair Barry Levitt. My close friendships with Kip Welborn, Chris Brashear, Mike Isaacs, Matt Lawrence, Sylvan Lee, George Gonos and Carlos Barrera have helped keep me passionate and engaged with the work that I do. Finally, my best friend and partner of over 30 years, Laura Leigh Rampey, is a constant source of love, support, and inspiration for me, which is a foundation for what I have been able to accomplish. My parents,

Rodgie and Janice Cox, are no longer with us, but will always have a special place in my heart, and I am thankful for the ongoing support and encouragement of my aunt, Linda Harris, and my wonderful brother-in-law, Clif Rampey.

Last, but not least, I want to thank the activists and organizers who are putting their lives on the line daily to struggle for a more just world. This book is dedicated to you as well, and hopefully these contributions will assist in some small way to move our struggle forward.

Figures and Tables

Figures

4.1   Saudi investment in U.S. industries by number of deals   96

Tables

4.1   Saudi investment in different U.S. business sectors by the source of investment   97
6.1   Canadian direct investment abroad: number of controlled subsidiaries   150
6.2   Canadian acquisitions abroad by industry, 1987–1990   150
6.3   Breakdown of Canadian and foreign bank revenue   167

Notes on Contributors

Melissa Boissiere
is a doctoral candidate in International Relations at Florida International University. She specializes in international political economy and regional trade agreements. Her dissertation is on the CARIFORUM-EU EPA trade agreement between the European Union and Caribbean countries. In the dissertation, she analyzes how corporations based in the EU used their power to affect the agenda and content of this trade agreement in the broader context of neoliberal global capitalism. She has published "Transnational Corporate Power: From Lomé to the CARIFORUM-EU EPA" in the journal *Class, Race and Corporate Power*.

Ronald W. Cox
is Professor of Politics and International Relations at Florida International University. He specializes in international political economy and U.S. foreign policy. He has published six books on corporate power in U.S. and global politics, most recently *Corporate Power, Class Conflict and the Crisis of the New Globalization* (Lexington Books, 2019). He is editor of the online open access journal, *Class, Race and Corporate Power*.

Aram Eisenschitz
is Senior Lecturer in Tourism Policy at Middlesex University Business School. His research interests include critical urban theory, tourism, power and class, and place branding. He is co-author with Raju Das and Jamie Gough of *The Challenges of the New Social Democracy: Social Capital and Civic Association or Class Struggle* (Brill, 2023). His other recent publications are "A Geography for the Common Good," *Journal of Geography in Higher Education*, 2022; "Place Branding and the Neoliberal Class Settlement", in *A Research Agenda for Place Branding*, eds. Medway, D., Warnaby, G., and Byrom, J. (Edward Elgar, 2021); and "Place Marketing for Social Inclusion", in *Inclusive Place Branding*, eds. Kavaratzis, M., Giovanardi, M., and Lichrou, M. (Routledge, 2018).

Jamie A. Gough
was a lecturer in human geography and urban studies before his escape into retirement. He has published widely on the labor process, local and regional economies, social life and politics, the capitalist state, the contradictions of neoliberalism and Keynesianism, the theorization of social space, and sexual politics. He is co-author with Raju Das and Aram Eisenschitz of *The Challenges*

of the New Social Democracy: Social Capital and Civic Association or Class Struggle (Brill, 2023). He is currently writing a book on the role of capital in Brexit. His website is jamiegough.info.

Adam D. Hernandez

holds a PhD in Political Science from Florida International University. His research focuses on computational propaganda, digital politics, and corporate power. His other areas of expertise include U.S. foreign policy, international political economy, sportswashing, and U.S.-Portuguese relations. He recently published "Bell Pottinger: Pre-Digital Fake News During the Rise of Neoliberalism" in the journal *Class, Race and Corporate Power*.

Tamanisha J. John

is an Assistant Professor of International Political Economy in the Department of Politics at York University. Her main research interests are Caribbean sovereignty and politics, imperialism, financial exclusion, corporate power, Canadian foreign policy, and Canadian overseas banking. Her most recent publications include: "Haiti in the Caribbean: A Political Economy Perspective on the Urgent Crisis of Imperialism" in the *Black Agenda Report*, "Canadian Financial Imperialism and Structural Adjustment in the Caribbean" in the journal *Class, Race and Corporate Power*, and "Racialized Financial Exclusion in the Anglophone Caribbean" in the *Social and Economic Studies Journal*.

Mazaher Koruzhde

is a visiting lecturer in the Department of Political Science at Howard University. He specializes in International Political Economy and the political economy of U.S. geopolitical strategy in the Persian Gulf. His recent article published in *Class, Race and Corporate Power* is entitled "The Iranian Crisis of the 1970s-1980s and the Formation of the Transnational Investment Bloc."

Rob Piper

is a doctoral candidate in International Relations at Florida International University. His research interests are international political economy, corporate power, U.S. politics and inequality. He recently published "The Institutional Drivers Contributing to Billionaire Wealth at the Sector Level" in the journal *Class, Race and Corporate Power*.

Bryant William Sculos

is Lecturer II in the Department of Political Science at The University of Texas Rio Grande Valley. He is the Politics of Culture section editor for the open-access journal *Class, Race and Corporate Power*. Sculos is the co-editor of *Teaching Marx & Critical Theory in the 21st Century* with Mary Caputi (Brill 2019/Haymarket, 2020) and author of *The Dialectics of Global Justice: From Liberal to Postcapitalist Cosmopolitanism* (SUNY Press, 2022).

CHAPTER 1

Introduction

Ronald W. Cox

This volume brings together scholars who analyze the relationship between capitalism, class power and the state.[1] The thread that ties most of these chapters together is a focus on how capitalist firms, sectors and policy planning organizations use their political power to affect state policies. This is the instrumental aspect of capitalist power—how capitalists are directly embedded within state institutions in a way that allows them to secure their policy preferences. The other aspect is structural power—the way that capitalism as a system generates outcomes independent of the specific agency of capitalists. Both are important features of capitalist power structures, and often cannot be neatly separated, but coexist as mutually interdependent.

We go beyond the often-simplified debates in the academic literature on business and the state that pit "instrumentalists" against "structuralists" (Reuss, 2020). Capitalists have market and political power that is reflected in their concentration of wealth within the economy and the use of that wealth to affect the politics of the capitalist state. Capitalism produces divisions within the capitalist class that result in divisions within and between sectors of capital regarding policy preferences. These battles between capitalists over policy preferences are often expressed within the capitalist state. Capitalist firms do unite at times as a broader set of class interests, especially when it comes to policies that produce universal gains for capitalist owners and reduce costs of capitalist production, including facilitating access to low-cost labor, but otherwise capitalist divisions emerge as a result of capitalist owners being situated within different sectoral and competitive locations, producing different policy objectives as a result of what capitalists produce and how (and where) they produce it (Ferguson, 1995; Cox, 2019).

At the same time, the political agency of the capitalist state is not completely reducible to capitalist interests. State officials within capitalist structures of power must navigate both instrumental pressures from dominant economic and political coalitions as well as maneuver within the space of

---

1 These chapters are revised and expanded versions of articles originally published in the online academic journal that I edit, *Class, Race and Corporate Power*.

electoral politics, which means political, economic, and ideological factors are intertwined when it comes to assessing why some policies are adopted and others are rejected. In capitalism, however, the instrumental and structural power wielded by capitalist owners of production shapes agenda-setting, decision-making and power relationships within countries and between powerful countries in the so-called Global North and the majority of the global population concentrated within the Global South. This book examines a wide range of these capitalist power structures within rich capitalist countries and within the context of North-South capitalist power dynamics, as well as providing a broader assessment of how capitalism is structured to produce poverty, exploitation, and oppression, regardless of whether it is labeled "neoliberal" or otherwise.

In Chapter 2, I write about the power of the military-industrial complex (MIC) in the United States as being deeply embedded within the policies advanced by the capitalist state. The MIC refers to military contractors, state bureaucracies and politicians that are interconnected in a policy apparatus that promotes the weapons industry to counter "threats" to U.S. national security. I locate the preferences of the MIC within the intersection of the profiteering interest of military contractors, the reliance on military weapons production for capitalist accumulation in the U.S., and the set of relationships cultivated by the MIC within the U.S. national security establishment.

I argue that the MIC has been consistently involved in shaping U.S. foreign policy agendas, specifically defining threats and how best to respond to these threats during critical junctures of U.S. foreign policy, which includes the beginning of the Cold War, the transition to the post-Cold War period, post-9/11 and the War on Terror, and the more recent shift toward war preparations against China and Russia. These critical junctures have provided an opportunity for the MIC to maximize profit-making by emphasizing the necessity of permanently expanding large-scale weapons systems. The fact that the MIC has been strengthened and consolidated after decades of increased militarization gives them even more power to set the foreign policy agenda. This is especially true given the lengthy history of military spending being used as a de facto industrial policy in the U.S. There has also been a dispersal of weapons production across a wider range of U.S. Congressional districts that has helped generate more political support for increased military spending. In summary, instrumental and structural factors within militarized capitalism have provided the conditions for explaining why military spending in the U.S. has long surpassed military spending at the height of the previous Cold War.

In Chapter 3, Rob Piper explains the increase in billionaire wealth in the U.S. during the period of neoliberal capitalism (1980 to the present) by analyzing the capitalist sectors where such wealth has been most concentrated: finance, information technology and food and beverage. In each sector, there has been a steady increase in the concentration of ownership over the past several decades, which has provided firms in each of these sectors with more wealth, market power, and political power. Piper identifies several "drivers" of such wealth accumulation, including financialization of the U.S. and global economy, the acceleration of "rentierism" or "the control of access to productive activities and assets for the sole purpose of extracting capital in the form of rents," and labor exploitation, all of which have contributed to greater concentration of wealth ownership by a billionaire class and growing inequality between capital and labor. Such trends have been facilitated by crony capitalism, or "collusion between business and government officials to preserve the interests of capital accumulation at the expense of labor and society."

Piper's chapter examines how market concentration has been facilitated by government policies that have deepened and reinforced this concentration of market power and wealth. The extent to which government has accommodated and accelerated the rise of billionaire wealth under neoliberal capitalism is not an extreme manifestation of government quiescence, but rather how capitalist governments have historically operated: in the service of large-scale and politically powerful capitalist firms who have relied on governments to facilitate private sector accumulation and, at times, restoration of profit rates. As numerous scholars have argued, the advent of neoliberal capitalism was due to the pressure of well-organized corporate political interest groups which sought to dismantle the previous system of "regulated capitalism" in order to reverse the long-term fall of the rate of profit. Therefore, as Piper documents, capitalist market power and political influence have increased in the U.S. and globally within the neoliberal capitalist period.

In Chapter 4, Mazaher Koruzhde and I identify a transnational investment bloc that links U.S. and Persian Gulf corporations in a political and economic alliance that has shaped U.S. policy toward the region from the late 1970s to the present. The U.S. military-industrial complex provided the policy planning agenda for a militarization of U.S. policy in the region during the late 1970s and early 1980s. Deeply embedded within the national security bureaucracy, the MIC advocated an increase in U.S. arms sales to Persian Gulf allies, an expansion of U.S. military bases and active engagement in military preparedness and conflict in the region (to defend allies and to weaken enemies), and a policy commitment for U.S. troops to protect access to oil reserves rather than rely on U.S. allies to police the region. The MIC became part of a durable coalition of corporate lobbies that had a material stake in expanding U.S. militarism in the Persian Gulf. Leading corporations in the U.S. energy sector established joint investments with Middle Eastern oil producers (states as well as private firms), which have grown more lucrative over time. U.S. commercial, investment banks and other financial firms have expanded linkages to Persian Gulf capital, which deepened during the oil price hikes of 1973, when leading OPEC states deposited dollar reserves in the Eurodollar accounts of private commercial banks. These financial, energy and military relationships between transnational capitalists from the U.S. and Persian Gulf elites in government and the private sector have expanded dramatically over time. This is most evident in the U.S.-Saudi transnational investment nexus, which has involved an expansion of joint global investments in a wide range of profit-making ventures, including the global information technology sector, increased financial ties between U.S. banks, financial investors and Saudi investors, a deepening of transnational energy joint ventures, and growing financial investment links between U.S. and Saudi/Persian Gulf capital to the most profitable sectors of global capitalist accumulation, including information technology.

The authors conclude that a transnational investment bloc has helped define U.S. national security toward the Persian Gulf to serve its members interest in maximizing profits through global accumulation strategies. U.S. foreign policy elites have defined "national interests" largely through the prism of well-embedded transnational capitalist political and economic networks whose influence is apparent when examining their financing of key policy planning organizations and steady access to the highest levels of policymaking and deliberation. The transnational investment bloc has helped perpetuate a steady militarization of U.S. policy in the Persian Gulf region that has contributed to two U.S. wars in Iraq, and a steady escalation of U.S. military engagement in conflicts within and around the Persian Gulf—including an escalation of U.S. counterinsurgency strategy and increased utilization of U.S. Special Forces in the region. These policies of expanded U.S. militarization have grown inside a radical expansion of the U.S. global intelligence-surveillance state, whose policies are increasingly clouded behind veils of secrecy and lack of accountability to the U.S. public.

In Chapter 5, Adam D. Hernandez analyzes the emergence of the global disinformation firm Bell Pottinger from its origins and links to the administration of Prime Minister Margaret Thatcher of Britain to the global expansion of the firm's profit-making activities. This includes case studies of how Bell Pottinger worked for the apartheid government in South Africa, the U.S.-backed government of Iraq during the U.S. occupation, and with several of the world's dictatorial governments. Hernandez argues that Bell Pottinger was not just a mercenary for hire, but instead originated within the same networks of political and economic power cultivated by the Thatcher government. The firm started as an extension of the Thatcher government's propaganda campaign designed to promote conservative political and economic policies, specifically privatization, deregulation, a reduction of progressive taxes on the wealthy and the corporate sector and less funding for social welfare—a range of policies often labeled "neoliberal." Bell Pottinger also pioneered many of the disinformation strategies that would later be used by the firm in its transition to information technology, specifically the use of social media platforms to spread narratives favorable to their clients, whether it be the Thatcher government in Britain, the U.S.-backed government in Iraq under U.S. occupation (Bell Pottinger would be a client of the U.S. Defense Department), or the apartheid government in South Africa or dictatorships in the Persian Gulf. The uprising of the Arab Spring ultimately helped expose Bell Pottinger and led to the firm's collapse.

As Hernandez makes clear, Bell Pottinger was the pioneer of global corporate disinformation campaigns which have been linked to far-right politicians and wealthy business elites around the world. Bell Pottinger developed extensive ties to benefactors that had an interest in using the latest advancements in information technology to maintain and expand their economic and political power. Bell Pottinger and firms that followed in their footsteps became more impactful in using social media and information technology to spread disinformation online to mass audiences, often for the purpose of redirecting the anger of the public away from powerful politicians or economic elites and toward vulnerable groups in society. For Hernandez, corporate disinformation campaigns have used populist rhetoric on behalf of powerful elites to safeguard and expand their own power by shaping online discourse around controversial public policy issues or individual personalities. These propaganda campaigns have been facilitated, expanded and accelerated by the profit incentives of social media corporations like Facebook, whose platform encourages a wide dissemination of targeted propaganda. The aim has been to promote and expand policies that disproportionately advance the interests of corrupt political and economic elites, to the detriment of the broader public.

In Chapter 6, Tamanisha J. John develops a framework for analyzing Canadian imperialism in the English-speaking Caribbean. She argues that large-scale chartered Canadian banks have used their economic and political power in Canada to shape domestic legislation favorable to their interests. In turn, these banks have become more powerful over time, entrenching themselves in the foreign policies of the Canadian government as Canada exploited the colonial and post-colonial power structures established by British imperial policies in the English-speaking Caribbean. John makes the case that the power of Canadian banks in the Caribbean region is a legacy that has grown and re-emerged in different forms over time. When some Caribbean governments, especially Grenada, started to assert greater independence from foreign investors and from foreign banks, including Canadian banks, during the 1970s, the Canadian government responded with a globally organized imperialist strategy led by the IMF, the World Bank, the U.S., and Canada, that was designed to provide penalties and incentives to Caribbean countries that would re-establish favorable policies for Canadian banks and foreign investors.

John provides a detailed history of how the Canadian government and Canadian chartered banks worked aggressively to promote structural adjustment programs throughout the English-speaking Caribbean that entrenched the privileges of Canadian banks and foreign investors while scaling back or eliminating social programs to uplift the working class and poor of the region. The result has been the privileging of the financial investments of the richest classes while contributing to rising indebtedness of the region. As John writes, "structural adjustment dramatically intensified the existing inequalities in states and removed the ability of governments to alleviate these situations." States such as Guyana and Grenada, which tried to develop nationalist alternatives to foreign investor privileges were met with coordinated campaigns of international repression and intervention, from both Canada and the U.S., in service of imperialist interests. John argues that wealthy states like Canada saw liberalization of global financial markets, in the Caribbean and elsewhere, as part of the solution to declining profit rates and reinvigoration of capitalist accumulation at home and abroad. The power of the financial sector in Canada gave chartered Canadian banks the opportunity to shape domestic and foreign policy in a way that favored their interests. John details how this financial power shaped the Canadian government responses to the economic and political crises of capitalism in the English-speaking Caribbean during the late 1970s and early 1980s, a historical turn that still weighs on the region today.

In Chapter 7, Melissa Boissiere details the history of how the structural market power of European-based transnational corporations allowed them to benefit disproportionately through various phases of EEC-Caribbean trade agreements, including the Lomé Conventions from 1975–2000 and the most recent CARIFORUM-EU Economic Partnership Agreement finalized in 2008. She documents the way that sectors of transnational capital used their structural and instrumental power within the EU to set the agenda for these negotiations. During the Lomé Conventions, this meant that trade agreements promoted a continuity of colonial power structures that locked-in Caribbean countries to export cheap raw materials for the European market while importing European manufactured goods. Over time, transnational corporations were able to use the terms of the Lomé Convention trade agreements, especially rules of origin requirements, to increase their market power in the region and to make it more costly for Caribbean manufacturing competitors to stay in business. Meanwhile the terms of "preferential access" of Caribbean agricultural producers to the EEC market did not enable Caribbean producers to increase their revenues and access to that market. More countries and regions had preferential access, increasing competition between low-cost suppliers, and therefore limiting the incentives for increased raw material production from the region. Transnational corporations in the EEC were also able to use their market power to keep raw materials cost low by diversifying their imports across different countries and regions.

As the Lomé agreements came to an end, transnational corporations in Europe, mobilized primarily within the European Roundtable of Industrialists (ERT), began to lobby for a shift in trade agreements toward content that provided greater protection for foreign investors, greater capital flow between investment partners and elimination of the preferential trade access that were extended to Caribbean countries (and other regions) during the Lomé Conventions. As Boissiere documents, the contemporary power of European transnational capital can be traced to the emergence of the ERT in 1983, when the corporate lobby consolidated its efforts in support of the single-market European Union. During the 1980s and early 1990s, in addition to working with EU policymakers to craft an EU single market that was highly favorable to corporate investors, the ERT used its lobbying networks and institutionalized policymaking connections to Brussels to set the agenda for neoliberal trade agreements. One of those agreements, the EU-CARIFORUM Economic Partnership Agreement, shifted the terms of trade heavily in favor of investment protection, expansion of capital flows at lower costs, and liberalization of trade across all trading partners and trading agreements. Transnational capital through organized lobbies led by the ERT had drafted position papers that were mostly adopted as frameworks for neoliberal trade agreements such as EU-CARIFORUM, further locking in the structural and instrumental power of corporate lobbies to have their policy priorities institutionalized.

In chapter eight, Jamie A. Gough and Aram Eisenschitz argue that the persistence of poverty in high-income countries is a direct product of capitalist exploitation and oppression. Capitalist investors require access to a low-cost pool of workers whose precarity works against their ability to negotiate higher wages and working conditions. The stratification of workers into different job classifications and opportunities is both a function of the capitalist market and of capitalist state policies which reinforce working class precarity and contribute to the persistence of poverty. Capitalists are able to take advantage of a labor market that divides workers by skill, spatial location, skin color and ethnicity, and employment/unemployment to keep aggregate wages low to support capitalist accumulation. The drive of capitalists for profit rates high enough to justify private investment means undertaking strategies of employment that take advantage of a divided and highly precarious labor market where the lowest tier workers are just a paycheck away from poverty, unemployment and immiseration. This structural feature of the capitalist marketplace locks in place persistent poverty that is designed to favor capitalist accumulation strategies.

The authors also provide considerable detail about the role of capitalist state policies in underpinning labor exploitation and oppression. While labor organizing and social movements have been able to secure social welfare benefits for workers and the poor, those benefits ebb and flow over time in response to the level of class struggle. What remains constant are policies that fall well short of what is needed to end poverty, let alone to provide a better set of conditions for workers to be able to establish their own terms for employment. In recent decades, made possible by reduced class struggle from below, the capitalist states in rich countries have attached more rigorous conditions for qualifications for welfare assistance, implemented more regressive taxes on the working class, transferred fewer benefits to workers in the form of employment protections or transfer incomes, and substituted tax credits to the poorest workers in place of redistribution of income. These policies have contributed to the persistence of poverty in higher income countries, helping to consolidate a precarious existence for the aggregate working class, whose ability to stay ahead of the poverty curve has necessitated more creative strategies, and more vigorous competition with a much larger pool of cheap and unprotected workers.

In Chapter 9, Bryant William Sculos argues that the use of the term "neoliberalism" suffers from conceptual and empirical problems, namely a lack of definitional clarity that shields capitalism from more direct interrogation and critique. For Sculos, the descriptions of individuals or policies as "neoliberal" are often too vague and disconnected from a more specific analysis of capitalism. One problematic result is the notion that if we can just get rid of "neoliberalism," as opposed to capitalism, many of our most pressing social, political and economic problems could be greatly resolved. Sculos details why many of the policies described as "neoliberal" are actually variants of standard capitalist "solutions" to economic problems. This is true in the healthcare policy debate in the U.S., where every dominant policy alternative was informed by capitalist profit considerations. Why use the term "neoliberal" instead of pointing out the extent to which a capitalist system constantly reproduces "solutions" that entrenches existing capitalist power relations and fails to address the relationship between capitalism and crises. Sculos also critiques the use of neoliberalism in the climate change policy discourse, which often obscured or negated the relationship between capitalism and climate change and paved the way for false solutions around "green capitalism," market incentives, regulatory capitalism and public-private partnerships which all fell considerably short of addressing the climate crisis.

Sculos concludes by arguing for a more vigorous policy intervention by leftists around an explicit critique of capitalism. He urges social movement activists and organizers to articulate anti-capitalist alternatives that explicitly identify the dynamics of a capitalist system that is inherently linked to exploitation and oppression in a way that impedes egalitarian and democratic solutions to urgent, existential crises. By trying to appeal to reformist critics of "neoliberalism," larger systemic critiques of capitalism easily get lost within the narrowness of language. Radical alternatives get submerged within a simplified and inconsistent discourse that often unwittingly (though sometimes deliberately) protects capitalism from the problems it causes.

In Chapter 10, I examine how these critiques of capitalist power can be used by academics and researchers to serve social movements and anti-capitalist organizing. All of these chapters indicate the extent to which capitalist power has been thoroughly entrenched in state policymaking in ways that further solidify exploitation and oppression on a global scale. The ultimate solution to this involves several components: first, understanding the roots of such capitalist power structures. The second is knowing how to use such understanding to identify causes of specific problems and/or crises points within the system. The third is identifying agents of change and methods best suited to promote change. In an increasingly stratified world economy, beset by uprisings among mass movements that are articulating, however incompletely and unevenly, the unfairness and injustices of the current capitalist system, it is increasingly urgent for the left to help people organize in a way that allows them to change the system, not to simply accommodate to the interests of those who benefit from it. That means academics and researchers need to be part of the solution by helping to empower working class movements seeking change. We need to serve as a bridge between those movements and the acquisition of theoretical and empirical knowledge necessary to inform the fight for systemic transformation.

References

Cox, Ronald W. (2019) *Corporate Power, Class Conflict and the Crisis of the New Globalization*. Blue Ridge Summit, PA: Lexington Books.

Ferguson, Thomas (1995) *Golden Rule: the Investment Theory of Party Competition and the Logic of Money Driven Political Systems*. Chicago: University of Chicago Press.

Reuss, Alejandro (2020) "The Power of Capital: an Introduction to Class, Domination and Conflict," *An ECI Teaching Module on Social and Economic Issues*, Economics in Context Initiative, Global Development Policy Center, Boston University.

CHAPTER 2

Class Power and the Military-Industrial Complex in the United States

Ronald W. Cox

1   Introduction[1]

Scholars focused on the military-industrial complex owe a huge debt to the pioneering work of elite power theorist C. Wright Mills, who was part of a history of U.S. academics who theorized about the influence of corporate interests within the political process. Mills emphasized an interwoven constellation of interests operating within the state that tied together the growth of large-scale bureaucracies such as the Defense Department with particular firms that profited from military procurement (Mills, 1956). The network of interests benefitting from military spending made it very difficult to change the embedded priorities of a military allocation system that profited from the perceptions of an ever-present threat to the security of the U.S. Ever since WWII, the features of U.S. foreign policymaking have heightened the influence of the military-industrial complex by centralizing authority for foreign policy decision making in the executive branch, and by creating a complex array of bureaucracies whose very existence is predicated on (and justified by) the presence of an external enemy.

Economic and ideological factors, as well as corporate interests, state bureaucracies and political elites, play a role in the calculation of external threats, and therefore levels of military spending to meet those threats. This makes assessments of which factors cause military spending hikes more complicated than they might be otherwise. In order to make sense of the politics of military spending escalation in the U.S. and elsewhere, we need to examine the divisions among powerful vested interests, especially corporate interests and corporate-based coalitions, as well as powerful political actors and bureaucracies, in order to develop a more complete understanding of the political economy of militarization. This analysis borrows from both elite power theory,

---

[1] This chapter is a revised and expanded version of an article by Ronald W. Cox (2014) "The Military-Industrial Complex and U.S. Military Spending After 9/11," *Class, Race and Corporate Power*, Vol. 2 (2): Article 5.

inherited from scholars like Mills, and instrumental and structuralist Marxist theory. These theories represent a considerable advance in explaining shifts in levels and types of military spending, as they stand alone in emphasizing the intersecting role of corporate power, class coalitions and state bureaucracies in determining military allocations.

Frameworks such as elite power theory insist that "national interest" does not exist apart from the clashing and competing definitions of "national interest" put forward by the most powerful domestic interest groups. Elite power theorists working in the C. Wright Mills tradition have long argued that the constellation of interests comprising the military-industrial complex have helped determine, shape, and refine the definition of "national interest" in order to maximize profits and to protect access to resources. This school acknowledges that the military-industrial complex does not define "national interest" in a vacuum, but is forced to compete with other powerful corporate interest groups over how to define "national interest." Business conflict theorists, heavily influenced by elite power theory, argue that capitalist firms located in different sectors of the capitalist economy will take varied positions on military expansionism, U.S. intervention in foreign countries, and levels of military spending necessary to meet security threats. In fact, corporate groups may define "threats" differently depending on their particular location within capitalist production, and how "threat definition" impacts on their ability to maximize profits and to maintain market share (Gibbs, 1991; Ferguson and Rogers, 1987).

Some variants of Marxist foreign policy theory overlap with elite power theory in its focus on the relationship between the capitalist class and the state. Instrumental Marxists have examined the history of competition among capitalist firms and groups for influence in foreign policy making (Miliband, 1969). Structural Marxists have advanced the theory of the "permanent arms economy" to explain the reliance of the U.S. state on military spending as a Keynesianism stimulus program designed to prop up capitalism through an infusion of fiscal spending to leading capitalist firms (Kalecki, 1971; Kidron, 1970; Baran and Sweezy, 1966). In addition, Marxists have rightly emphasized the relationship between sections of the capitalist ruling class and the military in safeguarding and providing the conditions for profitable foreign investment and trade.

The insights of instrumental and structural Marxists, as well as elite power theorists in the Mills' tradition, are blended in this chapter to develop a framework for understanding the influence of the military-industrial complex in structuring U.S. military spending during transition from the Cold War to the post-Cold War period, the so-called "war on terror" after 9/11, and the more recent shift to military spending escalation that anticipates war with Russia and/or China.

There are various components of the corporate and bureaucratic interest bloc which comprises the military-industrial complex. This includes the corporate sector that produces military weapons, as well as corporations that are contracted to perform a range of military and intelligence services. Also included are the bureaucracies that are linked in whole or in part to the military apparatus of the U.S. state, which includes most obviously the Defense Department, but also as many as 17 intelligence agencies that carry out a range of foreign operations that involve everything from espionage to low-levels of U.S. intervention, and other Departments, such as the Department of Energy and NASA and more recently the Department of Homeland Security, that devote a portion of their budgets to supplemental military spending and military preparation. In addition, congressional representatives and senators disproportionately tied to the military sector through campaign contributions or through districts that are heavily dependent on military spending, would be expected to be part of the military-industrial complex. Finally, the last ingredient to be included, but among the most important, are the lobbying networks and policy-planning organizations that attempt to influence the process of agenda-setting and therefore "threat definition" and "threat construction" in a way that is beneficial to their membership.

There are three features that define the military-industrial complex. The first is the centrality of corporations that depend on military production and arms sales for anywhere from 50 to 90 percent of their revenues. These corporations occupy a position of market and political power that has become increasingly concentrated over time. There are now just five prime U.S. military contractors that do business directly with the federal government, down from 51 contractors in 1991. These five contractors rely heavily on military contracts with the U.S. government for the majority of their annual revenues. Between 9/11 and 2021, Congress gave $2 trillion dollars to the top five: Lockheed Martin, Boeing, Raytheon, General Dynamics, and Northrop Grumman (Hartung, 2021; Semler, 2021). Unlike financial investors or corporations whose investments are based on provision of liquid capital, research and development financing, and/or the ownership of patents or civilian products, military producers' profits are derived from military hardware that cannot easily be transferred to a wide range of uses. The political implications are stark in that these firms have a vested interest in maintaining and expanding weapons systems that, absent external threats, would face a limited or nonexistent political justification.

Second, military contractors have a sustained relationship with key U.S. foreign policy bureaucracies, especially the Defense Department, but also a range of departments and agencies that utilize military equipment and engage in strategic or tactical deployment of such equipment (Harris, 2006: 119–148). Thus, key turning points in U.S. foreign policy, in which long-term threats are identified and long-term strategic plans are developed, provide an important critical juncture to observe the extent to which both corporations and bureaucracies work together to identify threats to U.S. security in a manner that maximizes access to government revenues and tax dollars.

Third, such critical junctures in U.S. foreign policymaking that are noteworthy for the identification of long-term threats to U.S. national security are opportune moments for policy planning organizations, especially those funded by self-interested military contractors and security ideologues, to exert influence in framing the policy debate. The end of the Cold War and the shift to post-Cold War strategic doctrines, the aftermath of 9/11, and the heightened rivalry between the U.S., Russia and China, are examples of critical junctures for assessing these propositions. I conclude here that the military-industrial complex was disproportionately involved in the policy-planning process in each of these critical junctures, based on evidence that all the key actors comprising the complex participated in the establishment of U.S. security doctrines during each of these transition periods. This included military contractors themselves, the defense and intelligence bureaucracies, congressional representatives and senators from districts and states distinguished by their dependence on military spending, and policy-planning organizations receiving disproportionate funding and influence from the military sector. More recently, after the major wars associated with 9/11 had ended and military spending briefly declined, the military-industrial complex has been a key actor in identifying China and Russia as the next high-level security threats, which has been used to justify higher military budgets in the contemporary period.

In short, the following analysis uses a military-industrial complex theoretical framework to explain why and how the U.S. government increased military spending during various critical junctures, from the end of the Cold War in 1989, through the "War on Terror" after 9/11, and the current war planning against China and Russia. The next section of the chapter examines the role of the military-industrial complex during critical junctures of U.S. foreign policy. Then I will examine the mechanisms used by the military-industrial complex to maximize policy goals after the Cold War, following 9/11, and in war planning against Russia and China.

2 The Military-Industrial Complex and Critical Junctures in U.S. Foreign Policy

There has been a strong continuity of military spending from the Cold War to the present. The only absolute reductions in Cold War spending occurred during the end or de-escalation of major wars such as the immediate aftermath of the Korean War (1953–1954) during the Eisenhower Administration, the de-escalation of the Vietnam War prior to 1973, and the reduction in military spending during the transition from the Cold War to the post-Cold War period and briefly after the end of the U.S. wars in Iraq and Afghanistan. Each of these reductions proved to be temporary. In the aftermath of the attacks of 9/11, U.S. military spending quickly escalated so that, counting the wars in Iraq and Afghanistan, the U.S. was spending more on its military by 2008 than it did at the height of the Cold War. After the end of the U.S. wars in Iraq and Afghanistan, the U.S. briefly reduced military spending before escalating spending to new heights over the past five years, in anticipation of wars with Russia and/or China.

Most measurements of U.S. military spending underestimate the total costs of the military budget. Typically, analysts focus on Defense Department expenditures, which do not include other sources of defense spending, such as NASA, the Atomic Energy Agency, and foreign military aid. In addition, there are the additional military spending items tracked by the U.S. National Income and Products account, which include "government consumption of fixed capital, cash payments to amortize underfunded liability for military and civilian retirement benefits, and expenditures recorded on a delivery rather than a cash basis" (Foster, Holleman and McChesney, 2008: 6). If we add all of these expenditures to Defense Department spending, plus interest payments on the debt deriving from past military spending, medical spending to military retirees or dependents at non-military facilities, and veterans' benefits, the overall military budget would have approached $1 trillion dollars by 2008 (Johnson, "Why Has the U.S. Really Gone Broke," LMD, Feb. 2008) and as much as $1.25 trillion by 2019 (Hartung, 2019). At the same time, military spending (then and now) accounts for over half of all discretionary spending in the U.S. budget, which is a better indication of the expansion of U.S. militarism that the often-used calculation of military spending as a percentage of GDP. The reason is that the U.S. government is incapable of taxing the 20% of corporate profits that are shifted offshore, equivalent to a third of corporate tax revenues, due to creative tax avoidance and evasion by corporations (Leslie, 2014: A19).[10] So the issue is not GDP, but the amount of taxable income available to the U.S. state. With these factors in mind, the key questions for this chapter are: Why was military spending higher in 2008 than at any year in Cold War history, despite the elimination of the Soviet Union as a threat to U.S. security interests? What was the role of the events of 9/11 in explaining the dramatic increases in military spending? What has been the impact on the military budget after targeting Russia and China as leading security threats?

The ongoing influence of the military-industrial complex is an important part of the answer to these questions. However, at the outset of this chapter I emphasized that the MIC does not have automatic influence in pushing the outer boundaries of military spending allocations. Their influence is conditioned by other factors which have helped explain strong continuities in military spending from the Cold War to the post-Cold War period. The presence of an external threat was always only one part of the explanation for high levels of U.S. military spending. The other factors include what some have called a "permanent war economy," in which military spending is used as "military Keynesianism" to help boost production and demand for a range of U.S. goods during times of recession or relatively high unemployment (Leslie, 2014: 1–5). The U.S. state has used military spending the way that other states use industrial policy to provide research and development support for industrial and technological innovation. Corporate interests in the U.S. have long preferred the use of military spending as industrial policy, rather than an expansion of the welfare state, which has been much more controversial for corporate elites. In addition, corporations outside the military-industrial complex have long seen the military as a way to protect investments in foreign countries.

However, during the period of détente in the 1970s and during the end of the Cold War in the late 1980s, there were divisions within the U.S. corporate sector about the relative merits of military spending. Business conflict split those corporations between those whose assets were most liquid and mobile (the banking community in particular, especially those banks who were not involved in financing military expansion) and those firms that were increasingly reliant on military production for a substantial share of their profits (Cox and Skidmore-Hess, 1999: 161–202). For financiers disconnected from military production, high levels of military spending pose a potential threat to the aggregate economy, especially during times when military spending is thought to be a leading cause of inflation or when such spending is thought to threaten the long-term stability of the U.S. dollar. Leading corporate interest groups and policy planning organizations such as the Business Roundtable and the Committee for Economic Development did not support increases in military spending during the 1970s or mid-to-late 1980s, meaning that they were often at odds with promilitary spending organizations such as the Committee on the Present Danger and the Heritage Foundation (Skidmore, 1996). The difference in the orientation of such corporate groups is most pronounced during times of easing tension between the U.S. and foreign rivals, such as the détente process of the 1970s and the negotiations that led to the end of the Cold War during the Reagan Administration's second term.

On the other hand, critical junctures in foreign policymaking can move the corporate policy planning organizations further to the right in favor of substantial hikes in military spending. For example, the key events of 1979, in which the USSR invaded Afghanistan, the Sandinista National Liberation Front took power in Nicaragua and the Iranian Revolution overthrew the pro-U.S. government of the Shah, led to a successful push by pro-military spending organizations to affect the implementation of policies that they had long advocated. At the same time, corporate groups such as the Council on Foreign Relations backed away from their support for the détente process. Corporations with fixed foreign investments in the developing world, especially oil corporations, also advocated U.S. militarization to protect those investments, especially during times of revolutionary upheaval in the developing world (Cox, 1994). Similarly, the attacks of 9/11 provided advocates of U.S. militarization with an opportunity to expand a Rogue Doctrine that had been developed at another key conjuncture in U.S. foreign policy history: the transition from the Cold War to the post-Cold War period.

During the transition to the post-Cold War period, advocates of U.S. militarization were faced with potentially substantial cuts to military spending, as former Cold War hawks began to advocate for a peace dividend. Former Defense Secretary Robert McNamara, alongside other former Defense Department officials, argued in 1989 that defense spending could safely be cut in half given the fact that the Cold War was coming to an end (Rosenbaum, 1989). In an effort to minimize cuts to military spending, policy planning organizations with close ties to military contractors worked to fashion a new defense doctrine that could provide a newfound justification for the retention of large-scale weapons systems long after the demise of the Soviet Union. The result was the Rogue Doctrine, which posited that the U.S. would still face considerable threats to its security after the Cold War, namely from rogue states in the developing world that possessed weapons of mass destruction and the capability to threaten vital U.S. geostrategic interests in key regions of the world (Klare, 1996). The transition from the Containment Doctrine to the Rogue doctrine solved two problems for military contractors dependent on high levels of U.S. military spending for profitability. First, it provided a justification for the retention of all large-scale military production lines that had been built with the Soviet threat in mind. Second, it also (much later) provided a justification for a response to the 9/11 attacks that targeted rogue states, in addition to non-state actors such as Al-Qaeda.

In the development of the Rogue Doctrine, military contractors and oil corporations were well-represented through their influence in the conservative think-tank, the Center for Strategic and International Studies, which drafted an influential 1988 report advising the Reagan Administration to move toward war preparation for potential hostilities with "maverick regimes" that constituted a new threat to U.S. national security interests (Homolar, 2010: 713). In addition, during the late 1980s, the Defense Department, the Joint Chiefs of Staff and the White House, first under Ronald Reagan and then under George H.W. Bush, produced a series of documents that provided the basis for a retention of all large-scale Cold War weapons programs that had been developed to counter the Soviet threat. In fact, none of the large-scale Cold War weapons systems would be eliminated in the transition to the post-Cold War period. The justification for the continuity in weapons systems was the newly emerging concept of "rogue state." Future U.S. security interests would be determined by the U.S. ability to effectively wage war against states in developing countries that were characterized by their links to international terrorism, their possession of weapons of mass destruction, and their threat to key regions of the world that constituted U.S. geostrategic interests. The first public iteration of the rogue state appellation was by President Reagan, who applied the term to "Iran, Libya, North Korea, Cuba and Nicaragua" (Homolar, 2010: 713). By the late 1980s and early 1990s, several new states joined the list, led by Iraq, which became the first test case for the Rogue Doctrine as the U.S. waged war against the country after the Iraqi invasion of Kuwait.

In 1988, the Center for Strategic and International Studies (CSIS) drafted a report that identified Third World states as posing new threats to U.S. national security due to their capacity to threaten U.S. interests in key regions of the world. The report urged the U.S. government to take steps to counter these threats by reorienting U.S. military readiness against these "maverick" regimes (Homolar, 2010). In their own 1986 report, the CSIS identified that much of its funding came from 26 companies that supplied weapons to the Pentagon, in addition to 8 U.S. oil firms. The CSIS had a history of promoting militarization of U.S. policy in the Middle East, including support for maintaining and reinforcing the U.S.-Saudi geostrategic alliance. Their own recommendations for the Rogue Doctrine focused heavily on the Middle East, and were buttressed by the reports of other influential strategic analysts such as Albert Wohlstetter, the father of neoconservatism who chaired the Commission on Integrated Long-Term Strategy established by the Reagan Administration in 1988, which also warned of the urgency of maintaining and expanding the U.S. defense budget in anticipation of newly emerging threats from the developing world (Homolar, 2011). In addition, the Chair of the Senate Foreign Relations Committee, Sam Nunn, met with the head of the Joint Chiefs of Staff Colin Powell, in 1988 to discuss the outlines of a new strategy which would involve the "search for new enemies" after the Cold War had come to an end (Klare, 1996). By 1990, the U.S. war against Iraq had produced an official commitment by the George H.W. Bush Administration to a Rogue Doctrine, which was outlined in "A White House Fact Sheet on the National Security Strategy Report" in March of 1990. As Alexandra Homolar has noted, "On the day Iraq invaded Kuwait, President George H.W. Bush officially announced that the new direction of U.S. defense planning was to prepare for regional contingencies in the face of "serious threats to important U.S. interests wholly unrelated to earlier patterns of the U.S.-Soviet relationship" (Homolar, 2011).

The shift toward a Rogue Doctrine only staved off more serious cuts in the transition to the post-cold war period, namely by preserving large-scale Cold War spending programs. It did not prevent cuts to the military budget, which declined by 17 percent under George H.W. Bush and by 12 percent during the first term of the Clinton Administration. Defense and aerospace contractors attempted to counter the reduced business opportunities through a mixture of economic and political strategies. Economically, the largest defense contractors restructured their operations through a combination of layoffs, selloffs of corporate divisions, and mergers and acquisitions of other firms (Brady and Greenfield, 2010: 288–306). The U.S. Defense Department helped to finance the mergers and acquisitions as early as 1993, which in combination with economy-wide trends, contributed to a defense sector whose top four firms were receiving a higher share of DOD contracts than had been true for most of the post-World War II period. The overall pattern of consolidation was the most dramatic in U.S. military history, essentially allowing the top four defense contractors to increase their share of prime weapons contracts from 18 percent in 1993 to 30 percent by 2003 (Brady and Greenfield, 2010).

Politically, the big four defense firms increased their lobbying expenditures and expanded their funding of conservative think-tanks committed to promoting increased military spending. Some of this mobilization paid off during the Clinton Administration, which became a strong advocate of increasing export subsidies to U.S. military contractors whose steady budget escalation had been briefly interrupted during the post-Cold War transition. Numerous scholarly studies provide support for this contention, including the work of William Hartung, Michelle Ciarrocca and David Gibbs (Hartung and Ciarrocca, 2003: 17–20; Gibbs, 2004: 293–321). Each of these scholars document the contributions of the largest defense contractors to the financing of conservative and neo-conservative think-tanks that emerged as prominent in defense policy discussions and debates from the mid-1990s through the attacks of 9/11. According to Hartung and Ciarrocca, the most important think tanks were the Project for the New American Century, also documented extensively by Gibbs, alongside the National Institute for Public Policy and the Center for Security Policy. For the purposes of this study, I have also traced an overlapping relationship between the boards of directors of the largest seven defense contractors, conservative policy planning organizations funded by these contractors, personnel in the Defense Department, and high-level cabinet executives within the administration of George W. Bush. These interests form the latest iteration of a military-industrial complex which has been actively involved in policy planning deliberations and discussions, both before and after 9/11. The 9/11 attacks become a pretext for a dramatic escalation of military spending, with the Defense Department elevated in importance relative to other Departments, and with the policy decisions of the administration borrowed directly from ideas developed by the three think tanks identified by Hartung and Ciarrocca.

It has long been true, as documented by C. Wright Mills in his pioneering study, that defense contractors have had a revolving door relationship with the U.S. state that has helped shape particular foreign policy strategies, military allocation policies, and the definition of strategic threats. However, there is considerable evidence that the revolving door relationships have only intensified in the years prior to 9/11 and in the decade after 9/11. According to Richard Skaff,

> A 2010 Boston Globe investigation revealed that the number of retired three-and-four star Generals and admirals moving into lucrative defense industry jobs rose from less than 50 percent between 1994 and 1998 to a stratospheric 80 percent between 2004 and 2008, findings that brought new scrutiny to this unethical revolving door ... A recent study found that when a defense company announced the hiring of a former defense department political appointee, on average, the company's stock price increased. The relationship was statistically weak but positive, suggesting investors believe such hires bring benefits ... In 2011 alone, the Department of Defense committed to spending nearly $100 billion with the five largest defense contractors—Lockheed Martin, Boeing, General Dynamics, Raytheon, and Northrop Grumman. At least nine of the top-level generals and admirals who retired between 2009 and 2011 took positions with those five companies. In addition, 12 generals who retired during that

period have gone on to work for Burdeshaw Associates, a "renta-general" consulting firm specializing in helping companies obtain defense contracts. Burdeshaw's clients have included Northrop Grumman.
SKAFF, 2012

The following section of this chapter examines the key role of corporate-funded think tanks in structuring the policy response of the George W. Bush Administration to the attacks of 9/11. The events of 9/11 provided an opportunity for defense corporations, ideologues based in corporate-funded think-tanks and key actors in the Bush Administration to use 9/11 as a pretext or justification for a wide-ranging expansion of the military budget. A close analysis of the budget increases suggests a tenuous relationship to the stated objectives of the war on terror, but a robust relationship to the militarization agenda advanced by the military-financed think-tanks. More recently, with the conclusion of the large-scale wars associated with the "War on Terror," in Iraq and Afghanistan, military-financed think-tanks have lobbied aggressively for the current and ongoing period of military escalation targeting Russia and China.

3   The Rising Power of the MIC Post-9/11

Critical junctures in U.S. foreign policy involve a key foreign policy event or set of events that increases the level of threat perception among the U.S. political and economic elite (Collier and Collier, 1991: 887–917). Certainly, the attacks of 9/11 qualify, as they constituted a foreign attack by a global terrorist network on U.S. soil. The severity of the attack and its consequences are not in dispute, nor is the fact that much of U.S. population was mobilized around support for the victims, and admonition for the perpetrators. The attack itself, however, says little about how the attack will be interpreted by political and economic elites, and about the strategies utilized to respond to the attack. In the case of the George W. Bush Administration, the first official response, the National Security Strategy of the U.S., was unveiled in September of 2002, when President Bush called for a full-scale global "War on Terror" that connected the perpetrators of the attack, Al-Qaeda, to the existence of "rogue states" which provided a safe haven and breeding ground for terrorist networks. The recommendations embedded in Bush's emerging security doctrine came directly from the policy goals of military-financed conservative and neoconservative think-tanks that had increased their level of mobilization prior the attacks of 9/11. The identification of rogue states, three of which Bush labeled the "axis of evil," had been central to the justification for the retention of large-scale

U.S. weapons systems in the transition from the Cold War to the post-Cold War period (Cumings, Abrahamian and Maoz, 2004). Now the Bush Administration was promoting a response to 9/11 that involved the expansion of large-scale weapons systems to be utilized against such states, in addition to a dramatic expansion of the U.S. military and intelligence bureaucracies that would be enlisted to fight a global war.

The Bush Doctrine, as it is often referenced, refers to three aspects of the Administration's policy response to 9/11. The first was a global militarization approach that promoted robust increases in all aspects of military spending, coupled with military intervention in rogue states. The second was a "preventive war" approach that justified U.S. strikes on rogue states by linking the long-term threat posed by these states to enhanced opportunities for Al-Qaeda and Al-Qaeda-linked terrorist networks to launch future attacks against the U.S. The third aspect was a rollback strategy that lent support to a U.S. overthrow and transformation of designated "rogue states" in favor of the construction of pro-U.S. states that would then be used to transform entire regions, especially the Persian Gulf. Each aspect of this policy agenda had been endorsed and anticipated, down to a strikingly similar level of detail and analysis, by both conservative and neoconservative think-tanks in the 1990s which were closely linked to the military-industrial complex, and heavily financed by military contractors. At the same time, the expansion of military spending accelerated an already growing lobbying network of defense contractors whose efforts had already contributed to significant increases in the military budget during the Clinton Administration's second term in office, specifically from 1998–2001 (Breslin, 2011: 316). Post-9/11, military contractors were actively involved in working with Defense Department officials to justify, promote and expand a range of weapons systems that had been carried over from the Cold War to the post-Cold War period. Just as these weapons systems were tested in the first Gulf War as a justification for the Rogue Doctrine, they were expanded and utilized in a two-war fighting strategy in Afghanistan and Iraq, a strategy that was anticipated by the Rogue Doctrine itself.

The argument advanced here is that defense contractors were active participants in the think-tanks and lobbying networks that contributed to the Bush threat definition of the 9/11 attacks. In order to demonstrate this, I examine the connections between military corporations, think-tanks, and key decision-makers in the Bush Administration after the attacks of 9/11. I also examine the ways in which 9/11 further centralized executive branch power and, in particular, expanded the power of the Defense Department in the aftermath of the attacks. This is especially significant given the close working relationship that military contractors have with the Defense Department bureaucracy. Critical junctures such as the 9/11 attacks contribute to heightened MIC influence in the policymaking process due to a further concentration of power and privilege within the executive branch and a weakening of checks and balances within the federal system. Critical junctures also tend to elevate the opinions of hard-liners in the executive branch at the expense of moderates, whose advocacy of approaches to conflict short of full-scale militarization are less effective in providing symbolic value to political elites during a time of strategic crisis.

The most effective transmission belt linking military corporations to the Bush Administration was the Project for the New American Century (PNAC) (Gibbs, 2004). First, PNAC was established in 1997, and was disproportionately financed and supported by military corporations and oil firms. Ideologically, its membership has close linkages to a history of MIC groups dating back to the Cold War, including the father of neoconservatism Albert Wohlstetter, whose mentorship at the University of Chicago gave rise to several prominent thinkers within the neoconservative movement (Bacevich, 2011). Going beyond the realist preoccupation with security measures necessary to maintain preponderance of power within the international arena and to check rival and potentially rival states from ascending in influence, the neoconservative movement borrowed aggressively from the rollback policy positions advocated by right-wing organizations during the Cold War. In fact, the membership of the Committee on the Present Danger, also heavily financed by military contractors during the Cold War period, overlapped with the membership of PNAC as it was established in 1997.

The Committee on the Present Danger, in both its first iteration in 1950, and its second iteration in 1976, called for an aggressive militarization that would weaken and ultimately help to destabilize or overthrow regimes sympathetic to or aligned with the Soviet Union. Similarly, after 9/11, PNAC called for a global militarization robust enough to effect regime change of rogue states, especially in the Persian Gulf region. The language of the PNAC mirrored the rollback language of the Committee on the Present Danger (CPD) and anticipated a third resurgence of the CPD in 2004. The influence of neoconservatives on the strategic posture of the U.S. was evident in the Defense Planning Guidance document drafted by Paul Wolfowitz in 1992 during the George H.W. Bush Administration, which called for a dramatic expansion of U.S. militarization on par with the earlier NSC-68, which advocated a similar robust expansion of militarization in 1950, just before the outset of the Korean War. In fact, the level of continuity of the rollback position in U.S. foreign policy is especially striking here, and the fact that PNAC was very well-represented in the Bush Administration and linked to earlier iterations of this position is noteworthy of the longstanding continuity of the MIC sector in U.S. foreign policymaking.

Just as with PNAC, the CPD had its greatest influence on policymaking during critical junctures, first during the Korean War of 1950, which provided a pretext for the most dramatic increases in the U.S. military budget in its history, and the perceived gains of the Soviet Union in 1979, including the Soviet invasion of Afghanistan. In 1997, PNAC had little direct influence in policymaking, but after the events of 9/11, its former members were elevated in stature as the Bush Administration used its long-time recommendations for full-scale militarization to respond to the 9/11 attacks. In addition to support for substantial increases in militarization, PNAC called quite explicitly for regime change, focusing heavily on the Persian Gulf region, and targeting Iraq as the country whose regime should be toppled to create a domino-effect of the toppling of dictators and the rise of pro-U.S. regimes in the region.

The interrelationships between PNAC and military contractors is best illustrated by the changing roles of Bruce Jackson, who alternated from being Bob Dole's campaign advisor in 1996 to executive director of PNAC by 1997, to director of strategic planning for Lockheed Martin.

Jackson also founded the Committee to Expand NATO in 1996, a key pillar of Lockheed Martin's efforts to aggressively promote the exportation of weapons abroad in the context of post-cold war reductions in the rate of growth of military spending. Similarly, he founded the Project on Transitional Democracies, advocating an expansion of NATO membership for Eastern European states and newly independent states that used to be part of the Soviet Union. By the late 1990s, Jackson was advocating for regime change in the Middle East, as part of PNAC and as a strategic lobbyist for Lockheed Martin. By 2002, and shortly after the 9/11 attacks, Jackson was invited into the office of Deputy National Security Adviser Stephen Hadley to discuss Jackson's role in founding the Committee for the Liberation of Iraq, which worked closely with former PNAC members who were now in key policy positions within the Bush Administration to help justify an occupation of Iraq in the aftermath of 9/11. Jackson acknowledged that he knew little or nothing about Iraq, but he boasted of the Iraqi exile contacts that his group was able to pull together in his newly emerging organization. These would become a focal point for efforts by administration hardliners to build a case that attempted to link the regime of Saddam Hussein to the events of 9/11 (R. Cumings, 2007).

Another right-wing advocacy group that helped provide the policy agenda for the Bush Administration's response to 9/11 was the National Institute for Public Policy, also closely linked to Lockheed Martin and the nuclear weapons industry. The Institute advocated the revitalization of a strategic campaign to increase the production and utilization of low-level usable nuclear weapons against terrorist groups that pose a threat to U.S. national security. According to William Hartung, three members of the Institute took significant positions with the Bush Administration's foreign policy bureaucracy, and the director of the NIPP was appointed by the Administration to lead the Nuclear Posture Review which recommended the adoption of most of the NIPP recommendations on increasing the stockpile of low-level nuclear weapons, in addition to creating a newer generation of "low-yield" nuclear weapons that could be deployed and used on the battlefield under scenarios in which the war on terror was expanded to enemy territory. The NIPP, like the PNAC, had very close ties to Lockheed Martin, including the presence of Lockheed Martin executive Charles Kupperman on the advisory board of the organization (Hartung and Ciarrocca, 2003).

Finally, the push for continued funding and expansion of a U.S. missile defense system, which had often been the most consistent high-ticket budget item in Cold War and post-Cold War military spending, was justified by a third think tank that also had close ties to the military industrial complex and the Bush Administration. The justification for expanding the missile defense system as part of the war on terror had been a long-standing position of Center for Security Policy, which received one-sixth of its funding from the defense industry (Hartung and Ciarrocca, 2003). The decision to expand National Missile Defense as part of the war on terror proceeded after 9/11 namely due to the influence and recommendations of members of this conservative think tank, several of which were represented in the Bush Administration and gained increasing influence in policy recommendations after 9/11. The missile defense program continued to be expanded and justified even though the National Intelligence Estimate argued that it was highly unlikely that the terrorist threat could be effectively countered by the development of a missile defense program, since terrorist cells were unlikely to be able to acquire long-range missiles and were much more likely to concentrate on small-scale explosives conveyed by "ships, trucks, airplanes and other means" (Hartung and Ciarrocca, 2003).

The lack of fit between the recommendations of the right-wing groups heavily financed and staffed by the military-industrial complex and the recommendations made by the 9/11 Commission to most effectively fight the war on terror are worth noting. The 9/11 Commission indicated that one of the most important avenues for an effective response to Al-Qaeda networks is a robust coordination of intelligence activities across the myriad intelligence agencies that historically had tried to protect their respective turfs in the years leading up to 9/11, which resulted in a lack of shared intelligence that contributed to the success of the 9/11 hijackers (9/11 Commission Report, 2004). Intelligence functions, if effective, needed greater coordination and oversight by a central source, which was supposed to be embodied by the newly created post of the Director of Intelligence. However, what has happened since these recommendations has been a further concentration of intelligence functions by the Defense Department, which now controls most intelligence spending. Such an increased concentration of power in the Defense Department has spawned an intelligence network that has become heavily privatized. Concentrated in the beltway, and specifically in northern Virginia, which has received a disproportionate share of post-9/11 funding, the privatized intelligence functions are increasingly carried out by private companies that have a stake in perpetuating the war on terror and the perpetual designation of new enemies. The privatization of intelligence has further expanded the ranks of the MIC into a myriad of private sector corporations that have benefitted from the widest distribution of intelligence contracts in U.S. defense history, reinforced by the emergence of a very powerful military-intelligence complex that is closely integrated with the profit-making activities of the 10 largest U.S. defense firms (Bamford, 2009).

The Defense Department also expanded its reach into areas previously controlled much more exclusively by the State Department, such as aid and development spending. The expansion of Defense Department supervision of the war on terror had become so pervasive by 2006 that it prompted a Senate Foreign Relations Committee Report chaired by Republican Richard Lugar, entitled "Embassies as Command Posts in the Anti-Terror Campaign" (Senate Committee on Foreign Relations, 2006). The Committee concluded that the Defense Department had begun to usurp the authority and influence of State Department personnel as the U.S. increasingly moved to militarize the war on terror through U.S. embassy compounds, a set of practices that former Defense Secretary Robert Gates argued had gone too far.

Furthermore, the allocations of funding for the war on terror have become very politicized, with disproportionate funding going to rural areas, and regions and states with low population density. This is partly designed to maximize support for military and intelligence spending within regions and localities that disproportionately depend on such spending as a high percentage of economic activity. Recent research has exhaustively confirmed a robust relationship between targeting military spending to rural areas and low population density regions and states as a way to maximize support for a high military budget. In fact, such regions and localities are much more likely to elect representatives who consistently vote for military appropriations, in comparison to large-scale allocations to urban areas where military spending is just one component of overall economic activity (Thorpe, 2014). If we chart the distribution of military spending across the U.S. from the Cold War to the present, the distribution of dollars is far more widespread today across the territorial

U.S. than it was at the height of the Cold War, which helps explain the difficulty in forming Congressional coalitions that are willing to challenge high levels of military spending.

One way of measuring the plausibility of the military-industrial complex as a significant causal factor in U.S. military spending hikes is to examine the "threat definition" used by policymakers and its relationship to the levels of U.S. military spending, especially during the aftermath of critical junctures such as 9/11. The level of escalation of U.S. military spending from 1998 to 2008 is unprecedented in U.S. foreign policy history, despite the fact that the U.S. faced no enemy state with anywhere near the capacity of the former Soviet Union. By 1998, U.S. military spending was already at the average level of spending during the Cold War, and by 2008, the U.S. budget was higher than at any time in Cold War history. What the MIC theory can predict better than realist theory are the types of weapons systems that received disproportionate shares of funding. Realism would expect military spending allocations to finance weapons systems that have a direct utility in countering the threats faced by the U.S.

Using a database developed by the Project on Defense Alternatives, the largest military spending increases after 9/11 were accounted for by the operations and maintenance budget, and by the modernization of existing large-scale weapons systems, most of which were well in-place before the events of 9/11 and were justified by a Rogue Doctrine that was then used as an umbrella strategy for prosecuting a global war on terror (Conetta, 2009). For example, the highest line-item on the Defense Wide Agency and Program Funding for 2010 remained the Missile Defense Agency, which received 7.8 billion dollars in budget allocations, second only to Defense Health Programs at 27.9 billion dollars. For the armed services, before and after 9/11, there has been a reliance on large-scale platforms, including big-deck aircraft carriers, intercontinental bombers, and stealth fighter jets that proved problematic if not useless for the type of counterinsurgency operations emphasized in the war on terror. As Carl Conetta noted in his study for the Project for Defense Alternatives:

> In the decade before the 9/11 attacks, the United States spent over $1 trillion dollars in military modernization. But most of this expenditure proved irrelevant to defending against the most serious attack on America in 60 years. Subsequently, three more years of funding after 9/11 added another $450 billion to modernization accounts, but still the nation found itself ill-equipped to execute the new tasks it had undertaken: counterinsurgency in Iraq and Afghanistan.
>
> CONNETTA, 2010: 10

4 The Post-9/11 Failures of Counterinsurgency

There is a wide body of mainstream and critical literature which concludes that the U.S. "war on terror" was a failure on many levels. First, there is considerable evidence that U.S.-led counterinsurgency campaigns increased support for terrorist groups. The U.S. increased its global military operations post 9/11 to carry out counterinsurgency campaigns in countries experiencing civil, political, economic, and social unrest. The magnitude of these campaigns has been extensively scrutinized by scholars, both outside and inside of the U.S. military, producing a sizeable body of literature concluding the U.S. counterinsurgency programs often increased support for terrorism due to unleashing the scope and scale of military operations targeting societal "enemies." The designation of "enemies" under counterterrorism often included a wide range of civil society groups, including unions, teachers, doctors, environmentalists, and political activists, as well as communities targeted because of their political opposition to the government or the military (Stokes and Rafael, 2010; Eland, 2013; Jeffrey, 2015; Hazelton, 2021).

Second, there has also been an extensive scholarly literature criticizing the scope and scale of U.S. bombing campaigns, particularly the use of drone strikes, expedited across numerous countries by Presidential edict and therefore subject to minimal checks and balances or oversight, and justified as necessary to isolate, defeat and curb the operations of terrorist cells. The release of classified documents pertaining to these programs has contradicted the official government narrative about their effectiveness in targeting terrorists and in avoiding civilian casualties. The evidence is clear that civilian casualties have been a routine product of these drone campaigns, which further risks increasing support for terrorist organizations rather than being an effective tool to fight terrorism (Scahill, 2017). The total costs of the war on terror from 2001 to 2021 has been estimated at $8 trillion, from the global counterinsurgency campaigns to the lengthy wars in Iraq and Afghanistan (Costs of War Project, 2021).

Third, the U.S. wars in Iraq and Afghanistan were failures on several measurements. The U.S. war in Iraq generated substantial support for terrorist organizations in the country, a product of the long-term political, economic, and social divisions that were created and accentuated by the U.S. occupation (Davies, 2010). As the U.S. troops left Iraq during the administration of Barack Obama, the legacy of U.S. prisons and detention centers had already helped produce a radicalization of the insurgency in the country that took the form of Islamic State of Iraq and the Levant (ISIL), whose ability to recruit followers and wage war across vast sections of the Middle East proved to be a major cause of future instability, generating a return of U.S. troops to Iraq in an effort to defeat this latest incarnation of the terrorist threat. The total cost of the Iraq War is estimated to be $2.2 trillion (Costs of War Project, 2021).

Since the U.S. war on ISIS, the U.S. once again has pulled its troops out of Iraq and Syria, a troop removal process that eventually included Afghanistan in 2021, at the beginning of the presidency of Joseph Biden. The war in Afghanistan became the longest ground war in U.S. history, with the result being little more than a return to the status quo as the U.S. failed to defeat the Taliban insurgency. After 20 years and an estimated cost of $2.3 trillion, the U.S. counterinsurgency campaign emerged as a colossal failure, with ample documentation that the Defense Department and U.S. intelligence agencies distorted the missions "successes" through decades long bureaucratic doublespeak that concealed the extent to which the U.S. military operations had further entrenched political, economic and social corruption by a narrow clique of Afghan powerbrokers and had provided further openings for a Taliban resurgence. As was the case with other counterterrorism operations, the U.S. presence in Afghanistan served to incentivize more openings for terrorists who thrived inside the violence, instability and corruption that was accentuated by the U.S. military campaigns (Whitlock, 2021).

5 The Continuity of the MIC from Bush to Obama to Trump to Biden

The circumstances of the post-9/11 period did not signify a dramatic change in U.S. foreign policy, but instead reinforced policy continuities long advocated by interests comprising the military-industrial complex. The opportunity for the MIC to use the events of 9/11 to pursue an agenda of expansive militarization is not unique to the 9/11 attacks, but has recurred throughout U.S. history, and is once again being utilized to construct the threat narratives associated with Russia and China. This pattern allows us to conceptualize an MIC that is deeply embedded as a policy current in establishing long-term strategic responses to perceived threats (Johnson, 2004 and 2007). The expansion of the MIC is most apparent in the revolving door of interests that link the executive branch, especially the Defense Department, to an increasingly consolidated group of military corporations that seeks expanded rents through "threat construction." As I have argued here, the growth of large-scale weapons systems do not represent a particularly useful fit for a war against a global terrorist network. The very presence of such large-scale weapons systems, however, can be explained in large part by the policy preferences and profit imperatives of the MIC itself. As documented here, the MIC utilized think-tanks as transmission belts to policymakers that helped craft the threat definition of 9/11 and the strategic response that followed. This process has real consequences in shaping how the U.S. state responds to critical junctures in U.S. foreign policy.

If we apply the MIC analytical framework to patterns of military spending after the financial crisis of 2008 and through the Biden Administration, the strength of the military-industrial complex appears to be quite robust by comparison with earlier periods of U.S. Cold War history. In fact, it's useful to think of the financial crisis of 2007–2008 as another critical juncture, but one that could have potentially contributed to absolute reductions in military spending similar to past critical junctures such as the de-escalation of the Vietnam War, when the U.S. faced a significant dollar crisis that divided U.S. corporate interests over the rates of military spending. The result at that time was an absolute reduction in military spending (in constant dollars) from $550 billion in 1968 to $400 billion in 1975, a reduction that contrasts with the large-scale increases in military spending during most of the post-Cold War period, despite the absence of any threat comparable to the Soviet Union. Despite the 2008 economic crisis, the worst since the Great Depression, military spending has mostly continued to escalate, in contrast to the reductions during the post-Vietnam critical juncture of U.S. policymaking. Even with the modest cuts to U.S. military spending in 2013, the U.S. military budget remained extraordinarily high compared to the Cold War period. This is due in no small part to the 15-year escalation of military spending, from 1998 through 2012, that has resulted in higher military budgets than at any other point after World War II. Most recently, after brief reductions of military spending in the mid-2010s associated with drawdowns of U.S. troops in Iraq and Afghanistan, the last seven years from 2017 to 2023 have seen the U.S. military budget reach new heights in dollar adjusted figures, exceeding $1 trillion dollars (Kaplan, 2023).

As the final section of this chapter will demonstrate, the lobbying power of the constellation of interests comprising the MIC has been central to constructing the most recent threats of Russia and China as the primary justification for the latest round of military spending escalation.

6   The MIC and the Threat Construction of Russia and China

The interests comprising the military-industrial complex have lobbied aggressively for maintaining high levels of military spending in anticipation of emerging "threats" to U.S. global power. Instead of lowering the scope and scale of U.S. global commitments to meet the realities of the end of the Cold War, the military-industrial complex has been a key player in using critical junctures in

U.S. foreign policy to justify maintaining and expanding U.S. military spending and U.S. global power projection. As I have documented thus far, the role of the military-industrial complex is especially clear when it comes to critical junctures in U.S. foreign policy. The interest groups within the MIC were active in justifying a retention of large-scale weapon systems after the end of the Cold War in preparation for a simultaneous two-and-a-half war scenario against "rogue states." The attacks of 9/11 provided a pretext for increasing the military budget to yearly levels that were higher than any military budget in Cold War history. U.S. national security planners treated the "war on terror" as legitimation for prosecuting two extensive wars in Iraq and Afghanistan and for undertaking a global counterinsurgency campaign utilizing U.S. special forces to train and equip foreign militaries and to participate in wars against designated enemies around the world, buttressed by U.S. drone warfare to target designated terrorists on foreign soil.

The costs of these wars, combined with the levels of secrecy, lack of accountability and unprecedented length, have been well-documented. The military-industrial complex has grown well-beyond the concerns expressed by President Dwight Eisenhower in his farewell address in 1961. Indeed, the MIC has become an even more far-reaching military-industrial-surveillance complex that is deeply entrenched in U.S. foreign policymaking, including identifying threats, and the policies deemed necessary to defend against those threats. As the costs and blowback of the war on terror mounted, the U.S. finally pulled back from its wars in Iraq and Afghanistan, but the military-industrial complex has emerged more powerful than ever. The Defense Department is alone among U.S. federal agencies that can repeatedly fail an audit of its finances and continue to receive appropriations that are the highest in its history (Knox, 2022).

After a brief period of military spending reduction in the aftermath of the Iraq War and during the second term of the Obama Administration, U.S. national security planners began to quickly pivot to the rise of China as the foremost threat to U.S. national security, essentially replacing the "war on terror" as the primary threat that would drive future military appropriations. As with other critical junctures identified in this chapter, the military-industrial complex would use the threat of China and Russia to justify substantial increases in U.S. military spending over the past six years. While the Obama Administration would begin to militarize the conflict with China as part of a "pivot to Asia," the Trump Administration would codify the threats of China and Russia into its yearly National Security Strategy reports. Starting in 2017, the emphasis of U.S. geostrategy was overwhelmingly focused on countering China and Russia as the foremost security threats to the U.S., justifying another period of escalation of the U.S. military budget that has continued under the Biden Administration.

The U.S. geostrategic rivalry with Russia had been building throughout the post-Cold War period. The U.S. decision to expand NATO after the Cold War ended represented a geopolitical continuity in U.S. power projection that started during the early stages of the Cold War, when NATO was seen as not just countering the Soviet Union but keeping Europe locked into U.S. security and economic objectives. After the collapse of the Soviet Union, U.S. national security strategists under the George H.W. Bush Administration drafted a defense guidance document in 1992 that called for maintaining and expanding U.S. global preponderance to counter any future threats to U.S. primacy. Part of this ongoing commitment to U.S. global preponderance has been the U.S.-led expansion of NATO. During the post-Cold War period, the purposes of NATO were redefined from "defending Western Europe" to a global NATO whose military operations would be expanded well-beyond Western Europe. This meant that NATO expanded more dramatically during the post-Cold War period than during the Cold War itself, notably by adding Eastern European countries to the Alliance. This NATO expansion was combined with the simultaneous expansion of the European Union to Eastern Europe, alongside billions of dollars in U.S. aid to pro-Western movements in Eastern Europe. For Russia, this constituted an encirclement of its own territorial and security interests. U.S. government officials even understood that NATO expansion would be a very risky undertaking, even potentially threatening all-out war, even nuclear war, with Russia.

The military-industrial complex has been directly involved in promoting NATO expansion from the very beginning. From 1996 through early 1998, the six biggest U.S. military contractors spent $51 million lobbying for NATO expansion. These lobbying dollars supported the work of the U.S. Committee to Defend NATO, which worked directly with national security officials in the Clinton Administration and in Congress to justify and promote an expanded role for NATO in the post-Cold War period, which would lead to a lucrative market for the sale of U.S. weapons, an arms market that the Clinton Administration supported aggressively during his second term in office (Seelve, 1998). As documented by historian David Gibbs, the U.S. policy of NATO expansion, and the role of the military-industrial complex, was a key factor in driving U.S. intervention in the former Yugoslavia, where U.S. policymakers insisted on a central role for NATO as a precondition for supporting peace talks (Gibbs, 2009). The expansion of NATO to Eastern Europe has been documented as one of the factors that led to the Russian invasion of Ukraine—certainly not the only factor, but one that has been emphasized for decades as having blowback consequences, including provoking a Russian military invasion of Ukraine, referenced as a potential outcome of NATO expansion even by U.S. national security planners (Schwartz and Layne, 2023).

To be clear, the above is not at all to excuse or to apologize for the barbarous Russian invasion of Ukraine, which has its origins in the ascendancy of Russian far-right nationalism, used aggressively by dictator Vladimir Putin to consolidate domestic power by using Russian chauvinism and foreign enemies as ideological weapons against domestic political opponents. Indeed, Putin's foreign policies are justified in Russian domestic politics by fascistic ideologies that are invoked to provide legitimacy for the invasion, which includes state propaganda of a Russian essentialism that denies the legitimacy of Ukraine as an independent country (Glazebrook, 2022).

However, the role of NATO expansion has at the very least helped to activate the most reactionary impulses of Vladimir Putin. From a strictly geostrategic analysis, the Russian invasion of Ukraine could have been seen as one of the ways that the Putin regime would decide to respond to decades of perceived geopolitical, geoeconomic and geostrategic challenges from the West. The fact that the U.S. national security establishment continued to expand its global military commitments, alliances, and capabilities, including by expanding NATO to the boundaries of a rival country armed with nuclear weapons, appears to defy rational foreign policy statecraft. The expansion of NATO indicates a unified political, economic, and ideological commitment of the national security establishment, and both U.S. political parties, to an unending and forever escalating global military commitments that are entirely compatible with, and justified by, the interests and directives of the military-industrial complex.

From the outset of the Russian invasion of Ukraine, the U.S. national security establishment has unequivocally endorsed, with Congressional bipartisan approval, over one hundred billion dollars in weapons sales to Ukraine that are intended to be used not just to aid Ukrainian troops, but as part of a proxy war of the U.S. targeting Russia. A recent release of classified U.S. classified documents has exposed the extent to which U.S. military and intelligence officials are directly involved "in virtually every aspect of the war," including identifying Russian targets (DeYoung, 2023). The direct engagement of U.S. military and intelligence personnel in the prosecution of the Ukrainian War has escalated the conflict from a war of liberation to a possible nuclear war between the U.S. and Russia. At the same time, the interests comprising the military-industrial complex are reaping outsized profits as a result of the escalation of U.S. weapons production, much of which will not even be produced for years and therefore unable to help Ukraine, but is being added to the bill of U.S. taxpayers as part of the long-term costs of the war, including long-term war-planning against Russia. Even before the war in Ukraine, the Pentagon was slated to receive $7.3 trillion over the next decade to pay for large-scale weapon systems. That figure could easily rise to an additional trillion dollars of expenditures (over the next decade) based on a range of long-term big ticket weapon systems that has been justified by the Ukraine War itself, most of which will never likely be used in the Ukraine War (Hartung and Gledhill, 2022; Klare, 2022).

As the Ukraine war continues, the U.S. has escalated its global campaign to wage economic, geopolitical, and geostrategic containment of China. Starting in 2017, the Trump Administration identified China and Russia as the primary threats to U.S. national security. Even earlier, the Obama Administration identified China as an increasingly hostile actor, which was based on an assessment of Chinese military, economic and political actions in Asia and globally. What is striking about these developments is the relative shift from decades of U.S. economic and political cooperation with China. By the middle of the 2010s, U.S. foreign policy shifted toward greater confrontation with China and less cooperation. What explains the pivot of the U.S. toward a more confrontational foreign policy strategy toward China?

For decades, the U.S. led the creation of a global neoliberal economic architecture that facilitated, rewarded, and encouraged an expansion of transnational capitalist investment through global value chains. As part of this approach, U.S. policymakers supported giving China most-favored nation status and entering the World Trade Organization. Transnational capitalist investors, especially in the information technology sector, lobbied U.S. policymakers to pursue policies that lowered the costs of expanding global value chains to China, a process that I have written about extensively (Cox and Lee, 2012; Cox and Wartenbe, 2018). From the early 2000s to the 2010s, China has been at the center of transnational globalization, partnering with transnational capitalist investors in a mutually profitable wave of foreign direct investment strategies, focusing China's economic policies toward an export-led growth model that has integrated China with Western financial and investment markets.

The business and political coalitions in U.S. foreign policy advocating political and economic cooperation with China have been eclipsed from the mid-2010s to the present. Global capitalist crises, starting with the 2008 global recession, have sharpened the tensions between U.S. corporations who have long benefitted from locating their global value chains within the China market and those corporations who have long felt threatened by the competition posed by Chinese exports (Cox, 2019). Meanwhile the Chinese government has sought to exert more concessions from foreign investors and to increase the scope and scale of state intervention toward an upscaling of Chinese capacity in 5G technology and artificial intelligence. An acceleration of Chinese nationalist political strategies in recent years, combined with the global political and economic crises of the COVID pandemic, have increased the costs of foreign direct investments for Western corporations. Corporations that have long been in competition with China, especially in the steel and aluminum sectors, have aggressively led the campaign for sanctions against China (and were major contributors to President Trump's campaign). At the same time, interest groups within the military-industrial complex, which have long sought to identify China as a threat justification for higher military budgets, have identified an expansion of Chinese military capacity and utilization, especially in the South China Sea, but also throughout East Asia, as a threat to U.S. extra-regional hegemony in Asia (Grazier, 2021). The rise of China's economic and military capacity in Asia and its long-term claim to the island of Taiwan, with newly rising military maneuvers and tensions in recent years, has accelerated an increasing confrontational posture between the U.S. and China (Grazier, 2022).

The national security establishment in the U.S. has used the threat of China to justify another round of large-scale increases in the U.S. military budget. At the very moment when it appeared that lowering the military commitments associated with the war on terror would provide the space for reductions in military spending, the China (and Russia) threats have been utilized as a broad-brush for justifying a new period of robust expansion in U.S. military expenditure. The U.S. could have acknowledged China's rise as an economic competitor and responded with its own government economic policies designed to fortify U.S. capacity to acquire, develop and profit from 5G and AI technologies. That is certainly part of what the Biden Administration and the U.S. Congress has done with the CHIPS Act, providing large-scale subsidies to corporations locating their high technology production activities within the United States. However, the U.S. government and national security officials have not stopped there: the escalation of global sanctions against China that started under Trump has intensified under Biden, alongside dramatic increases in military spending that has provided military contractors with large-scale appropriations extending through the 2030s and 2040s, consistent with the expectation of prolonged global military conflict with China. Indeed, the voices of the national security establishment, as well as both wings of the two U.S. corporate-backed political parties, are increasingly (and openly) talking about war scenarios with China (Klare, 2022).

As with past escalations of U.S. military spending, this current escalation is very much tied to the agenda-setting architecture of lobbying networks and think-tanks of the military-industrial complex, which has a profit-making interest in a hawkish diagnosis of, and response to, the "China threat." The public affairs database Quorum provides tracking of policy issues in the U.S. Congress through how often particular mentions of issues occur within specified time intervals. There have been spikes in references to "Chinese military" in Congressional floor debates that have been especially pronounced from 2018 to the present. Similarly, use of the LexisNexis database shows how articles focused on the "Chinese military" and threats posed by that military, have increased dramatically in recent years, especially in the U.S. and Western press (Grazier, 2022).

The framing of the Chinese military threat, as it pertains to U.S. national security, is being led by think-tanks directly tied to the military-industrial complex, who are well-represented in the U.S. Congress in terms of lobbies, campaign donations and networks that connect U.S. government officials directly to military contractors when it comes to yearly appropriation decisions. These think-tanks are the sources for Congressional testimony pertaining to the "China threat," and for news reports about the "China threat" (Grazier, 2021). In contrast, there is no comparable alternative set of policy voices representing a different assessment of Chinese military power, capability, and intent. There is also an absence, or at least a very limited presence, of any alternative think-tanks or scholars or activists who are recommending an alternative set of policy responses. The dominance of the military-industrial complex is consistently unchallenged in legislative forums, executive branch deliberations, media coverage and cultural propaganda. As William Hartung has noted, the influence of the military-industrial complex is at an all-time high, which in turn has kept military spending at the highest levels since World War II:

> Lobbying expenditures by all the denizens of the MIC are even higher during the last two election cycles. Such funds are used to employ 820 lobbyists, or more than one for every member of Congress. And mind you, more than two-thirds of these lobbyists had swirled through Washington's infamous revolving door from jobs at the Pentagon or in Congress to lobby for the arms industry. Their contacts in government and knowledge of arcane acquisition procedures help ensure that the money keeps flowing for more guns, tanks, ships and missiles. Just last month, the office of Senator Elizabeth Warren (D-Mass.) reported that nearly 700 former high-ranking government officials, including former generals and admirals, now work for defense contractors. While a few of

them are corporate board members of highly paid executives, 91 percent of them become Pentagon lobbyists, according to the report.

HARTUNG AND FREEMAN, 2023

The MIC political and economic power structure has been fully institutionalized across all branches of the U.S. government. The result has been a threat inflation that is almost never subject to serious public debate or scrutiny. This is evident in the policy rhetoric about China, whose recent increases in military spending have still kept Chinese military spending three times lower than the U.S. and nowhere near the global capacity of the U.S. military, especially when combining U.S. military power with that of countries allied with the U.S. In fact, China's focus on military expansion and modernization is overwhelmingly focused on creating a "defensive buffer extending outward from the Chinese coast" (Grazier, 2022). As a 2022 report by the Project on Government Oversight concludes, "In many discussions about China's intentions, the strategy is understood to create an exclusion zone inside the so-called 'first island chain.' This defensive line extends from the southern tip of Japan through the Ryukyu Islands, past the western edge of the Philippine Islands, and then curls around the edge of the South China Sea. Taiwan, notably, sits inside this line" (Grazier, 2022).

In contrast, the commentary emerging from well-entrenched MIC lobbying networks, think tanks and the Defense Department extrapolate global ambitions and long-term global expansionism as the aim of Chinese military spending. In this way, the current alarmist propaganda serves the same political and economic functions as previous MIC propaganda. First, the China threat is escalated for domestic political purposes, to deflect attention from policy failures in the U.S. by blaming China for these failures. This was evident during the global COVID pandemic (Layne, 2020). Second, the speculation about Chinese long-term global military ambitions allows for a perpetual escalation of U.S. military spending across the next few decades, including planning for hypothetical wars with China or with China and Russia simultaneously (Klare, 2023). Third, the escalating U.S. military budgets lock-in U.S. discretionary spending overwhelmingly towards war preparation and war itself, linking U.S. industrial policy to military spending and threat inflation, while there is less room for social welfare spending or industrial policy that can be directed toward public purposes. The emphasis is on focusing expenditures toward private sector military accumulation at public expense, which satisfies financial investors who move large pools of money liberally around profitable investment opportunities.

7 Conclusion

What explains the resistance to cuts in military spending, despite the absence of an external threat comparable to the Soviet Union, and despite an economic crisis that in the past has led to more significant cuts to the military budget? The first factor is the long-term centralization of power within the executive branch that has occurred as an outgrowth of the Cold War and has been extended and further institutionalized as part of the never-ending war on terror. The centralization of executive branch power has contributed to a threat definition that favors bureaucracies that have disproportionate control over military and intelligence resources. The Defense Department exerts considerable influence over threat definition, and therefore over recommendations for how resources are to be allocated to respond to foreign threats. This also gives military corporations added leverage in decisions pertaining to military spending. As I have documented here, the largest defense contractors have an active engagement in policy-planning organizations that include military contractors and former defense department officials. But there is an even more embedded set of institutional relationships that Jerry Harris has documented:

> The symbiotic relationship between state and industry can be seen in the National Defense Industrial Association (NDIA). An organization with 9,000 corporate affiliates, 26,000 individual members, and no foreign membership. The Association maintains close coordination with the DOD functioning through 56 chapters and 34 committees, each with direct access and a working relationship with the DOD. Divided up among these contractors is the largest single slice of the Pentagon's budget.
> HARRIS, 2008: 129–130

The political strength of military corporations has been further enhanced by their economic consolidation, which allows a smaller number of firms to secure a higher percentage of prime military contracts. The top five military contractors are heavily engaged in political mobilization and in the disproportionate financing of think-tanks and policy-planning organizations advocating increases in spending for big-ticket weapons items, regardless of whether or not they are appropriate to counter the type of enemies the U.S. is most likely to face over the next decade. In addition, the top military contractors increasingly produce military weapons systems through a supply chain that connects them with other sectors of the corporate economy which then have a vested interest (at least in the short-term) of supporting military spending increases. Many of the broadest cross-section of corporate interests, prominent military contractors included, are working inside the "Fix the Debt" coalition, which recommends cuts to the federal budget that are disproportionately focused on entitlements such as Social Security and Medicare, while military spending is spared similar cuts.

While progressive groups were arguing for larger cuts in military spending to help spare social programs, the "Fix the Debt" corporate coalition advocated smaller cuts in military spending and much more significant cuts to entitlement programs (Confessore, 2013: A1). What is instructive about the "Fix the Debt" corporate coalition is how dispersed its ranks are across just about all corporate sectors, from finance to a range of manufacturing interests to military contractors. The current MIC agenda is being given at least tacit support from a range of non-MIC corporate interests that are in favor of preserving high levels of military spending while expanding cuts to entitlements. This is primarily due to the overlapping interests of large-scale institutional financial investors and military contractors, as well as the supply chain relationships that link military contractors with a base of manufacturing firms that produce goods for the military (D'Eramo, 2023).

In addition, the ability of military contractors to preserve big-ticket items is further entrenched by institutional and economic relationships between military firms and Congressional power-brokers, whose districts include significant military contracts. When those districts are spread out across the country, including to rural and relatively isolated areas that disproportionately depend on defense spending, then military contractors have more leverage in preventing the elimination of weapons systems—even when the Pentagon no longer wants those weapons systems (Thorpe, 2014).

In short, the balance of institutional and economic power has tilted aggressively in favor of the military-industrial complex, to the point where numerous corporate, executive branch, Congressional and bureaucratic allies are linked in favoring the maintenance of relatively high levels of military spending. It will take a vigorous political response to dislodge such an embedded political force. That means building social movements which can link antiwar and antimilitarization with a progressive social spending agenda that has suffered from the priorities of the military-industrial complex.

References

Bacevich, Andrew (2011) "Tailors to the Emperor," *New Left Review* 69: 101–124.
Bamford, James (2009) *The Shadow Factory: the NSA from 9/11 to the Eavesdropping of America*. Milwaukee, WI: Anchor Press.

Baran, Paul and Paul Sweezy, *Monopoly Capital*. New York: Penguin 1966.

Brady, Ryan R. and Victoria R. Greenfield (2010) "Competing Explanations of U.S. Defense Industry Consolidation in the 1990s and Their Policy Implications," *Contemporary Economic Policy* 28 (2): 288–306.

Breslin, Thomas (2011). *The Great Anglo-Celtic Divide in the History of American Foreign Relations*. Westport, CT: Praeger.

Collier, David and Ruth Collier (1991) *Shaping the Political Arena*. Princeton, NJ: Princeton University Press.

Conetta, Carl (2010) "Undisciplined Defense," *Project for Defense Alternatives*, Jan. 18.

Confessore (2013) "Public Goals, Private Interests in Debt Campaign." *New York Times*, Jan. 9: A1.

Costs of War Project, "2021 Report," Brown University.

Cox, Ronald W. (2019) Corporate Power, Class Conflict and the Crisis of the New Globalization. Lanham, MD: Lexington Books

Cox, Ronald W. (1994) *Power and Profits: U.S. Policy in Central America*. Lexington: University of Kentucky Press.

Cox, Ronald W. and Daniel Skidmore-Hess (1999) *U.S. Politics and the Global Economy: Corporate Power, Conservative Shift*. Boulder, CO: Lynne Rienner Publishers.

Cox, Ronald W. and Sylvan Lee (2012) "Transnational Capital and the U.S.-China Nexus," chapter 2 in *Corporate Power and Globalization in U.S. Foreign Policy*, ed. Ronald W. Cox. New York: Routledge Press.

Cox, Ronald W. and Michael Wartenbe (2018) "The Politics of Global Value Chains," in *The Political Economy of Robots*, edited by Ryan Kiggins 17–40. New York: Palgrave Macmillan.

Cumings, Bruce, Ervand Abrahamian, and Moshe Maoz (2004) *Inventing the Axis of Evil*. New York: New Press.

Cumings, Richard (2007) "U.S.: Lockheed Stock and Two Smoking Barrels," *Corpwatch*, Jan. 16.

Davies, Sandy (2010) *Blood on Our Hands: the American Invasion and Destruction of Iraq*. Ann Arbor, MI: Nimble Pluribus.

D'Eramo, Marco (2023) "Death Merchants?" *Sidecar, New Left Review*, May 11.

DeYoung, Karen (2023) "An Intellectual Battle Rages: Is the U.S. in a Proxy War with Russia?" *Washington Post*, April 18.

Eland, Ivan (2013) *The Failure of Counterinsurgency: Why Hearts and Minds Are Seldom Won*. Westport, CT: Praeger.

Ferguson, Thomas and Joel Rogers (1987) *Right Turn: the Decline of the Democrats and the Future of American Politics*. New York: Hill and Wang.

Foster, John Bellamy, Hannah Holleman and Robert McChesney (2008) "The U.S. Imperial Triangle and Military Spending," *Monthly Review.org*, October 1.

Gibbs, David (2009) *First Do No Harm: Humanitarian Intervention and the Destruction of Yugoslavia*. Nashville, TN: Vanderbilt University Press.

Gibbs, David (1991) *Political Economy of Third World Intervention*. Chicago, IL: University of Chicago Press.

Gibbs, David (2004) "Pretexts in U.S. Foreign Policy: the War on Terrorism in Historical Perspective," *New Political Science* 26 (3): 293–321.

Glazebrook, Dan (2022) "Alexander Dugin and Fascism on the Left." *Counterpunch +*, April 10.

Grazier, Dan (2021) "The China Threat Is Being Inflated to Justify More Spending." *Project for Government Oversight*, February 17.

Grazier, Dan (2022) "Chinese Threat Inflation and America's Nonsensical Plans," *Project for Government Oversight*, Dec. 7, Washington, DC.

Harris, Jerry (2006) *The Dialectics of Globalization: Economic and Political Conflict in a Transnational World*. London: Cambridge Scholars Publishing.

Hartung, William (2019) "Merger Mania: The Military-Industrial Complex on Steroids," Salon, July 22.

Hartung, William (2021) "Profits of War: Corporate Beneficiaries of the Post-9/11 Pentagon Spending Surge," *Center for International Policy*, September 13.

Hartung, William and Michelle Ciarrocca (2003) "The Military-Industrial Think Tank Complex," *Multinational Monitor*, Jan.-Feb.: 17–20.

Hartung, William and Ben Freeman (2023) "Unwarranted Influence, Twenty-First Century Style: Not Your Grandfather's Military-Industrial Complex," *TomDispatch*, May 4.

Hartung, William and Julia Gledhill (2022) "Ukraine and the Profits of War," *TomDispatch*, April 17.

Hazelton, Jacqueline L. (2021) "The Hearts and Minds Myth: How America Gets Counterinsurgency Wrong," *Foreign Affairs*, July 15.

Homolar, Alexandra (2010) "Rebels Without a Conscience: the Evolution of the Rogue State Narrative in U.S. Security Policy," *European Journal of International Relations* 17 (4): 705–727.

Jeffrey, James F. (2015) "Why Counterinsurgency Doesn't Work," *Foreign Affairs*, March/April.

Johnson, Chalmers (2004) *Blowback: the Costs and Consequences of American Empire*. New York: Holt Paperbacks.

Johnson, Chalmers (2007) *Nemesis: the Last Days of the American Republic*. New York: Metropolitan Books.

Kalecki, Michael (1971) *Selected Essays on the Dynamics of the Capitalist Economy*. London: Cambridge University Press.

Kaplan, Fred (2023) "President Biden's Proposed Budget for National Security is Wild," *Slate*, March 14.

Kidron, Michael (1970) *Western Capitalism Since the War*. New York: Penguin.

Klare, Michael (1996) *Rogue States and Nuclear Outlaws: America's Search for a New Foreign Policy*. New York: Hill and Wang.

Klare, Michael (2022) "The Ukraine War's Collateral Damage," *TomDispatch*, May 22.

Klare, Michael (2023) "Spurring an Endless Arms Race," *TomDispatch*, April 16.

Knox, Jennifer (2022) "Defense Spending Reaches Record High as Pentagon Fails Its Audit for Fifth Time," *The Equation*, Union of Concerned Scientists, Dec. 14.

Layne, Christopher (2020) "Preventing the China-U.S. Cold War from Turning Hot," *The Chinese Journal of International Politics* 13 (3): 343–385.

Leslie, Jaques (2014) "The True Cost of Hidden Money: a Piketty Protégé's Theory on Tax Havens," *New York Times*, June 15: A19.

Miliband, Ralph (1969) *The State in Capitalist Society*. London: Weidenfeld and Nicolson.

Mills, C. Wright (1956) *The Power Elite*. London: Oxford University Press.

9/11 Commission Report (2004) "Reorganization, Transformation and Information Sharing," *U.S. Government Accountability Office*, August 3.

Rosenbaum, David (1989) "Spending Can be Cut in Half, Former Defense Officials Say," *New York Times*, Dec. 13: p. B14.

Scahill, Jeremy (2017) *The Assassination Complex: Inside the Government's Secret Drone Warfare Program*. New York: Simon and Schuster.

Schwartz, Benjamin and Christopher Layne (2023) "Why Are We in Ukraine?" *Harper's* 346: 23–35.

Seelve, Katherine O. (1998) "Arms Contractors Spend to Promote an Expanded NATO" *New York Times*, March 30.

Semler, Stephen (2021) "The Top Five Military Contractors Ate $2 Trillion During the Afghanistan War." *Speaking Security*, Substack, August.

Senate Committee on Foreign Relations (2006) "Embassies as Command Posts in the Anti-Terror Campaign," Dec. 15.

Skaff, Richard (2012) "The Military-Industrial Complex: a Capitalist System Run Amok," *Global Research: Centre for Research on Globalization*, Dec. 14.

Skidmore, David (1996) *Reversing Course: Carter's Foreign Policy, Domestic Politics and the Failure of Reform*. Nashville, TN: Vanderbilt University Press.

Stokes, Doug, and Sam Rafael (2010) *Global Energy Security and American Hegemony*. Baltimore: Johns Hopkins University Press.

Thorpe, Rebecca (2014) *The American Warfare State: the Domestic Politics of Military Spending*. Chicago: University of Chicago Press, 2014.

Whitlock, Greg (2021) *The Afghanistan Papers*. New York: Simon and Schuster.

CHAPTER 3

The Billionaire Dimension of Class Power within Economic Sectors

Rob Piper

1 Introduction[1]

Ever since the beginning of what scholars have referred to as the period of neoliberal capitalism (roughly forty years ago), the national wealth of the United States has reached unprecedented levels. The Federal Reserve reported back in 2019 that national wealth in the U.S. had reached $126.08 trillion ($396.85 trillion in assets minus $270.77 trillion in liabilities) (*U.S. Federal Reserve*, 2020: 3). This is double the national wealth in 2012 of $60.09 trillion ($226.89 trillion in assets minus $166.79 trillion in liabilities) (*U.S. Federal Reserve*, 2013: 2).

Despite this dramatic increase in national wealth, an increasing amount of American wealth has found its way into the hands of a smaller percentage of the population. Americans in the bottom half of the income distribution only saw their average pretax income rise from $16,000 to $16,200, while those in the top 10% saw their income more than double, those in the top 1% saw theirs more than triple, and those in the top 0.001% saw theirs more than septuple (Giridharadas, 2018: 16).

Indicative of this class disparity, a peculiar trend has emerged during the period of neoliberal capitalism: the number of individuals that have achieved a net worth of $1 billion (billionaires) has increased more than any other time in American history. Most economic historians agree that before 1970 there were not even five billionaires in the United States, but between 1982 and 1987, the number of American billionaires grew from 15 to 44 (*Lovemoney*, 2019). By March of 2020 the number of U.S. billionaires had reached 610; over a forty-fold increase since 1982 (*Americans for Tax Fairness*, 2020). By comparison, this rate of increase outpaced inflation, which increased over six-fold since 1970! And it far surpassed real U.S. GDP growth since 1970, which only increased three-fold. And the rate of billionaire proliferation easily dwarfs the rate of increase in

---

1 This chapter is revised and expanded from Rob Piper (2023), "The Institutional Drivers of Billionaire Wealth at the Sectoral Level," *Class, Race and Corporate Power*, Vol. 11 (1): Article 3.

national wealth by an immense margin. What factors have contributed to this trend of billionaire proliferation during the neoliberal period?

2 Theoretical Framework

Explaining the increase in billionaires during the period of neoliberal capitalism requires an analysis of the U.S. economy at the macroeconomic level. Descriptive evidence from literature explaining billionaire proliferation at the macroeconomic level highlights major economic, social, and political themes that correlate with the concentration of wealth in the U.S. during neoliberal capitalism. These themes resemble comprehensive, interrelated, structural, and institutional aspects of capitalist power (or drivers as I will refer to them) that led to a massive increase in billionaires (and the class disparity that comes with them). They include:

1. *Financialization*: the accumulation of capital mainly through financial activities. Contains the components of "debt" (collection of interest on loans in order to accumulate capital), "securitization" (turning non-financial assets into tradable financial instruments), "capital mobility" (the ease in which capital is moved around for conducting financial activities), "financial shift" (the move by different economic sectors from productive non-financial activities to less productive financial activities), and "intermediation" (when middlemen act as financial facilitators between multiple economic sectors).
2. *Rentierism*: the control of access to productive activities and assets for the sole purpose of extracting capital in the form of rents. Contains the components of "subsidization" (the act by capital accumulators to benefit from state support and investments) and "concentration" (small numbers of firms controlling access to a sector and its market).
3. *Labor Exploitation*: the exploitation of labor exclusively for the benefit of capital accumulation. Possesses the two components of "labor devaluation" (ensuring that less capital is expended for the benefit of labor) and "worker displacement" (displacing workers from their jobs or vice versa).
4. *Shareholder Culture*: the societal reverence for capital accumulation that creates a permissive environment for billionaire wealth proliferation. Consists of the following components: "maximization of shareholder value" (giving precedence to the maximization of profits and the interests of shareholders), "market fundamentalism" (the ideology that society benefits only when markets are structured for the advantage of capital accumulation), and "manipulation of perception" (the effort by

capital accumulators to influence societal perceptions of their actions in positive ways).
5. *Crony Capitalism*: collusion between business and government officials to preserve the interests of capital accumulation at the expense of labor and society. Has the components of "lobbying" (influence of current government officials to ensure favorable policies), "regulatory capture" (control of government regulatory structures to ensure favorable policies), and "campaign finance" (monetary support to candidates for elected office to ensure favorable policies).
6. *Tax Policy*: the decisions that have manipulated the tax code to prioritize the capital accumulation that leads to billionaire wealth over all other societal investments. Tax Policy contains the component of "loopholes" (ambiguities or inadequacies within the tax code that can be exploited in a beneficial way by capital accumulators).

The above institutional drivers and their components provide a comprehensive framework for explaining billionaire proliferation at the macroeconomic level. But there is no analysis that explains billionaire proliferation at the lower, meso-economic (economic sector) level. The purpose of this chapter is to fill this gap in the literature by 1) fully examining the characteristics associated with economic sector wealth that are responsible for billionaire wealth and 2) analyzing how certain institutional drivers may have most contributed to billionaire wealth at this level. The chapter will achieve this by identifying the sectors where billionaire wealth is most concentrated, and then creating a sectoral analysis framework to analyze why billionaire wealth is concentrated in these sectors.

For the purposes of this analysis, a sector is defined as a distinct area of economic activity. As there are multiple sectors in the U.S. economy it is impractical to try and trace the patterns in all of them. Further, many of these sectors overlap with one another and there is not a single authority or consensus on just what constitutes a distinct economic sector in the U.S. economy. Therefore, it becomes essential to choose a sample of the most relevant sectors for which to focus this meso-economic analysis of billionaire wealth. Choosing which sectors to analyze requires one to consider factors that will best help to illustrate and analyze the patterns that led to the concentration of billionaire wealth during the neoliberal period.

The number of billionaires within a sector will be the metric used for sector selection (the most obvious factor to consider). Billionaire wealth signifies a concentration in the distribution of capital, as such, if capital was distributed evenly within a sector there would be more millionaires and fewer billionaires. Based on the review of the U.S. economy through the lens of these criteria, the following three sectors are chosen to be analyzed in detail: finance, information technology, and food and beverage.

3   Sector Overview

The U.S. finance sector provides financial services to people and businesses and consists of sub-sectors like banking, investment services, tax preparation, accounting, and insurance. According to the financial media website Investopedia, this sector provides the processes that ensure that businesses and individuals obtain capital to pay for goods and services and to finance the means of production (Kenton, 2021). The relevance of the U.S. financial services sector to this analysis is due to its dominance of billionaire wealth. According to Forbes Magazine, most U.S. billionaires in 2022 either worked, obtained income, or acted as stakeholders in this sector (Dolan and Peterson-Withorn, 2022). Other sources in financial media highlight that "with senior bankers on Wall Street and the City of London paid well above €1 million ($1.3 million) on average" that this sector was (in 2021) the top industry most likely to make one a millionaire (*Business Insider India*, 2021).

Current assets of U.S. financial institutions amounted to approximately $123.1 trillion by 2020 (*Statista*, May 2022). Even further, the sub-sectors of commercial banking, life insurances and annuities, and retirement and pension plans were among the sectors with the highest amounts of revenue in 2023 (the fifth, seventh, and ninth highest respectively), totaling $3.27 trillion (*IBISWorld*, 2023). As far as net income, multiple sub-sectors of the financial services sector such as banks and investment management firms were among the top ten industries with highest net profit margins as early as 2017, with finance and insurance possessing the fourth highest GDP share: 7.2% of U.S. GDP totaling $1.26 trillion (banks, insurance carriers, investment funds, etc. add up to about 1/14th of U.S. total economy, with the Federal Reserve Bank alone constituting 3.1% of total GDP) (*Blue Water Credit,* 2017). As expected, the financial services sector has become an increasingly large source of profit over the last several decades, with sector profits accounting for approximately 40 percent of total U.S. economy profits and nearly half of total U.S. corporate profits by the turn of the 21st century (Krippner, 2012: 28, 33). The financial sector accounts for a significant and growing share of U.S. wealth and profits, but only 15% of the funds generated by this sector go to businesses in non-financial sectors with the rest simply being traded between firms within the sector that provide services for moving money around (i.e., intermediation) (Mazzucato, 2018: 136).

The information technology (or "tech") sector is described by Investopedia as being "comprised of businesses that sell goods and services in electronics, software, computers, artificial intelligence, and other industries related to information technology (IT)" while investing heavily in research and development for risky projects with great potential for growth (like social media platforms and search engines) (Frankenfield, 2022). According to Forbes Magazine, the U.S. tech sector had the second highest number of billionaires in 2022 (Dolan and Peterson-Withorn, 2022). As discussed in the financial press, tech sector billionaires in 2021 made the greatest wealth gains during the COVID-19 pandemic. Like finance, it was the industry second most likely to make one a millionaire in 2021 (*Business Insider India*, 2021). In fact, of the eight people that controlled more wealth than the bottom half of humanity in 2017, five were heads of U.S. tech companies: Bill Gates of Microsoft, Mark Zuckerberg of Facebook, Jeff Bezos of Amazon, Larry Ellison of Oracle, and Michael Bloomberg of Bloomberg L.P. (Giridharadas, 2018: 86).

Businesses in the tech sector may not have assets since they may carry little to no inventory or take on large venture capital investments or issue large amounts of debt to fund research and development (Tarver, 2021). Despite these deficiencies, tech sector businesses are extremely profitable. Information tech and services was tenth on the list of biggest industries in the U.S., ranking second overall in profits, with a stunning $17.5 billion in profits in 2016 (*Blue Water Credit*, 2017). Other sub-sectors like tech services, biotech, and internet software and services ranked among the top 10 industries in the country for net income (*Blue Water Credit*, 2017). While the information sub-sector (internet publishing, broadcasting, media, sound recording, motion pictures, etc.) has the tenth largest share of U.S. GDP (4.6%) at $807.9 billion (*Blue Water Credit*, 2017).

According to Investopedia, the food and beverage (or "food") sector in the U.S. is a broad industry that "covers household consumer staples, restaurants, socially conscious food-related companies, grocery stores, and food distribution companies," (Twin, 2022). According to Forbes Magazine, this sector had the third highest number of U.S. billionaires in 2022 (Dolan and Peterson-Withorn, 2022). It was also the 16th most likely to sector to make one a millionaire in 2021 (*Business Insider India*, 2021).

The U.S. food sector is a highly diverse collection of valuable sub-sectors. For example, the U.S. packaged food market was valued at $1.03 trillion in 2021 and is expected to expand at a compound annual growth rate (CAGR) of 4.8% from 2022 to 2030 (*Grand View Research*, 2022). The food sector also includes the sub-sector of agriculture, which contributes input to the food industry as a whole. Agriculture, food, and related industries contributed $1.055 trillion to the U.S. gross domestic product (GDP) in 2020, a 5% share (Kassel and Martin, 2022).

4 Method of Sector Analysis

Explaining the billionaire wealth in the above sectors can be done by examining how this billionaire wealth correlates with the wealth concentration in these sectors. Descriptive evidence will be provided to show how this wealth concentration occurred and why. Key questions to ask are 1) how heavily concentrated is ownership within the above sectors (as compared to other sectors)? 2) How much of the wealth generated in these sectors stays with the individual billionaires as opposed to the sector's individual workers? And 3) how heavily subsidized (tax incentives, public money, etc.) are these sectors by the state when compared to other sectors? Answering these questions is crucial in meeting the purpose of this sectoral analysis.

Capital concentration within a sector is relevant in analyzing the causes of billionaire wealth in a sector simply because a more equal distribution of wealth in the U.S. would net fewer billionaires. Data that measures concentration within economic sectors is available from the U.S. Census Bureau. It has created a matrix that is useful for analyzing concentration in the above sectors in comparison with others (*United States Census Bureau*, 2017). Although the most recent matrix was completed in 2017 and the sectors may be delineated differently than in other sources of economic data (there are 17 designated economic sectors), the Census Bureau matrix is a good start to answer questions about ownership concentration within the three sectors. It includes the Herfindahl-Hirschman Index (HHI), which is used by antitrust regulators to score concentration within economic sectors and is based on how big a sector's 50 largest firms are in relation to the rest of their industry. It also breaks down other metrics such as the value of total sales as well as what percentage that the 50, 20, 8, and 4 largest firms each sector possess of these sales.

Individual income distribution is another relevant factor in analyzing billionaire wealth in a sector for the same reasons mentioned above. To answer the question about how much wealth in a sector stays with the billionaires, the Census Bureau's matrix is also useful for tracking the distribution of pay within the three sectors. It breaks down the total annual payroll and employees of all the firms in each sector as well these values for the 50, 20, 8, and 4 largest firms in these sectors. While it is impractical to determine the net worth of each employee in the sectors, one can examine the Census Bureau's data to determine if a correlation exists between the number of billionaires in each sector and the average pay for each employee.

And finally, answering the question of how much state subsidization has occurred in each sector is relevant because there is a possible correlation between the level of state subsidies and the amount of billionaire wealth in a sector. For the purposes of this discussion, subsidies are any form of financial aid, support, or benefit authorized by state entities and extended to an economic sector with the aim of promoting economic and social policy. State subsidies in the form of tax incentives, patent sales, access to public money, and research and development investments are all types of wealth (i.e., capital) infusion that, when combined with the revenue generated by sales and production, add to sector wealth and likely correlate with the billionaire wealth in said sector. Measuring state subsidization requires specifically defining its aspects, applying a dollar value, and using descriptive evidence from the last 40 years to show its level of prevalence in each sector.

5 Level of Concentration in the Finance Sector

Within the finance sector, data from the Census Bureau reveals a noticeable correlation between the level of concentration and the extent of billionaire wealth. The finance sector contained the most billionaires in 2022 while even as far back as 2017, this sector showed some of the highest levels of concentration, with an HHI rank being fifth among the other 17 sectors. In addition, out of the 236,950 firms in the finance sector back in 2017, almost half (45.7%) of its $4.34 trillion in revenue and sales was achieved by only the top 50 (0.02%) of these firms. This percentage of revenue and sales by the top 50 firms was the fourth highest of all other sectors in 2017.

Of note, these levels of concentration decrease the further one goes up the wealth scale in the finance sector. The further up you go, the less of a share of total revenue and sales is enjoyed by the firms that sit at the top. The percentage of total revenue and sales drops to only 29% for the top 20 firms (sixth out of 17), 16.2% for the top 8 firms (sixth out of 17), and only 9.3% for the top 4 firms (seventh out of 17). Despite this decrease in upward concentration, the data suggests that within the finance sector there are still significant levels of concentration, as only 0.02% of all the sector's firms amassed nearly half of its revenue back in 2017 and have likely amassed more by 2022.

This finance sector concentration grew during the neoliberal period due to certain economic conditions. This dynamic was especially true in the subsector of banking. In the 1980s state legislatures began removing restrictions on intra and interstate bank expansion, resulting in the number of banks falling from 14,000 to 10,000 between 1980 and 1995 thanks to mergers and acquisitions (Zhang, 2017: 6). In the 1990s, banks enjoyed increasing profits, a favorable interest-rate environment, and unprecedented values on the stock market, thereby encouraging them to use their stocks to acquire other banks (Zhang, 2017: 8). By 1994 the Riegle-Neal Interstate Banking and Branching Efficiency Act effectively removed any remaining geographical barriers to banking in the United States, and mergers and acquisitions in the banking subsector occurred in masse (Zhang, 2017: 2).

This proliferation of bank mergers led to greater asset control and market power for large banks across the country. The amount of assets involved in interstate mergers between 1980 and 1998 increased significantly despite fewer mergers, with interstate mergers involving amounts of more than $1 billion in assets increasing to 68 percent of all interstate mergers (Zhang, 2017: 5). Even further, the share of banking assets controlled by large banks (banks with assets exceeding $10 million) increased from 42 percent in 1984 to 73 percent in 2003 (Zhang, 2017: 7). As large banks continued to cross state lines and gobble up smaller community banks via mergers, more concentration in the finance sector occurred. Even worse, overall concentration of all U.S. wealth was present in the finance sector because of the banks. By 2000, the top five banks held only 30% of ALL the assets in the United States, but by 2015, these banks held nearly half (Howe, 2015). The above factors contributing to finance sector concentration resulted in excess capital accumulation by increasingly fewer firms as well as growing wealth disparity, which is indicative of the proliferation of billionaire wealth.

6   Level of Income Distribution in the Finance Sector

The data from Census Bureau's concentration matrix reveals a correlation between a concentration of employee pay and the existence of billionaires. In 2017, a significant amount of annual payroll was paid out to a noticeably lower number of sector employees (when compared with data from other sectors). For example, the finance sector had the fourth highest annual payroll out of the 17 sectors ($638.82 billion), but only had the eighth highest number of employees (6.5 million). This averaged out to an annual pay of $98,282 per employee (the third highest amount amongst all of them).

This concentration of income distribution was even more pronounced when focusing on the top 50 firms in the sector. Finance's top 50 firms boasted an annual payroll of $ 206.91 billion, making it the top sector, averaging out across 1.91 million employees (5th out of 17) was a $108,584 average annual payroll per employee (the third highest among sectors). Like the previous metric of total sales and revenue, employee pay became less concentrated farther up the wealth scale, with payroll averages declining among the top 20, 8, and 4 firms within the finance sector.

What this data indicates is a greater concentration of income among employees in the finance sector when compared to other sectors. But what contributes to this? One factor is the extractive nature of the finance sector activities, which are capital extractive versus capital producing. Finance sector firms tend to not produce anything tangible, but merely extract value from other productive and employee driven sectors. When firms in a sector are less dependent on employees for productive activities, there is less of a need for them. A significant number of finance sector employees are engaged only in the activities of financialization (intermediation, securitization, debt proliferation, capital mobility, etc.). This results in a greater share of income doled out to a fewer number of employees.

The extractive nature of the finance sector further translates into higher income gains concentrated at the very top. Financial wealth formed 13% of the total wealth of the top 10% (most of it concentrated in the top 1%), but less than 4% for the bottom 50% (Sayer, 2016: 13). The richer people are, the more of their wealth tends to be in financial form. Individuals in the top 1% are likely to be involved in the financial sector with a greater reliance on income from capital gains, dividends, stocks, shares, and other financial assets (Sayer, 2016: 15).

Further evidence of the extractive nature of the finance sector is the way capital is gained even when assets lose value. Billionaire hedge fund managers made a fortune during the Financial Crisis by betting on the collapse in value of securitized mortgages. In 2008 hedge fund manager John Paulson got $3.7 billion by helping the investment banking firm Goldman Sachs put together the very securitized mortgage packages that he was betting against (Sayer, 2016: 201). Carl Icahn secured bankrupt Las Vegas property for approximately $155 million, or about 4% of the estimated cost to build the property, only to sell the unfinished property for nearly $600 million in 2017, making nearly four times his original investment (Furhmann, 2022). Finally, JP Morgan CEO Jamie Dimon used fear to his advantage during the Crisis, acquiring distressed banks in 2008 for a fraction of their value only to make huge gains for his bank in the following decade (Furhmann, 2022).

Another factor contributing to the concentration of income among finance sector employees is the exploitative nature of the activities in which this sector engages. Financial activities (intermediation, securitization, debt proliferation, capital mobility) are *not* labor intensive, but labor exploitative. This results in an advantage over other sectors whose firms were subjected to the financial shift from productive non-financial activities (like manufacturing) to less productive (but profitable) financial activities (like finance and lending). Throughout the neoliberal period, there was a shift from the managerial model to a financial model for businesses. In the managerial model, a productive workforce, needed to produce goods and services with the goal of generating profit, can share in the productivity gains and benefit from increased wages (Appelbaum, 2017: 6). In the financial model, assets were no longer viewed as fixed resources for investment but as Lego pieces to be bought and sold with the goal of increasing shareholder returns (Appelbaum, 2017: 13). In this situation, the finance sector firms and employees that facilitated this process benefitted more as a result.

More than any other economic sector, the growth of finance has fed the growth of income inequality across other economic sectors, not least by adding to the influence and lobbying power of financiers who tend to favor reductions in taxes and social expenditures and promoting the financial market volatility that boosts the fortunes derived from it (Mazzucato, 2018: 127). This cronyism has created a pseudo-aristocratic class that undermines economic equality and destroys the social mobility that accompanies quality job growth. The intermediary jobs in the finance sector are highly paid and contribute to the widened wage and income gap across the U.S. economy (Milanovic, 2016: 54). The move by other, non-financial sectors to the exploitative financial model has led to a lower concentration of income among employees in these other sectors.

7 Level of State Subsidization in the Finance Sector

The U.S. finance sector is heavily subsidized by the state. There are many ways that financial sector firms benefitted from state support during the neoliberal period. The most glaring example is the bailout of the industry as result of the Financial Crisis. As of 2019, the U.S. Treasury has disbursed $443 billion to banks and other financial institutions as part of the Troubled Asset Relief Program (TARP) authorized by the Emergency Economic Stabilization Act of 2008 (*ProPublica*, 2019). Although a sizable portion of these funds were paid back, the initial funding constitutes a subsidy, as the U.S. government purchased billions in toxic securitized assets and the U.S. Federal Reserve sent $16 trillion in bailouts to financial institutions (both U.S. and European) in an effort support the sector and save it from collapse.

The finance sector also benefits from U.S. government sponsorship of certain financial institutions. This support is subsidization in the form of guaranteed insurance in the event of extreme losses. The bailout of both the Federal National Mortgage Association (Fannie Mae) and Federal Home Loan Mortgage Corporation (Freddie Mac) are examples of this. While Fannie Mae and Freddie Mac are both private mortgage companies, they are sponsored by the U.S. government, who disbursed billions of dollars ($120 and $71.6 billion respectively) to them as part of the Housing and Economic Recovery Act in 2008 (*ProPublica*, 2019). This form of guaranteed government aid in times of crisis extends even to non-government sponsored entities, who often enact self-serving strategies to ensure this support. Banks will deliberately enter mergers and/or acquire other banks to make themselves larger and less agile. The result is that federal deposit insurers might consider these combined banks "too big to fail" (TBTF), which allows all uninsured liabilities to have de facto insurance coverage and thereby maximizes the value of the implicit guarantees received from the government (Penas and Unal, 2004: 149–150). Financialization infects the entire economy with debt and risk, and finance sector firms will securitize this risk to extract wealth from it. When the U.S. government underwrites this risk with guaranteed bailouts, it effectively subsidizes these institutions, allowing them to privatize their profits while socializing their losses at the expense of taxpayers.

The benefits of state subsidization are not just limited to insurance in the form of taxpayer funded bailouts or government sponsorship. Finance sector firms also benefit from their access to pension funds at all levels of U.S. government (federal, state, municipal, etc.). Hedge funds and private equity firms received millions in fees for managing these public workers' pension funds (often with very little transparency). One 2020 analysis by Oxford professor Ludovic Phalippou found that private equity firms have raked in nearly a quarter trillion dollars in performance fees in the last 15 years (Sirota, 2021). One pension fund in California alone has shelled out more than $3.4 billion in fees, while in Pennsylvania, pension officials admitted to paying $4.3 billion worth of fees to these firms (Sirota, 2021). Even more shocking, a forensic investigation in Ohio reported that the state teachers' pension fund was likely paying $143 million in fees to private equity firms on money merely set aside *for investments that haven't even been made* (Sirota, 2021).

In addition to the exorbitant fees, firms in the hedge fund and private equity sub-sectors benefit from the leverage that these pension funds provide. Pension funds are large pools of capital that can be used to as collateral for increasingly risky investments. And the financial firms can reap immense profits when successful but shield themselves from losses when they aren't. And these firms continue to reap the benefits of this subsidization even when they underperform. Public pension funds experienced large market losses during the market downturns of 2000–2002 and 2008, with their funding levels declining from more than 100 percent in 2000, to 85 percent in 2006 (well before the onset of the Great Recession) and to 72 percent as of 2012 (*Pew Charitable Trusts* et al., 2014: 3). By 2020, private equity firms were only performing at 3.40%, well below returns on several broad U.S. stock indexes, including the S&P 500 (performing at 7.51%), the Russell 1000 Index (performing at 7.48%), and the Wilshire 5000 Total Market Index (performing at 6.78) (Joffe, 2021).

Finally, the finance sector benefits from state subsidization via tax breaks that allow its firms to hold onto much of the wealth it extracts from the rest of society. The private equity firms that drain so much wealth from government pensions retain an estimated $75 billion a year by funneling their earnings through private equity partnerships, while helping their managers avoid income taxes on the roughly $120 billion the industry pays them each year (Drucker and Hakim, 2021). Then there is the carried interest loophole, which allows private equity fund managers to treat their compensation as capital gains vice actual earned income (thus having it taxed at a lower rate), which becomes an annual subsidy estimated at $1.4 billion (Sullivan, 2022). Bailouts, insurance, access to cash, and tax breaks are the multiple ways that the finance sector benefited from billions of dollars in state subsidies, which in turn fueled much of the billionaire wealth in this country.

8 Level of Concentration in the Tech Sector

For the tech sector, data from the Census Bureau reflects even higher levels of concentration than even finance. For one, despite having fewer billionaires than finance in 2022, the tech sector had a higher HHI. In fact, it had the highest HHI of all economic sectors in 2017. Within the tech sector, more than half (61.7%) of a total $1.58 trillion in revenue and sales in 2017 was achieved by the top 50 firms (a mere 0.06% of the sector's 79,418 firms). This share of sales and revenue by the top 50 was the second highest among the 17 sectors in 2017.

It is especially telling that within the tech sector (unlike finance), levels of concentration increase the further one goes up the top. The total percentage of sales and revenue by the tech sector's top 20 firms was the highest of all sectors in 2017 (a 51% share at $806.27 billion). Even further, the tech sector remained the top sector for the percentage of sales and revenue by its top 8 firms (36.4% share at $576.53 billion) as well as its top 4 firms (25.7% share at $406.74 billion). This data suggests that in 2017, more than in any other sector, tech firms at the top enjoyed a significant share of sales and revenue. This dynamic exemplifies high levels of concentration that has likely increased by 2022.

Tech sector concentration proliferated in the neoliberal period due to several factors. For one, the dynamic of first mover advantage contributed to the first tech sector firms gaining early market share and cornering the initial demand for products and services. A certain number of tech firms were able to achieve significant first mover advantage despite rapidly evolving technology and increasing market demand. For example, the tech company Intel made the best use of its technical and marketing muscle for product development to stay one step ahead of its competition to dominate its industry while Apple was able to achieve an 82% share in the portable media player market with its iPod by the end of 2004 due to its strength in marketing, R&D, and design (Suarez and Lanzolla, 2005). Advantages by tech sector first-movers facilitated concentration in this sector.

Corollary to this first mover advantage is the factor of geography. First mover firms tend to arrive first and set up shop in certain American cities. As a result, these firms gobble up resources and human capital in these areas and press their competitive edge. By 2020, despite the tens of thousands of digital services jobs sprouting in up-and-coming towns in the U.S. heartland, 90% of the nation's tech sector employment growth in the last 15 years was generated in just five major coastal cities: Seattle, Boston, San Francisco, San Diego, and San Jose, California (Muro, 2020). These geographic hubs began with a high individual attainment of educational degrees and became centers of big platforms, command-control centers for the largest tech firms, and places with high amounts of human capital around skills acquisition (Pethokoukis and Muro, 2022). Geographic concentration fueled the concentration that correlated with billionaire proliferation in the tech sector.

Another factor that contributed to tech sector concentration is the growing impact of virtually unlimited economies of scale. In traditional industries, firms can become less efficient once they exceed a certain size, but in the tech sector, firms like Google and social networks like Facebook can generate revenue from ads that reach millions of new users at little or no marginal cost (Howe, 2015). Platforms similar to Google and Facebook, like Uber and Amazon, seem to have no limit to their size simply because (due to the network effects that pervade online markets) a tech firm's dominance (once in a market) self-perpetuates and increases automatically (Mazzucato, 2018: 217–219). These tech sector firms managed to achieve infinite levels of production at very little cost because the digital nature of their products (raw data, information, etc.), which helped them acquire a disproportionate share of resources, revenue, and profits.

Finally, the global dominance of multiple tech subsectors fuels the immense levels of capital that contribute to the concentration in the U.S. tech sector. Six tech subsectors occupied the top 15 most profitable industries in the world in 2021. These include the software systems and application subsector, which was the most profitable in the world in 2021 with a net income of $81.3 billion, capital returns of 32.07%, and a gross profit at $339.9 billion (Karlo and Tottoc, *Insider Monkey*, 2021). Growing at exponential rates, the global computer service subsector had a global net income of $41.5 billion, a return of 21.92% on capital, and a gross profit of $209.7 billion (Karlo and Tottoc, *Yahoo!Finance*, 2021). Finally with the global dependence on data, the information services industry had a net income of $29.5 billion, a 23.40% return on invested capital and a gross profit of up to $108 billion (Karlo and Tottoc, *Yahoo!Finance*, 2021).

9 Level of Income Distribution in the Tech Sector

Like the finance sector, the Census Bureau data shows a correlation between concentration of employee pay and the existence of billionaires in the tech sector. Tech had an annual payroll of only $360.58 billion in 2017 (in the middle of the pack at 9th out of 17 sectors) and a relatively low number of employees (only 3.6 million which was 12th out of 17 sectors in 2017). This made the tech sector possess some of the highest paid employees among all economic sectors, with an average of $101,143 average per employee (second out of 17 sectors).

The concentration of employee pay was even more pronounced when going up the scale for tech sector firms. The number of employees boasted by the top 50 firms in the tech sector was only 1.4 million in 2017 (seventh out of 17 sectors), but it paid out the second highest in annual payroll ($179.27 billion). This payroll by tech's 50 top firms produced an average of $127,032 per employee (the highest average among all sectors for the 50 top firms). This disparity of payroll between tech and the other sectors repeated itself among the top 20, top 8, and top 4 firms. Tech's top 20 firms boasted an annual payroll of $141.3 billion (first out of 17) distributed among only 1.1 million employees (seventh out of 17) for an average of $129,208 per employee (first out of 17 sectors). Payroll for the top 8 firms ($94.54 billion) was first among sectors and distributed to only 814,628 employees (seventh out of 17) for an average of $116,047 per employee (second out of 17 sectors). And finally, the top 4 firms had the second highest payroll when compared to their counterparts in other sectors ($64.49 billion). Distributed to only 593,411 employees the average was third among sectors at a $108,673 average per employee.

This data shows that the tech sector (even more than the finance sector) had a great concentration of income among its employees in 2017 (especially among the sector's top firms). But like the finance sector, extraction and exploitation are factors most responsible for this trend. Tech firms can take advantage of artificial intelligence (AI), surveillance capability, economies of scale, and global connectivity to obtain data and information that allows them to undermine traditional services (lodging, transportation, retail, etc.) by cornering demand and markets with its predictive and surveillance capabilities. The result is an ability to extract capital from productive activities despite having a low number of employees. With the rise of the "gig economy" and the replacement of waged jobs with precarious "self-employment," tech is lucrative for Silicon Valley firms at the expense of employees (Scrivener, 2018). For example, the founder of Uber, Travis Kalanick, used technology to exploit the gig economy and collect rents from the labor market via a platform monopoly. Uber's driver terms and conditions casts each driver as an entrepreneur, a free agent choosing hours but receiving none of the regulatory infrastructure and protections that employees in other sectors depend on (Giridharadas, 2018: 30–31). This type of arrangement allows tech firms to extract billions in revenue without the expense of providing for millions of employees.

The trend of extraction became even more pronounced by 2022. A crisis makes for a good opportunity for a sector's firms to extract wealth. Like the Financial Crisis did for the finance sector, the COVID-19 pandemic performed this role for the tech sector. As millions of U.S. employees found themselves out of work, tech sector employees found themselves still employed and making more money. In 2020, the five tech superpowers, Amazon, Apple, Google, Microsoft, and Facebook, had combined revenue of more than $1.2 trillion (Olvide, 2021).

As alluded to above regarding Uber, the tech sector's extractive ability simultaneously exploits labor. Tech firms will take advantage of a system of production or a weakness in an economy to acquire the most productivity from workers, even while paying them sub-standard wages. Examples abound of real-life firms that have facilitated this kind of individual inequality among employees. Amazon CEO Jeff Bezos took advantage of the technological innovations that allowed him to exert greater control of a production network, all while paying the employees in his fulfillment centers extremely low wages and squeezing as much productivity out of them as he could. And at Google, more than half of its workforce was on temporary contracts by 2019, with these workers being paid less without job protection despite doing the same work as Google's direct employees (*The Socialist*, 2019). Others will boost their profits by cutting jobs. Yahoo CEO Scott Thompson (while being paid $27 million a year) axed 2000 jobs in 2012 (14% of the company's workforce) following four major layoffs over the previous six years (Sayer, 2016: 120).

The technological tools available to the tech sector make it easy (easier than the tools of financialization for the finance sector) to extract from productive activities all over the world (at very little expense). Amazon is already big in places like India and Mexico, taxi drivers in places like Uganda and Bangladesh pay large chunks of their income to Uber, and homestays and small hotels across the global south pay hefty commissions to Airbnb (Scrivener, 2018). Even worse, U.S. tech firms are multinational corporations that rely on an exploitative global network of smaller companies that are often based in underdeveloped countries; child laborers are used in the Democratic Republic of Congo to mine the cobalt used in electronic components, which are assembled in Chinese factories by workers paid as little as $2 an hour (*The Socialist*, 2019). Specifically, Apple has the bulk of its manufacturing workforce in China, particularly at one of its chief suppliers, Foxconn, a company that made headlines for the high number of worker suicides, under-age labor and oppressive working conditions (Sayer, 2016: 127). These global workers do not factor into the employee numbers of U.S. tech firms, but they are critical in ensuring the massive amounts of capital responsible for this sector's high payroll.

What the above trends highlight is that the tech sector's lack of income distribution is made possible by its ability to extract capital and exploit labor. The top firms in the tech sector (and those they employ) benefit handsomely in this situation. The high level of income concentration correlates with the concentration of wealth indicative by this sector's number of billionaires, as enormous amounts of capital flow into the sector among a relatively smaller number of employees.

10 Level of State Subsidization in the Tech Sector

State subsidization includes any form of support that results in a monetary benefit. This includes state funded research and development (R&D) that contributes to the creation of technologies from which tech firms can derive profit. Through this kind of state subsidization, the U.S. tech sector has received billions in dollars of monetary benefit in the form of decades of profit due to its firms' control of technology only made possible by initial state funding. For the purposes of this discussion, it is impractical to track every specific transaction that directly or indirectly resulted from state funding, but it is necessary to highlight the most significant instances across the neoliberal period.

Tech sector firms accumulate and concentrate capital in the form of rent derived from the usage of or access to digital platforms under control of these firms. The largest U.S. tech sector firms deriving the most benefit from digital platforms (Amazon, Google, and Facebook) each made $470 billion (*Macrotrends*, 2023), $257 billion (*Statista.com*, 26 July 2022), and $118 billion (*Statista.com*, 27 July 2022) in revenue in 2021 respectively. These platforms would never exist without the decades of state funded research and development that went into the Internet and World Wide Web. The Internet has its origins from U.S. government research that led to the establishment of the Advanced Research Projects Agency Network (ARPANET) of the U.S. Department of Defense. And although not funded via U.S. state subsidization, the World Wide Web was created as part of European state subsidization via funding by the European Organization for Nuclear Research (CERN). This state investment has ensured infinite rates of return for tech sector companies.

Like the Internet and World Wide Web made possible billions in dollars in digital platform rent for tech sector firms, computer technology made possible billions in dollars in sales and revenue for these firms. The innovations in computer technology would never be possible without the initial state-funded R&D that led to the development of computer hardware and software. In computing, the graphical user interface that involves the mouse, pointer, icons, and hypertext, was invented by state agencies before it was adopted by Apple and Microsoft; key innovations in electronics, including the microchip, were funded by the Department of Defense, while the technologies behind the iPhone (the GPS and touchscreen display) were dependent on state funding (Sayer, 2016: 126). And this subsidization continues now in 2022 with the passage of the Creating Helpful Incentives to Produce Semiconductors (CHIPS) and Science Act, which is a $280 billion dollar spending package that includes about $50 billion in spending on increasing domestic semiconductor production and $39 billion in incentives to build chip manufacturing plants in the U.S. (*USA Facts*, 2022).

Finally, patents are examples of state authority that grant exclusive rights for tech sector firms to take advantage of making, using, and/or selling technological inventions. Patents are a type of government support (subsidization) given to private tech sector firms who in turn benefit monetarily by having exclusive rights to these inventions. Since these inventions were made possible by state funded R&D, the resulting patents are an even greater example of state subsidization as they are made possible by state authority. In some cases, the patent is also a vehicle for labor exploitation if a tech company profits from the research and innovation done by its employees and fails to compensate them adequately. Examples of patents owned by U.S. tech sector companies that benefitted from U.S. Government R&D are Apple's original iPhone (Bennet, March 2022) and Qualcomm's several Third Generation Wireless Mobile Telecommunications (3G) patents (Goodman and Myers, 2015), none of which would have been possible without the Internet.

Technological innovation is necessary for a country's economic development, as such, state subsidization of the R&D that leads to this innovation is crucial. But when a disproportionate share of wealth is created for those in a sector that exclusively profit from this innovation, billionaire wealth is the result within said sector. The U.S. tech sector is an example of this problem, as it has accumulated and concentrated capital to such a degree that billionaire proliferation is inevitable.

11 Level of Concentration in the Food Sector

The 2017 Census Bureau data shows that the food sector experienced some of the lowest levels of concentration among the other sectors. Despite having the third highest number of billionaires by 2022, the food sector's HHI rank in 2017 was 12th out of the 17 other sectors. In addition, the sector's top 50 firms only possessed only 19.2% share of the sector's $938 billion in total revenue and sales (ranking only 13th out of 17 sectors). This distribution was confirmed even when going further up the scale. The share of the food sector's total revenue and sales by its top 20, 8, and 4 firms consistently ranked at only 13th out of 17 sectors. The data suggests that in 2017 the food sector revenue was evenly distributed among the sector's firms.

Unlike the previous two sectors, the wealth concentration in the food sector as noted in 2017 does not correlate well with its level of billionaire wealth in 2022. But this trend has reversed itself as evidenced by how concentration proliferated across the sector. By 2021, only four firms controlled 53% of the meat processing market, four companies processed 85% of America's beef and 65% of its chicken, four companies owned 80% of the beer market, four others controlled 83% of the ready-to-eat cereal market, only one company (J.M. Smucker) had a 45% share of the U.S. jelly market, and one (Frito-Lay) controlled 60% of the potato chips market (*Food Processing*, 2021).

Food sector concentration after 2017 is attributed to multiple factors. For one, international phenomena caused a small amount of U.S. based global corporations to increase their wealth. During the COVID-19 pandemic, when processing plant closures led to shortages in global food supply, the overall wealth of food sector firms and billionaires swelled by 45% in a mere two years to a mammoth $382 billion because of the global rise of food prices (which went up by over 33% in 2021) (Sethi, 2022). Another contributing factor is the large amount of generational wealth transfer within families owning food sector businesses. For example, thanks to the food price inflation caused by the COVID-19 pandemic, the Cargill Family (owners U.S. Cargill Corporation) added four more billionaires to its group of fifth generation heirs and heiresses for a total of 12 billionaires as of 2022 (Sethi, 2022). Cargill is one of four companies that control over 70% of the global market for agricultural commodities (wheat, soy, and cocoa) and reaped record profits, increasing the family fortune by 65% since 2020 to a whopping $42.9 billion (Canning, 2022).

Concentration proliferated in the food sector as opportunities for mergers and acquisitions kept presenting themselves to food sector firms. The incentives for these transactions (increased market share, economies of scale, reduced competition, etc.) became harder for food sector firms to resist. This pace of mergers was reinforced by lax anti-trust enforcement that shaped the pace of concentration in the food sector (*Food Processing*, 2021). Corollary to lax anti-trust enforcement is the industry collusion and cronyism that are allowed to emerge as a result. Instances include coordinated price-fixing among meat and poultry companies, which finally led to indictments by the U.S. Justice Department of executives in this subsector in 2020 (*Food Processing*, 2021). Other cronyism is facilitated by international phenomena, specifically the COVID-19 pandemic. A major egg supplier in the Northeast was charged by the New York State attorney general with taking advantage of egg shortages during the pandemic by hiking prices by almost 500% in 2021 (*Food Processing*, 2021). The factors of international phenomena, wealth transfer, lax anti-trust enforcement, and cronyism explain food sector concentration despite what the Census Bureau data revealed in 2017.

12   Level of Income Distribution in the Food Sector

Based on Census Bureau data, distribution of income within the food sector in 2017 was not as concentrated as the finance and tech sectors. This sector had the third highest number of employees in 2017 (14 million) while having an annual payroll in the bottom half of all the sectors (tenth out of 17) at only $264.6 billion. Even more telling, its payroll average per employee was in last place at only $18,897 per employee. And this disparity for average payroll per employee repeated itself in the top 50, top 20, top 8, and top 4 firms in the food sector, with each of these brackets coming in last among their counterparts within the rest of the 17 sectors.

But despite this low level of income distribution in 2017, the sector managed to have the third highest number of billionaires by 2022. This is largely because the extractive activities of the industry combined with its exploitation of workers and producers caused sector capital to wind up in the hands of a limited few. While the finance and tech sectors extract capital from and exploit labor in other sectors, the food sector does this within itself. Even worse, like finance and tech, the food sector can extract from productive activities outside of the U.S. (at very little expense). Cargill has made billions trading cocoa, while West African cocoa farming families earn, on average, less than $1 per day (Canning, 2022). Research by Oxfam found that employees and workers in global supply chains are those who suffer when corporations like Cargill protect their profits, and that just 5.9% of the value of an average basket of groceries reaches small-scale farmers (Sethi, 2022).

As the food sector tends to be more labor intensive than most sectors, it continues have a larger number of employees than most sectors. Concentration of power for the top food sector firms allows them to easily exploit these workers while extracting immense wealth from their efforts. Researchers maintain that food sector concentration (despite lower food prices) facilitates exploitation of farmers, plant workers and others (*Food Processing*, 2021). Across the food sector, as workers (and even their children) continue to be exploited, powerful interests protect the industry and block progress against the exploitation that's baked into its business model (Canning, 2022). For example, in 2019 an agricultural employers' association sued in federal court to cut the wages of migrant farm workers (the suit was rejected) (Martin, 2019). Corporations like Pepsi and McDonald's hide behind trade associations like the National Restaurant Association (NRA) to resist efforts to raise the minimum wage in the U.S. Congress (Sullivan, 2021). And according to research done by the advocacy group Feed the Truth, in the 2020 election cycle alone, the entire agribusiness sub-sector spent $186 million on campaign contributions, nearly four times more than the defense industry, and on par with the oil and gas industry (Sullivan, 2021).

13 Level of State Subsidization in the Food Sector

The level of state subsidization to the food sector is not as high as with the finance and tech sectors, but it is significant, nonetheless. This is especially true in the farm sub-sector, where the U.S. government provides massive subsidies via costly programs like a highly restrictive sugar import and domestic production quota system, a federal crop insurance program, and price and income support programs for major crops such as corn and wheat (Smith and Goren, 2021). The extent to which the farm sub-sector benefits from direct federal subsidies was significant, averaging at $15 billion annually from 2000 to 2008, surging to $30 billion in 2019, and then to $52 billion in 2020 (reaching record levels to compensate for losses from the trade wars with China and the COVID-19 related market disruptions) (Smith and Goren, 2021).

This subsidization of the farm sub-sector has been a key contributor to the wealth concentration in the entire food sector, as the U.S. government has become an important source of income for many farms, especially larger "commercial farms" where most of the benefits are concentrated (Smith and Goren, 2021). And these federal farm subsidies further prop up the global conglomerates like Archer Daniels Midland, Cargill, and Bayer, while America's smaller family farms decline by the thousands each year (Sullivan, 2021). This situation is exacerbated when these smaller farms are purchased by asset-collecting billionaires in other sectors solely for the purpose of extracting rents. The U.S. Department of Agriculture estimated in 2021 that approximately 39% of the 911 million acres of farmland across the U.S. is rented out to farmers, and 80% of that rented farmland is owned by landlords who don't farm themselves (Lee, 2021). In 2020 for example, tech billionaire Bill Gates became the largest private farmland owner in the U.S., having accumulated more than 269,000 acres of farmland across 18 states in less than a decade (Lee, 2021).

And these subsidies continue to benefit the richest of the rich and create more billionaire wealth, even in other sectors. According to an analysis by the Environmental Working Group (EWG), fifty members of the 2016 Forbes 400 richest Americans list (with a combined net worth of $331.4 billion) received at least $6.3 million in farm subsidies between 1995 and 2014, and this doesn't include the subsidies likely received through the federal crop insurance program (Coleman, 2016). Like other farm subsidies, the greatest share of crop insurance subsidies flows to the most successful farm businesses; per an EWG analysis of USDA data, the top 1% of crop insurance subsidy recipients received on average nearly $227,000 a year in crop insurance premium support in 2011, while the bottom 80% of recipients received only about $5,000 a year (Coleman, 2016).

Despite lower levels of concentration in the food sector in 2017, there is a correlation between its current level of billionaire wealth and the level of state subsidization received over the years. Subsidies from the U.S. government are an investment in food sector firms that the firms do not have to make themselves. As such, they can accumulate wealth at a faster rate. And this is true for other sectors that can take advantage of this situation by acquiring food sector assets.

14 What Patterns Have Been Identified

Now that the characteristics responsible for billionaire wealth at the sector level have been examined, it is possible to draw certain conclusions from the findings. Analyzing the three most billionaire heavy sectors through the lenses of concentration, income distribution, and state subsidization reveals some telling patterns. Chief of which is the degree that the institutional drivers of billionaire wealth discussed above (and their individual components) are represented by the actions of firms within these sectors. This degree of representation provides clues as to the most relevant drivers and components to the proliferation of billionaire wealth.

15 Financialization

From this sectoral analysis it can be gathered that the driver of Financialization (which is defined at the accumulation of capital mainly through financial activities) is an extremely relevant contributor to billionaire wealth. For one, the entire finance sector and all its activities is the absolute manifestation of Financialization, and the components described above. Firms in the finance sector use the components of "debt" (collection of interest on loans in order to accumulate capital), "securitization" (turning non-financial assets into tradable financial instruments), "capital mobility" (the ease in which capital is moved around for conducting financial activities), "financial shift" (the move by different economic sectors from productive non-financial activities), and "intermediation" (when middlemen act as financial facilitators for multiple economic sectors) to achieve dominance over the U.S. economy. As discussed above, financial firms managed to sell debt in the form of mortgages throughout the U.S. economy and securitized this debt via the creation of tradable financial assets. In addition, large banks used the mobility of capital across state lines to gobble up smaller banks and facilitated the financial shift that led other sectors to move from a managerial model to a financial model. And finally, finance sector actors like pension funds, private equity firms, hedge funds, and sovereign wealth funds also used their capital mobility to swiftly move capital into the food sector during the Financial Crisis and made investments in agriculture and farmland as promising alternatives to their floundering investments (Stephens, 2022).

The low levels of income distribution in the finance sector are indicative of Financialization's component of intermediation. Finance sector firms amassed tremendous amounts of wealth and speculative profits because what they were selling did not require purchase of goods, products, or supplies from other sectors (just lots of mobile capital). As a result, finance sector employees like bankers, financiers, and hedge fund managers received massive salaries thanks to their skills as intermediaries between their sector and others. Between 1985 and 2012, the average bonus of an employee on Wall Street has increased by 409% (from $29,809 to $121,890) (*Financial Planning*, 2013). These intermediaries got paid massive amounts of money to orchestrate Financialization's components to extract more and more capital from other sectors across the U.S. economy.

The financial shift across the U.S. economy was massive and pervasive during neoliberalism. As discussed above in the section on income distribution in the finance sector, firms in other sectors shifted from productive activities to non-productive financial activities. This dynamic could not be better represented than in the automobile sector. Before the 1980s, the main function of finance companies within automobile manufacturers like General Motors and Ford was to provide their customers access to credit to increase car sales. Starting in the 1980s, however, these firms broadened their portfolio to include mortgage lending, savings and loan markets, insurance, banking, and commercial finance (*Mises Institute*, 2020). Other sectors followed suit, and this embrace of Financialization has led to more billionaires, a concentration of wealth, and greater inequality across non-financial sectors.

Among the sectors that followed suit were the other two billionaire heavy sectors in this analysis: tech and food. If the finance sector is the manifestation of the driver of Financialization, then the tech and food sectors are extreme beneficiaries. Currently, tech companies are increasingly practicing financial activities by pulling tech sector resources away from innovation and entrepreneurism and toward the creation of platforms to facilitate financial asset trading (which helped push finance sector growth during the Financialization boom of the 2000s) (Smith, 2022). While China is leaping ahead in semiconductor innovation and leading the world in drone technology, America's brightest minds are spending their time and energy thinking of new ways to trade tokens back and forth (Smith, 2022). And in the food sector, agricultural trading firms such as Cargill are increasingly involved in financial activities to generate profit by structuring themselves into several business units and subunits for trading seed, feed, fertilizer, and agrochemicals all while providing financial services through subsidiaries like Black River Asset Management (Stephens, 2022). Financial activities track robustly across both the tech and food sectors and the driver of Financialization is implemented heavily in these sectors, ensuring the proliferation of billionaires more than any sector of the U.S. economy.

16   Rentierism

All three sectors engaged in the driver of Rentierism, which was defined above as the control of access to productive activities and assets for the sole purpose of extracting capital in the form of rents. In discussing the prevalence of Rentierism among the finance, tech, and food sectors, it is useful to note how they engage in the multiple types of rentierism as highlighted by Brett Christophers in *Rentier Capitalism*. Christophers' concepts complement the theory of Rentierism as an institutional driver very well, and there are multiple examples of how the firms in the analyzed sectors comport to Christophers' types of rentierism.

The extractive nature of the finance sector is indicative of what he refers to as *financial rentierism,* which he describes as receiving rents by limiting access to capital and collecting them in the form of interest, capital gains, and dividends from financial assets (Christophers, 2020: xxxi–xxxii). As discussed in the section about the finance sector, an excessive number of mergers and acquisitions in the banking subsector led to concentration. This concentration gave banks greater control over the access to capital which helped them achieve higher rents. In addition, other financial firms collected rents by selling debt, collecting fees, and securitizing assets and liabilities. And finally, state subsidization of these financial firms ensured even greater financial rents as these businesses benefitted from exclusive access to state capital in the form of bailouts, government sponsorship, insurance against loss, and access to state pension funds.

The tech sector overlaps with other sectors (financial, services, medical, etc.) and is responsible for engaging in what Christophers describes as *platform rentierism* since they derive rents (income) by controlling access to platforms either through subscription charges, fees, commissions, and/or advertising (Christophers, 2020: xxxiii). Firms in the tech sector like Google, Facebook, and Uber, collected rent from their control of platforms and technology that were heavily subsidized by state funded R&D and these platforms used powerful AI and surveillance capability to extract value from productive labor and activities from all over the U.S. and the world (at very little expense). Closely related to platform rentierism, with their reliance on state enforced patents and subsidized R&D, tech sector firms took part in what Christophers describes as *intellectual property rentierism,* which he characterized as rents coming from the ownership of intellectual creations as recognized by law (Christophers, 2020: xxxii–xxxiii). Patented technologies like the previously mentioned graphical user interface, iPhone, and 3G technology allowed their respective tech sector owners to collect billions in rents as they retained exclusive control and government protection of these assets.

Service contract rentierism is practiced by firms in all three sectors as they have benefitted from what Christophers describes as "a veritable explosion in the outsourcing industry" and "awarding contracts for the services to be provided," (Christophers, 2020: xxxiii–xxxiv). The management of state pensions by hedge funds (as discussed above in the section on finance sector subsidization) includes firms that typically enter into exclusive contracts with state government agencies, including the Kentucky Public Pension Authority, which had contracts with several investment firms from 2011 to 2016 (Sonka, 2022). Tech sector firms that benefitted from the previously mentioned state subsidized R&D include computing firms like Amazon Web Services, which has contracts with the U.S. Federal Government (*Amazon Web Services*, 2022). And subsidized agriculture firms like Cargill are contracted by government agencies like the U.S. Department of Agriculture's Farm Service Agency to support U.S. midwestern farms (*USASpending.gov*, 2022).

As highlighted above, "subsidization" (the act by capital accumulators to benefit from state support and investments) and "concentration" (small numbers of firms controlling access to a sector and its market) are components of the institutional driver of Rentierism. As revealed repeatedly in this sector analysis, these concepts have emerged via the blatant practices of firms in all three sectors. First, the concentration in the three sectors has meant less competition for a minority of the firms in those sectors. When facing little or no competition, these companies can extract excess returns on their capital (i.e., rents) from their customers in the form of higher prices (thus deepening income inequality). As economist and Nobel laureate Joseph Stiglitz states, "In a competitive economy, the real return to capital would be much smaller," (Porter, 2014). And second, this lack of competition has also led to greater subsidization as these firms have gained exclusive access to state resources and benefits. As components of Rentierism, concentration and state subsidization has led to increased rents for businesses in all three sectors, and these rents come in the form of more sales, higher prices, a rising share of national income, and a proliferation of billionaires, showing just how prevalent Rentierism is at the sector level.

17   Labor Exploitation

All actions within the three sectors show the prevalence of the driver of Labor Exploitation, which was defined above as the exploitation of labor exclusively for the benefit of capital accumulation and possesses the two components of "labor devaluation" (ensuring that less capital is expended for the benefit of labor) and "worker displacement" (displacing workers from their jobs or vice versa). What makes Labor Exploitation so relevant to billionaire wealth proliferation at the sector level is how its components perpetuated an unequal capital-labor relationship in the three sectors of this analysis.

As noted above in the section on income distribution in the finance sector, the financial shift in other sectors was characterized by businesses practicing a financial model instead of a managerial model to increase shareholder returns. With the move to a financial model, investment in the skills, productivity, and benefit of workers became less a priority as businesses sought to increase their earnings by paying lower wages; exploitation of workers was the result. But while the financial shift component of Financialization resulted in the exploitation of labor across the U.S economy, the Labor Exploitation is seen as a separate driver simply because it has directly contributed to billionaire wealth in other sectors.

Labor Exploitation's contribution to billionaire wealth is especially obvious in the tech and food sectors, both having glaring examples of this driver as shown above in this analysis. As noted in the section on income distribution in the tech sector, tech firms created multiple technological platforms that controlled access to the productive activities of other sectors and exploited these workers in the process. Labor Exploitation's component of "labor devaluation" was facilitated by tech companies like Uber who profited off driver labor without providing them with the wages and benefits of regular employees (which enabled it to attain billions of dollars in profit). Amazon used technology to squeeze productivity out of its workers without paying them the requisite compensation while Google didn't even bother to give them the protection of full-time work. Making increased investments in worker pay, benefits, and well-being would effectively mean a greater distribution net-profits between capital and labor within these sectors. This would result in less wealth for these firms and make billionaire proliferation less likely.

Labor devaluation combined with the component of "worker displacement" was the result of actions exemplified above in both the tech and food sectors. As mentioned, both Apple and Uber displaced jobs from U.S. workers when they outsourced labor to countries with more exploitative laws. In the food sector, firms that weren't guilty of paying U.S. workers sub-standard wages, were busy displacing as many of these jobs as they could into the Global South where wages are even lower. Research suggests that, thanks to globalized food chains, jobs in industrialized countries are impacted from the outsourcing and relocation of this work to lower-cost destinations; as relocation of manufacturing and processing facilities to lower-cost regions has been practiced by American food companies (*Issues paper* 2007: 20). By analyzing the sectors through the lens of income distribution, the driver of Labor Exploitation and its components among the respective firms are revealed in a very visible way.

18 Shareholder Culture

A connection can be also made between the other three institutional drivers discussed above and the actions of firms in the three sectors. For example, all the actions discussed so far in the three sectors would be less likely without the driver of Shareholder Culture. Shareholder Culture was characterized as the societal reverence for capital accumulation that creates a permissive environment for billionaire wealth proliferation and consists of the following components: "maximization of shareholder value" (giving precedence to the maximization of profits and the interests of shareholders), "market fundamentalism" (the ideology that society benefits only when markets are structured for the advantage of capital accumulation), and "manipulation of perception" (the effort by capital accumulators to positively influence societal perceptions of them). This driver and its components permitted large banks in the finance sector to gobble up smaller banks with impunity, expected taxpayers to subsidize financial losses, permitted tech companies to exclusively reap the benefits of taxpayer funded R&D while using the same technology to exploit workers, and allowed food sector firms to collect the benefits of federal subsidies while using their increasing market share to fix prices. The permissive attitude for these actions in turn further paved the way for more of billionaires. As author Anand Giridharadas makes clear, billionaires exist at society's collective pleasure, but if enough people made the decision, there could be labor, tax, antitrust and regulatory policies enacted to make it hard for anyone to amass that much wealth (Giridharadas, 2022). Thanks to the existence of Shareholder Culture, the activities revealed in this sector analysis make it clear what society has chosen.

Although Shareholder Culture is an important driver that leads to billionaire wealth at the macroeconomic level, it contributes to a lesser degree at the meso-economic or sector level. Shareholder Culture's and its respective components were not crucial to making the finance, tech, or food sectors billionaire heavy. Shareholder Culture simply provides justification for the changing of rules that elevate the power of sector actors who create wealth for shareholders and justify their position, while giving the ideological cover that legitimizes the changing of these rules and the power received. Shareholder Culture therefore emerges as an effect of the existing power relationships that allow *all* sectors to amass wealth and proliferate billionaires in the first place. While the actions of the finance, tech, and food sectors continue and receive greater legitimacy because of Shareholder Culture, the effect of this driver doesn't necessarily make billionaires any more likely in these sectors than in other sectors.

19   Crony Capitalism

Although minimal descriptive evidence was revealed, instances of the institutional driver of Crony Capitalism has been shown in this sectoral analysis. As stated above, this driver is characterized as collusion between business and government officials to preserve the interests of capital accumulation at the expense of labor and society and has the components of "lobbying" (influence of current government officials to ensure favorable policies), "regulatory capture" (control of government regulatory structures to ensure favorable policies), and "campaign finance" (monetary support to candidates for elected office to ensure favorable policies).

As discussed above in the income distribution sections for both the finance and food sectors, the "lobbying" component was regularly practiced; actors in the finance sector used their resources to influence elected officials for policies favoring financial market volatility while firms in the restaurant and farm subsectors worked to ensure the continued existence of low wages. The component of "regulatory capture" was demonstrated above thanks to the weak antitrust enforcement that permitted the high levels of concentration in all three sectors (along with the instances of criminal price fixing in the meat and poultry industry). And finally, the component of "campaign finance" was exemplified above through the agribusiness sub-sector's $186 million in contributions during the 2020 election cycle. Crony Capitalism has run rampant at the macroeconomic level during the neoliberal period, and its presence at the meso-economic level is revealed through this analysis of the finance, tech, and food sectors.

Despite its presence at the sector level, Crony Capitalism does not stand out as a critical institutional driver of billionaire wealth in the three most billionaire heavy economic sectors. As a driver, Crony Capitalism has the same effect across all economic sectors. The existence of this institutional driver does not create billionaires but allows them to persist and thrive. Furthermore, the existence of Crony Capitalism (like Shareholder Capitalism) does not have a crucial role in making the finance, tech, and food sectors billionaire heavy in a way that is unique to other sectors. Through Crony Capitalism and its components, economically powerful actors in ALL sectors use their position to dominate the political arena. Subsequently, they can increase their market power through regulatory favoritism and state policy.

20   Tax Policy

Finally, this sector analysis has revealed a small amount of descriptive evidence of the institutional driver of Tax Policy. Tax Policy was defined above as the decisions that have manipulated the tax code to prioritize the capital accumulation that leads to billionaire wealth over all other societal investments. Obviously, tax policy can be structured to prevent billionaire wealth, but for the purpose of this discussion, Tax Policy as an institutional driver is tax policy that has been structured to perpetuate it. Without the driver of Tax Policy, billionaire wealth would be less likely because the tax code would be more progressive and financiers, rentiers, and shareholders would surrender more of their wealth in the form of taxes, making them less likely to be billionaires.

This sector analysis showed how the Tax Policy component of "loopholes" (ambiguities or inadequacies within the tax code that can be exploited) were exemplified by actors in the finance sector that used certain loopholes to retain billions of dollars in the capital they extracted. As stated above regarding the finance sector, private equity firms funneled $75 billion in profits through private equity partnerships as their managers managed to avoid taxes on $120 billion in earnings. This was complicated by their use of the carried interest loophole to have their earned income taxed as capital gains, saving $1.4 billion in the process. Tax Policy as an institutional driver permits finance sector actors to retain growing amounts of capital and ensures this sector's spot as the most billionaire heavy sector.

It must be noted that although Tax Policy is an important institutional driver for billionaire wealth at the macroeconomic level, at the meso-economic level it is less so because it doesn't necessarily contribute to a sector's number of billionaires any more than in other sectors. Like the previous two drivers of Shareholder Culture and Crony Capitalism, Tax Policy functions the same way in the finance, tech, and food sectors as it does in others. It also only accentuates gains and advantages initially secured by the most powerful actors in a market. And these initial gains and advantages are made possible by the effects of other drivers, with Tax Policy acting as a tool to preserve them. Hedge fund manager John Paulson, Amazon CEO Jeff Bezos, and the family of owners of food conglomerate Cargill did not become billionaires because of Tax Policy, they merely remain billionaires because of it.

21   Conclusion

Existing research has established the economic, social, and political themes contributing to billionaire wealth during the period of neoliberal capitalism. Most of this research into those institutional themes (or drivers) deal with the effects at the macroeconomic level. Research on the effects at the mesoeconomic (or sector) level is not as robust. This chapter has filled this gap in the research using an analysis of a sample of the three most billionaire-heavy economic sectors. Thanks to the methodology used in this sector analysis (concentration level, income distribution, and state subsidization), it has been revealed just how relevant the institutional drivers are to billionaire proliferation at the sector level.

Even though the methodology used in this sector analysis appears totally unrelated to these drivers, their presence still managed to emerge and allows researchers to draw certain conclusions. For one, there is a greater degree of certainty of the institutional drivers that contribute to billionaire wealth across sovereign economies. The United States is by no means an outlier in this phenomenon. While the increase in billionaire wealth has been more intense in the United States, this trend has occurred on a global scale, with individuals crossing the billionaire wealth threshold in every continent.

Two, this sector analysis has determined the most relevant drivers of billionaire wealth (Financialization, Rentierism, and Labor Exploitation). Because these drivers emerged as the most prevalent factors in the three U.S. sectors containing the most billionaires, one can ascertain that these sectors could not have achieved their dominance without their extensive use of these mechanisms. The other three drivers (Shareholder Culture, Crony Capitalism, and Tax Policy) have perpetuated billionaire wealth but could not have pushed its current level without the existence of the previous three.

And finally, an even stronger theoretical foundation has been built for explaining billionaire wealth (and by extension the intersection of capitalism with class power) during the neoliberal period. Achieved is an excellent start towards useful policy discussions on economic inequality and class disparity. As a concept, economic inequality is vague and solutions for its eradication can lack enough focus to be effective. Billionaire wealth is a stronger representation of class disparity because it is more specific and therefore easier to target. Along with this ease in targeting, a determination of the contributing institutional factors gives policy experts, elected officials, and academics better tools in finding solutions. The institutional drivers are the contributing factors, and with their identification they can also be targeted with solutions to reverse or counter their effects on sovereign economies.

References

Amazon Web Service (2022) "AWS Public Sector Contract Vehicles," https://aws.amazon.com/contract-center/federal-contracts/.

Americans for Tax Fairness (2020) "Billionaires by the Numbers," 18 March. https://americansfortaxfairness.org/billionaires/.

Appelbaum, Eileen (2017) "What's Behind the Increase in Inequality," *Center for Economic and Policy Research*, September 2017, https://cepr.net/images/stories/reports/whats-behind-the-increase-in-inequality-2017-09.pdf.

Bennet, Jay (2022) "15 Patents that Changed the World," *Popular Mechanics*, 25 March, https://www.popularmechanics.com/technology/design/g20051677/patents-changed-the-world/.

Blue Water Credit (2017) "Ranking the Biggest Industries in the U.S. economy," 18 March, https://bluewatercredit.com/ranking-biggest-industries-us-economy-surprise-1.

Business Insider India (2021) "The 16 Industries Most Likely to Make You a Millionaire," 26 July, https://www.businessinsider.in/finance/the-16-industries-most-likely-to-make-you-a-millionaire/slidelist/53396564.cms#slideid=53396587.

Canning, Anna (2022) "Child Labor is on the Rise. So are the Billionaires in the Food System," *Fair World Project*, 8 June, https://fairworldproject.org/child-labor-is-on-the-rise-so-are-billionaires-in-the-food-system/#:~:text=Our%20Food%20System%20Prioritizes%20Profits,an%20increase%20of%20%24382%20billion.

Christophers, Brett (2020) *Rentier Capitalism: Who Owns the Economy, and Who Pays for it?* New York: Verso.

Coleman, Robert (2016) "The Rich Get Richer: 50 Billionaires Got Federal Farm Subsidies," 18 April 2016, https://www.ewg.org/news-insights/news/rich-get-richer-50-billionaires-got-federal-farm-subsidies.

Dolan, Kerry A. and Chase Peterson-Withorn (ed.) (2022) "World's Billionaires List: the Richest in 2022," *Forbes*, 13 September, https://www.forbes.com/billionaires-2022/.

Drucker, Jesse and Danny Hakim (2021) "Private Inequity: How a Powerful Industry Conquered the Tax System," *The New York Times*, 12 June, https://www.nytimes.com/2021/06/12/business/private-equity-taxes.html.

Financial Planning (2013) "Wall Street Salaries and Bonuses," 28 March, https://www.financial-planning.com/slideshow/wall-street-salaries-bonuses-1985-2012.

Food Processing (2021) "The Food Industry's Market Concentration Problem," 25 February, https://www.foodprocessing.com/business-of-food-beverage/mergers-acquisitions/article/11298617/the-food-industrys-market-concentration-problem.

Frankenfield, Jake (2022) "Technology Sector: Definition, 4 Major Sectors, Investing in Tech," *Investopedia*, 2 January, https://www.investopedia.com/terms/t/technology_sector.asp#:~:text=The%20technology%20sector%20is%20comprised,to%20information%20technology%20(IT).

Furhmann, Ryan (2022) "5 Top Investors Who Profited from the Global Financial Crisis," *Investopedia*, updated 10 June, https://www.investopedia.com/financial-edge/0411/5-investors-that-are-both-rich-and-smart.aspx.

Giridharadas, Anand (2018) *Winners Take All: the Elite Charade of Changing the World*. New York: Vintage Books.

Giridharadas Anand (2022) "This Week, Billionaires Made a Strong Case for Abolishing Themselves," *The New York Times*, 19 November, https://www.nytimes.com/2022/11/19/opinion/musk-trump-bezos-bankman-fried-billionaires.html.

Goodman, David J. and Robert A. Myers (2015) "3G Cellular Standards and Patents," *IEEE Wireless Communications*, 13 June, https://patentlyo.com/media/docs/2009/03/wirelesscom2005.pdf.

Grand View Research (2022) "U.S. Packaged Food Market Size, Share & Trends Analysis Report By Product (Bakery & Confectionary Products, Snacks & Nutritional Bars, Beverages Sauces, Dressings, & Condiments), By Distribution Channel, And Segment Forecasts, 2022 – 2030," https://www.grandviewresearch.com/industry-analysis/us-packaged-food-market.

Howe, Neil (2015) "Why Markets Keep Concentrating and How That Hurts Our Economy," *Forbes*, 30 December, https://www.forbes.com/sites/neilhowe/2015/12/30/why-markets-keep-concentrating-and-how-that-hurts-our-economy/?sh=6ba5d0337959.

IBISWorld (2023) "The Biggest Industries by Revenue in the U.S. in 2023," 1999–2023, https://www.ibisworld.com/united-states/industry-trends/biggest-industries-by-revenue/.

Issues paper for discussion at the Tripartite Meeting to Examine the Impact of Global Food Chains on Employment (2007) "The Impact of Global Food Chains on Employment in the Food and Drink Sector," *International Labour Office Geneva*, https://www.ilo.org/sector/Resources/publications/WCMS_161663/lang--en/index.htm.

Joffe, Mark (2021) "Private Equity Returns Stumbled in 2020, Hurting Public Pension Plans," *Reason Foundation*, 27 April, https://reason.org/commentary/private-equity-returns-stumbled-in-2020-hurting-public-pension-plans/.

Karlo, Jose and Mari Tottoc (2021) "5 Most Profitable Industries In the World in 2021," *Insider Monkey*, 18 June, https://www.insidermonkey.com/blog/5-most-profitable-industries-in-the-world-in-2021-946645/5/.

Karlo, Jose and Mari Tottoc (2021) "15 Most Profitable Industries In the World in 2021," *Yahoo!Finance*, 18 June, https://finance.yahoo.com/news/15-most-profitable-industries-world-173731858.html.

Kassel, Kathleen and Anikka Martin (2022) "Ag and Food Sectors and the Economy," *USDA Economic Research Services*, 24 February, https://www.ers.usda.gov/data-products/ag-and-food-statistics-charting-the-essentials/ag-and-food-sectors-and-the-economy/.

Kenton, Will (2021) "Financial Sector: Definition, Examples, Importance to Economy," *Investopedia*, 29 June, https://www.investopedia.com/terms/f/financial_sector.asp#citation-1.

Krippner, Greta R. (2012) *Capitalizing on Crisis: the Political Origins of the Rise of Finance*. Cambridge MA: Harvard University Press.

Lee, Nathaniel (2021) "Here's Why the Ultra-wealthy like Bill Gates and Thomas Peterffy are Investing in U.S. Farmland," *CNBC.com*, 20 August, https://www.cnbc.com/2021/08/20/heres-why-the-ultra-wealthy-like-bill-gates-investing-to-farmland.html.

Lovemoney (2019) "How the Number of Billionaires has Changed Over the Last Century," 13 November, https://www.lovemoney.com/gallerylist/90301/how-the-number-of-billionaires-has-changed-over-the-past-century.

Macrotrends (2023) "Amazon Revenue 2010–2023," https://www.macrotrends.net/stocks/charts/AMZN/amazon/revenue.

Martin, Nick (2019) "American Farming Runs on Exploitation," *The New Republic*, 17 October https://newrepublic.com/article/155403/american-farming-runs-exploitation.

Mazzucato, Mariana (2018) *The Value of Everything: Making and Taking in the Global Economy*. New York: PublicAffairs.

Milanovic, Branko (2016) *Global Inequality: a New Approach for the Age of Globalization*. Cambridge, MA: Harvard University Press.

Mises Institute (2020) "Financialization: Why the Finance Sector now Rules the Global Economy," 18 March, https://mises.org/wire/financialization-why-financial-sector-now-rules-global-economy.

Muro, Mark (2020) "No Matter Which Way You Look at it, Tech Jobs are still Concentrating in Just a Few Cities," *Brooking Institute*, 3 March, https://www.brookings.edu/research/tech-is-still-concentrating/.

Olvide, Shira (2021) "How Big Tech Won the Pandemic," *The New York Times*, 12 October, https://www.nytimes.com/2021/04/30/technology/big-tech-pandemic.html.

Penas, María Fabiana and Haluk Unal (2004) "Gains in Bank Mergers: Evidence from the Bond Markets," *Journal of Financial Economics*, February (74), https://www.sciencedirect.com/science/article/pii/S0304405X04000108.

Pethokoukis, Jame and Mark Muro (2022) "Is the Tech Sector Too Concentrated? My Long-Read Q&A with Mak Muro," *American Enterprise Institute*, 15 April, https://www.aei.org/economics/is-the-tech-sector-too-concentrated-my-long-read-qa-with-mark-muro/.

Pew Charitable Trusts, et al. (2014) "State Public Pension Investments Shift Over the Past 30 Years," June, https://www.pewtrusts.org/~/media/assets/2014/06/state_public_pension_investments_shift_over_past_30_years.pdf.

Porter, Eduardo (2014) "Concentrated Markets Take Big Toll on Economy," *The New York Times*, 27 May, https://www.nytimes.com/2014/05/28/business/economy/concentrated-markets-take-big-toll-on-economy.html.

ProPublica (2019) "Bailout Tracker," https://projects.propublica.org/bailout/initiatives/2-emergency-economic-stabilization-act.

Sayer, Andrew (2016) *Why We Can't Afford the Rich*. Bristol UK: Policy Press.

Scrivener, Alex (2018) "Big Tech is an Extractive Industry, it Must Be Regulated as Such," *Al Jazeera*, 9 May, https://www.aljazeera.com/opinions/2018/5/9/big-tech-is-an-extractive-industry-it-must-be-regulated-as-such.

Sethi, Vaamanaa (2022) "The Pandemic Created 62 New 'Food' Billionaires and the Ukraine War Will Make Them Richer," *Business Insider India*, 23 May https://www.businessinsider.in/thelife/news/rising-food-prices-made-62-new-food-billionaires-and-the-dynasties-could-get-richer-this-year/articleshow/91738259.cms.

Sirota, David (2021) "Workers are Funding the War on Themselves," *The Daily Poster*, 7 July, https://www.dailyposter.com/workers-are-funding-the-war-on-themselves/.

Smith, Noah (2022) "The Financialization of Tech," *Substack*, 26 July, https://noahpinion.substack.com/p/the-financialization-of-tech.

Smith, Vincent H. and Benjamin J. Goren. 2021. "Farm-Sector Spending on Federal Campaign Contributions and Lobbying Expenditures: Evidence from 2003 to 2020," *American Enterprise Institute*, December, https://www.aei.org/wp-content/uploads/2021/12/Farm-sector-spending-on-federal-campaign-contributions-and-lobbying-expenditures.pdf?x91208.

The Socialist (2019) "Tech Industry, Super Profits from Super Exploitation," 15 February, https://thesocialist.org.au/tech-industry-exploitation/.

Sonka, Joe (2022) "Long-suppressed Report on Kentucky Pensions' Hedge Fund Deals is Public at Last," *Louisville Courier Journal*, 7 September, https://www.courier-journal.com/story/news/politics/2022/09/06/report-on-kentucky-pensions-hedge-fund-deals-finally-made-public/65476649007/.

Statista (2022) "Total Assets of Financial Institutions in the United States from 2002 to 2020," 31 May, https://www.statista.com/statistics/421697/financial-institutions-assets-usa/#:~:text=The%20total%20assets%20of%20financial,approximately%20123.1%20trillion%20U.S.%20dollars.

Statista.com (2022) "Annual Revenue of Google from 2002–2021," 26 July https://www.statista.com/statistics/266206/googles-annual-global-revenue/.

Statista.com (2022) "Meta's (formerly Facebook Inc.) Annual Revenue from 2009 to 2021," 27 July, https://www.statista.com/statistics/268604/annual-revenue-of-facebook/.

Stephens, Phoebe (2022) "Perspective: the Financialization of Food," *University of Ontario Open Library*, https://doi.org/10.22215/fsmmm/sp46.

Suarez, Fernando F. and Gianvito Lanzolla (2005) "The Half-Truth of First-Mover Advantage," *Harvard Business Review*, April, https://hbr.org/2005/04/the-half-truth-of-first-mover-advantage.

Sullivan, Becky (2022) "A Tax Loophole Made Fund Managers Rich: Closing it may Help Pay for the Climate Bill," *NPR*, 3 August, https://www.npr.org/2022/08/03/1115218183/carried-interest-close-tax-loophole.

Sullivan, Lucy Martinez (2021) "Op-Ed: We Need to Get Food Industry Dollars Out of Our Politics to Save Our Democracy," *Civil Eats*, 26 February, https://civileats.com/2021/02/26/op-ed-we-need-to-get-food-industry-dollars-out-of-politics-to-save-our-democracy/.

Tarver, Evan (2021) "Key Financial Ratio to Analyze Tech Companies," *Investopedia*, 31 May, https://www.investopedia.com/articles/active-trading/082615/key-financial-ratios-analyze-tech-companies.asp.

Twin, Alexandra (2022) "Food Industry ETF," *Investopedia*, 26 July, https://www.investopedia.com/terms/f/food-industry-etf.asp#:~:text=This%20broad%20industry%20covers%20household,stores%2C%20and%20food%20distribution%20companies.

United States Census Bureau (2017) "Selected Sectors: Concentration of Largest Firms for the U.S. (2017)," https://data.census.gov/cedsci/table?q=concentration&tid=ECNSIZE2017.EC1700SIZECONCEN.

U.S. Federal Reserve (2013) "Z.1 Financial Accounts of the United States: Flow of Funds, Balance Sheets, and Integrated Macroeconomic Accounts, First Quarter 2013," https://www.federalreserve.gov/releases/z1/20130606/z1.pdf.

U.S. Federal Reserve (2020) "Z.1 Financial Accounts of the United States: Flow of Funds, Balance Sheets, and Integrated Macroeconomic Accounts, Second Quarter 2020," https://www.federalreserve.gov/releases/z1/20200921/z1.pdf.

USA Facts (2022) "What's in the Recently Passed CHIPS Act?" 12 August, https://usafacts.org/articles/whats-in-the-recently-passed-chips-act/.

USASpending.gov (2022) "Contract Summary: Cargill, Inc.," accessed 17 December, https://www.usaspending.gov/recipient/a31654c7-f5ff-71fe-90d8-91a59745fb51-C/latest.

Zhang, Jeffery (2017) "The Rise of Market Concentration and Rent Seeking in the Financial Sector," *Harvard Law School*, No. 72, April.

CHAPTER 4

The Transnational Investment Bloc in the U.S. and Persian Gulf

Mazaher Koruzhde and Ronald W. Cox

1   Introduction[1]

We develop a critical political economy framework to explain U.S. foreign policy toward Saudi Arabia and the Persian Gulf. In doing so, we argue that U.S. policy in the Persian Gulf goes well beyond the geopolitics of "oil for security," which has been the focus of many scholarly studies. In our framework, U.S. policy can best be understood as protecting the economic and geopolitical interests of a U.S.-Saudi transnational capitalist investment bloc that derives steady profits from the Persian Gulf. This transnational investment bloc intersects and informs the geopolitical strategy of U.S. foreign policymakers in privileging U.S. ties with Saudi Arabia and Gulf Cooperation Council states. The lengthy history of U.S. military expansion in the Persian Gulf has been supported and encouraged by a transnational investment bloc that benefits directly from U.S. foreign policies that enhance the commercial and profit-making opportunities of this bloc. The deepening ties of transnational investors to Saudi Arabia and the Persian Gulf has become a much more important explanation for recent U.S. policies in the region than the standard framing of U.S. policy as "oil for security." U.S. policies have worked to maintain and increase investment opportunities that favors a U.S.-Saudi transnational investment bloc.

We refer to several groups of U.S.-Saudi investment partnerships as part of an investment bloc due to their mutual geostrategic and economic interests in enhancing the overall investment climate in Saudi Arabia and throughout the Persian Gulf, where profit-making opportunities have expanded over the decades and are increasingly connected to joint ventures both in the Persian Gulf and the U.S. This has provided the economic foundations for a politically powerful investment bloc that has a strong economic interest in maintaining U.S. foreign policies that support Saudi Arabian interests in the region.

---

1 This chapter is a revised and expanded version of Mazaher Koruzhde and Ronald W. Cox (2022) "The Transnational Investment Bloc in U.S. Policy Toward Saudi Arabia and the Persian Gulf," *Class, Race and Corporate Power*, Vol. 10 (1): Article 1.

Contrary to accounts of Saudi Arabia that separate U.S.-based transnational energy corporations from the state-owned Saudi Aramco, we show that prominent U.S. transnational energy corporations have significant investment partnerships with Saudi Aramco that have become more important over the decades. We also discuss the deepening investment ties between U.S. military contractors, weapon sales, and security assistance to Saudi Arabia, which have become lucrative sources of profits for U.S. defense and security firms. The mutual interests of U.S. defense and private security firms in the stability of the Saudi state provides direct profits to military contractors. These relationships also function to ensure profit-making opportunities for current and future investors in Saudi Arabia and the Persian Gulf.

As we also discuss, the Saudi Sovereign Wealth funds provide important sources of capital for U.S. commercial and investment banks, as well as sources of support for U.S. financial markets, start-up funds for commercial ventures, and investment funds for an expansion of U.S.-Saudi business projects in the U.S. market. These financial investments link transnational capitalists from Saudi Arabia to the U.S. to the global economy, providing economic incentives for a transnational capitalist investment bloc to favor pro-Saudi policies in the Persian Gulf. We develop an overview of the transnational investment bloc as a political power-broker in helping to shape U.S. foreign policy in the Persian Gulf. Transnational investors that profit from the U.S.-Saudi investment nexus are deeply embedded within think-tanks and interest groups that influence the direction of U.S. policy in the Persian Gulf, including hardline policies toward Iran.

Only when a comprehensive picture of the economic links between U.S. and Saudi Arabia is drawn can we fully grasp the political and security implications of these links for the Persian Gulf and the Middle East. In the remaining sections, we will examine the historical foundations of the transnational investment bloc, followed by an analysis of how various sectors of U.S. capital have operated as part of this investment bloc to influence U.S. foreign policy toward Saudi Arabia and the Persian Gulf.

2   The Historical Foundations of the Transnational Investment Bloc[2]

As an interwoven network of state and corporate elites, the transnational investment bloc has used its political power to shape U.S. economic and

---

2 In another study, Mazaher Koruzhde (2022) shows how the events surrounding the 1979 Iranian crisis, namely the fall of the Shah, the hostage crisis, and the Iran-Iraq war played a

security policies toward the Persian Gulf region, particularly Saudi Arabia. Due to sitting at the crossroads of U.S. geostrategic interests and its linkages with the global economy, the bloc gains more authority and legitimacy in times of perceived crises in the Persian Gulf. The bloc has used its political influence to directly impact U.S. policy toward Saudi Arabia, and the region in general, by working closely with high-level U.S. policymakers in corporate-funded political think tanks and policy-planning organizations to advance the following agendas: 1) Deepening the trade and investment ties between the U.S. and the Gulf Cooperation Council (GCC) member states, particularly Saudi Arabia, and integrating their economies into transnational capital; 2) Militarization of the U.S.-GCC relations through arms sales, prolonged military training programs, material pre-positioning and basing arrangements, joint exercises, and direct military interventions. As a result, the bloc secures the stability of the global energy and capital markets and maintains the status quo (at lease in the short term) through promoting pro-Saudi policies in the region.

Transnational investors that profit from the U.S.-Saudi investment nexus are well-organized through such economic bodies as the U.S.-GCC Corporate Cooperation Committee (referred to as the Committee herein), U.S.-Saudi Arabia Business Council (the U.S. has joined the same councils with other GCC members), and Business Initiative. In addition, this investment bloc is deeply embedded within a wider network of think-tanks and interest groups that have influenced the direction of U.S. policy in the Persian Gulf over the past four decades. The last years of the 1970s witnessed a remarkable mobilization of these groups. Their influence consolidated during the Regan administration and their narrative of U.S. "national interests," "national security," and "threats" to "U.S. interests" in the Persian Gulf became the political consensus-building strategic wisdom ever since. Together, they have manufactured this image of vitality of U.S.-Saudi Arabia and U.S.-GCC countries for strategic and economic interests of the U.S. as a whole. The goal is to create a barrage of analysis papers and policy recommendations to sell this picture to the White House, Congress, and American public. As a result, the bloc has become hegemonic over time and to a great extent blocks any other policy initiative that endangers its profitability.

---

crucial role in the formation of the transnational investment bloc by first, accelerating the breakdown of liberal internationalism represented by détente and second, facilitating the replacement of the Shah as an ally with the Saudis.

3 Agenda's in U.S.-Arab Relations

GCC countries, particularly Saudi Arabia, were placed squarely at the center of the Carter administration's energy policies extracted directly from the energy recommendations of Trilateral Commission (TC). The TC was the dominant foreign policy-planning organization during the Carter administration. Consisting of largely internationally oriented corporations, intellectuals, and government officials, the TC predominantly represented the leading sectors of transnational capital. It was also closely tied to other similar organizations such as the Brookings Institute and the Council on Foreign Relations. The TC "can be conceived" Richard Falk points out, "as a geoeconomic search for managerial formula" that intended to keep the concentration of wealth in the three centers of global wealth- North America, Japan, and Western Europe- intact, and its vistas "can be understood as the ideological perspective representing the transnational outlook of the multinational corporation [which] seeks to subordinate territorial politics to non-territorial economic goals" (Falk, 1975: 1005). This is the reason why Jeffery Frieden contends that the TC constituted "the executive advisory committee to transnational finance capital" (Frieden, 1980: 69).

The foundation of the Trilateral Commission's energy policies was based on integrating oil producing countries, and Saudi Arabia in particular, into the international energy and financial markets. The goal was twofold: create a "many-sided structure of cooperation with [oil] producers," primarily Saudi Arabia, due to its production capacity and more freedom of its petrodollars compared to others like Iran and Venezuela; and stabilize energy prices through a "mutual entanglement" with the Saudis. As a congregation of internationally oriented businesses, the Commission relied on a variety of areas to accomplish these goals. Increasing ties with the Saudis, as planned in the Commission, was through getting them to invest their petrodollars in U.S. banks and Treasury bonds, selling oil in dollars, massive purchases of weapons, hosting a myriad of multinational corporations, and the like (Bird, 1980).

The TC institutionalized the U.S.-Saudi special relationship. Two main organizations in the Trilateral system carried out this task: The U.S-Saudi Joint Commission on Economic Cooperation and the Arabian American Oil Company (ARAMCO). The Joint Commission was created in 1975 at the height of U.S. concerns about international oil and of Saudis' international influence. It was meant to provide the Saudis with technical and managerial assistance and administer multibillion dollar development projects in the Kingdom. Chaired and administered by the U.S. Treasury Department, the Joint Commission was an opportunity for U.S.-Saudi interests to elevate their partnership beyond a military-political one. Following the 1974 oil/dollar negotiations, the Joint Commission institutionalized the U.S.-Saudi initiative for recycling petrodollar surpluses and securing U.S. access to steady and stable oil flow through an ambitious $140 billion industrialization program (Harbinson, 1990). It also worked in close tandem with the Saudi Planning Commission in the implementation of a $140 billion Five Year Plan. The other institutional pillar of the U.S.-Saudi investment bloc was ARAMCO, representing Mobil, Exxon, Texaco, and Standard Oil of California (Bird, 1980: 347).

The efforts to hold the special relationship between the U.S. and Saudi Arabia continued more aggressively in the 1980s through The National Council on U.S.-Arab Relations (NCUSAR) as an organization whose specific focus was U.S. economic and security policy in the Persian Gulf. Founded in 1983, the NCUSAR serves as the Secretariat of the Committee in Washington D.C which coordinates its public affairs programs and implements its events and activities.[3] The founding president and the CEO of the NCUSAR, John Anthony, has worked closely with the Committee and is well connected to its corporate members- like Burton P. Bacheller from Boeing and then chairman of the Committee- as well as its state members. He has been the only American who has ever attended the GCC ministerial and heads of State summits since the inception of the GCC in 1981. He has access to Department of Commerce through senior officials like Jan H. Kalicki, a counselor to the Department of Commerce and exceptionally active member of the Council on Foreign Relations (CFR). As part of the revolving door between the state and corporate actors, Anthony is also a lifetime member of the CFR since 1986.[4]

Anthony is the editor of the U.S.-GCC Occasional Paper Series published by the Committee. The sixth paper, written by Anthony himself in 1999, indicates the extent to which the Committee and the NCUSAR are aware of the U.S.-GCC strategic interests and involvement in the region. Immediately after pointing out the mutual benefits of economic restructuring of the GCC energy sector, and the profitability of deepening the trade and investment ties with the GCC countries for American corporations, the paper links "defense with commerce and commerce with defense." It explicitly advertises the value

---

3 Such important events as the 1993 U.S.-GCC Private Sector Business Conference which was organized by the Committee for the first time and held in Washington DC. The conference attracted hundreds of public and private sector leaders and officials in order to further promote the agenda of strengthening business and security ties to the region.

4 Dr. Anthony currently serves on the United States Department of State Advisory Committee on International Economic Policy's Subcommittee on Sanctions. The political implications of his role will be examined in the next section.

of defense arrangements between the U.S. and the GCC member states. In doing so, it acknowledges that the realities of mutual interests in protecting the "vital assets and interests" of both sides "provide context for the fact that most GCC countries are co-signatories to defense cooperation agreements with the United States ... They provide context also for what the agreements make possible: continuous consultation, joint training maneuvers, and the pre-positioning of allied forces' defense equipment. As testimony to the overall credibility and operational success of these agreements, the last aggression against the GCC countries occurred nearly a decade ago" (Anthony, 1999: 5).

It is not a coincidence that the policy paper emphasizes the value of defense cooperation in securing business prosperity in the region at the same time the governments of the U.S. and the GCC members were weighing the costs and benefits of the Cooperative Defense Initiative proposed by Secretary of Defense, William Cohen, in 1998.[5] In fact, the GCC members considered the Initiative extravagant and showed resistance in embarking on the project, notwithstanding the recovery of oil prices which gave them their required budget (Henderson, 2001). The paper rebukes the opposition to the U.S. military expansion in the region by capitalizing on the fear of having another Iraqi invasion of the 1980s and resorts to what-if-isms, asking: "What if the views of those who claim the threats to the member-states to be non-existent, minimal, manageable, or exaggerated happen to be wrong, as has happened twice in the past two decades? How much more expensive might the cost be in the event current deterrence and defense arrangements were absent and another war were to occur? Were armed conflict to recur, given present world financial circumstances, which country or countries would likely be able and willing to assume the multibillion-dollar cost of the massive mobilizations and deployments that would likely be required to end it?" (Anthony,1999: 6).

The Committee and the NCUSAR have been very effective in promulgating these ideas within the U.S. and GCC governments as well as the American public. In most of the meetings they sponsor, they host GCC's Secretary Generals and state officials and make sure to invite senior officials from the White House, National Security Council, and Departments of State, Defense, Commerce, and Treasury. They also arrange meetings between GCC officials and U.S. Senators and Representatives and their staffs. They have also delivered these messages to a broader public through the National Press Club, the World Affairs Council,

---

5 The Initiative would establish a military communication network linking the GCC member states and a missile warning system. The Initiative was proposed to link the network to U.S. systems in order to integrate GCC defenses within the region as well as with the United States.

The CFR, and the U.S Foreign Service Institute, in addition to universities, conferences, public policy research institutions, and making appearances on talk shows in national TV and radio (NCUSAR, 1994).

4 Petrodollars and the Expansion of the Transnational Investment Bloc

The 1970s and the shifting global economy structured U.S.-Arab relations and U.S. geopolitical goals within a petrodollar interdependence that later became solidified in the 2000s petrodollar boom and has persisted up to the present (Wight, 2021). Major Arab states in the Persian Gulf became the agents of "statist globalization" (Harris, 2009) in an effort to integrate their economies into the U.S.-led global capitalist economy. Through these phases, the U.S.-GCC relationship weaned away from one founded on cheap oil for security. Instead, it gravitated toward putting the petrodollars into investments in various sectors, giga-project constructions, energy joint ventures, arms and military service developments, and financing the U.S. empire's debt. The transnational investment bloc has expanded over the decades through the establishment of economic bodies such as the Arab Bankers Association of North America (ABANA), U.S.-GCC Corporate Cooperation Committee (the Committee), U.S.-Saudi Arabian Business Council (as well as the same bilateral council established with other GCC countries), and U.S.-GCC Business Initiatives. Over the years, these organizations institutionalized and solidified the economic and political power of the transnational investment bloc by incorporating corporations from diverse sectors of the transnational capital.

In 1983, a group of Arab investors, including Hutham S. Olayan, the head of the Olayan family- one of the major private investors in U.S. capital market (see below)- founded ABANA. According to the official page of the organization, they founded ABANA because they "identified the need for an organization to foster professional exchange and promote the business interests of the Arab and Arab-American financial community in the United States." ABANA began its life with fourteen financial institutions and forty banking professionals as its inaugural members, but it very quicky became recognized, as the page emphasizes, "as an essential bridge between the financial sectors in North America and the MENA region, and it developed a reputation as a unique forum for policy discussions that enhance understanding of the business culture and capital flows between North American and the MENA region." Over the decades, ABANA has incorporated more actors from diverse sectors in MENA and American financial markets such as private banking, asset management and real estate, private equity and venture capital, consulting, and other fields related to the financial service industry. The organization has managed to diversify its members' professional and geographic composition along with the changing global financial sector to catch up with an increasingly interconnected global economy (ABANA, 2022).

Working in close cooperation with ABANA in thickening the ties between the U.S. and GCC countries in the private sector was the U.S.-GCC Committee. Over the years, the Committee has increasingly integrated major American transnational corporate investors. The members of the Committee with key positions included: AT&T (Vice President for Telecommunications), the Boeing Company (Chair), Lockheed Martin (Vice Chair, Vice Chair for Government Relations), Northrop Grumman and Raytheon (Vice President for Aerospace, Defense, and Electronics), Parson Corporation[6] (Vice Chair), Mobil Oil Corporation (Vice President for Energy), Fluor and Bechtel (Vice President for Construction). Other corporations, including AlliedSignal Aerospace, General Dynamics Land Systems, General Electric, Exxon Company International, Adams & Associates, Inc, Booz Allen & Hamilton, Inc (management and information technology), Bryan Cave LLP (law firm), Eli Lilly & Company (pharmaceutical), FMC Corporation (chemical), Foster Wheeler Corporation (engineering), Lucent Technologies (telecommunication), SAIC (information technology), and TRW (aerospace).

"The Committee's objective," as acknowledged in its report under the title of Building Bridges; Business to Business and People to People, "is to enhance American awareness of the innumerable benefits to the United States from increased relations with the six GCC countries. Among the Committee's programs and activities are public affairs forums that inform American leaders and the public in general about the shared interests and common concerns between the U.S. and the GCC countries." Over the years, with the help of the NCUSAR (discussed earlier), the Committee has been very influential in bringing the U.S. and GCC business elites together in different conferences, summits, and seminars. For example, in its 1997 seminars, the Committee addressed, among other topics, "the 1997 International Defense Exhibition in Abu Dhabi; economic offsets in the GCC; comparative methods of international project finance; and Bahrain's and Kuwait's economic and political situations. In addition, the Committee co-sponsored the U.S. Mideast Policymakers Conference which brought key public and private sector leaders from more than 14

---

6 An American technology-oriented defense, intelligence and security firm headquartered in Centreville, Virginia.

countries together to discuss U.S. commercial, economic, defense, and political objectives in the region in the context of globalization." (Anthony, 1997: 2).[7]

What has been very instrumental in expanding the transnational investment bloc is the support that the U.S. government has provided for the business ties established by the private sector. It has done so by fortifying its relationships with the GCC countries through establishing bilateral Business Councils with them. The most important of these councils is the U.S.-Saudi Arabian Business Council that was established in 1993 as a spin-off of U.S.-Saudi Arabian Joint Economic Commission (established in 1975). Over the past two decades, according to its official website, "the Council has evolved from an organization focused on disseminating information on trade and investment opportunities to an entity recognized today as the premiere U.S.-based bilateral business promotion organization working with Saudi and American companies." Today, the Council has a membership base of approximately 250 major American and Saudi companies. The Council's Board of Director composition mainly consists of senior executives from leading American corporations with powerful economic and political clout. They include, Bechtel, Citigroup, General Electric, ExxonMobil Corporation, Morgan Stanly, and the Boeing Company. The Arab component of the Board of Director is also made of powerful actors such as Saudi Aramco, SABIC, Ma`aden, Zamil Group, and Xenel Group.

Through broadening its membership base to incorporate more powerful economic actors, The Council has improved its political influence in the public sector, thus facilitating the expansion of the transnational investment bloc. "The Council," as acknowledged in its website, "plays an advocacy role by working with the American and Saudi public and private sectors on issues affecting trade and investment." In this regard, over the years the Council has organized and convened formal discussions between senior executives of Saudi and American companies and government officials from the Saudi Ministries Foreign Affairs, Commerce, and Health and the U.S. Departments of State and Commerce. The opinions and commentary from these gatherings have informed both governments through policy papers and recommendations from business (The U.S.-Saudi Business Council, 2022). The same role in supporting the expansion of the transnational investment bloc is played by other bilateral councils such as the U.S.-Qatar Business Council (1996) and the U.S.-UAE Business Council (2009).

---

[7] The Committee also publishes special reports and analyses, including Occasional Papers, Gulf Link, Gulf Wire, and Issue Briefs.

The most recent attempt of the U.S. government to bolster the economic and security ties with the GCC countries has been launching of U.S.-GCC Business Initiatives in 2014 under the aegis of U.S. Chamber of Commerce. In addition to managing the important bilateral economic relationship with the GCC countries, the Initiative is launched with the purpose of following the significant interests of U.S. corporate members and also supporting GCC companies interested in making inward investment into the U.S. In its official page, the Chamber acknowledges: "Leveraging our institutional partnerships and nine American Chambers of Commerce in the region, the Chamber is expanding our work to engage GCC states to deepen bilateral trade and investment. Opportunities for commercial engagement between the United States and the GCC countries extends to a wide variety of sectors, from energy to healthcare and education, to culture and defense, and the Initiative works to develop and expand these key partnerships" (U.S. Chamber of Commerce, 2022).

It is very crucial to know that the energy, financial, and military corporations that put the building blocks of the transnational investment bloc have been central to the entire architecture of the expanding ties between the U.S. and GCC countries through these economic bodies. The leading corporations in these sectors, such as Boeing, Lockheed Martin, Chevron, ExxonMobil, and Bechtel, usually occupy influential positions within these organizations. They are mostly on the board of directors or have a special membership that distinguishes them from less prominent members. For example, in the case of U.S.-Saudi Arabian Business Council, the majority of these corporations have "Chairman's Circle" and "Platinum" membership which implicitly amounts to having a higher status, thus more influence in the overall policy direction of the organization.

5 Saudi Arabia's Role

Saudi Arabia, among other GCC countries, has played an integral role in the formation as well as the expansion of the transnational investment bloc. In the 1970s, the Saudi government gradually asserted ownership and control of Aramco, an oil corporation that had been owned and operated by a consortium of U.S. energy corporations as part of a "participation agreement" with the Saudi government. By 1980, after a decade of negotiations steadily increased the ownership stake of the Saudi government, the transition to complete Saudi government control of oil production and revenues was essentially completed- though the name change from Aramco to Saudi Aramco would not be official until 1988. Like other GCC countries, Saudi Arabia benefited from the oil price boom of 1970s and 2000s.[8] The Saudi government invested petrodollars in global markets, providing sources of capital for U.S. commercial banks located in the deregulated Eurodollar markets of London and Paris. These dollar deposits, made possible by a petrodollar surplus emerging from the oil price hikes of 1973–74 and again from 1979–81, were recycled by U.S. banks to finance Third World debt. In addition, the Nixon Administration, led by U.S. Treasury Secretary William Simon, negotiated a deal with Saudi Arabia in July of 1974 to agree to sell its oil in dollar and invest their surplus petrodollars in U.S. Treasury Bonds, which helped underwrite U.S. debt and finance the U.S. empire. In return, Nixon officials promised Saudi Arabia increased arms sales and defense commitments in exchange for assurances from Saudi Arabia for Western access to Middle Eastern oil and for assistance in helping to stabilize oil prices in global markets. The U.S. also promised to help build the Kingdom a modern infrastructure, using American companies (Koppelaar and Middelkoop, 2018: 136).

Since this agreement was reached, over $6 trillion Saudi petrodollars have flowed through U.S. financial markets over the next four decades (al-Labbad, 2013). These petrodollars have linked Saudi investors to the U.S. financial market by providing major sources of credit for the U.S. Treasury, and as important sources of capital for U.S-based transnational commercial banks, buttressing their capital reserves as they sought to manage their leveraged position during the debt crisis in the developing world during the 1980s. Petrodollars also functioned as a key element in sustaining the high levels of U.S. debt and global imbalances that have been an important characteristic of the structure of the global economy in the post-2000 era (Hanieh, 2011: 97).

With the decline in oil prices that occurred after 1981, Saudi Arabia began to use petrodollars to transition to foreign direct investment strategies that offered investment opportunities to transnational capital in the areas of defense contracting, commercial manufacturing and service sector investment. According to the World Investment Report of 1997, "the share of inward FDI stock in GDP increased from 6.6 percent to 39 percent between 1980 and 1990" (Bardesi, Davies and Ozawa, 2002). Some of the most significant partnerships were in the petrochemical sector, led by the Saudi Basic Industries Corporation (SABIC), a subsidiary of Saudi Aramco, established in 1976. SABIC undertook joint ventures with a wide range of transnational energy firms, including U.S. firms such as Shell Oil, Exxon Chemical, Mobil Oil (all three were previous investors in

---

8 From $9.76/barrel in 1999 to $90.32/barrel in 2007 and to over $145 in the first half of 2008. See (Hanieh, 2011).

Aramco), Hoechst-Celanese, and Texas Eastern. There were also numerous joint ventures with a consortium of Japan corporations led by Mitsubishi, as well as German, Finnish, South Korean, Italian and Taiwanese corporations. In the non-energy sector, foreign investors were concentrated in the defense market, including U.S. transnationals General Dynamics, General Electric, McDonnell Douglas, Hughes Aircraft and United Technologies, Lockheed-Martin, Raytheon, TRW, and Northrup Grumman (Bardesi, Davies and Ozawa, 2002).

After the initial growth of foreign direct investment in the 1980s, the next surge of FDI took place from 2000 to 2008, made possible by a tenfold increase in oil prices from 1999–2008, driven largely by rising demand from China. Saudi Arabia and the UAE used Sovereign Wealth Funds, quasi-government agencies that managed the revenues from natural resources, to invest heavily in GCC and foreign markets. The exponential growth of petrodollar revenues led to the emergence of a heavily consolidated capitalist class in the GCC with an ownership stake in petrochemicals, construction, real estate, financial investments, and services. By the 1990s and early 2000s, GCC governments worked together and in coordination with international financial institutions and trade organizations (including GATT and the WTO) to lower trade barriers and capital restrictions among GCC countries. Large-scale corporations from Saudi Arabia and the UAE benefited the most from this market liberalization. Foreign investors, led by U.S. corporations, also increased their FDI during this period, building on earlier joint venture partnerships in petrochemicals, manufacturing, military contracting and services (Hanieh, 2011: 87–94).

Today these investment ties between U.S. and Saudi Arabia have expanded across a variety of areas. There has been a dramatic expansion in U.S.-Saudi relations as even a wider range of transnational investors have committed substantial capital in Saudi Arabia as part of the restructuring of the Saudi economy. Now, more than before, the two sides have a mutual interest in maintaining the stability of this system. Recent developments in Saudi Arabia's economic strategies have further tied this country to the U.S. capital markets. Data provided by the Saudi Ministry of Investment show that the ten largest U.S. investments in the Kingdom have a combined paid-in capital of over $56 billion (Kenner and Al-Ahmad, 2021: 13). According to the Department of Commerce's Bureau of Economic Analysis (BEA), the U.S. cumulative investment in the Kingdom rose from $3.7 billion in 2000 to nearly $11 billion in 2019, about 200% increase (U.S. Department of Commerce, Bureau of Economic Analysis, 2021). This amount has been increasing as Prince Mohammed Bin Salman has been trying to reduce oil dependency and turn Saudi Arabia into a foreign investment hub. In order to accomplish this task, Saudi Arabia has been notably investing, largely through its Sovereign Wealth Fund, known as Public Investment Fund

(PIF), in the U.S. financial and capital markets, which includes Silicon Valley and many others. Here are some of the investment ties that Saudi Arabia has established with the U.S., particularly over the last five years.

6 Energy Ties

In accordance with the Trilateral program the U.S.-Saudi energy ties increased significantly. This was while these ties were decreasing between U.S. and non-Arab sources. In 1975, imports of Saudi oil increased 45 percent, while oil imports from Canada declined 21 percent. By 1976, Saudi crude oil alone accounted for over 23 percent of U.S. oil imports (Bird, 1980: 344–45). Over the following decades, the rise of U.S. domestic production, due to drilling technologies and imports of crude oil from Canada, has not dramatically affected Saudis' share of the U.S. oil market and its commercial and political outcomes (Kemp, 2016).[9]

Today the U.S.-Saudi Arabia energy connection is no longer limited to crude oil export.[10] There have been multiple energy joint ventures (JV) between U.S. oil companies and Saudi Aramco both in Saudi Arabia and in the U.S. a few examples of these JVs inside Saudi Arabia are Aramco's partnership with Shell known as SASREF[11] and between Petromin[12] and Mobil known as PEMREF.[13] Shell is a key partner in Saudi projects as it has joined SABIC[14] in Saudis' biggest petrochemical venture and "Saudi Aramco's partner in the biggest export refinery" (Shammas, 2000: 48). ExxonMobil is also, as mentioned in its website, "one of the largest foreign investors in the Kingdom and also one of the largest private sector purchasers of Saudi Aramco crude oil." The company has participated in the petroleum refining and petrochemicals manufacturing industries in the Kingdom through three JVs: SAMREF- a refining 50–50 JV with Saudi

---

9   In order to defend its market, Saudi Arabia has tapped into its historic ties with the U.S., downstream integration, strategic marketing relationships and competitive pricing (Kemp, 2016).
10 Here are some activities that are far more lucrative for both sides and have created a tremendous amount of wealth for them: "energy research and technology development; oil and gas exploration and production; the construction and operation of fuel storage tanks and marine terminals; reservoir and onshore as well as offshore drilling platform maintenance, pipelines, pumping stations, refineries, shipping, marketing, and management and operations" (Anthony, 1999: 2).
11 Saudi Aramco bought Shell's share for $631 million in September 2019 (Shell).
12 The General Petroleum and Mineral Organization.
13 It was merged into Saudi Aramco in 1993.
14 Saudi Arabia Basic Industries.

Aramco; Kemya; and Yanpet- both chemical JVs with SABIC. The company also owns fifty percent of two equity companies, Saudi Aramco Mobil Refinery Ltd. (in the downstream segment) and Saudi Yanbu Petrochemical Co. (in the chemical segment).

Except for these JVs that are in Saudi Arabia, Saudi Aramco and SABIC have considerable investments in U.S. oil companies, mostly through Saudi Aramco's International Division, founded in 1991. To understand the scope of Saudi Aramco, one needs to think of it not "just as a national oil company," to borrow from Young (2018), but "a global energy company with aims to expand its production cycle to refineries globally and vast petrochemical operations." The company is the Saudis' largest investment arm and holds more than seven U.S.-based subsidiaries (Kenner and Al-Ahmad, 2021: 21). Of particular significance are three remarkable enterprises, Star, Motiva, and GCGV (Gulf Coast Growth Ventures). Star Enterprise was Saudi Aramco's first major foreign JV through which [Saudi Refining, Inc- SRI][15] partnered with Texaco in 1988. The focus of the enterprise was to refine, distribute, and market petroleum in 26 Southern and Eastern states in the U.S. and in the district of Columbia (Saudi-Texaco Joint Venture, 1989; Shammas, 2000: 48). Motiva Enterprise was founded in 1998 as a JV between Shell (%35), Texaco (%32.5), and SRI (Shammas, 2000). What makes it a very special case is that later in 2017 it became fully owned by Saudi Aramco. Through this acquisition, now Saudi Aramco owns the largest refinery in the U.S. in Port Arthur, Texas, worth$13.8 billion (by the end of 2018) and capable of refining 635,000 barrels of crude oil per day (Saudi Aramco Prospectus, 2019). As the largest gasoline processor in the U.S. now Saudi Aramco "markets gasoline, diesel and other refined products in 26 states and the District of Columbia under the Shell brand as well as through unbranded wholesalers" (Kemp 2016).[16] The Motive project has been expanding its operations as in 2019 it acquired Flint Hills, which owns and operates a chemical plant in Port Arthur (Kenner and Al-Ahmad, 2021: 22).

Finally, there is SABIC partnership with ExxonMobil. In May 2018, they announced that they created a new JV to advance development of the Gulf Coast Growth Ventures project, a 1.8 million ton ethane cracker planned for

---

15 U.S. unit of Saudi Aramco.
16 According to Shell's announcement in May 2017, Saudi Aramco "assumes full ownership of the Motiva Enterprises LLC name and legal entity, including the refinery at Port Arthur, Texas and 24 distribution terminals. Additionally, Motiva has the right to exclusively sell Shell-branded gasoline and diesel in Georgia, North Carolina, South Carolina, Virginia, Maryland and Washington, D.C., as well as the eastern half of Texas and the majority of Florida" (Shell, 2017).

construction in San Patricio County, Texas. According to a study by Impact DataSource, this project is estimated to create over 6,000 jobs for Americans and "generate more than $22 billion in economic output during construction and $50 billion in economic benefits during the first six years of operation." "We look forward to the next phase of the project," said SABIC Vice Chairman and CEO Yousef Al-Benyan, "which supports not only our goals for global diversification, but also supports Saudi Vision 2030" (ExxonMobil, 2018). After the two parties decided to proceed with the project in June 2019, Al-Benyan stated that "with this project, we look forward to further building our business presence in the U.S. and serving the communities and customers in the North and South American markets even more effectively" (ExxonMobil, 2019). It is also notable that the profitability of U.S.-Saudi JVs has, in some cases, led to their partnership outside the U.S. and the Kingdom. For example, ExxonMobil-Saudi Aramco entered a partnership with Sinopec and Fujian Province to build the first integrated Sino-foreign petroleum refining, chemical and marketing operation in China. ExxonMobil and Saudi Aramco each have a 25 percent share in this JV (ExxonMobil, 2017).

In addition to the state-owned oil company, there are several private Saudi businesses that have built up an impressive overseas presence. The one which is active in the U.S. is Nimir Petroleum Co. LTD (NPC) that is linked to Saudi Royal Family whose activities range from the upstream end to oil refining and distribution (Shammas, 2000: 50). All things considered, we can safely say that even if the U.S. is less dependent on Saudi oil, the energy links between the two countries are profound enough to keep them into each other's orbit. As Young (2018) correctly points out "It might not be Saudi oil that is fueling Americans' cars, but the downstream revenue is going to Saudi Arabia."

7   Defense Contracts

After the fall of the Shah of Iran, Saudi Arabia became the main recipient of U.S. Foreign Military Sales program. Even before the Iranian Revolution, Saudi Arabia made up 99% of U.S. Foreign Military Construction Sales agreements (total of $10.3 billion) and deliveries ($4 billion) from 1971 to 1977 (Wight, 2021: 109–111). Today U.S. arms sales to Saudi Arabia is no longer bound to its "energy security" as some argue (Stokes and Raphael, 2010) and cannot be considered only as a function of U.S. energy dependency. The records of military sales during the past decade, indicate that weapons export means more to U.S. corporate profits than they do to the Saudis as the biggest customer of the U.S. weapons producers (Ivanova, 2018). According to Stockholm International

Peace Research Institute (SIPRI), during this period, the U.S. top defense contractors have received permission to sell roughly $140 billion worth of military equipment and service to Saudi Arabia (Layne, 2018). Data show that these defense contracts contribute a great deal to corporate profits and for jobs in key Congressional districts which provide further political support for ongoing arms sales.[17] This is captured in a 2016 Deloitte study (Deloitte, 2016) that introduces the U.S. Aerospace & Defense (A&D) sector as one the key taxpayers and employers in the U.S. economy. Based on the data from 2014, this sector has employed, directly and indirectly, 4.1 million workers (640,000 employees in the top 20); paid roughly $116 billion in wages (to those directly employed) and about $54.3 billion in taxes. The economic benefit of military sales is even far more vital to districts whose regional and local economies are disproportionately dependent on the production of weapons as the foremost driver of jobs and employment (Thorpe, 2014).

The "Arms Transfer Initiative" policy put forth by the National Security Council is a recent policy measure that highlights the economic underpinnings of security policies. This policy strengthens the traditional linkage between weapons sales and alliance with the U.S. as it cuts regulations and waiting time in tandem with weapons sales, all in exchange for the promise of economic growth (Ivanova, 2018; Yglesias, 2019). As Tina Kaidanow, a State Department diplomat pointed out, the policy is explicitly meant to "expand opportunities for American industry [and] create American jobs" (Ivanova, 2018). This policy is a vivid manifestation that U.S. foreign policy is increasingly linking arms sales to the profits of defense corporations (Yglesias, 2019). However, the officials do not usually admit that the sole purpose of the arms transfer is economic. They often cite some rationale for the sale in order not to be viewed as "merchants of death" but instead guarantors of U.S. "national interests," "regional stability," and eventually "world peace." In fact, sometimes they tend to characterize arms sale in positive terms to have the public support by designating sale programs with the prefix "peace"; as in the sale of F-15 to Saudi Arabia under "Peace Sun" (Klare, 1984: 27).[18]

The U.S. government has long been protecting the military industry in its efforts to extend its market to the Persian Gulf. This support spans consecutive administrations. During the Ford administration, Congress passed a bill

---

17 Although economists believe that federal spending on health care, education, and infrastructure can be more economically effective in terms of creating jobs and opportunities than that on defense spending (Garrett-Peltier, 2017).

18 Other examples are sale of F-15 and F-16S to Israel, "Peace Fox" and "Peace Marble" respectively; sale of F-4S to Egypt, "Peace Farrow"; sale of F-15S to Japan, "Peace Eagle."

to restrain U.S. military sales to Saudi Arabia. In 1976, Congress objected to the sales of 2,000 Sidewinder air-to-air missiles and 1,800 Maverick air-to-surface missiles, manufactured by Raytheon, to Saudi Arabia. Ford vetoed the bill arguing that the bill "obstructs U.S. industry from competing fairly with foreign suppliers," not to mention that it would jeopardize the security of U.S. allies in the region and the U.S.-Saudis relations (Wight, 2021: 155). Only after Kissinger met with the Congressional leaders and warned them about the possibility of straining the U.S.-Saudis relation due to the arms sale restriction did Congress agree to the sales (although with modified numbers: 850 and 650). The latest example of when the profit-making of U.S. defense contractors from their deals with Saudi Arabi trumped other foreign policy concerns was when President Trump downplayed the assassination of Jamal Khashoggi- despite mounting evidence that the Saudi Prince was involved- and promoted the sales of over $100 billion worth of military equipment to Saudi Arabia. He emphasized that the Saudis were spending $450 billion in the U.S. which would "create hundreds of thousands of jobs, tremendous economic development, and much additional wealth for the United States. Of the $450 billion, $110 billion will be spent on the purchase of military equipment from Boeing, Lockheed Martin, Raytheon, and many other great U.S. defense contractors."[19]

Arms sales to Saudi Arabia [as well as other GCC countries] have become a much easier task due to the great ties between the Saudis and the entire range of actors involved in arms transfer which constitute the nerve center of foreign military sales. These actors fall into three categories of private arms suppliers, governmental arms exporters, and governmental arms regulators. The link between the Arab leaders and the U.S. large defense contractors such as Boeing, Lockheed Martin, Raytheon, McDonnell Douglas, Northrop Grumman is established mostly through the economic bodies mentioned before. These institutions provided the testing ground for the U.S.-Saudi military ties to further evolve into a private enterprise. U.S. private military contractors are the major beneficiaries of these ties which benefit from arms sales and military service programs. Saudis' petrodollars tempted the U.S. government to allow the privatization of services that were previously the exclusive domain of the Pentagon and the U.S. military. In the 1970s, Saudi Arabia "hired California-based Vinnell Corporation to train the twenty- six thousand members of the Saudi National Guard in modern weapons use and military tactics under the supervision of former U.S. army officers. This deal was the first instance of

---

19   Of course, the argument for the job creation, as mentioned before, is very controversial. Paul Krugman and Bernie Sanders cast doubt on the validity of this argument at the time the deal was in process.

the Pentagon outsourcing the training of foreign armies to a private contractor ... Faced with declining construction profits in the late 1960s and early 1970s, Vinnell decided to diversify its services by offering military training to foreign armies" (Wight, 2021: 121).

Saudis also have had influence within the U.S. Defense and State Department mostly through what is known as the "Arab Lobby" (Brad, 2010). This way the Saudis are connected to those agencies in charge of making decisions on arms sales before Congress and the public know about such transfers. Some of these agencies that are poised at the core of U.S.'s arms export establishment and manage arms trades are: Office of Munitions Control (OMC) and Office of Security Assistance and Sales (OSAS) in the State Department; and the Office of the Assistant Secretary of Defense for International Security Affairs (ISA) and the Defense Security Assistance Agency (DSAA) in the Pentagon (Klare, 1984: 55).

These ties prove more crucial as we realize that the process of arms sales begins well before the formal request from buyer states to the U.S. government. Arms sales are initiated through informal negotiations between U.S. officials and foreign military officials, as well as "promotional activities" conducted by U.S. defense contractors. It means that the military firms with close ties to Arab leaders (deepened by the Business Dialogues and U.S-GCC economic councils) engage in a wide range of activities to promote their products against their competitors and ensure that the leaders already have a "brand name" when approaching the U.S. government to supply a particular system. These activities entail advertising and other marketing techniques but has also included extensive use of bribery and other illicit practices. Through its investigation into Lockheed Martin's alleged controversial payments abroad, the Senate Subcommittee on Multinational Corporations of the Senate Foreign Relations Committee found that the company had made $200 million of such payments, of which $38 million had gone to bribery and kickbacks. Of course, Saudi Arabia was one of the recipients. Other major defense firms including McDonnell Douglas, Northrop Grumman, and Raytheon, also admitted making such bribes to their potential customers. Today, even though federal regulations have imposed more restrictions on such firms' activities, "there is no way to prevent company personnel from making an informal agreement with prospective buyers over drinks in the nearest cocktail lounge or in the 'hospitality suits' maintained by all the major suppliers in adjacent hotels" (Klare, 1984: 64–66). The point is that all of these activities occur before the buyers place their official request to the U.S. government. Saudis have had an edge when it comes to establishing such informal ties.

8 Saudi Investment in U.S. Companies and Financial Markets

As mentioned in the previous chapter, Saudi Arabia (as well as other Arab oil producers) found the U.S. debt market a secure place to park the petrodollars that was pouring to the Kingdom following the spikes in its oil revenues. The latest updates show that Saudi Arabia now holds $134.4 billion in U.S. Treasury securities, making the Kingdom the fourteenth largest creditor of U.S. debts (U.S. Department of the Treasury-Federal Reserve Board, 2021). This shows a whopping 1000% increase in Saudis holding over the last two decades ($11.7 billion in 2000) (U.S. Department of the Treasury-Federal Reserve Board, 2016).

Beside U.S. debt markets, Saudis have long been interested in investment in U.S. technology and financial markets. Figure 4.1 shows Saudi Arabia's investment in U.S. companies 2008–2018.

Saudi investors are now the single largest source of capital for U.S. startup companies. Since 2016, Saudi's Sovereign Wealth Fund (SWF) has flowed roughly $60 billion in U.S. Silicon Valley directly or indirectly (through financing half of SoftBank Corp's $100 billion Vision Fund), investing in companies like Lucid, Sisco Systems, Lyft, Uber, WeWork, Slack, and Magic Leap (Brown and Bensinger, 2018; CFR, 2018; Layne, 2018). Table 4.1 shows the top investment rounds by Saudi investors:

Like in industry sectors, SWF is also the most prominent Saudi investor in U.S. equity markets. According to Securities and Commission filling in May 2020, the Saudis' SWF investment in U.S. stock market quadrupled in value and reached nearly $10 billion (Mohamed, 2020). The investment portfolio contains a variety of companies' shares ranging from Citigroup and Bank of

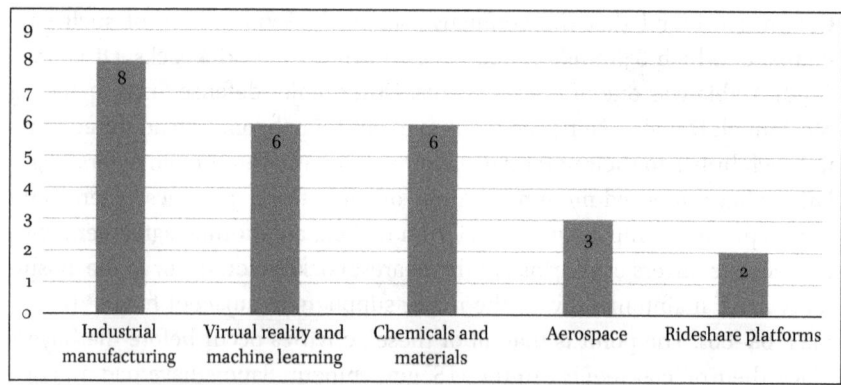

FIGURE 4.1 Saudi investment in U.S. industries by number of deals
SOURCE: (COREN, 2018)

TABLE 4.1 Saudi investment in different U.S. business sectors by the source of investment

Company	Sector	Investment round (millions USD)	Saudi investor
Uber	Rideshare platform	$11,321	SWF
Lyft	Rideshare platform	$4,915	Kingdom Holding
Magic Leap	Augmented reality	$1,888	SWF
Lucid Motors	Car manufacturer	$1,131	SWF
Virgin Galactic	aerospace	$280	SWF
Desktop Metal	Industrial manufacturing	$273	Saudi Aramco Energy Venture
Beamreach Solar	Energy	$239	Riyadh Valley Company
Snap	Social media network	$250	Prince Alwaleed Bin Talal of Saudi Arabia
Siluria Technologies	Oil and gas	$151	Saudi Aramco Energy Venture
Digital Signal	Facial recognition technology	$125	Technology Control Corporation
Rive Technology	Oil and gas	$85	Saudi Aramco Energy Venture

SOURCE: (COREN 2018)

America to Boeing and Shell (Jones and Said, 2020).[20] There is also a tangible pivot in SWF's strategy to invest in social media (Twitter, Snapchat, and Facebook) as well as entertainment industry (Disney and Hollywood)[21] which may have more pronounced political implications (Young, 2018). In this regard, Saudis' donations to major U.S. higher education institutions are of stark importance. In the 1970s, Georgetown University and the University of Southern California (USC) were the biggest recipients of Saudis' petrodollars. The Saudis donated

---

20 Saudi investors traded $86 billion worth of American stocks in 2020. See (Capital Market Authority, 2020).
21 Production firms like William Morris Endeavor Entertainment LLC.

$3.4 million to Georgetown for launching its Center for Contemporary Arab Studies (CCAS) and $1 million to USC's chair of Arab and Islamic studies. The Saudis also made American companies with significant investment ties to Saudi Arabia pledge over $22 million to establish a Center for Middle Eastern Studies at USC. (Doran, 2012: 286). There were also other recipients of such gifts like Harvard's Arab Studies, University of Texas Middle East Studies, Johns Hopkins, MIT, and Princeton (U.S. Department of Education, n.d.).

It must be noted that SWF is not the only source of Saudis' money flooding the U.S. markets. Private investors have their own high stakes in these companies. Prince Alwaleed Bin Talal, among others, has had great stakes in companies like Twitter, Lyft, Snapchat, Citigroup, etc. (CFR, 2018; Manjoo, 2017). Olayan Group of Saudi Arabia (in private sector) is another Saudi family-owned conglomerate which has invested mostly in U.S. financial institutions. CS First Boston, Transamerica (5.3%), First Chicago (6.8%) and J.P. Morgan (1%), Merrill Lynch ($6.6 billion) and also companies like Thermo Electron (5%) and Occidental Petroleum (4%) are among few businesses this group has invested in.[22]

9 U.S. Banks, Financial and Non-financial Sectors, and Saudi Arabia's Transformation

Saudi-U.S. financial ties are not just limited to Saudi investments in the U.S. The Saudi Prince's decision to open the country to foreign investors as a necessary step to diversify away from oil exportation has created another grid of financial ties between the two countries. Especially since 2015, American firms, banks, financial institutions, consultancies[23] and private investors have made large commitments to Saudi Arabia and invested a significant amount of energy to win access to the liberalization and privatization plans in the country. Firms like Goldman Sachs, JPMorgan, Morgan Stanly, Citigroup, Blackrock, to name a few, registered to attend the Vision 2030 conference in Riyadh and set themselves up for huge profits stemming from investments and deals following the Prince's decision to transform the country's economy (Horowitz and Egan, 2018; Young, 2018).[24] The profitability of their engagement with the

---

22 For more on Olayan Group's investments see (Bartlett, 1991; Dealbook, 2008; Shepherd Jr., 1987).
23 They have a key role in transforming Saudi Arabia. There is an influx of giant consultant companies like McKinsey, Boston Consulting Group (BCG), A.T. Kearney, Strategy&, and Oliver Wyman to this country. See (Consultancy.uk, 2016).
24 As they had already made over $300 million by advising Saudis on debt deals and mergers (Horowitz and Egan, 2018).

Saudi modernization programs adds to the profits that they accrue from channeling Saudi petrodollars to the U.S. that are stored and passed through the six largest private U.S. banks.

Bin Salman's transformative strategy manifested in Vision 2030, which includes building a futuristic emission-free mega-city known as NEOM and new refinery and petrochemical sites like Jazan, is an extremely expensive undertaking, and at the same time, a beneficial opening for the dominant actors in global capital markets which converge on Wall Street. To finance its transformation, Saudi Arabia has been on a "spending spree" over the past five years. For 2018, Saudi Arabia added up $90 billion in capital expenditure to its normal budget (Young, 2018). The declining oil revenues of 2016 led Saudi Arabia to borrow over $60 billion in international debt markets, particularly from U.S. banks which have had a significant role in facilitating Saudi Arabia's dollar-dominated bond sales amounting to $52 billion since 2016. As an illustration, in only one contribution a consortium of banks including Goldman Sachs, Citigroup, and JPMorgan lent Saudi SWF $11 billion in September 2016 (Horowitz and Egan, 2018). This and other such examples indicate that Wall Street is a significant component in financing Saudi Arabia's attempted economic transformation.

In addition to borrowing, Prince Bin Salman has counted on a public offering of 5 percent of Saudi Aramco as a foundational component of his Vison 2030. Since the release of the blueprint for this large sell in 2016, American banks have been increasingly involved in the processes of valuation and preparation of deals for the sales to public investors across the world. JPMorgan, Morgan Stanley, HSBC, Moelis (a boutique investment bank) and later Bank of America are among the banks that expect a boon by making profit from this public sale (Horowitz and Egan, 2018; Layne, 2018). The footprint of U.S. banks' profit-making is even noticeable in Saudis' partnership with American companies. For instance, Blackstone has managed a $20 billion fund that Saudi Arabia has injected into U.S. infrastructure. Even after the tech companies and startups bear fruit and "go public," it is U.S. banks who "expect to cash in on underwriting fees." That is why it seems as if "[everything] is all about Wall Street looking for opportunities" (Horowitz and Egan, 2018).

At the same time that the U.S. financial sector is financing the attempted industrial restructuring of Saudi Arabia, the U.S. non-financial sector is reaping profits from the industrial implications of Vision 2030-led transformation. For example, there is a significant American firms' involvement in the Kingdom's projects to expand arts, entertainment, sports, and tourism industry. The Prince has allocated over $60 billion to these sectors. In another instance, on May 2017 General Electric announced that it signed a $15 billion contract with Saudi Arabia that includes a $7 billion package focusing on "the kingdom's power, healthcare, energy and mining sectors, as well as skills training and digital analytics running on Predix, the company's software platform for the Industrial Internet" and a $4 billion project that includes partnerships with Saudi Aramco and focuses on "efficiency savings by digitizing its operations" (Kellner, 2017). This contract is in addition to a $1 billion power contract with the Saudi Electric Company that GE announced in 2015 to "supply gas, steam and solar power generation technology to the Waad Al Shamal combined cycle power plant" (Kellner, 2017).

The construction sector is one the most awarded beneficiaries of the Saudis' Vision Realization Program. In 2019, the Kingdom awarded $52.6 billion worth of contract to boost spending on sectors ranging from housing to oil and gas development (Kenner and Al-Ahmad, 2021: 16). American construction firms have been increasingly involved in expanding the Kingdom's infrastructure. Bechtel company is an old ally in this sector that has been active in Saudi Arabia since 1940s when it built the railway that linked the capital with the oil-producing east (Wald, 2018: 31). The company has been working on the Jubail project in Eastern Province of Saudi Arabia since the mid 1970s, which is the "biggest civil engineering project in modern times," Bechtel claims (Bechtel Corporation, n.d.).[25] The company was asked to manage the expansion of the project to Jubail II (2006–2016) which required another $11 billion funding totaling the cost of the project over $20 billion. In 2016, the project was further expanded for another five years that makes Bechtel involved in a fundamental aspect of Saudi Arabia's agenda for providing educational facilities and residential accommodation in Jubail.[26] The construction giant is the key developer of the NEOM project and won another contract in August 2020 to develop NEOM's primary infrastructure, which will include a "highly advanced transport system" (Bechtel Corporation, 2020).

According to data from MEED Projects,[27] the projects won by American companies in the Kingdom are worth more than $700 billion. Jacobs Engineering Group, Fluor Corporation (in 1970s won a $14 billion project to construct a natural-gas-gathering system), and KBR Inc. have received major parts of these projects amounting to a total value of $225 billion. American companies are

---

25 In 1983, the Guinness Book of Records listed this project as the largest undertaken in history (Wight, 2021: 122).

26 Which means the involvement of other American tech companies like Amazon, Apple, and Snap in order to contribute to building Saudis' tech-focused cities (Layne, 2018).

27 The statistics are available at: https://www.meedprojects.com/sectors/construction-projects-overview/.

the leading firms in Kingdom's giga-projects. Beside Bechtel's role in the NEOM project, Six Flags is the key company in developing Qiddiya, Air Product & Chemicals Inc. is part of a $5 billion joint venture in Neom. If accomplished as stated, the project will be the largest green hydrogen facility in the world which will be eighty times bigger than its nearest rival (Matthews and Blunt, 2021). Other U.S. architecture, engineering, and design firms are also contributing to giga-projects like the Red Sea Development Project. The most notable example so far is Aecom which won a contract to oversee the supervision of the project's airport.

Although not as visible as projects in the entertainment sector or giga-projects, the mining sector has witnessed incredible expansion over the last decade. American mining companies have been very interested in partnering with the Saudis in the joint ventures in this sector. According to the Saudi Ministry of Investment, three of the top ten largest U.S. Saudi joint ventures in terms of paid-in capital are in the mining industry. Alcoa, The Mosaic Company, and Tronox Limited have partnered with the Saudi Ma'aden company in several joint ventures that are worth over $20 billion in total.

10 The Political Implications of U.S.-Saudi Economic Ties

We have documented the influence of an integrated transnational capitalist bloc on U.S. policy toward Saudi Arabia and the Persian Gulf over the past four decades. Transnational capital has pooled its efforts in corporate-funded think-tanks that integrate the interests of U.S.-based defense, energy, and financial corporations across a wide network of growing U.S.-Saudi investment ties. It is no longer possible, if it ever was, to neatly separate the interests of a transnational investment bloc, focused on maximizing their own profits, from how the U.S. foreign policy establishment defines "strategic" interests. As we have shown, a transnational investment bloc led by defense contractors, as early as the 1970s, was instrumental in working with U.S. policymakers to identify U.S. military expansion in the Persian Gulf region as central to U.S. national security. They were joined as early as the 1980s by an emerging transnational investment coalition that included U.S. energy and financial corporations.

These relationships have expanded dramatically over the decades, as an even wider range of U.S. transnational investors have committed substantial capital in Saudi Arabia as part of the restructuring of the Saudi economy. Furthermore, the substantial growth of Saudi Public Investment funds into a wide range of U.S. investments have further solidified and deepened the lobbying power of this transnational investment bloc, which operates as a two-directional lobbying network that attempts to influence a wide range of policies. Although the broader political goals of this investment bloc are beyond the scope of this paper, there is considerable evidence that this transnational investment bloc linking U.S., Saudi Arabian and GCC investors has been prominent in successfully working to scuttle the Iranian nuclear deal negotiated by the Obama administration.[28] This bloc has also continued to lobby for increasing U.S. weapons sales to Saudi Arabia and supporting Saudi foreign policy ventures in Syria, Yemen and Bahrain.

Countering this bloc in U.S. foreign policy would require building a broad coalition that could link the concerns of human rights groups, social welfare organizations, labor unions and peace organizations in a campaign to reverse U.S. militarization abroad and at home. The fact that the U.S. Congress voted in 2019 to cut off U.S. military assistance to Saudi Arabia's war in Yemen and, in a separate vote in 2020, to block $23 billion in arms sales to the United Arab Emirates that had been approved by President Trump, indicates that there is some momentum to challenge some aspects of status quo policy (despite President Trump's successful vetoes).

Whether this momentum can continue will be largely dependent on the ability of critics of the U.S. militarization of the Persian Gulf to build a broad enough coalition to challenge the power of the well-financed and deeply entrenched transnational investment bloc. Contrary to accounts that speak of U.S. "strategic interests" without referencing how the transnational investment bloc defines those interest, our account emphasizes the profit-making motives behind those "strategic" choices. We hope this helps to advance a broader politicization about the relationship between this transnational investment bloc, U.S. militarization, and the efforts to build constructive alternative definitions of "security" and human welfare.

References

ABANA (2022) *About ABANA*. Available at (consulted May 10 2020) at: https://www.abana.co/about/?pu=.

Al-Labbad, Mustafa (2013) *Obama's Presidency Brings Uncertainty to Saudi-U.S. Relations*. Available (consulted April 12 2020) at: http://www.al-monitor.com/pulse/politics/2013/03/obama-us-saudities.html.

---

28 For other accounts of the failure of the Iran nuclear deal see (Koruzhde and Popova, 2022).

Anthony, John Duke (1997) *The 18th GCC Heads of State Summit: Consultation and Consensus in Kuwait.* Washington: U.S.-GCC Corporate Cooperation Committee, Inc.

Anthony, John Duke (1999) "U.S.-GCC Trade and Investment Relations." *U.S.-GCC Occasional Paper Series; U.S.-GCC Corporate Cooperation Committee*, 1–16.

Aramco (2019) *Saudi Aramco Prospectus.* Available (consulted November 8 2021) at: https://www.aramco.com/-/media/images/investors/saudi-aramco-prospectus-en.pdf?.

Bardesi, Hisham J., Davies, Stephen and Ozawa, Terutomo (2002) "Transnational Corporations-Cum-Host Collaborative Growth: Structural Transformation in Saudi Arabia." *Journal of Energy and Development* 28(1): 41–56.

Bartlett, Sarah (1991) *Saudi Group Now Owns Over 5% of Chase Stock.* Available (consulted June 1 2020) at: https://www.nytimes.com/1991/04/23/business/saudi-group-now-owns-over-5-of-chase-stock.html?searchResultPosition=2.

Bechtel Corporation (2020) *NEOM Selects U.S. Construction Leader Bechtel to Accelerate Primary Infrastructure Development for Its Cognitive Cities.* Available (consulted November 8 2021) at: https://www.bechtel.com/newsroom/releases/2020/08/neom-selects-bechtel-infrastructure-development/.

Bechtel Corporation. n.d. *One of the Largest Civil Engineering Projects in the World Today.* Available (consulted January 10 2020) https://www.bechtel.com/projects/jubail-industrial-city/.

Bird, Kai (1980) "Co-opting the Third World Elites: Trilateralism and Saudi Arabia." In Sklar, Holly (ed.) *Trilateralism: the Trilateral Commission and Elite Planning for World Management,* 341–351. Boston: South End Press.

Brad, Mitchell (2010) "The Arab Lobby: the American Component." *Middle East Quarterly,* Fall: 3–15.

Brown, Eliot and Greg Bensinger (2018) *Saudi Money Flows into Silicon Valley – and with it Qualms; the Kingdom is now the Largest Single Investor for U.S. Startups, an Unsettling Fact for Silicon Valley.* Available (consulted August 8 2020) at: http://ezproxy.fiu.edu/login?url=https://search-proquest-com.ezproxy.fiu.edu/docview/2120249852?accountid=10901.

Capital Market Authority (2020) *Fourth Quarter 2020.* Available (consulted November 8 2021) at: https://cma.org.sa/en/Market/Reports/Documents/Q4_2020_EN.pdf.

CFR (2018) *U.S.-Saudi Arabia Relations.* Available (consulted July 5 2020) at: https://www.cfr.org/backgrounder/us-saudi-arabia-relations.

Consultancy. UK (2016) *Saudi Arabia a Lucrative Battleground for Management Consultants.* Available (consulted July 11 2020) at: https://www.consultancy.uk/news/12082/saudi-arabia-a-lucrative-battleground-for-management-consultants.

Coren, Michael J. 2018. *Silicon Valley is awash with Saudi Arabian Money. Here's what they're Investing in.* Available (consulted August 8 2020) at: https://qz.com/1426370/silicon-valley-is-awash-with-saudi-arabian-money-heres-what-theyre-investing-in/.

Dealbook (2008) *When Elbows Rub, Can Deals Be Far Behind?* Available (consulted June 1 2020) at: https://dealbook.nytimes.com/2008/01/22/amid-the-big-ideas-some-flirt-with-deals/?searchResultPosition=8.

Deloitte (2016) *U.S. Aerospace and Defense Labor Market Study; Employment Outlook Upbeat, Reversing Job Losses.* Deloitte Development LLC, 1–56.

Doran, Christopher (2012) *Making the World Safe for Capitalism: How Iraq Threatened the U.S. Economic Empire and had to be Destroyed.* New York: Pluto Press.

ExxonMobil (2017) *ExxonMobil in the Kingdom Today.* Available (consulted November 13 2021) at: https://corporate.exxonmobil.com/Locations/Saudi-Arabia/ExxonMobil-in-the-Kingdom-today.

ExxonMobil (2018) SABIC *and ExxonMobil Advance Gulf Coast Project with Creation of a New Joint Venture.* ExxonMobil. Available (consulted November 14 2021) at: https://corporate.exxonmobil.com/News/Newsroom/News-releases/2018/0501_SABIC-and-ExxonMobil-advance-Gulf-Coast-Project-with-creation-of-a-new-joint-venture.

ExxonMobil (2019) *ExxonMobil,* SABIC *to Proceed with Gulf Coast Growth Ventures Project.* Available (consulted November 13 2021) at: https://corporate.exxonmobil.com/News/Newsroom/News-releases/2019/0613_ExxonMobil-and-SABIC-to-proceed-with-Gulf-Coast-Growth-Ventures-project.

Falk, Richard (1975) "A New Paradigm for International Legal Studies: Prospects and Proposals." *The Yale Law Journal* 84(5): 969–1021.

Frieden, Jeffry (1980) "The Trilateral Commission: Economics and Politics in the 1970's" in *Trilateralism: the Trilateral Commission and Elite Planning for World Management*, edited by Holly Sklar, 61–75. Boston: South End Press.

Garrett-Peltier, Heidi (2017) *Job Opportunity Cost of War.* Costs of War, Watson Institute International & Public Affairs, Brown University, 1–7.

Hanieh, Adam (2011) *Capitalism and Class in the Gulf Arab States.* New York: Palgrave Macmillan.

Harbinson, David K. (1990) "The U.S.-Saudi Arabian Joint Commission on Economic Cooperation: a Critical Appraisal." *Middle East Journal* 44(2): 269–283.

Harris, Jerry (2009) "Statist Globalization in China, Russia and the Gulf States." *Science and Society* 73(1): 6–33.

Henderson, Simon (2001) *The Gulf Cooperation Council Defense Pact: an Exercise in Ambiguity.* Available (consulted January 1 2020) at: https://www.washingtoninstitute.org/policy-analysis/gulf-cooperation-council-defense-pact-exercise-ambiguity.

Horowitz, Julia and Egan Matt (2018) *For America's biggest banks, Saudi crisis strains a lucrative relationship.* Available (consulted June 11 2020) at: https://www.cnn.com/2018/10/16/investing/saudi-arabia-complicates-american-bank-deals/index.html.

Ivanova, Irina (2018) *Saudi Arabia is America's No. 1 Weapons Customer.* Available (consulted June 20 2020) at: https://www.cbsnews.com/news/saudi-arabia-is-the-top-buyer-of-u-s-weapons/.

Jones, Rory and Said, Summer (2020) *Saudi Sovereign Wealth Fund Buys Stakes in Facebook, Boeing, Cisco Systems; the Fund also bought Financial Stocks, Including Citigroup and Bank of America.* Available (consulted August 8 2020) at: http://ezproxy.fiu.edu/login?url=https://search-proquest-com.ezproxy.fiu.edu/docview/2403300137?accountid=10901.

Kellner, Tomas (2017) *Saudi Arabia and GE Partner On $15 Billion in New Projects.* Available (consulted August 10 2020) at: https://www.ge.com/news/reports/saudi-arabia-ge-partner-15-billion-new-projects.

Kemp, John (2016) *How Saudi Arabia Successfully Defended Its U.S. Oil Market Share.* Available (consulted August 8 2020) at: https://www.reuters.com/article/us-usa-refining-kemp-idUSKCN0V7231.

Kenner, David and Al-Ahmad, Kameal (2021) *The U.S.-Saudi Economic Relationship: more than Arms and Oil.* Special Report, Kingdom of Saudi Arabia: King Faisal Center for Research and Islamic Studies, 32.

Klare, Michael T (1984) *American Arms Supermarket.* Austin: University of Texas Press.

Koppelaar, Rembrandt, and Willem Middelkoop. 2018. *The Petrodollar and the Geopolitics of Oil: Why Big Oil Has Lost the Energy War.* Amsterdam: Amsterdam University Press.

Koruzhde, Mazaher (2022) "The Iranian Crisis of the 1970s-1980s and the Formation of the Transnational Investment Bloc." *Class, Race and Corporate Power* 10(2): 1–10.

Koruzhde, Mazaher and Popova, Valeriia (2022) "Americans Still Held Hostage: a Generational Analysis of American Public Opinion about the Iran Nuclear Deal." *Political Science Quarterly* 137(3): 511–537.

Layne, Rachel (2018) *Corporate America's deep ties to Saudi Arabia.* Available (consulted June 15 2020) at: https://www.cbsnews.com/news/corporate-americas-deep-ties-to-saudi-arabia/.

Manjoo, Farhad (2017) *Saudi Money Fuels the Tech Industry. It's Time to Ask Why.* Available (consulted July 12 2020) at: https://www.nytimes.com/2017/11/06/technology/unsavory-sources-money-fueling-tech.html.

Matthews, Christopher and Blunt, Katherine (2021) "Green Hydrogen Plant in Saudi Desert Aims to Amp Up Clean Power." *The Wall Street Journal,* February 8.

Mohamed, Theron (2020). *Saudi Arabia Plowed Billions into U.S. Stocks Including Boeing, Disney, and Facebook Last Quarter.* Available (consulted August 8 2020) at: https://markets.businessinsider.com/news/stocks/saudi-arabia-pif-invested-billions-boeing-disney-facebook-stocks-2020-5-1029210234#.

NCUSAR (1994) *U.S.-GCC Corporate Cooperation Committee – Building Bridges: Business to Business and People to People*. Available (consulted January 7 2021) at: https://ncusar.org/pubs/1994/01/us-gcc-ccc/.

Shammas, Pierre (2000) *Saudi Arabia: Petroleum Industry Review*. Nicosia: Arab Press Services (APS) Group.

Shell (2017) *Shell Announces the Completion of the Transaction to Separate Motiva Assets*. May 1. Accessed August 6, 2020. https://www.shell.com/media/news-and-media-releases/2017/completion-transaction-to-separate-motiva-assets.html.

Shepherd Jr., William G. (1987) *For Saudi Investor, Many U.S. Stakes*. July 14. Accessed July 14, 2020. https://www.nytimes.com/1987/07/14/business/for-saudi-investor-many-us-stakes.html?searchResultPosition=5.

Stokes, Doug, and Sam Raphael (2010) *Global Energy Security and American Hegemony* Baltimore: John Hopkins University Press.

The New York Times (1989) *Saudi-Texaco Joint Venture*. The New York Times, January 3. Available (consulted August 7 2020) at: https://www.nytimes.com/1989/01/03/business/saudi-texaco-joint-venture.html.

The U.S.-Saudi Business Council (2022) *Council History*. Available (consulted December 2 2022) at: https://ussaudi.org/about-us/company-profile/.

Thorpe, Rebecca U. (2014) *The American Warfare State: the Domestic Politics of Military Spending*. Chicago: The University of Chicago Press.

U.S. Chamber of Commerce (2022) *U.S.-GCC Business Initiative*, June 5. Available (consulted October 23 2022) at: https://www.uschamber.com/program/international-affairs/middle-east-and-turkey-affairs/us-gcc-business-initiative.

U.S. Department of Commerce, Bureau of Economic Analysis (2021) *Saudi Arabia – International Trade and Investment Country Facts*. Available (consulted November 8 2021) at: https://www.bea.gov/data/intl-trade-investment/direct-investment-country-and-industry.

U.S. Department of Education. n.d. *College Foreign Gift Reporting*. Available (consulted November 9 2021) at: https://sites.ed.gov/foreigngifts/.

U.S. Department of the Treasury, Federal Reserve Board (2016). *Holdings by Twelve Foreign Oil Exporters of U.S. Treasury Securities – December 1974 to March 2016*. May 16. Accessed January 27, 2020. https://ticdata.treasury.gov/Publish/oilexp_hist_to 2016mar.txt.

U.S. Department of the Treasury, Federal Reserve Board (2021) *Major Foreign Holders of Treasury Securities*. Available (consulted April 10 2021) at: https://ticdata.treasury.gov/Publish/mfh.txt.

Wald, Ellen (2018) *Saudi Inc*. New York: Pegasus Books Ltd.

Wight, David M (2021) *Oil Money: Middle East Petrodollars and the Transformation of U.S. Empire, 1967–1988*. London: Cornell University Press.

Yglesias, Matthew (2019) *Trump's Weird Ideas on the U.S.-Saudi Relationship, Sort of Explained*. Available (consulted July 2 2020) at: https://www.vox.com/policy-and-politics/2019/9/17/20868358/donald-trump-saudi-money.

Young, Karen E. (2018) *U.S.-Saudi Economic Ties: Why Saudi Arabia Matters*. Available (consulted June 20 2020) at: https://agsiw.org/u-s-saudi-economic-ties-why-saudi-arabia-matters/.

CHAPTER 5

Fake News and Social Media: Neoliberalism and the Case of Bell Pottinger

Adam D. Hernandez

1   Introduction[1]

The case of Bell Pottinger showcases the rise of the disinformation firm as a key player within the corporate power structure during the period of neoliberal capitalism. While Bell Pottinger survived through the 2010s, making a transition into the field of computational propaganda as the internet became more readily available, this chapter will mainly focus on the firm's genesis and actions until before the period of the Arab Spring, which was both a turning point for neoliberalism internationally and reflected the vast scale of utilizing the internet and social media in producing political propaganda. The case of Bell Pottinger showcases how the disinformation firm used the expertise of public relations professionals within the UK and internationally to promote a political and economic agenda backed by corporate lobbyists and think-tanks. Bell Pottinger assisted Margaret Thatcher in securing electoral victories domestically, while also advancing a neoliberal policy agenda abroad, often by aligning with autocrats who took advantage of neoliberal policies to secure political power. Bell Pottinger utilized the connections its founder Tim Bell had formed under Thatcher to win lucrative contracts abroad.

In truth, Bell Pottinger has taken multiple forms during its lengthy span of existence. It was founded by Tim Bell, a prominent figure in public relations who earned his prominence thanks to his work in getting Margaret Thatcher elected. Bell was working under Saatchi & Saatchi throughout the first half of the 80s. He would leave in 1985 to form the PR firm Lowe Bell, which would then be subsumed into Chime Communications in 1994 and become Bell Pottinger. For the sake of simplicity and to not get lost in focusing on just the man known as Tim Bell himself, the work of Lord Bell, his inner circle, and his employees will be put under the "Bell Pottinger" umbrella during this analysis.

---

1   This chapter is a revised and expanded version of Adam D. Hernandez (2023) "Bell Pottinger: Pre-Digital Fake News During the Rise of Neoliberalism," *Class, Race and Corporate Power*, Vol. 11 (1): Article 2.

This then allows for a focus on the analysis of the creation of the disinformation firm rather than a historical piece on the multitude of forms Tim Bell's firm has taken (Bates, 2019).

Bell Pottinger is the precursor to the modern disinformation firm, one of a generation of PR companies that rose to prominence at a key moment in the 20th century which saw a transformation of liberalism across the globe. The post-WW2 status quo in nations such as the United States and United Kingdom saw the use of regulated capitalism. This period saw strong state intervention and Keynesian economics derived from a compromise between corporations and labor that was made possible by the fears associated with the rise of communism at the time. Under regulated capitalism, a regulatory state used a mix of taxation, spending and regulatory policies to increase the role of the state in curbing practices conducted by the private sector. Under this system, there was greater taxation of corporate entities, more limits on international trade and capital flows, and greater social spending. This period saw trade unions grow in strength and numbers, albeit integrated into the management structure of big business. There were stable labor relations, a rise in economic growth and productivity compared to previous capitalist eras, and a lack of severe recessions until the stagflation of the 1970s (Kotz, 2015: 62).

The mid-1960s and 1970s saw the beginning of the end for this status quo as dominant economic powers with welfare systems in place were challenged by economic competition from states like Germany & Japan. The challenges this competition posed to already established global corporations began to produce cracks in the system. The stagflation crisis of the 1970s suddenly saw broader corporate support for a rollback of state regulation, taxation, and intervention in the economy (Cox and Skidmore-Hess, 1999: 8–10). The corporate coalition of economic elites who had supported regulated capitalism since the Great Depression began to fracture in the face of stagnating profits (Cox and Skidmore-Hess, 1999: 6). In the United Kingdom dominant firms in the finance, oil, gas, and real-estate sectors began to oppose regulated capitalism by the 1970s. When these firms began to see dips in their long-term profits, they began to develop and fund neoliberalism as a project to alleviate their profit losses (Christophers, 2020: 24).

The rate of profit for the globally dominant Fortune 500 corporations experienced a steady decline from 1965–1982. As a result, the most global and profitable corporations began to aggressively lobby for the reversal of policies implemented by governments during the period of regulated capitalism. This was advocated publicly as a necessary solution to the economic woes that had impacted the general public, but also served as a means of keeping these entrenched economic elites in power. There were greater calls to reduce taxation on corporations, reduce social regulation, and increase subsidies to incentivize investment. Corporate coalitions began a systematic critique of the welfare state and the left-leaning political parties that supported it (Cox and Skidmore-Hess, 1999: 161). Corporate lobbies, think tanks and conservative political movements promoted powerful neoliberal figures such as Thatcher and Reagan, who fought for these policies with the support of a coalition of powerful economic elites. These politicians emerged at the beginning of neoliberal policy changes in their respective nations, in part due to their promises that their policies would alleviate the economic burden on the middle class and put their nations' economic elites back on top. The liberalization of the global market and reduction of social benefits were the means by which they could bring about these promises (Cox and Skidmore-Hess, 1999: 167).

These investment coalitions shape policy agendas, provide a conduit between the private sector and the state, and as such are institutionalized within dominant governing coalitions, enabled by blocs of investors and voting coalitions (Ferguson and Rogers, 1987: 45). As corporate profit rates had been in long-term decline, corporations responded by increasing their lobbying, investing greater amounts of money into the political sphere, and using think-tanks to pressure political parties to move towards the right, particularly in terms of economic policy (Ferguson and Rogers, 1987: 105).

In *A Brief History of Neoliberalism*, David Harvey argues that neoliberalism was created as a project designed to substantially enhance the power of domestic and global elites (Harvey, 2007: 19). Neoliberalism is associated with utilizing political policies that favor enhancing the power of private actors while reeling back institutions and policies that protect the middle and working class. This includes shifting the tax burden from the rich to the middle class, the privatization and monetization of markets, weakening unions, and seeking to expand markets abroad by opening up other nations to similar neoliberal practices (Harvey, 2007: 33).

Many of these policies are ones that would not be traditionally popular among the working class of a nation, as they would involve deliberately weakening institutions that directly assist them in favor of policies which further empower already powerful economic actors. Furthermore, most industrialized countries post-ww2 favored a strong welfare state which neoliberal actors would need to tear down. As such, political actors favoring neoliberalism would need to go about the construction of a "new common sense," a pitch in which they argue that these policies will eventually yield greater benefits to individuals through empowering the market rather than through the provision of state welfare. Political parties were still required to win elections, even if their financers vastly supported neoliberal politics. The success of the neoliberal project relied on broad public support for politicians who favored neoliberal policies and solutions. Rejection from the general public threatened to prevent neoliberal policies from fully being implemented, and as such, the reversal of the policies of regulated capitalism and subsequent greater increase of privatization was dependent on their ability to sell neoliberalism as the best solution possible for the problems ailing the public at the time (Harvey, 2007: 19).

It is at this crossroads where the Disinformation Firm exists within democratic politics. These firms were enlisted by politicians and corporations to promote neoliberal policies as in the best interests of middle- and working-class voters. Disinformation firms used their expertise associated with selling a product in consumer markets to sell neoliberalism as an ideology so that enough voters could be convinced to give up a welfare state that provided social benefits in favor of policies that offered direct assistance to economic elites. For this to work, corporate elites and politicians promoting neoliberalism enlisted PR firms to garner public support by any means necessary. The methods of corporate PR firms included propaganda, disinformation, and utter ruthlessness towards political opponents who threatened to obstruct neoliberal hegemony. The rise of disinformation firms would be a political innovation that would change the nature of democratic politics.

This was something beyond the government-produced political propaganda of the past, or the use of mainstream news media to spin certain narratives. This was about getting experts who knew how to produce commercials, who knew how to run broad public relations campaigns to get the general public to buy a product. This was a huge, powerful sector, already entrenched within a corporate advertising and PR sector that had rapidly expanded since the end of World War 2. What separates the actions of the world of PR from previous political propagandists can be best summed up by Nigel Oakes, former employee of Bell Pottinger and founder of Cambridge Analytica's holding company SCL Group, who said "The greatest change that has happened with influence occurred when the scientific world began to realize that it wasn't about what you said ... the answer was in the audience." These are experts who innovated how to sell messages to human beings, who used scientific and business know-how to truly understand how to best sell one product against another in the most efficient way possible (Nielle and Poplack, 2020: 24:00–25:30).

The economic crises of the 1970s, which impacted the economies of nations like the U.S. and United Kingdom, allowed advocates of neoliberalism a chance to convince the public that neoliberal policies were a favorable solution for their economic woes. Supporting political parties advocating for neoliberal politics, including powerful political figures such as Ronald Reagan and Margaret Thatcher, firms such as Bell Pottinger, who already originated from the private sector, could apply their expertise in public relations to efficiently convince the general public that these solutions were the best solutions to vote for. These practices continue to this day, having evolved from the time of printed press into the digital age with firms such as Cambridge Analytics and the Archimedes Group. Today these firms operate in a very different status quo, one in which neoliberalism is in far greater crisis in a post-great recession world, but their support for neoliberal policies and their use of disinformation continues. These campaigns are run by professionals from a line of work that had expanded greatly and revised its toolsets constantly in order to maximize profits for their clients.

In the United Kingdom, corporate access to policymaking increased dramatically during the 70s, and especially the 80s, as a result of this broad push for neoliberal policies (Christophers, 2020: 17). This led to a reduction of taxation, the privatization of previously public services, and a rise of public subsidies for British corporations that allowed for a rentier class of economic elites to increase profits at the expense of societal growth. The post-WW2 economy of Britain saw financial and land-owning interests, the dominant forms of rentierism, limited by the government. By the 1950s, there were some who would predict that there would be full land nationalization in the future. The economy was tightly directed in this time period, but the 1970s brought crisis to the British economic model, and the 1980s provided opportunities for corporate elites to promote changes to the system. The rise of neoliberalism in this period brought about mass privatization, corporate subsidization, financialization that strengthened private sector power within the state, a process that would be facilitated with the rise of Bell Pottinger (Christophers, 2020: 4).

The founder of Bell Pottinger would be Tim Bell, who masterminded the "Labour Isn't Working" campaign for Margaret Thatcher's electoral efforts. Bell Pottinger as a corporate entity did not exist yet. Instead, Tim Bell was working for Saatchi & Saatchi, one of the largest PR companies in the world. Saatchi & Saatchi's status as a powerful PR company allowed it to secure a contract with the Conservative Party, and the Conservative Party's great wealth allowed for it to afford Saatchi & Saatchi. The success of "Labour Isn't Working" allowed for Tim Bell to score a notable reputation as a PR expert and granted him numerous connections in the world of politics needed to eventually found Bell Pottinger. These connections could then be leveraged to find Bell Pottinger work not just locally but abroad. Thanks to his connections with Thatcher, Tim Bell could get through the door to sell his services to other political allies of the Conservative Party abroad. Likewise, you could now hire the company founded by the man who helped Thatcher secure her political victories, for a price. Bell Pottinger suddenly found itself operating in South Africa, Iraq, Chile, Belarus, and numerous other nations across the globe. As money flooded in support for privatization and other neoliberal policies, Bell Pottinger was a potential service to purchase for powerful political and economic actors attempting to secure victory and power. In this, we see Bell Pottinger acting as a champion for the defense and adoption of neoliberal politics at a time where it was well-positioned within international politics. In doing so, we can clearly see the firm acting as a privatized political actor seeking to protect and expand the interests of important sectors of Britain's economy as well.

2 Bell Pottinger and the Rise of Neoliberalism

The rise of neoliberalism did not come overnight to Britain. Unlike the United States, the nation had a relatively entrenched welfare state post-WW2. It was well-developed and politically accepted. Thus, the rise of neoliberalism was not an inevitability, rather it was a conscious movement by powerful economic actors within the nation. The Labour Party had succeeded in securing a great amount of political power since the 1930s, many of the United Kingdom's most successful industries were nationalized, and even when in power, the Conservative Party rarely attacked the nation's welfare structure (Christophers, 2020: 55). However, a financial crisis in the 1970s substantially damaged Britain's economy. It would be this financial crisis which would give right-wing political actors the opportunity to pitch neoliberal politics as a solution to the nation's economic woes (Rustin, 2010). These actors did not come out of nowhere, many of them had been pitching such policies since the 1950s but had yet to pierce the mainstream. Their rise to power was gradual. The UK government began securing London's place as a financial power, one of the last vestiges of Great Britain's old imperial power structure. However, the stagflation the UK suffered from in the 70s was what truly allowed for the corporate sector, led by London's financial district, to pitch neoliberalism as a powerful economic solution (Harvey, 2007: 56).

Much of the early support for neoliberalism originated from corporate-funded think tanks. Neoliberal policies had been slowly pitched to professionals, academics, and the public by institutions such as the Centre for Policy Studies, the Adam Smith Institute, and the Institute of Economic Affairs since the 1950s. These actors did not just sell neoliberalism to professionals and politicians but were among the first organizations to understand that they had to pitch their ideas to the press. They also received considerable contributions from corporate interests, such as from powerful economic elites like Rupert Murdoch. Experts such as Keith Joseph, who originated from the IEA, and would go on to be a key advisor for Margaret Thatcher, rose to prominence among experts in the 1970s. These think tanks were very successful at taking advantage of youth groups, particularly within universities at the time. They did this through advocating neoliberalism through individualist ideals and presenting it as an ideology which challenged traditional class structures (Harvey, 2007: 57). Corporate lobbyists, oftentimes funded by the actors already described, were essential to pitching neoliberalism to politicians. Lobbyists convinced politicians that neoliberalism would be quite profitable. After all, many of Britain's largest and most lucrative industries, such as coal, steel and automobiles were nationalized. Privatizing these markets would generate a significant windfall of profits (Cave and Rowell, 2014: 648).

Powerful players within the press such as Rupert Murdoch were also important in not just funding think tanks such as the IEA but also using his publishing company, Murdoch Press, as a means of advertising neoliberalism as an economic solution to the financial crisis. The influence of Rupert Murdoch and News Corp on British politics cannot be understated. News Corp, Rupert Murdoch's company, has long been able to hold great political power due to its ability to control critical nodal points in modern society, such as the media, business, and economic networks. News Corp has managed to sway political narratives, and thus controlling the conversation in politics, through political brokering, leveraging public opinion, institutionalizing sensationalist media, and diversifying media holdings. Significant power-brokers within corporate elite networks already supported neoliberal policies, which provided the foundations for leveraging financial support that could help politicians supporting these policies get elected (Arsenault and Castells, 2008: 488). This would mean convincing the public to vote for politicians advancing neoliberal policies.

Margaret Thatcher emerged as a central figure in the ascendancy of neoliberal ideology. Thatcher was the president of the Centre for Policy Studies, a prior-mentioned thinktank which developed neoliberal policies and strategies for how to advocate for them (Cave and Rowell, 2014: 641). Margaret Thatcher's political program advanced the goals of corporate lobbyists. From 1984 to 1990, the Thatcher administration privatized more than 42 businesses. In addition, her policies were particularly aimed towards weakening unions and dismantling the welfare state (Cave and Rowell, 2014: 657). Thatcher's influence did not even end with the conclusion of her administration. Her policies did not just successfully implement neoliberalism in England, but also created a status quo that institutionalized business lobbying within British politics. Her influence on neoliberalism can even be felt today, as many of her allies still maintain influential positions in political lobbying. This includes figures such as Nigel Lawson, a former chancellor of Margaret Thatcher who has written for

Global Warming Policy Foundation, a climate skeptic policy group (Cave and Rowell, 2014: 2102).

This is where Tim Bell, the eventually founder of Bell Pottinger steps in. Bell was working in PR in the firm Saatchi & Saatchi at the time, having been picked by the Saatchi brothers who ran the company to work on the company's lucrative contract for Margaret Thatcher and the conservatives as she ran for office. This would come as no surprise. Saatchi & Saatchi is one of the largest PR companies in the world. Furthermore, the company has typically had ties to the conservative wing of British politics. In 1983, Saatchi & Saatchi would work for the Tories, notably creating a "Labour says he's black. Tories say he's British" poster depicting a black man. In 1992, they would once again take a contract with the Conservative Party, with two of their prominent works from this campaign being their "Defence" poster depicting a porcupine with a full back of pricks labeled "Conservative," alongside a smaller, prickles porcupine labeled "Labour" in addition to a poster of a bombshell labeled "You'd pay 1250 (pounds) more tax a year under Labour" (Townshendj, 2010). The company would also have a contract for the conservatives in 1997, conducting the "New Labour, New Danger" campaign. In addition, one of the brothers who owned the company, Maurice Saatchi, was an outspoken conservative who joined the House of Lords in 1996, often arguing for the cutting of taxes (BBC, "Profile: Lord Saatchi," 2003).

Tim Bell's work for Thatcher was considered revolutionary at the time. He was the mastermind behind the "Labour Isn't Working" campaign in 1979, a campaign which proved to be very successful for the Conservative Party. Bell's expertise in PR was essential to revolutionizing the political campaign and in getting the public to accept neoliberalism. As a PR consultant, Bell advised Thatcher's interviewing techniques, regulated how she dressed, and even how her hair was styled. The "Labour Isn't Working" campaign sought to discredit the left of Britain, blaming them and the welfare state for the country's financial crisis. It was this campaign which ingrained itself in the UK's public consciousness, convincing the nation's population that public institutions, unions, and leftwing policies were bad for the economic state of the country. Most infamously, this campaign involved a flier which depicted long lines of unemployed workers. In reality, the lines depicted on these fliers did not even exist, as they were nothing more than conservative party volunteers posing for the campaign (Shipman, 2015). Ultimately, Tim Bell was a PR man, and his strategy for a Conservative Party victory favored playing on the emotions of voters, even at the expense of the truth, as long as it secured victory. Bell's expertise involved selling customers a product, and this was evident in his public presentations. When speaking about his political work, Lord Bell wrote in his memoirs "Why tell the truth when a lie will do?" He would write: "I am a moral man (but) there were many times when I would adopt the same philosophy." In his own writings, he admits to his distortion of the facts, "We could in those days find statistics that proved anything ... you could argue we were always trying to stretch the truth, but then everybody was at the time" (Bates, 2019).

Margaret Thatcher and the Conservative Party's electoral success would see the UK adopt many neoliberal policies, as promised. The government sold off more than 42 businesses which employed nearly a million workers. Working class institutions were weakened, trade unions were weakened, and there was a privatization of public utilities. These were changes that left the bargaining power and morale of workers weakened and created a status quo that favored economic elites within British society. Lord Bell's campaign was so successful that he and Thatcher were said to have maintained personal ties even after they stopped working together. Thatcher's political successes changed the status quo of British politics to the point where, when the Labour Party rebranded itself in 1997 successfully and won, it did little to change what the Conservatives had done and made little attempts to go back to the welfare state of old (Rustin, 2010).

While Bell Pottinger as a company would not exist until after the rise of Thatcher, its origins ultimately lie in the "Labour Isn't Working" campaign, which is essential to understanding the company's origins. Tim Bell left the Saatchis in 1985, a departure that led to the creation of Bell Pottinger. The company, founded in 1994 as Lowe Bell, would eventually be known as Bell Pottinger by 1998 after co-founder Frank Rowe quit and requested that his name no longer be associated with the company (Bates, 2019). He founded the company with another PR figure, Franke Rowe, who ultimately split from Bell's company and had very little influence on its long-term narrative. The company was first named Lowe Bell before, in 1998, it was renamed to Bell Pottinger after Franke Rowe demanded the company be renamed (*The Guardian*, 2006). Without the political infamy Bell's work for Saatchi & Saatchi earned him, Bell Pottinger may not have been founded, and it definitely would not have won the company the lucrative contracts abroad it would gain over the years. This success cemented a relationship between the corporate power structure and Bell Pottinger, which would then go about enforcing the political ideology abroad, both to secure political allies and bring about new allies. We can see how Bell Pottinger's prior connections with the neoliberal movement helped it secure success early on in its existence from Tim Bell himself. Tim Bell has publicly spoke about how he used Margaret Thatcher's support to get him phone calls straight to world leaders, such as FW de Klerk. Politicians, particularly allies of Margaret Thatcher, were well-informed of Tim Bell's work for her campaign, and his PR work was given a lot of credit for its success by the Conservative Party. (Nielle and Poplack, 2020: 28:30-29-30). This allowed for Bell Pottinger to not only a lot of room to navigate politically in terms of finding clients interested in its services, it allowed the company to charge a great amount of money for its services.

Bell Pottinger would take on numerous contracts of a political sort from its founding to before the Arab Spring in 2011. These would range from being hired by arms manufacturers such as BAE and former neoliberal despots such as Pinochet. However, the two most prominent and striking cases that point towards Bell Pottinger's role within a corporate power structure are its contracts with FW de Klerk during South Africa's first post-Apartheid elections in 1994 and with the U.S. military during the occupation of Iraq during the War on Terror. These cases showcase Bell Pottinger's willingness to work with neoliberal autocrats who seek to use their state power to open up new markets for Britain.

3 Early Bell Pottinger in South Africa

Bell Pottinger's ties to the corporate power structure and neoliberalism deepened beyond its British origins to include a significant impact on global politics. As Harvey describes, a key component of the corporate lobbying for neoliberal policies was to increase profits and to reduce costs. As part of that strategy, corporate support for neoliberalism involved using neoliberal ideology to promote opening new markets for trade and foreign investment, which has historically been viewed as part of the "solution" to capitalist crises. The global expansion of neoliberalism became a key concept of Bell Pottinger's mission statement. Bell Pottinger promoted policies that sought to advance the "increasing geographical mobility of capital," as Harvey puts it, or the outsourcing of labor and production contracts within an increasingly globalized system of capitalist production which would help define neoliberal capitalism (Harvey, 2007: 92). One of Bell Pottinger's first international contracts highlights this, as the company found itself working for FW de Klerk, who was running against Nelson Mandela in a post-Apartheid South Africa. The National Party, to whom Bell Pottinger was working for, was championing neoliberalism as its main solution to economic crises. This came to no surprise, as the National Party was mainly made up of figures from the Apartheid state, who had adopted these policies in the 1980s due to its close connections to the United Kingdom, United States, and World Bank, who were all advocating for neoliberal policies (Narsiah, 2002: 33).

FW de Klerk represented a status quo that had existed before the fall of Apartheid. It has been argued that neoliberalism has deep historical roots within South Africa. The political crisis of 1976 saw South Africa's Apartheid government in crisis, with it quickly becoming apparent that reforms were needed for elites to maintain their power. In response to this, government-aligned economists began to use the writings of neoliberal thinkers such as Hayek for their own policies in an effort to legitimize their minority rule (Von Schnitzler, 2016: 53). This crisis was joined by the global finance crisis of the 70s, which resulted in the South African government borrowing a great amount of money that grew considerable public ire into the 1980s. UK economists were among those who criticized South Africa's borrowing of funds, criticizing public corporations as bad economics (Guy et al., 1999: 151). Margaret Thatcher, a key ally to Bell Pottinger, was often a reliable although critical ally of the Apartheid government, holding off from imposing sanctions on the South African government in a time where her opponents were calling for such measures to take place (O'Meara, 1996: 399). The 1980s saw Apartheid political elites increasingly favoring neoliberal policies to solve their political issues. The Ministerial Committee for Privatization and Deregulation was created to oversee a reformation of South Africa's public corporations. It was headed by Wim de Villiers, a man who loudly criticized the post-war welfare state as "Post-War socialism" (*Business Day*, 1989) All in all, the Apartheid government favored neoliberal solutions post-1970s. Apartheid needed neoliberalism to extend its lifeline, because it needed economic policies that weakened the bargaining power of its (mostly African) working class and boosted the power of its (White) ruling class.

Bell Pottinger's PR campaign for South Africa's first democratic election was one of its first major contracts outside of the UK, and its connections with South Africa would continue through the existence of the firm. The election involved FW de Klerk running against Nelson Mandela for president. This PR campaign involved films which cast doubts on the results of the 1994 election, suggesting that the National Party's percentage of the vote was not actually its real percentage but part of an agreement by ruling powers. This placed a lot of focus on the potential corruption of the National Party's political opponents, designed to hurt their political legitimacy. It also focused on black-on-black violence between the ANC and Inkatha Freedom Party, with the goal being to split and create fear within their respective voting bases. This strategy was twofold: it sought to create wedges within the National Party's political foes while also painting its enemies as violent to their own supporters (Kemp, 2020). Ultimately, de Klerk would not win the 1994 election.

While the National Party was defeated, this would not be the defeat of neoliberalism in South Africa. Its very nature meant that Mandela would simply inherit a government that had already given away much of its political power to economic elites, the very same economic elites who had been in power in Apartheid were here to stay. Ultimately, it could be argued that it would be difficult for anything to truly change, even after the end of Apartheid. Apartheid had already created inequalities based on race, and unless those inequalities were fixed through direct action after Apartheid, they would remain. Looking at it this way, it can be easy to see claim that the privatization process described above was more of an exit strategy for the Apartheid government than anything, an exit strategy intended to maintain the majority of the prior status quo. The United States, United Kingdom, and many global financial institutions were practicing privatization at the time. By practicing privatization as well, the National Party elites enacting these privatization strategies began to build alliances with elites from the larger neoliberal power structure. By enacting these policies and further embedding South Africa in a larger global corporate power structure, these elites created a dependency that would make it difficult for substantial reforms to take place to reform South Africa's inequalities (Narsiah, 2002: 6).

The techniques that Bell Pottinger used in the election were similar to what they had done with Thatcher. They did not just create products for the National Party and de Klerk, they advised de Klerk on how to speak and present his political ideas. They had even dressed de Klerk in traditional African clothes in an effort to win over voters. In a similar manner to how Thatcher was advised towards coming across as a powerful leader who could keep "socialist leftists" in check, de Klerk and the National Party were depicted as rational men who would prevent the ANC from taking any "radical" steps once taking power. Bell Pottinger understood that the National Party could not get more votes than the ANC, so the goal was about positioning the status quo powers as rational figures looking out for South Africa's well-being, rather than the holdovers from a cruel and racist regime. Particularly, a focus in their speeches were aimed at the importance of the National Party in creating South Africa's new constitution. In addition, a great amount of political violence was still transpiring within the nation. Bell Pottinger worked with the media in South Africa to depict this violence as evidence of the potential chaos that could ensue alongside a transition of political power. This violence was constructed to paint a negative image of the changes going through South Africa at the time, depicting the ANC's rise and the end of Apartheid as the beginning of a great rise of black violence. Of course, this campaign was being made to advance the political status of the National Party, which would be projected as the "strongman" leaders who would play the protector in this narrative. The National Party would be the ones pulling back from any scary reforms the ANC wanted to make to prevent any further chaos. Through depicting the explicit political violence that was taking place at the time, Bell Pottinger could leverage support for the National Party's message of being "rational political figures against radicalism." Bell Pottinger's PR campaign focused on calling upon voters to vote for the National Party to undercut "radicals" and depicted the ANC as communists (Nielle and Poplack, 2020: 27:20-35:00).

This campaign was one of the first of its nature for Bell Pottinger. The company saw itself as an agent capable of shaping the reputations of its clients. Even when dealing with overt political actors, it saw its goal as "enhancing their "clients" brand and deliver(ing) commercial success." According to Bell Pottinger itself, they had eight rules for managing crises: Do not panic, work out a plan, avoid blame; but take responsibility, accept help; but never lose control, manage expectations, be there and be available, be as transparent as possible, and understand your media and audience (Mance, 2014). While many of these statements are clearly insincere, it illustrates Bell Pottinger's cold, analytical approach to politics. While the National Party did not win the majority of the vote, Bell Pottinger's support was still central to the party gaining 20% of the vote. This gave the National Party the 2nd most amount of the votes in South Africa's first post-apartheid election. This allowed the National Party to remain influential during the formative years of South Africa's democracy while the ANC did not have the 2/3rds of the vote they needed to rewrite the constitution. According to South African journalist Diana Neille, "It had massive implications for South Africa," speaking on how Bell Pottinger helped the National Party influence South Africa's new constitution. The new constitution was very protective over the ownership of property and land rights, the biggest concern for the white-ruling class during the Apartheid government. This constitution allowed for the same elites from apartheid to maintain economic control (Shoba, 2020).

The firm had managed to use fear to drum up support for the National Party by depicting violence between the ANC and Inkatha Freedom Party. This played upon the anxieties of certain elements of the voting base of South Africa. There is no doubt Bell Pottinger was creating a narrative that the fall of Apartheid would bring about political violence from those who had managed to overturn it, in hopes of garnering voters who would believe that support for the National Party would help stabilize this perceived chaos. While they did not manage to overcome Nelson Mandela in the election, that was never the goal. Mandela was too popular. All Bell Pottinger needed to do, however, was help de Klerk gather just enough support to ensure the National Party had a seat at the table. This way, it could fight for the policies it needed to back up South Africa's existing economic elites. While it is easy to dismiss Bell Pottinger's support of the National Party in 1994 as nothing more than a footnote building towards a larger campaign in 2017, it is important to note here that Bell Pottinger's work for de Klerk was part of why it had the influence to win another contract in South Africa in the first place. Bell Pottinger's work in helping the National Party secure votes to eventually influence land rights in the country cannot be understated. Here lies the use of such tools as Bell Pottinger, who successfully managed to manifest an air of anxiety among the National Party's political base. Because the ANC could not secure the 2/3rds needed to make the substantial reforms it needed to make to South Africa's constitution, it was inevitable that the ANC would need to adopt neoliberal policies to be successful within its status quo. We can see this through cases such as the ANC's more socialist-leaning Reconstruction and Development Plan transforming into a far more liberal Growth Employment and Redistribution policy (Narsiah, 2002: 3). The truth of the matter was that the ANC had to act within the institutions that it was operating within as a political party. These institutions had been reformed throughout the 70s and 80s by the Apartheid government as it privatized. Many of the inequalities perpetuated had become systemic, and the ANC could not help but be influenced by the discourse and institutions already embedded into South Africa by this process (Narsiah, 2002: 6).

Bell Pottinger would return to South Africa throughout its existence, with the country being one of its first and last international contracts. The company's work in South Africa showcases Bell Pottinger's commitment as an enforcer of the neoliberal ideology abroad. This was not a company content with championing neoliberalism at home. The South Africa case showcases the establishment of the relationship between Bell Pottinger and neoliberal autocrats whose power is reinforced by larger neoliberal nations such as the United Kingdom and United States. Bell Pottinger would return to South Africa in favor of the ANC in 2016, ironically, a show of how far the ANC had endeared itself into a system it had previously been hostile to in the past. Aligning with the wealthy-billionaire Gupta family and ANC president Zuma, Bell Pottinger ran a social media campaign stoking anger over "white monopoly capital" and "economic apartheid" in order to distract from the corrupt practices of the Gupta family, who had used its ties with Jacob Zuma to extract billions out of the state (Neate, 2017).

4   Bell Pottinger in Iraq

In *The Shock Doctrine: The Rise of Disaster Capitalism*, Naomi Klein argues that after nations are shocked by wars or other political crises, they are then shocked by corporations and aligned politicians who exploit the vulnerabilities left by the crises to implement "economic shock therapy." If, after this process, there is still resistance, they are then again "shocked," albeit this time by police, prisons, and other autocratic tools (Klein, 2007: 25–26). This is dubbed the "shock doctrine" by Klein, who argues in her book that the case of the Iraq War is one of the most comprehensive implementations of the practice. The 2003 invasion of Iraq and its subsequent occupation saw the privatization of state-owned enterprises, which included thousands being laid off, which then contributed to insurgency and greater political turmoil. The post-occupation Iraqi government, initially under the direction of a Coalition Provisional Authority established by the United States, had a bottom-line that favored insiders and economic elites (Klein, 2007: 381). The profits international businesses made from contracts related to the occupation of Iraq are well documented, including UK-based private firms. CorpWatch reports that at least 61 British Companies accumulated at least £1.1 billion on contracts and investments in the new Iraq (Verkaik, 2006). The case of Iraq sees Bell Pottinger champion neoliberalism once again; this time amassed by a small army of corporate actors all seeking to expand their businesses. As described prior, a key element of neoliberalism is the expansion of capital investment into new markets. The occupation of Iraq was a major opportunity to do so. The nation saw this happen through an economy of homeland security, privatized war, and failed reconstruction, which only led to the foundation of a privatized police state (Klein, 2007, 299).

The 2003 invasion of Iraq effectively dismantled the nation's status quo as it found its economic and political paradigms shifted. The nation was integrated into the global markets through the use of neoliberal legal frameworks and laws that trans-nationalized the Iraqi state, utilizing it to effectively create new means of transnational capital from the nation. The new laws imposed by the U.S. occupation opened the nation to global investors regardless of their international origins, showcasing that the invasion of Iraq often served trans-national business interests (Baker, 2014: 121).

The U.S. Defense Department awarded Bell Pottinger one of its largest contracts, which paid the firm at least $540 million between 2004 and 2011. This placed Bell Pottinger at the center of the United States "psy-ops" efforts in the midst of its War on Terror (Gaffey, 2017). On the eve of the 2003 invasion of Iraq, political commentator Michael Ignatieff described the United States' global efforts as "an empire lite, a global hegemony whose grace notes are free markets, human rights, and democracy, enforced by the most awesome military power that the world has ever known" (McCoy, 2017: 43). These words best describe America's mindset heading into the Iraq War and the War on Terror as a whole. The United States' actions in the Middle East best represented the nation's ambitions in the absence of any challenges on the global stage. The USSR had fallen, and China, while seen as a threat, was not viewed in the way it would become in the 2010s. The United States' efforts in Iraq, regardless of what motivations one may argue were behind it, clearly involved liberalizing the state. This meant neoliberal policies: A democratic state that looked more like the U.S., and especially a free and open economy. This fit in with Bell Pottinger's modus operandi thus far, and so it would come to no surprise that the PR firm would be hired to assist the United States in its efforts in Iraq. There was money to be made, and British companies such as Bell Pottinger made a fortune from the occupation of Iraq.

Bell Pottinger's efforts in Iraq were vast and complicated. To meet the conditions of their Pentagon paymasters, all content was signed off by the then-commander of Iraq's coalition forces, General David Petraeus. Bell Pottinger was said to have worked directly with military forces in Camp Victory, Baghdad. They reported directly to The Pentagon, CIA, and National Security Council. The work the firm had done was unlike anything it had done before, and clearly a huge step forward for the scope of Bell Pottinger's actions. It is why the case of Bell Pottinger in Iraq represents a clear point of transformation that would shape the modern disinformation firm of the 2010s. Being paid over a hundred million dollars a year, and employing at least 300 British and Iraqi staff, this was a huge campaign. In 2004, it was tasked by Iraq's temporary administration to promote democratic elections in the country.

During its tenure in Iraq, Bell Pottinger's contractual assignments from 2007 to 2011 are significant in helping to pioneer techniques that would later be more widely used by modern disinformation firms. According to Martin Wells, a video editor working for Bell Pottinger during this time, the company engaged in a systematic disinformation campaign that produced three related public relations products. The first products were television commercials meant to depict Al-Qaeda in a negative light. The second products would be news items meant to look as if they had come from Arabic TV. This involved using low-definition cameras to apparently film bombings, although the exact source of the footage is unclear. These first two products were designed to be sent to TV stations all over the Middle East to paint the U.S. military in a more positive light, with the fact that they were propaganda manufactured by the military itself often not being disclosed to viewers. What is clear is that the United States had also contracted the Lincoln Group around the same period to place Pentagon articles in Iraqi newspapers, framed as unbiased news. The technique of creating a piece of propaganda but disguising it to appear as if it came from a separate, more legitimate news source will be one that we will see repeated many times by successor disinformation firms (Black, 2016).

The goal of these products was to win the hearts and minds of Iraqis and other regional citizens for the occupational forces in the same way "Labour Isn't Working" won the hearts and minds of British voters. "I was really dead set on going to Iraq and I wanted to do it in the space of countering the extremism on the ground of giving the new state a chance" said Kirsten Fontenrose, Strategy Consultant of the Multi National Forces in Iraq. "It was not naïve in the beginning to bring in marketing expertise (...) who does it better? Who's ever done it before at all?" She spoke when speaking on her rationale behind bringing in experts from firms such as Bell Pottinger. These products were sensational and contained shocking imagery. One such TV spot created for Iraqi citizens involved a lone Iraqi woman watching over a newborn baby, presumably her child, humming Iraq's national anthem. Other spots included scenes of violence, including imagery of men using firearms to gun others down to depict the chaos that insurgents had created within the nation. Another spot involved a middle-aged Iraqi woman crying over a small casket, presumably a child. A soap opera-like program was produced in which a young man from an Iraqi family falls into the wrong crowd and is recruited by Al-Qaeda, ending in tragedy. Supposedly, at least 13 of these products were created a month for use as propaganda pieces by the occupational forces. Looking at the kinds of products Bell Pottinger made, they were clearly interested in both nation building and combating support for insurgents in Iraq. These products were created by non-Iraqis, funded by the U.S. government, and focused on cultivating Iraqi nationalism, support for occupational forces, and swaying support for insurgencies (*Influence the Film*, 2021).

Fabricated Al-Qaeda propaganda films were produced. Martin Wells was given exact instructions for how to construct these films to appear as legitimate as possible. They had to look and feel like real Al-Qaeda propaganda films, even being encoded in the same way as if they were being produced by Al-Qaeda itself. Reportedly, U.S. forces were told to drop these films as CDs in the middle of scenes of chaos, often in the aftermath of violence so that they may be picked up and watched afterwards by insurgents. The CDs were meant to be played on Real Player, a media streaming application connected to the internet that allowed for the United States to collect IP addresses of where the video was played. The point was to track the locations of insurgents using these IP addresses. In doing so, Bell Pottinger did not just act as propagandists, they literally assisted the U.S. military in tracking and killing Iraqi insurgents during the occupation. Through this act, the U.S. government could even tell if these CDs were circulated outside of Iraq. Although multiple PR firms were utilized by the United States within this period, including Leonie Industries and the aforementioned Lincoln Group, Bell Pottinger's contract would be the most lucrative (Black, 2016).

In many ways, nothing that has been described about Bell Pottinger's operations thus far is particularly new. This could arguably be true for any of the case studies, as propaganda has existed as long as politics have. Most of the techniques described above have appeared in the Cold War, the World Wars, and other conflicts long before these. Regardless, Bell Pottinger's work in Iraq remains important for two reasons: First, it represented Bell Pottinger's growing prestige and the acknowledgement of its high position in promoting neoliberal policies on a global stage. Second, we saw the first uses of the internet in their product. Although not entirely relevant in terms of content, and the use of the internet to track IP addresses is likely The Pentagon's idea rather than Bell Pottinger's, we can see the start of the internet's importance here. The influence of which will eventually become vital to the scope and power of disinformation firms.

5 Bell Pottinger's Promotion of Neoliberalism Pre-Arab Spring

South Africa and Iraq were only two major contracts Bell Pottinger had during the 1990s and 2000s. However, there were many more operations of lesser scale that the firm undertook in this time period which shared similar features with their contracts in South Africa and Iraq. The company worked with autocrats such as Pinochet, the Al-Assad Family, Shinawatra in Thailand, and the supposed "last dictator of Europe," Lukashenko of Belarus. These contracts are similar in nature to the contractual work in South Africa in showcasing a pattern of behavior in which Bell Pottinger takes contracts from autocrats who either already have ties with neoliberal superpowers or are showing a willingness to adopt neoliberalism in order to reconsolidate their power. Meanwhile, contracts with the Kirchners in Argentina and BAE show Bell Pottinger's willingness to promote international business, even in the face of controversy. Bell Pottinger's contracts with the Kirchner family and BAE saw the company promoting the arms manufacturing and international tourism industries, respectively, even as both their clients were highly criticized for their practices.

The history of the firm's relationship with autocrats is highlighted by their defense of Augusto Pinochet when he was detained in Spain in 1998. Pinochet's regime in Chile had close ties with imperial powers such as the United States since its inception, when it paved the way for the adoption of neoliberal policies long before the days of Reaganism or Thatcherism. Therefore, the fact that Bell Pottinger was willing to defend Pinochet's legacy should come as no surprise (Hutchinson, 2014: 438). Tim Bell had actually done work with associates of Pinochet before, as he had actually helped run a campaign for Hernan Buchi, Pinochet's successor, during Chile's 1989 elections as it was transitioning away from dictatorship, the campaign being similar in nature to Bell Pottinger's work for de Klerk (Nielle and Poplack, 2020: 23:23-24:07). Upon being hired, Bell Pottinger created the "Chile reconciliation" website in defense of their new client, whom had been arrested in Spain for the actions of his regime in Chile. The narratives used by Bell Pottinger and other actors organized by the Pinochet Foundation painted Pinochet's detainment and the reports of the cruelty of his regime as one created by "Marxists" who wished to destroy Pinochet and his legacy for their own economic agenda, not through any sense of justice. Numerous narratives were constructed in the Pinochet Foundation's efforts to defend its founder. A pamphlet was circulated arguing that while Pinochet's police may have committed atrocities, there was no concrete proof that Pinochet himself was involved. It was also argued that the real reason the Spanish courts made an extradition request was because they were being masterminded by Joan Garces, a former political advisor to Salvador Allende, the president that Pinochet had overthrew (Honigsbaum, 1999).

Bell Pottinger was then hired by the wife of Syrian President Bahas Al-Assad in 2006. Reportedly, Asma Al-Assad wanted Bell Pottinger to grow her public profile in the same vein as the first ladies of other world leaders. Bell Pottinger did not work directly for her but did advise Asma on how to portray her own international image and set up her own communications office. Following Bell Pottinger's advice, favorable coverage of Asma Al-Assad began to increase. It chose to create some distance from itself and the Syrian dictatorship in this case but was still willing to share its expertise for the right price. A 2011 Vogue article on Syria's first lady referred to Syria's ruling family as "wildly democratic." Although Bell Pottinger kept the Al-Assad regime at arm's length, it is clear that Syria's first lady attempted to use Bell Pottinger's advice for navigating the west's media landscape to build a positive reputation for herself. The Vogue article being a clear case of this (Gaffey, 2017).

The firm also had a contract in Belarus in 2007. Bell Pottinger's work in Belarus focused on shifting Belarus' image over to one that would benefit a greater transition to neoliberalism under infamous despot Lukashenko. The plan was to promote Belarus as a nation that could be attractive for international investment as an alternative to Russian support in the nation. (Meduza,

2020) The 2007–2011 period would actually see Bell Pottinger taking on even more controversial clients. This included Thaksin Shinawatra, former Prime Minister of Thailand, who contracted Bell Pottinger to build his reputation after he bought the Manchester City Football Club (Holmes, 2014). Thaksin Shinawatra was ousted in a military coup in 2006, and was controversial, accused of both corruption and abuse of power before being removed from office. Shinawatra was also a champion of neoliberal politics before being ousted, seeking to open Thailand to international business (Hewison, 2010: 121).

In 2003, BAE Systems, the United Kingdom's largest defense company, hired Bell Pottinger to improve its public relations (Freeman, 2014). BAE Systems is one of the world's top arms producers, generating sales of about $20 billion a year. It has a unique relationship with The Pentagon, which treats the company as a domestic arms contractor. BAE systems has repeatedly been accused of corruption, polluting the environment, and selling arms to autocratic states. Bell Pottinger's work was primarily focused in counteracting the controversy BAE often finds itself garnering. The company has sold arms to Saudi Arabia, Indonesia, Zaire, and Tanzania, sales that would be impossible without the sanctioning of the United Kingdom. British Conservative leaders such as Tony Blair, Margaret Thatcher, and John Major were major supporters of the company, and of the arms industry in general (Lilley, 2003). In 2009, under the controversial Kirchner government, Bell Pottinger would be hired to improve Argentina's image to make it attractive for international tourism and foreign investment using similar strategies to the Belarus case (Cañas, Maria, and Estay-Nicular, 2013: 206). After the death of Hugo Chavez, Bell Pottinger briefly fought to improve the image of Venezuelan energy firms Trafigura and Cuadrilla in order to make them attractive for international investment, despite both being tied to the authoritarian Chavez regime. Bell Pottinger argued that the market would naturally set the moral standards for the behavior of corporate entities (Sloan, 2017).

In each of these cases, we can see Bell Pottinger acting as an operative for the greater international market, even if it means operating with authoritarian actors. In some cases, such as with the Al-Assad Family, we can see how great wealth can be leveraged to acquire their services. With companies such as BAE, we see Bell Pottinger acting as a defensive agent to protect the right of a large corporate entity to act without any regulation from the public or government. The biggest pattern between them, however, as can be seen in Thailand, Argentina, Belarus, Chile, Syria, and Chile, is that autocrats will align themselves with neoliberal policies, or even just flirt with the idea of privatizing public assets, paths that would establish relationships with a firm such as Bell Pottinger, who would then attempt to shape the public perception of them into something more favorable. This allows for autocrats to essentially form alliances with wealthy elites to secure greater power and support, at the expense of democracy itself in many cases.

6 Conclusion

Bell Pottinger arose in British politics just when it was needed and was used as a tool to aggressively promote new neoliberal policies. Its main purpose was to normalize neoliberal policies as a means of solving political crises while simultaneously dispelling competing solutions as corrupt and inefficient. Without these firms as a conduit for neoliberalism, political actors dependent on such messaging may not have been able to communicate their policies effectively to their audiences. The pattern of operations Bell Pottinger followed strike eerily similar to digital "fake news" firms that operate on social media such as Cambridge Analytica, with the two companies actually operating similarly in the same timeframe for a small period. South Africa and Iraq shows the extent to which Bell Pottinger was employed to lead disinformation campaigns. In both cases the firm advanced the objectives of powerful imperial powers as a means of asserting neoliberalism abroad, namely by supporting autocratic leaders in their efforts to manipulate public opinion. As seen by their contracts with Pinochet, the Al-Assad family, Shinawatra, Lukeashenko, Kirchner, and BAE, the cases of South Africa and Iraq are not isolated cases but rather significant examples of the kind of work Bell Pottinger did.

Truth and political transparency were never once considered in any of the cases described here. In South Africa, Bell Pottinger relied on disinformation to portray political opponents as violent and radical. In Iraq, they were willing to proliferate fake media for use by Iraqi insurgents and produced propaganda for the U.S. military. In Spain, Syria, Thailand, and Belarus, they transparently attempted to rewrite history to sugarcoat the violent atrocities, human rights violations and ulterior motives of some of the worlds' most infamous autocrats. They promoted tourism in Argentina for the Kirchners and defended BAE Systems' business practices, despite both clients being under harsh scrutiny for corrupt practices. All of this happened before social media really took any kind of grip on modern society. If anything, the examples of this case showcase that the disinformation firm has existed long before the age of Facebook fake news.

7   Reflections

The case of Bell Pottinger should not by any means be seen as extraordinary. The uniqueness of the firm is not where its importance lies. Bell Pottinger would meet its end in 2016 after being hit by harsh criticism for its campaign in South Africa, which saw it once again sow racial divisions under the employ of the Gupta Family. This campaign made use of modern social media platforms and strategies more akin to the activities we associate with fake news on Twitter and Facebook today (Sloan, 2017). By that point Bell Pottinger had already gone from using traditional forms of marketing to a more digital-based approach, much like any other legitimate PR company would be doing by the mid-2010s. Barring the adoption of new technologies, however, BP had changed very little since the campaigns described here. Now consider that even in a pre-digital world, Bell Pottinger was not alone. The Bureau of Investigative Journalism found that the U.S. had hired at least 40 companies to work on behalf of the occupation for jobs similar to what Bell Pottinger was asked for. This includes U.S. firms such as Lincoln Group and Leontie Industries, in addition to Iraqi corporations such as Babylon Media and Iraqi Dream (Black, 2016).

The invasion of Iraq was clearly a profitable venture for many companies. Bell Pottinger was not unique, rather, it merely shows that there has always been a willingness from political entities to hire private companies to spin political propaganda campaigns for them. This holds particularly true for those rich enough to afford to continually hire such firms. It logically follows by the rise of neoliberalism saw the adoption of entities such as BP: It has always largely been constructed and supported by rich elites who could afford to use such firms to not just spread neoliberal economic policies but defend their place in the status quo as well.

But if disinformation firms have been in use since far before the widespread adoption of social media, then why are we so much more aware of it all now? Why was Cambridge Analytica immediately identified as a problem after the U.S. 2016 presidential elections when Bell Pottinger's role in Iraq wasn't located until the mid-2010s? The answer is two-fold: The first element of the modern digital media landscape we live in today is that it is just far easier to get information, and thus misleading disinformation, into the public sphere than before. A small, dedicated PR company in the Philippines can run a few Facebook groups and Twitter pages and then hire influencers to promote their disinformation, a relatively cheap affair, and still be highly influential to Rodrigo Duterte's presidential campaigning. Duterte also had firms like Cambridge Analytica, which were far larger in size and scope, working on his campaign as well (Elemia, 2021). Meanwhile, barring a few exceptions like the Pentagon, the hiring of Bell Pottinger in the pre-digital age was a far costlier affair on both sides. You would need someone with media connections like those in charge of BP to make a difference. Now, relatively small companies can have their posts go viral on the internet with relatively more ease. The second element of the modern digital media landscape is that it is also far easier to call out these kinds of operations publicly thanks to social media. Most of the operations described in this chapter were met by limited criticism: Mostly by small groups of protestors, experts, or through limited reporting by traditional media outlets. Meanwhile, the controversies surrounding BP's 2016 campaign in South Africa was the result of concentrated criticism and attacks by concerned individuals on social media for months (Sloan, 2017).

Ultimately, the relative cheapness of disinformation today allows for a greater proliferation of activities described in this chapter, and the relative ease of publicly calling these acts out makes it far likelier for us to hear about them. What we are seeing now is a greater proliferation and awareness of disinformation campaigns, but nothing about fake news itself is new by any means.

References

Arsenault, Amelia, and Manuel Castells (2008) "Switching Power: Rupert Murdoch and the Global Business of Media Politics: a Sociological Analysis." *International Sociology* 23, no. 4: 488–513.

Baker, Yousef K. (2014) "Global Capitalism and Iraq: the Making of a Neoliberal State." *International Review of Modern Sociology*: 121–148.

Bates, Stephan (2019) "Lord Bell Obituary." *The Guardia*, August 26, 2019. https://www.theguardian.com/media/2019/aug/26/lord-bell-obituary.

BBC (2003) "UK | Politics | Profile: Lord Saatchi." *BBC News*, Nov. 10. http://news.bbc.co.uk/2/hi/uk_news/politics/3256185.stm.

Black, A. F.-S. and C. (2016) "Fake News and False Flags." *The Bureau of Investigative Journalism*, October 2. http://labs.thebureauinvestigates.com/fake-news-and-false-flags/.

Business Day (1989) "De Villiers Wants to Make Capital Work," March 14.

Cave, Tamasin, and Andy Rowell (2014) *A Quiet Word: Lobbying, Crony Capitalism and Broken Politics in Britain*. New York: Random House, E-book.

Christophers, Brett (2020) *Rentier Capitalism: Who Owns the Economy, and Who Pays for It?* London: Verso, 2020.

Cox, Ronald W., and Daniel Skidmore-Hess (1999) *U.S. Politics and the Global Economy: Corporate Power, Conservative Shift*. Boulder, CO: Lynne Rienner Publishers.

Echeverri Cañas, Lina María, and Christian A. Estay-Niculcar (2013) "The Role of Tourism in the Country Brand Consolidation of Argentina." *Revista Científica Visión de Futuro* 17, no. 2: 186–200.

Elemia, Camille (2021) "Stars, Influencers Get Paid to Boost Duterte Propaganda, Fake News." RAPPLER, June 25, https://www.rappler.com/newsbreak/investigative/celebrities-influencers-get-paid-to-boost-duterte-propaganda-fake-news/.

Ferguson, Thomas, and Joel Rogers (1987) *Right Turn: the Decline of the Democrats and the Future of American Politics.* New York: Macmillan.

Freeman, G. (2014) "BAE Hires Bell Pottinger Following Press Attacks." *PR Week*, July 10, https://www.prweek.com/article/170781/bae-hires-bell-pottinger-following-press-attacks.

Gaffey, C. (2017) "Assad, Pinochet and the Pentagon: Bell Pottinger's Most Controversial Clients." *Newsweek*, September 13, https://www.newsweek.com/bell-pottinger-pentagon-al-qaeda-south-africa-assad-664180.

Guardian (2006) "82. Sir Frank Lowe." *The Guardian*, July 17, 2006. https://www.theguardian.com/media/2006/jul/17/mediaguardiantop100200664.

Guy, Simon, Stephen Graham, and Simon Marvin (1999) "Splintering Networks: the Social, Spatial and Environmental Implications of the Privatization and Liberalization of Utilities in Britain." In The Governance of Large Technical Systems, pp. 149–170. Routledge, 2002.

Harvey, David (2007) *A Brief History of Neoliberalism.* London: Oxford University Press.

Hewison, Kevin (2010) "Thaksin Shinawatra and the Reshaping of Thai Politics." *Contemporary Politics* 16, no. 2: 119–133.

Holmes, P. (2014) "Bell Pottinger to Represent Controversial Man City Owner. Provoke Media," October 24, https://www.provokemedia.com/latest/article/bell-pottinger-to-represent-controversial-man-city-owner.

Honigsbaum, M. (1999) "Pinochet Groupies Fly in to Combat 'Vendetta' against their Hero." *The Guardian*, Jan. 24, https://www.theguardian.com/world/1999/jan/24/markhonigsbaum.theobserver.

Hutchison, Elizabeth Quay, Thomas Miller Klubock, Nara B. Milanich, Peter Winn, eds. (2014) *The Chile Reader: History, Culture, Politics.* Durham: Duke University Press.

Influence The Film (2021) "INFLUENCE: Cut scene | Bell Pottinger Goes to War in Iraq" Youtube Video. 16:36, July 20th. https://youtu.be/GELEVZJjdlU.

Kemp, G. (2020) "Doccie Dives into Bell Pottinger PR Nightmares." *Citypress*, Aug. 9. https://www.news24.com/citypress/trending/doccie-dives-into-pr-nightmares-20200808.

Klein, Naomi (2007) *The Shock Doctrine: the Rise of Disaster Capitalism.* New York: Macmillan.

Kotz, David M. (2015) *The Rise and Fall of Neoliberal Capitalism.* Boston: Harvard University Press.

Lilley, S., Chatterjee, P. C., Fox, T. (2003) BAE System's Dirty Dealings. *CorpWatch*, Nov. 11. https://www.corpwatch.org/article/bae-systems-dirty-dealings.

Mance, H. (2014) "Lord Bell's Textbook for Old School Public Relations," *Financial Times* October 9.

McCoy, Alfred W. (2017) *In the Shadows of the American Century: the Rise and Decline of U.S. Global Power*. Chicago: Haymarket Books.

Meduza. (2020) "Guys, get out: How British spin-doctors and Boris Berezovsky tried to help Alexander Lukashenko win over the West," *Meduza*, Oct. 10, https://meduza.io/en/feature/2020/09/10/guys-get-out.

Narsiah, Sagie (2002) "Neoliberalism and Privatisation in South Africa." *GeoJournal* 57, no. 1: 3–13.

Neate, Rupert (2017) "Bell Pottinger Faces Hearing Over Claims it Stirred Racial Tension in South Africa." *The Guardian*, August 13, https://www.theguardian.com/world/2017/aug/13/bell-pottinger-pr-industry-hearing-secret-south-africa-campaign.

O'Meara, Dan (1996) *Forty Lost Years: the Apartheid State and the Politics of the National Party, 1948–1994*. London: Ravan Press.

Poplack, Richard, co-director; Neille, Diana, co-director (2020) "Influence." *EyeSteelFilm*, 1 hr., 30 min. https://www.influence.film/influence-watch-the-film.

Rustin, Mike (2010) "From the beginning to the End of Neo-Liberalism in Britain." *OpenDemocracy*, May 19, https://www.opendemocracy.net/en/opendemocracyuk/after-neo-liberalism-in-britain/.

Shipman, Alan (2015) "How(e) 'Labour Isn't Working' Did the Job for the Conservatives." *OpenLearn*. The Open University, March 31, https://www.open.edu/openlearn/people-politics-law/howe-labour-isnt-working-did-the-job-the-conservatives.

Shoba, Sandisiwe (2020) "Encounters Film Festival: Bell Pottinger Exposed: Influence Unpacks the Evils of Disinformation." *Daily Maverick*, August 21. https://www.dailymaverick.co.za/article/2020-08-21-bell-pottinger-exposed-influence-unpacks-the-evils-of-disinformation/.

Sloan, Alastair (2017) "Bell Pottinger Got What It Deserved." Corruption | *Al Jazeera*. Al Jazeera, September 18, https://www.aljazeera.com/opinions/2017/9/18/bell-pottinger-got-what-it-deserved.

Tim-Bell-Theres-never-been-so-much-tension-between-business-and-politicians.html.

Townshendj (2010) Archives and Manuscripts at the Bodleian Library. *Bodleian Libraries*, March 26, https://blogs.bodleian.ox.ac.uk/archivesandmanuscripts/tag/m-and-c-saatchi/.

Verkaik, R. (2006) IRAQ: British Companies Making a Fortune out of Iraq Conflict. *CorpWatch*, March 13, https://www.corpwatch.org/article/iraq-british-companies-making-fortune-out-iraq-conflict.

Von Schnitzler, Antina (2016) *Democracy's Infrastructure*. New Jersey: Princeton University Press.

CHAPTER 6

Canadian Imperialism in Caribbean Structural Adjustment, 1980–2000

Tamanisha J. John

1   Introduction[1]

This chapter analyzes the causes, characteristics, and consequences of the new global international architecture of the 1980s to the 2000s, looking at new opportunities for foreign investors that arose in the 1980s, and how these changes strengthened the already powerful Canadian banks and investors in the English-speaking Caribbean. I address the effects of the Canadian banking oligarchy on Caribbean development by focusing on the consequences of outsized foreign ownership of capital in the region as broader changes in the international financial system were occurring. The main point being that Canadian interests in the region continued to play an important role in the consolidation, concentration, and domination of Canadian banks there. During the late 1970s and early 1980s, international financial institutions (IFIs) used the economic crisis faced by Caribbean states to impose structural adjustment policies as a condition for those states in need of financial assistance. Financial assistance was necessary for states in the region which needed to address their balance of payments problems, the fall in their export revenues, and lowered prices for their oil and other raw materials.

From the start of the early 1980s, structural adjustment was already normalized in the Caribbean given the power of a variety of self-interested actors, including the U.S., IFIs, and Canadian investors who continued to advance and support – by any means necessary – structural adjustment policies in the Caribbean. Debt traps, coupled with incursions on Caribbean state's sovereignty would see the neoliberal and capitalist doctrine accepted by all of the independent states in the English-speaking Caribbean region by the mid-1980s. Structural adjustment drastically intensified the existing inequalities in states and removed the ability for governments to alleviate these situations. Aiding

---

1   This chapter is a revised and expanded version of Tamanisha J. John (2021) "Canadian Financial Imperialism and Structural Adjustment in the Caribbean," *Class, Race and Corporate Power*, Vol. 9 (2): Article 1.

structural adjustment policies (SAPs) in the Caribbean during the 1980s, was a successful wave of imperialist (anti-socialist and anti-communist) propaganda to counter influential Marxist-Leninist ideologies which were popular in the region. The result of imperialist propaganda being that many of the independent states in the region would see moderate and left governments replaced with reactionary conservative ones (e.g., in Jamaica, Manley was succeeded by Seaga). And a small number of states that nationalized (e.g., Guyana) would witness harsh retaliation from Canada and the U.S., ultimately causing them to confess themselves to be socialist and/or Marxist-Leninist to receive help from other socialist (and non-aligned) states like Cuba and the Soviet Union.

Although initially enveloped in the general trends of the region under the Gairy regime, Grenada became an exception to the situation engulfing the rest of the English-Speaking Caribbean. This is because after its successful revolution in March of 1979, the revolutionary government went to work on improving the economic situation within Grenada, until its untimely end in October 1983. Within the chapter, while the English-Speaking Caribbean region maintains the focus, special attention is given to the case of Grenada, given that it attempted to distance itself from the burgeoning neoliberal system of the 1980s that relegated English-speaking Caribbean states as sites of imperial domination. The untimely demise of the revolution in Grenada would witness Grenada's reintegration back into the neoliberal system,[2] facilitated by Western states like Canada and the U.S., and international organizations like the World Bank and International Monetary Fund (IMF) which acted as financial disciplinarians.

The IMF's involvement is worth paying close attention to, given that the IMF mandate changed from the 1940s when it assisted European countries, to how it would assist countries in the Global South. IFIs like the IMF were created in 1944 during the aftermath of WWII to address the balance of payment problems experienced by European countries. At that time, European countries received generous assistance from the IMF to "rebuild their economies and societies" (Phillips, 1993: 1). However, in the 1980s when developing countries were experiencing balance of payment problems the IMF restructured its

---

[2] When we think about neoliberal policies, the ideological underpinnings of said policies, and how they impact us domestically, internationally, socially, politically, and economically – Klak (1998) reminds us that neoliberalism "serve[s] to perpetuate the highly unequal power distributions at the national and international levels" (4), while maintaining the exploitative (fundamentally capitalist) status quo; In the Caribbean, neoliberalism often refers to "that nexus of socioeconomic and political forces referred to variously as 'neoliberalism,' 'the Washington consensus,' 'corporate globalization,' or simply 'globalization'" (Scott, 2006: 2).

lending policies (Phillips, 2002; Melville, 2003 Ramesh, 1992), to focus more on "conditional lending," acting as "fiscal disciplinarian[s] for distressed sovereign borrowers, monitoring their compliance with loan conditions" (Roos, 2019: 14). This stood in stark contrast to the "social democratic order of the post-1948 period" (Gordon and Webber, 2016: 129) which stressed rehabilitating distressed societies and economies in need of financial assistance. Instead, SAPs decreased the relative autonomy of developing states, by providing supra-specific mandates for financial and economic stabilization. The IMF justified this shift due to its changed focus on restoring macroeconomic stability in countries experiencing crisis, with attention to recovering and promoting economic growth (Melville 2003: 3). These new policies were in direct response to the restructuring of the capitalist world economy that elevated the role of finance (Gordon and Webber, 2016; Roos, 2019).

According to Ramsaran (1992), during the 1970s and 1980s states in the Caribbean were often subjected to policies at odds with their development and economic objectives. These policies nonetheless reflected the priorities of dominant financial relations within the international system. During the late 1970s, as states in the English-speaking Caribbean faced economic crisis, financial conglomerates and other large corporations from developed countries were operating in an uncertain environment of increased internationalization and global competition for foreign markets. Larger countries saw trade liberalization, especially in capital markets, as a way to address economic crisis, including the falling rate of corporate profits, rising inflation and unemployment (Moseley, 1990). Toward this end, financial capitalists "played a central role in the renewed project of capitalist imperialism" in its time of crisis, via the "neoliberalization of the globe" (Gordon and Webber, 2016: 12).

Grenada's aggressive reinsertion back into this system happened in the aftermath of Maurice Bishop's assassination, the subsequent United States invasion of Grenada, and the mass arrests of party leaders from Bishop's People's Revolutionary Government (PRG). The main takeaway from the invasion into Grenada is that states in the Caribbean which did not accept the terms of the neoliberal doctrine were subject to military and political interventions, followed by the imposition of neoliberal economic policies. The policies themselves, which made these states available to imperial penetration being the end goal. That the U.S. decided to invade Grenada, although it had no significant investments or trade with the island prior to the invasion, says as much. This has led some to call the U.S. invasion of Grenada "the first neoliberal war" (Forte, 2013). It was also the case that an invasion into Grenada under their revolutionary government by the U.S. was imminent, if not, outright planned. Two years prior to the actual invasion, "NATO exercises in 1981" on Vieques, Puerto

Rico carried out a "practice operation"[3] in which the scenario included "occupy[ing] an imaginary Caribbean Island state called 'Amber and the Amberines' (read 'Grenada and the Grenadines'), [to] rescue American citizens resident therein and replace its hostile government by one friendly to the USA" (Searle, 1984: xxi). The aforementioned being the exact justification used in the aftermath of Bishop's assassination and the quick timing/ease of U.S. forces invading the island.

Given lack of tangible U.S. interests in states like Grenada, the post-invasion environment proved that Western-led capitalist reintegration was the goal. Canadian financiers were trusted by both the U.S. and IFIs to advance the broader strategic and economic goals of structural adjustment, in Grenada post-invasion. Adherence to the failed neoliberal doctrine for development in the Caribbean region would be accepted by all states by the mid-late 1980s, given the international mishandling of Grenada. In the post-invasion period, other newly independent Caribbean states placed a lot more emphasis on state police forces to limit rebellions against reformist and revolutionary agendas. For instance, the Dominica Defense Force (DDF) was utilized multiple times in the aftermath of its independence to put down legitimate civilian protests and mass movements (Phillips, 2002: 52).[4] Canada has also been crucial to "training police and security forces in the Commonwealth Caribbean" (Momsen, 1992: 506).

Generally, Canada's role in imperialist domination of its Global South neighbors, in both the Caribbean, Central and South America, receives little theoretical and analytical attention. This chapter is an indictment of Canada's role in ensuring states in the English-speaking Caribbean (as well as the rest of the Global South) remain subservient to Western and other foreign capital. The case of revolutionary Grenada is telling, given that during the revolutionary government's tenure, the Grenadian economy grew at a 3% annual rate. This was true even as most other English-Speaking Caribbean states experienced stagnation and decline – even with the enforced structural adjustment policies from international organizations that alleged structural adjustment policies would lead to economic developments and growth. Nonetheless, the post-revolutionary environment in Grenada would see Canadian advisors pursue these same failed policies in Grenada. The effect being that the post-revolutionary environment would witness an influx of Western capital but

---

3   It should be noted that during this mock/practice operation, "over 120,000 troops, 250 warships and 1,000 aircraft [were deployed] to Vieques Island" (Searle, 1984: 37).
4   Under Charles regime, Dominica was extremely close with the Reagan administration in the U.S.

limited economic developments and growth. This is precisely because in the Caribbean region, the neoliberal doctrine as championed by Western states like Canada, only serves to enrich external capitalists and local elites supporting their policy preferences.

2 The Neoliberal Turn: Canada and the English-Speaking Caribbean

It should be noted here that all state relationships were impacted by the neoliberal turn. Prompted by the U.S. and Western European states, Canada's acceptance of the neoliberal doctrine was spottier, and it was not until the late 1970s that capitalist governments in Canada also accepted the neoliberal structuring of the global financial system. Given the crisis of the dollar (thus the Bretton Woods system) Canada was pushed to adopt a policy of "monetary gradualism" in the early 1970s, which "w[as] supplemented by wage and price controls introduced from 1975–1978" including anti-inflation laws "which restricted or rolled back union wage increases" (King, 2001: 116, 122). This was because "exchange rates ha[d] always played an important role in Canadian politics," and the Canadian government and financial sector did not want to spook any of its financial investments given its "high integration" in "international financial markets" and the "importance [of its] traded sector" (King, 2001: 116). At the time, the most effective lobbying group in Canada was the Canadian Bankers Association (CBA) – which was able to bring about a "financial sector [with] unified preferences," even in the midst of fragmentation, "due to the presence of universal banking and a central bank [in Canada] that was not [actually] responsible for banking regulation" (King, 2001: 127, 137).

Financial sector power in Canada, largely based on the strength of Canada's chartered banks, allowed neoliberal policy prescriptions to occur on the terms of the financial sector. This was because "rising government deficits and intermediate government debt levels [in Canada] suggested that politicians were dependent on [the financial] sector for financing" (King, 2001: 137). Although there was opposition in Canada by manufacturers, exporters, and unions not yet covered by collective wage agreements – they had "weaker lobbying effectiveness" (King, 2001: 137). Unsurprisingly, by 1981–1982 governments in Canada successfully "reversed union's collective bargaining rights and right to strike, and imposed wage controls ... [which] led to a significant decline in union membership and power in Canada" (King, 2001: 122) to the benefit of big corporations and the changed neoliberal landscape. While already competitive abroad, Canadian banks restructured their international operations at this time, given the uncertainty of the unstable global monetary system.

The most notable restructuring happened during the 1980s when the Royal Bank divested from a large portion of its Caribbean (and Latin American) operations. After leaving Grenada in 1983, the Royal Bank of Canada (RBC) would leave Guyana in 1984 and then by 1985 pull out from most of its Caribbean operations in Trinidad, Jamaica, St. Vincent, etc. (Garrod, 2018: ix; McDowall, 1993: 406). RBC publicly blamed its divestments in Latin America and the Caribbean on deteriorating economic conditions in the region given the debt crises. Prior to the debt crisis, RBC utilized its operations in the region for accumulating financial assets. While profits did decrease during the debt crisis, the inability of Caribbean states to pay back loans is what ultimately led RBC to divest. RBC publicized its divestment to restore its "damaged public credibility" in Canada, given perceptions of it as a predominantly international bank influencing Canadian austerity (McDowall, 1993: 417). Within Canada, growing anti-financial sentiments from other productive sectors of the economy bemoaning the influence of finance in the wake of increasingly austere and conservative politics worried the banks. Ultimately, conservative governance – pushed by both the conservatives and labor parties – became the norm in Canada (strengthening the power of smaller parties, like the New Democratic Party (NDP), but not enough to challenge austerity) as elsewhere in the developed world.

While more developed states had more say (choices) in how they would accept or respond to neoliberal changes, developing countries faced structural adjustment programs as a condition to receive needed financial assistance. These programs integrated developing states into the broader global financial system. The debt crisis helped wealthier countries expand neoliberal capitalist policies into more states. Liberalization, deregulation of financial activities, and reduced government spending all aimed to serve the interests of financial capital – and in the Caribbean this often meant foreign and external capital. These policies often increased foreign direct investments into developing countries, albeit with no real development objectives outside of economic growth, and returns to shareholders, of which private industry benefited. Speaking at a board of governors meeting at the IMF in 1977, a representative from the Bank of Trinidad and Tobago – "on behalf of six Caribbean countries" – noted that while they "accept the need for conditionality in the disbursement of Fund resources ... there is increasing concern among [them] that the conditionality at present attached to the use of [the Fund's resources] may serve to impair the effectiveness of Fund assistance" (Owen and Rhodin, 1977: 7).

The main concerns expressed by the local bankers in the Caribbean revolved around the negative social outcomes which resulted from the conditionalities, including the power that the conditions afforded a few private and foreign industries, as well as the high interest rates which made some of the debt expensive to Caribbean states (both at the time of acceptance and in the future). IFI conditionalities were recognized as problems early on by Caribbean states given the recent history of political movements opposing neocolonial policies, and broader movements calling for a new international economic order (NIEO). However, their concerns were brushed aside by the policy directives from the IMF board, which concluded that: States that come for assistance "do so because they are in a difficult payments situation … that will have to be remedied, whether the member draws on the Fund or not … the adjustment measures that are required in a particular case are worked out very carefully between a member and the Fund" (Owen and Rhodin, 1977: 7). Essentially, both the debt crisis and the neoliberal turn cemented further, albeit coercive, buy-in to the system.

States, including those in the Caribbean, were bound by rules established by IFIs in a more global and financialized system that made developing states' governments "subservient to international creditors for their own survival" (Roos, 2019: 11). States which sought and received help from IFIs in times of crises, all liberalized their financial systems and opened their economies. Deregulation during this period also had the effect of limiting the amount of corporate competition which existed. Big multinational corporations, given financial deregulation and liberalization, were allowed to merge with and/or acquire their competitors which helped them become bigger – as they relied on corporate takeovers to consolidate power in global markets in attempts to lessen the effects of market competition. This led to further concentration of different private industries within countries, including (and especially) in the financial sector.

Within the English-speaking Caribbean context, during the late 1970s Canadian banks faced the dual challenges of declining investments and the rise of political opposition in the Caribbean by protestors identifying their presence as a manifestation of neocolonialism. However, in the aftermath of the debt crisis, Canadian banks would find themselves better positioned in the region, precisely because of IFI conditionalities accepted by Caribbean states seeking credit (Canterbury, 2016: 116). As was the case during independence, foreign investors and their capital yet again became positioned as 'saviors' for the region's economic crisis. Given the longer history of Canadian financial interests in the region, they necessarily became placed as advisors on the kind of SAPs designed for the region by IFIs, which expanded their growth.[5]

---

5 "Advisor" is being quite lenient in regards to the role of Canadian banks, as they played a direct hand in creating the types of adjustment packages states in the English-speaking

Reminiscent of the post-colonial laws in the late 1950s and the industrialization by invitation policies of the mid and late 1960s – sans former colonial preferences – IFI stipulations yet again reduced "the scope for national discretionary control of the monetary system [maximizing] the unfettered action of foreign private investors" (Thomas quoted in Canterbury, 2016: 122). Foreign ownership and foreign investments became the 'answer' to Caribbean development without any "real commitment to the [local] development of the region" (Canterbury, 2016: 122). This locked these states further into the dependent and colonial relations that already existed. The IMF and World Bank were allowed to set the terms of Caribbean engagement in the global economy to the benefit of foreign capitalists that already controlled much of the region's finance.

Expectedly, neoliberal policy prescriptions in societies that already had limited amounts of capital for government spending, high unemployment rates, and crisis management – only deepened the effects of crisis. Neoliberal policy prescriptions also reduced governments' policy autonomy and their ability to address mass social and economic inequalities – especially those stemming from the practices of foreign corporations. Not unlike the 1970s, during the 1980s states like Jamaica, Guyana, Trinidad and Tobago – and to a lesser extent Barbados – continued to make attempts to curb foreign bank (and other foreign industries) repatriation of profits in their countries. While governments would have small successes in attempting to localize developments in their financial sectors, states facing financial crises would see Canadian reinvestments back into the region at profitable margins in the 1990s. Nonetheless, throughout the 1980s and 1990s brief periods of local bank development in the Caribbean region would emerge to provide financial alternatives to Caribbean people not being serviced by big foreign banks. Ultimately, with few exceptions (e.g., Trinidad and Tobago), local bank developments would be short-lived due to undercapitalization and renewed competition from Canadian (and other) banks in waves throughout the 1980s and 1990s. The number of choices available to English-speaking Caribbean states regarding their own development were limited, and dependent on the whims of big private, external and foreign interests.

To illustrate this point, Guyana stands out as a case where a Caribbean country attempted bold legislation to address foreign currency exchange shortages in the country during the 1980s. Guyanese legislators identified lax repatriation laws as a major contributor to Guyana's exchange shortage, and in

---

Caribbean would come to accept. CIDA, for instance, was directly involved in Guyana first structural adjustment loan from the World Bank (Engler, 2009: 77).

1985 passed legislation that "required foreign banks to bring in capital to back their operations in Guyana" (Khan, 2001: 47). With little room for maneuver, the Guyanese government positioned itself as willing to "assume control over [it's] banking system, since foreign banks were unwilling to bring in new capital when there was no assurance that they would be allowed to repatriate profits" (Khan, 2001: 47). This bold piece of legislation backfired, however, because while Canadian (and other foreign) banks chose to sell to the government, they left Guyana further indebted to IFIs and other agencies. By bucking the neoliberal orthodoxy, Guyana suffered an even larger decline in foreign investment and capital. By late 1980s-early 1990s, the Guyanese government abandoned this position and "announced its commitment to lowering its participation in the financial sector through restructuring and privatisation" (Khan, 2001: 50). A neoliberal success, only at the expense of Guyana(/ese).

The Guyanese example is provided to demonstrate two things: First, the neoliberal turn required compliance with the Western liberal capitalist system. Second, non-compliance left states stuck in economic crisis, unable to amass both capital and credits as investors snubbed them. As no surprise, many states in the English-speaking Caribbean would find the costs of non-compliance too high. Unlike the previous decades, domination by Canadian banks as further assisted by IFIs in the late 1970s-1990s, would lack strong political, social, and movement resistance from states in the region (e.g., the 1970 February Revolution in Trinidad and Tobago). Instead, Caribbean governments increased spending on police and militaries to quell protests and rebellions in their states, sparked by their own citizens feeling the disastrous effects of neoliberal policy, aided by Western military interventions in the region which sought to maintain the status quo.

To think about it in another way, English-speaking Caribbean states faced a crisis during the 1980s that had all the hallmarks of the 1960s: states needing capital, economies controlled by foreign corporations, a local elite that benefitted from and accepted the situation, governments that focused on reforms that would attract foreign aid and investments, and a need to import food and other necessities from more developed countries. However, unlike the 1960s, the 1980s witnessed greater coordination between multinational banks and other global financial institutions in response to a crisis of global capitalism. This drastically limited the number of already limited choices Caribbean states could make. IFIs worked with the largest commercial and investment banks to coordinate the enforcement of structural adjustment conditionality during vast increases in the internationalization of capital flows, that exposed banks to potential large-scale insolvency during the financial crises of the early 1980s. Changes in the international financial system during the 1980s saw "[t]otal earnings on international assets peak in 1981 at $815 million after which they fell – in part because of the provisions for the possibility of large loan losses" (Kaufman, 1985: 67). The IFIs and commercial banks coordinated with junior partners in the Caribbean who were dependent on establishing solvency for creditors through structural adjustment conditionality.

The emergence of Caribbean governments that were willing to cooperate with these demands facilitated the conditions for a resumption of foreign investment to the region. These developments proved especially beneficial to Canadian banks and firms which already had investments in the region, putting them in a stronger position to compete for market share because of the terms of structural adjustment. As investment conditions improved for Canadian banks, they became even more profitable in the region by the late 1980s and 1990s. Bank Act revisions in Canada at this time made deregulatory changes that allowed Canadian banks "to develop into financial conglomerates with [increased] involvement in a wide variety of financial areas." (Freedman, 1998: 13–15). These changes would once again see foreign currency assets and liabilities emerge as important components of Canadian banks balance sheets, reflecting "retail operations abroad, especially in the Caribbean" (Freedman, 1998: 34–35).[6] Indicative of these changes, during the mid-1980s the English-speaking Caribbean region saw an increase in mergers, acquisitions, and take-overs in its financial services industry (Khan, 2001). This helped Canadian banks grow bigger in the region, solidifying their 'competitive edge.'

The changed environment of a new international financial architecture solidified Canadian banks as dominant financial institutions in the Caribbean by the 1990s, despite the brief period in the early 1980s when two of the major Canadian banks briefly reduced their investments, albeit using different strategies. Scotiabank's broad range of services and overseas locations during the 1970s and 1980s made its experiences much different from RBC and the Canadian Imperial Bank of Commerce (CIBC), both of which undertook more divestments from their overseas operations in the early 1980s. For instance, in the 1970s and early 1980s, "the Royal had been making most of their profits by recycling Eurodollars[,]" as well as Petrodollars from the oil booms of the early 1970s, "through huge loans to Third World governments" (Garrod, 2018: 217). Meanwhile, CIBC took a more nationalist, approach due to anti-financial sentiments within Canada, which resulted in an emphasis on North American

---

6 Freedman also notes that in the 1970s and the first half of the 1980s Canadian bank expansion into the Euro-market and increased lending to less-developed countries (LDCS) also contributed to the growth of Canadian dollar assets and foreign currency assets (Freedman, 1998: 35).

expansion. While CIBC made public claims that they "are a Canadian bank and [thei]r priority is to serve Canadian customers" (Darroch, 1994: 188), their North American expansion was mostly in the U.S. to address volatile earnings within Canada. Both examples stood in stark contrast to Scotiabank, which continued to successfully expand its operations in both the U.S. and Asia during crisis, as well as venture into gold markets – making Scotiabank's capital base stronger than its competitors (Darroch, 1994: 98–100). Thus, unlike CIBC and RBC, Scotiabank did not close or divest from any of its Latin American and Caribbean operations, choosing instead to expand into even more areas.

As increased privatizations and expanded access to financial markets became pivotal to development strategies of the 1980s, Scotiabank continued to increase its overseas operations and expand its loan portfolio even further in the Caribbean. Not surprisingly, changes in the global landscape of international finance during the 1980s, made it so that by 1981, "[o]ver half [of] the profits of Scotia-bank [were] generated internationally ... and roughly half the profits of the Royal in 1982" (Kaufman, 1985: 71). On the other end, by the mid-1980s CIBC maintained that expanding its international presence would bode well for its domestic operations – explicitly making the case that its international activities would help financing in Canada. Thus, it resumed its investments in the Caribbean region. The results happened quite quickly. By 1983, the top five Canadian-owned chartered banks controlled 85% of total bank assets in Canada (Canada, Department of Finance). Of the top five, RBC and CIBC comprised the top two on the list, with Scotiabank placing fourth. Together, these three banks comprised 54.2% of total Canadian bank assets (Canada, Department of Finance). And, using the dynamics of the debt crisis, Canadian banks were able to expand – albeit unevenly – throughout the Caribbean (and Latin America) by the mid 1980's, even as the states in the region experienced debt crises.

Crucial to the success of Canadian banks reassertion in the region during the 1980s was the increasing market power of finance which harmonized well with IFI SAPs that reinforced their financial power. To drive home the instrumentality of SAPs one could look at RBCs divestment and then reinvestment back into the region. In the late 1970s and briefly during the early 1980s, the devaluation of Caribbean currencies and the losses RBC experienced in the region due to Caribbean governments' non-payments on loans led to large divestments from RBC. However, RBC's increased investments into the region during the mid-late 1980s and 1990s would rival that of Scotiabank, which never left the region. For RBC, financial losses during the late 1970s and early 1980s were minimal in comparison to the gains to be made in the post structural adjustment period. The aftermath of structural adjustment provided more guarantees that debtor states in Latin America and the Caribbean, who received assistance from IFIs in the 1980s, were bound to repay their debts in the system given the consequences of default (Roos, 2019).

3   IMF and World Bank Structural Adjustment in the 1980s and 1990s: New Reinvestment Opportunities for Canadian Banks and Financial Interests in the Caribbean

During the economic crises which shook the Third World from the late 1970s-1980s, foreign financial banking institutions like RBC started to sell interests to local capitalists and regional governments with prices ranging between $1 dollar to $6 million dollars (Hudson, 2010: 44). These developments were initially welcomed by states looking to assert economic autonomy and sovereignty from their economically dependent situation. However, what is most telling about this selling of interests, is these corporations buy-back into the region which happens vigorously towards the middle of the 1980s given the introduction of IMF SAPs that they helped to write. The adjustment period of the 1980s-1990s highlights the relationship between Canadian banks, the Canadian government, global financial institutions, and political classes in the Caribbean whose interests align with the region's dependence on foreign capital. IFI SAPs in the 1980s-1990s could best be described as one of the tools utilized to address the crisis of capitalism which began in the late 1960s. As such, the goals of the packages discussed below aimed to integrate developing states into a changing financial architecture by further opening their markets to Western capitalists who faced declining profits and increased global competition for foreign markets.

In 1984, Canada's RBC bank "sold its assets in Guyana to the Guyanese government for $1 dollar (a transaction repeated by both National City Bank and Barclays)" (Hudson, 2010: 44).

During 1984, Guyana's government borrowed money from the IMF due to balance of payments problems which the loan would not help to fix. By 1985 Guyana would be ineligible to receive further funds without the implementation of IMF SAPs, due to the continued deteriorating condition of its economy (Ramesh, 1992: xi). By 1989, Guyana became the poorest country in the Western Hemisphere, which was the first time that another country surpassed Haiti (which has suffered from economic isolation) for that position (Stabroek, 2016). When Guyana underwent structural adjustment, strict adherence to the SAP policy was overseen by a Canadian support group. Canada's support was to turn the Guyanese economy around by facilitating the raising of funds for the

Guyanese government through the privatization of state-owned enterprises, and the opening of other sectors for foreign (and private) ownership and investment (Ramesh, 1992: xi–xii). In other words, a Canadian support group oversaw the privatization of the Guyanese economy under the SAP and chose to privilege foreign and private investments.

To say that structural adjustment was harsh would be an understatement. Austerity in Guyana would see the workforce unable to secure jobs, and without capital necessary to meet basic living expenses. By the late 1980s, bauxite miners, sugarcane cutters, students, and teachers within Guyana could no longer afford bus fare. In response to the drop in living standers workers and demonstrators in Guyana picketed the Canadian High Commissioners Office. There was "widespread recognition that Canada was the architect of the new austerity" and that Canada was also overseeing strict adherence to the new set of policies (Swift and Tomlinson, 1991: 22). The Canadian support group recommended that Guyana undertake an intensive SAP that "involved a 230 per cent currency devaluation, a rise in interest rates to 35 per cent, and a wage rise of only 20 per cent" (Swift and Tomlinson, 1991: 80). By 1990, the Canadian Council for International Cooperation (CCIC) "referred to the austerity scheme [in Guyana] as an "economic assault."" (Swift and Tomlinson, 1991: 80) Although the Canadian High Commissioner, Frank Jackman at the time admitted that these budgetary measures were unpopular, Jackman contended on a local broadcast, that the Guyanese people should be reassured and "take heart [because the] austerity package would encourage Canadian multinational corporations to look favourably on Guyana in making decisions about where to invest" (Swift and Tomlinson, 1991: 80). As such, Canadian purchases and investments would service debts (exceeding $1.8 billion) that the Guyanese government could not – yet alarmingly at the same time, profit repatriation from Guyana far exceeded any capital or loan servicing provided by foreign takeovers and other privatizations.

While a harrowing story about the social consequences of austerity, the Guyanese example is not an outlier. The IMF pursued a similar corporate development strategy throughout the region, encouraged by the Canadian banking community – especially RBC which wanted to regain its investment base in the region. RBC had sold its interests in Trinidad and Tobago in 1987 as part of its restructuring plan, then when in1989 Trinidad and Tobago underwent IMF SAP to service their debts, RBC buy-back of its interests in the country started (Ramesh, 1992: xi). This, even as Trinidadians maintained negative views of foreign investment, and Canada, given direct protests towards these corporations' decade prior (Meyer, 1995: 143). The outcome of protests in Trinidad during the 1970s, would see the state pursue stronger pushes for government and/or local ownership over its resources and profitable sectors – including "uncompetitive corporate tax rates," at 45%, to discourage overwhelming foreign investment (Meyer, 1995: 143). Thus, the introduction of the SAP by the late 1980s in Trinidad rubbed many the wrong way. Due to the SAP, Trinidad and Tobago would instead pursue "a more liberalized approach toward direct investment to attract more foreign capital" (Price Waterhouse quoted in Meyer 1995: 143). This same story is repeated in Jamaica and Belize in the late 1980s. In 1987 Canadian banks sold their 48 per cent stake in Jamaica's Royal Bank to Jamaica Mutual Life Assurance, and in 1989 with the implementation of IMF SAPs, Canadian investors (along with American and European buyers) swooped back in (Ramesh, 1992: xi; Hudson, 2010: 44). Belizean investors in 1987 bought large stakes in Canadian banks, only to go under an IMF SAP two years later, and Canadian buybacks started. These opportunities were also extended to U.S. and European investors – Canada happened to take the most advantage, given their history in the region.

As privatization ruled by foreign capitalists persisted in the Caribbean region during the late 1980s, Canadian investors faced less competition and more opportunity as they re-invested. At this time, many European and some American investors were starting to look towards Russia and Eastern Europe, given the decline of the Soviet Union (Watson, 2016: 49). This eastward outlook was compounded by increased investments into China, given the lower production costs, there and "the negative impact of NAFTA on foreign investment inflows to the Commonwealth Caribbean for export production" (Watson, 2016: 49). Essentially, the Caribbean region was not the only space which opened itself up for foreign investors in the 1980s, as investment options abroad for investors increased. In a nutshell, as developing states 'competed' for foreign investment given monetary crises – investors which did go to specific countries, entered those spaces with more power. Because Eastern Europe and China piqued the interests more from other Western states, Canadian interests were allowed to have an even bigger role in the English-speaking Caribbean region – from local legislations to SAP rules and conditionalities. These developments entrenched the monopoly power of the dominant Canadian financial institutions in the region and given the limited amount of 'developed' state competition, Canadian investors and other Canadian interests pushed Caribbean states towards IFIs, and other debt acceptance.

As such, the crises did not mark the end of Canadian banking dominance in the region, but rather a brief hiatus for some of the banks. During the late 1980s and into the early-to-mid 1990s, Canadian banks would make their biggest push back into the region since their colonial introduction. In 1989, the then Chairman of the Royal Bank, Allan Taylor, convinced the IMF – with the appraisal of the Canadian banking community – that Canadian support groups were instrumental in advancing the position that "foreign investment in the borrowing countries would have to play a much larger role in resolving [their] debt[s]" (Swift and Tomlinson, 1991:95). Thus, towards the latter half of the 1980s, "financial regulation" in some Caribbean states "tended to have a Canadian focus" (Williams, 1989: 181). These regulations largely aimed to exclude foreign branch operations from the general rules governing banks in the region; meaning that Canadian interests were able to legislate provisions to not regulate foreign bank branches. Minimal regulation of Canadian financial investments abroad has always been considered a 'problem,' according to American and European competitors against Canadian investors. In the 1980s, this was not any different, as "Canada ha[d] few policies on outgoing investment; a situation that before [NAFTA], was often met with disfavor by American officials" because Canada would regulate and "screen" foreign investors while "not regulat[ing] their own multinationals" abroad (Meyer, 1995: 40).

Canadian financial institutions with overseas operations not only benefitted from lax legislation within Canada on their behalf – but given the need for foreign investment (per IFIs) in the Caribbean region, Canadian banks were also able to craft and avoid legislation there. For example, in Barbados "stipulations relating to capital requirements [did] not apply to branch operations, so that foreign branch operations [would be] excluded from provisions" stipulating capital requirements (Williams, 1989: 182). This meant that in Barbados, of the seven banks that this general rule could have applied to – only two banks, which were not foreign, were subjected to bank regulations on capital requirements. This regulation was also utilized by states in the Eastern Caribbean Community (ECC), of which 22 of the 38 commercial banks operating in the ECC were foreign; meaning that the regulation would only apply to 16 or 42% of the banks there (Williams, 1989: 182). It would not be unfair to assume that declining profitability in the Caribbean region during the mid and late 1980s contributed to favorable legislation towards foreign banks, to keep those entities within the region. This period was notably marked by decreased corporate tax rates on foreign entities, to disincentivize withdrawal and capital flight from the region (Williams, 1989: 191–192). However, these corporate friendly policies towards foreign business and investments did little to help Caribbean societies themselves. The local banks who were subjected to these rules and capital requirements would find themselves unable to compete with foreign owned Canadian banks, only capturing small portions of their own local markets. Instead, Canadian banks would use declining foreign investments in the Caribbean to entrench their own power with the help of structural adjustment and conditional lending to states.

Given the backlash of the previous decades to Canadian financial power in the Caribbean region, Canadian banks supplemented their Caribbean expansion during the late 1980s-2000s pursuing two strategies to stave off scrutiny from countries levying critiques of neo-colonialism. First, Canadian banks sought to promote Canadian investment through acquisitions and mergers which would make it so that local market shares could be retained in the region. Mergers and acquisitions became a way for Canadian banks to consolidate power during the privatizations of the 1980s, by insulating themselves from critiques because the symbol of the merged and/or acquired entities remained 'local' and/or 'Caribbean.' In other words, Canadian banks became majority owners (50% +) in Caribbean companies that became privatized – after having seen increased government ownership or outright takeovers during the 1970s and early 1980s. Although the transition from state ownership to privatization put the control of these companies in Canadian hands, the companies still maintained their 'Caribbean-ness,' since small shares remained held by more affluent Caribbean people.

Mergers and acquisitions also seemed to be preferred by Caribbean governments – who pushed nationalization and state ownership in the 1970s, as the strategy implied that at some point in the future local shares, as well as government ownership of majority shares, had the potential to increase. Additionally, the language of 'partnership' around merging and acquisitioning staved off some scrutiny against governments, "even as control of these foreign subsidiaries remain[ed] highly spatially concentrated in Canada" (Meyer, 1995: 73). Put together, there were increasing incentives towards merging and consolidating, which allowed large financial institutions to exercise monopoly power (Worrell, 1997: 69). The uneven competition landscape also acted as an incentive to merge, because no matter how "numerous their smaller rivals, small size ma[d]e their services expensive" and unable to be a "competitive challenge" to these foreign banks (Worrell, 1997: 69). In sum, government constraints due to crisis and backlash against foreign ownership within states, allowed merging and acquisitioning (privatization) to be seen as a strategy to address crisis (development). While the Caribbean faced a "lost decade"[7] from the 1980s to

---

7 According to Dr. Juliet Melville on the *Impact of Structural Adjustment on the Poor*: "the 1990s is regarded as a lost decade precisely because of the absence of economic growth and significant reversals on the social front. Szekely (2001) argued that SAPs in the 1980s resulted in the dismantling of the previous social development strategy, whilst the restraint of government spending across the board, the removal of subsidies, cost-based pricing for publicly provided goods and services and cuts in social spending adversely affected the poor disproportionately" (Melville, 2003: 4).

1990s, given the negative social situation and deepening inequality between people because of the neoliberal policy prescriptions in the 1980s – it was a booming year for big multinational corporations. Towards the latter half of the 1980s and heading into the 1990s, Canadian banks' lending and expansion – via incremental takeovers and mergers,[8] grew (Tables 6.1 and 6.2).

By the late 1980s a few regional trends in the Caribbean for foreign banks included (1) decreased market share (of about 1–3% in different Caribbean states) overall, and (2) an increase in market share for 'indigenous banks' (Juan-Ramón et al., 2001). Unlike previous Canadian bank divestment, this decrease in regional market shares for foreign banks were mostly due to U.S. and European banks pull-outs in the region. Although there is no one reason, it is the case that "the latter part of the 1980s [was] a period of retrenchment and sovereign debt rescheduling," (Létourneau and Heidrich, 2010: 6). Of Canadian banks, it was RBC in 1988 that sold an important part of its Caribbean operations – the Royal Bank of Trinidad and Tobago, to local interests (Létourneau and Heidrich, 2010). RBC would do the same in Jamaica which accounted for some market loss for Canadian banks overall. What is interesting is that sell offs by RBC hindered CIBCs expansion into these states, given past skepticism of RBC and CIBC divestments in the region almost a decade before. Noteworthy, Scotiabank continued expanding into the region – having never left even when RBC and CIBC divestments occurred earlier – operating in 24 Caribbean markets with 172 locations in 1992. CIBC opted instead to take advantage of new opportunities for merging and acquisitions which helped it expand.

As it solely relates to Canadian banks, heading into the 1990s, it was predicted that the three big Canadian banks in the Caribbean would "continue their long-standing, stable, profit-earning operations. Some less-productive branches [would] be phased out," but even then, "the large network [would] be maintained and in a few cases[,] extended" (Kaufman 1985, 74). Towards the latter half of the 1990s and early 2000s CIBC, RBC, and Scotiabank continued to grow in the Caribbean region, largely through pursuing acquisitions and setting up branch plants where possible. A large part of the acquisitions would take place in Guyana and Jamaica – two states that had nationalized more of their economies before the crisis of the 1980s. In 1995, "more than 36 state-owned banks were privatized with total assets amounting to more than US$8 billion, representing approximately three quarters of total commercial bank assets" in the region (Clarke and Danns, 1997: 154). The countries with the

---

8 Deregulation has a substantial impact on merger decisions.

TABLE 6.1   Canadian direct investment abroad: number of controlled subsidiaries

Central America and the Caribbean*	1974	1979	1984	1989	1992
(#)	140	207	220	230	279
(%)	12.2	9.4	7.1	6.1	7.2

Note 1: "The distribution of Canadian FDI activity among Central America [and the] Caribbean countries has been quite uneven [...] all countries within Central America are represented within this sample of outward direct Canadian investment, but the quantity of investee firms in these countries lag well behind those of the Caribbean" (Meyer, 1995: 70–72)
Note 2: The table shows a steady increase in the number of controlled Canadian subsidiaries from 1974–1992, with a noticeable decrease in the overall percentage given the decreases in market share due to competition.
SOURCE: *WHOM OWNS WHOM, NORTH AMERICA*. DUN AND BRADSTREET INTERNATIONAL (VOLUMES 1974, 1979, 1984, 1989, AND 1992); REPRINTED IN MEYER, 1995

TABLE 6.2   Canadian acquisitions abroad by industry, 1987–1990

Industry	(%)
Manufacturing	38.8
Financial	18.7
Resources	14.0
Services	8.3
Unclassified	6.9
Utilities	5.3
Merchandising Trade	5.0
Construction	3.0
Total	100.0%

SOURCE: KNUBLEY, J. W. KRAUSE AND Z SADEQUE (1991). "CANADIAN ACQUISITIONS ABROAD: PATTERNS AND MOTIVATIONS." IN CORPORATE GLOBALIZATION THROUGH MERGERS AND ACQUISITIONS, 36–37. REPRINTED IN MEYER, 1995

highest number of banking privatization were Guyana and Jamaica (ECLAC, 2001: 6). Illustrative is that RBC would open in several Caribbean locations, after having withdrawn from countries in the region during the mid-1980s – of which Jamaica and Guyana were early parts of (Garrod, 2018: x).

According to Alleyne and Waithe (2011), "one of the defining characteristics of the 1990s onwards [were the] mergers and acquisitions" which took place in the Caribbean (11). Whereas "from 1980 to 1989 there were only 83 mergers and acquisitions in the Caribbean ... in the 1990's there was a marked increase in activity, with 515 takeovers" (Wood and Wood, 2013: 38).

Illustrative is the experience of Trinidad and Tobago, where from 1985 to 2009, 52% of the takeovers in that country resulted in foreign companies acquiring Trinidadian firms, "with the first of these acquisitions occurring in 1990" (Wood and Wood, 2013: 38). During this same time in Barbados, Canadian banks would come to control over 49% of the country's commercial bank assets (RBC 18.8%, Scotiabank 14%, and CIBC 16.5% respectively) – in large part due to an increase in credit demand, and their ability to provide (Clarke and Danns, 1997: 154, 160). What is interesting about Canadian renewed interest in the Caribbean region, is that the banks chose to remain there – even as they generally sought to expand into other countries experiencing their own periods of increased privatizations.[9]

Canadian banks benefited greatly from Canadian aid entering the region in the 1980s and 1990s which contributed to their growing political and economic power there. Aid from Canada was highly conditional and based on the extent to which states followed SAPs which largely worked to integrate them into the Western capitalist system. The Canadian International Development Agency's (CIDA) 1982–1983 report "singled out Cuban revolutionary activity as the main threat to political and thus economic stability in the [Caribbean] region and implied that developmental aid staved off Cuban interference" and other revolutionary bents (Maloney, 1988: 155). CIDA aid to the Caribbean in the 1980s required that "80% of all aid be spent on the purchase of goods and services in Canada" (Ambursley 1985, 244). Although aid is typically thought of in altruistic development terms, Canadian aid sought to aid its own global corporations in their accumulation processes while further denying financial control to Caribbean people in the region. Not surprisingly, the intensification

---

9   Scotiabank, RBC, and CIBC positioned themselves strongly in Caribbean markets; Scotiabank into Mexico and Latin America as well. Scotiabank, RBC, and BMO are trying to break into Asian markets, specifically in China. Scotiabank wants to also extend its operations into Malaysia, Thailand, and India as well, going beyond China. Both TD and BMO have been more focused on North American markets, the U.S. in particular – with RBC, Scotiabank and CIBC also having U.S. operations (Létourneau and Heidrich, 2010: 6–20).

of Canadian aid programs to the region were praised by the IMF and others as proof of Canada's 'good-will,' versus rank neocolonialism towards its neighbors.

In 1990 Canada forgave $182 million worth of debt for 11 Caribbean countries – after the unfairness of Canadian trade deals in the region faced scrutiny (Chaitoo, 2013: 41). Of course, the forgiveness amount did not compensate for the total lost to states in the region due to unfair trade deals, but it did allow Canada to quiet off some criticisms, while overall ensuring neoliberal adherence in the Caribbean region. The framework that Canadian aid and debt forgiveness was grounded upon was laid out in the 1980s by Canada's Secretary of State, Mark MacGuigan, in a speech to the Caribbean Community (CARICOM): Canadian assistance to the region would be to "assist your states to cope with the rapid changes and economic difficulties which beset the region" via "emergency balance of payments assistance available to [Caribbean] states that had concluded remedial programmes with the IMF" (Basedeo, 1992: 198).

Thus, Canadian aid and loan assistance to states in the region was strictly dependent on states acceptance of IMF SAPs and meeting schedules for loan repayments. Further, Canadian aid to the region saw an "increase in the levels of technical assistance" to the region by Canada, and that assistance was "concentrated on economic and financial management in the public sectors [which included a budget for] the hiring of Canadian advisors to assist" in implementation (Basdeo, 1992: 198–199). Canadian aid and debt forgiveness stressed the role of the private sector – specifically in relation to foreign interests within the private sector – as the solution to the Caribbean regions development. In the post-debt forgiveness period of 1990, Canadian Prime Minister Brian Mulroney announced the funding for a new office of cooperation between Canada and the Caribbean, as realized through the Canada-Caribbean Business Cooperation Office (CCBO). The office itself made it clear that "if the Canadian government is to continue to ... assist the region, as it most certainly will do, it will be in the form of the private sector initiatives and not government hand-outs" (Basedeo, 1992: 213).

Essentially, the Canadian overseas business class – including Canadian banks – relied on their sheer size and market power to continue to influence markets in the Caribbean region without serious competition. They were backed in their dealings by the Canadian state – whose aid and debt forgiveness initiatives prioritized the private sector over the government in the region. Market liberalization, as preached by international financial institutions, aided Canadian financiers' concentration in the Caribbean – despite the liberal doctrine that liberalization would lead to increased competition (Worrell, 1997: 66). Canadian banks already in the region had the advantage of not incurring start-up costs, thus avoiding competition with competitive newcomers (Worrell, 1997: 66). Canadian bankers themselves were also uniquely positioned by the Canadian state and IFIS to act as advisors for 'stability' in the region, meaning that Canadian banks played a crucial role in mediating, determining, and benefiting from structural adjustment policies of the 1980s. Increases in private capital to the Caribbean region allowed Canadian financial institutions – uniquely situated in these states – to facilitate these transactions. Their advice changed economies in the region from the sole reliance on agricultural (and other resource) products to tourism and manufacturing, which ensured that Canadian banks would continue to service wealthy foreign clientele in the private sector, and those visiting from Western states.[10] These structured incentives allowed foreign owned private industrial sectors to be stronger in the region, relative to national ones. Although IMF SAPs and Canadian advice provided incentives for all foreign banks and corporations seeking to operate in the Caribbean region, by the 1990s financial liberalization in the developing world more broadly led to an overall reduction in U.S. and European interests in the Caribbean. The only exceptions for U.S. and European interests were in offshore hubs located in the Bahamas and Barbados. Although U.S. and European banks were unable to compete with the already established Canadian banks, they were content with simply avoiding taxes in their Caribbean offshore hubs, taking their investments to places in Asia and Eastern Europe instead (Worrell et al., 2001: 9–10; Ogawa et al., 2013). Although it began in the 1980s, by the 1990s it was clear that the debt crisis which had increased poverty in the Caribbean region had also "simultaneously enrich[ed] international banks and ruling elites" there, and that this phenomenon wouldn't be restricted to the 1980s (Swift and Tomlinson, 1991: 81).

4 Structural Adjustment as International Order: Canadian Banks, Financial Interests, and the Caribbean

Unlike the first wave of English-speaking Caribbean states that were granted independence by Britain, the potential for state nationalization projects did not exist for the second wave of states that would become independent. In other words, these state's independence process was pre-structured by structural adjustment policies, capitalisms aggressive reassertion via the neoliberal turn, and attracting tourists, foreign aid and investments. On the eve of its

---

10   Canadian corporations' own airlines, tour operators, and hotels in the region, and is second only to the U.S. in supplying visitors (tourists) to these states (Momsen, 1992: 510).

independence, St. Lucia implemented a "tax holiday," a "tariff-free import of industrial inputs [and the] unlimited repatriation of capital and profits" for foreign industries – with the included 'benefit' to St. Lucia being "worker training programs" for 'development' (Klak, 1998: 74). Worse, debt traps by IFIs, coupled with incursions on Caribbean state's sovereignty would see the neoliberal and capitalist doctrine accepted by all the independent states in the English-speaking Caribbean region by the mid 1980s. When the Bahamas (1973), the four Windward islands of Grenada (1974), Dominica (1978), St. Lucia (1979) and St. Vincent and the Grenadines (1979), and Belize (1981) were granted independence – their development routes were severely limited. While the height of the U.S. ideological war with the Soviet Union factored heavily into the acceptance of structural adjustment policies in this period; it had been the case that Canadian banks market power extended itself into these states even prior to their independence and the ideological battle which dominated global politics. As such, newly independent states remained highly tied, and dependent on, Canadian banks, as well as dependent on strategies aimed to attract additional aid and foreign investment pushed by them.

Simply stating that limited choices existed does not cover the depth of those limits, so I provide additional insight with Grenada as a case study. The main takeaway from the invasion into Grenada is that states who did not accept the terms of the neoliberal doctrine were subject to military and political interventions, followed by the imposition of neoliberal economic policies. If those states happened to be in the Caribbean region, the U.S. and IFIs trusted Canadian financiers to advance the broader strategic and economic goals of structural adjustment, in line with the system. Adherence to the failed neoliberal doctrine for development in the Caribbean region, would be accepted by all states by the mid to late 1980s, given the international mishandling of Grenada. In the post-invasion period, other newly independent Caribbean states placed a lot more emphasis on state police forces to limit rebellions against reformist and revolutionary agendas. For instance, the Dominica Defense Force (DDF) was utilized multiple times in the aftermath of its independence to put down legitimate civilian protests and mass movements (Phillips, 2002: 52). Not surprisingly, Canada has been crucial to "training police and security forces in the Commonwealth Caribbean" (Momsen, 1992: 506).

When Antigua and Belize gained independence (1981), it was thought that the Black Power Movements in Antigua would pose a challenge to the system. However, state policies checked the effectiveness of these movements through both political repression and economic liberalization. St. Kitts and Nevis, Belize, and Antigua would all pursue a neoliberal strategy of "industrialization by inducement" promising foreign businesses and investments "lucrative tax holidays, and to indiscriminately lease and purchase land" (Simmonds, 1987: 285). Canadian experts advised these governments about how to attract their businesses to their states. The independence parties in St. Vincent and the Grenadines did not even lay out a path for independence, instead choosing to forge closer ties "with the relatively centrist [and already independent] governments of Trinidad and Tobago and of Barbados [,]" (Niddrie and Tolson, 2019). Meanwhile, in the Bahamas, the constitution stressed its commitment to neoliberal development noting that it would not change its financial sector given the "confidence displayed by the banking community in the government's reaffirmation of the principles of democracy and its pledge for continued political stability" (Francis, 1985: 94). This is important because in the aftermath of the invasion of Grenada, state elites in the English-speaking Caribbean made it clear that revolutionary fervor would be contained as they simultaneously pledged allegiance to the Western capitalist system, to maintain state sovereignty from unwanted physical interventions.

4.1 The Case of Grenada: Going against Structural Adjustment as International Order

Given the severely limited development options for English-speaking Caribbean states that became independent during this second independence wave, Grenada tried to undergo a revolutionary path to circumvent powerful foreign interests – regarded as inimical to the interests of the Grenadian public. However, while initially successful, the outcome of the Grenadian revolution would reveal that powerful foreign interests were not above supporting ultra-asymmetrical military invasions to re-insert a Caribbean country within the preferred international financial architecture to the benefit of foreign investors. This revelation would make future revolutionary attempts unlikely, given the immense punishment enacted against Grenada after its attempt. In 1979 the Grenadian public supported the New Jewel Movement (NJM)[11] led by Maurice Bishop in overthrowing its then incumbent ruling party, the Grenada United Labour Party (GULP). GULP was backed by local elites within Grenada and external foreign interests. NJM made the explicit case that the present international order locked Caribbean states into unequal capitalist relations to the detriment of Caribbean people. The NJM identified Canadian financial

---

11   NJM in Grenada was a product of the Black Power Movement in Grenada during the late 1960s to early 1970s. This is why Black Power movements in newly independent Caribbean states (like Antigua and Dominica) were targeted as having the potential to become communist/Marxist/socialist in orientation.

institutions as having an outsized and negative role in the financial affairs of Grenada both before and after independence.

Prior to the coup, the incumbent (and illegitimate)[12] GULP ruling party, facilitated bilateral agreements with Canada granting Canadian banks an outsized role in Grenadian commercial industries. Although really small, by 1976 Grenada would have 6 commercial banks – all foreign – of which RBC, CIBC, and Scotiabank had the biggest hand (Paxton, 2016: 552). As was seen elsewhere in the region, "the requirement of the four foreign-owned commercial banks – Barclays Bank International, Royal Bank of Canada, Bank of Nova Scotia, Canadian Imperial Bank of Commerce –" meant that most people living in Grenada could not access the Canadian banking facilities (Ambursley, 1985: 32). Prior to the Grenadian Revolution, government economic planning in the aftermath of Grenada's independence "was limited to the preparation of lists of investment projects which were virtually 'shopping lists for aid'" (Kirton, 1989: 3). Within Grenada, local and foreign capital functioned in a laissez-faire way whereby "there were no controls on their operations and no regulation of foreign trade, prices or any other important economic variables" (Kirton, 1989: 3). As mentioned before, this was due to the overwhelming influence of Canadian financial institutions and IFIs who structured Caribbean economies to act and respond in this way.

In 1979, the NJM staged a successful coup d'état against the GULP government, given majority support amongst the Grenadian population, and formed the People's Revolutionary Government (PRG) of Grenada. The PRG's mission, as broadcast over radio, was outlined clearly with the description of the situation facing Grenada:

> We are a small country, we are a poor country, with a population of African slave descendants, we are part of the exploited Third World and, definitively, our challenge is to seek the creation of a new international order that puts the economy at the service of the people and social justice. -Maurice Bishop.
> Radio Free Grenada. April 13, 1979

Unlike most of the other independent governments in the region at the time, which geared policies towards the illusion of social progress while allowing the economic sectors to remain largely friendly towards foreign capital, the PRG set out to implement specific economic policies that would use state funds in

---

12   Illegitimate, as elections were understood to be rigged against opposition parties.

a productive manner. Part of this recognition included the outsized Canadian banking interests in Grenada, and in the Caribbean region. The PRG's concern was warranted, given the uncompetitive environment that has been established for the benefit of Canadian banks, which made it so that "by 1983, there were approximately 330 branches of Canadian banks, their subsidiaries, and affiliates in the [English-speaking] Caribbean" (Kaufman, 1985: 72). The focus on finance by the PRG government did frighten Canadian bankers. Shortly after the revolution, the Canadian Imperial Bank of Commerce "announced its intentions to cease operations on the island for financial reasons" (Ambursley, 1985: 207). CIBC may have been worried about the potential for its employees to unionize under PRG governance. A few months before the revolution in 1979, CIBC "strenuously opposed previous attempts by some of their staff to unionize," like the majority of foreign owned banks at the time, and "workers from [CIBC]" had approached revolutionary leaders about this (Coard, 2017: 40). The fundamental right to work in dignity, by forming a union, heavily concerned the PRG – thus, they aggressively tackled employment rights and redress in their policies.

Inheriting a 49% unemployment rate from the Gairy GULP regime,[13] in just three years the PRG would reduce the unemployment rate to 14.7% in 1982. During the PRGs short tenure, trade unions in Grenada became "vibrant organizations" with "active participation in international and other labour conferences" (Aberdeen, 1986: 37). Unionization of bank workers in the foreign banks were a top priority, and the recognition of the CIBC union under PRG leadership "had an electrifying effect among workers at all four foreign-owned banks in Grenada. The PRG used CIBC leaving Grenada as an opportunity to "acquire ownerships of [CIBC] bank facilities" and established the first state bank (Ambursley, 1985: 207). Thus, in 1979, the National Commercial Bank (NCB) became the first state bank in Grenada given CIBCs divestment, and "enjoyed the confidence of the Grenadian people" becoming "the second largest bank in the country" (Aberdeen, 1986: 26). Outside of establishing a dignified working environment, state banks like NCB placed top priority on lending to productive industries within Grenada, like agriculture, which also made it preferable

---

13   70% of those unemployed were women (Aberdeen, 1986: 37). During the revolutionary period in Grenada, the situation of women drastically improved given employment opportunities in education and other community sectors. After the invasion of Grenada, the situation of women in the country both notably and drastically declined. The post-revolutionary government defunded dramatically education and community services – given the belief by U.S. policy makers and the Grenadian elite, that it was through these sectors and institutions that communist propaganda spread.

for Grenadians. Seeing the success of NCB, management of the un-unionized banks immediately offered substantial salary and fringe benefit increases" to workers (Coard, 2017: 41).

A year after the revolution, the Royal Bank made announcements that "it would cease its operations in Grenada" as part of a broader trend with the Royal at this time to "rationalize its activities in the Caribbean" given the debt crisis (Ambursley, 1985: 210).[14] The "PRG bought the head office of the Royal Bank of Canada" which they initially noted as a "concern," and established a second state bank in Grenada (Ambursley, 1985: 210). After purchasing the Royal Bank, the PRG renamed the bank "the Grenada Bank of Commerce (GBC)" and "in order to encourage maximum efficiency through competition between" the GBC and NCB – thus the GBC "had been set up as a separate bank" (Aberdeen, 1986: 27). The GCB had acquired the holdings of the Royal Bank after its departure, meaning that capital between the two banks were also unshared and could truly operate as separate competing entities.

The PRG utilized the rules of the system to its advantage in consolidating its ownership of financial institutions. With the already established framework of mergers and acquisitions during the 1980s, the PRG came to buy off, or become majority shareholders in, the head offices of RBC and CIBC. And, in addition to buying off Canadian banks intent on leaving the country, the PRG also developed its own state banks not affiliated with its Canadian purchases. These state banks were to be government controlled and not beholden to a shareholder framework, so that foreign shareholders would not come to control the banks in the future. According to Bernard Coard, the former deputy Prime Minister of the PRG, if they incorporated purchased Canadian banks with the state banks "[Canadians] would have had fifty percent of all deposits in Grenada" (Grenade, 2010: 148). Thus, it was reckoned that to truly localize investments in needed industries and sectors, the PRG would need financial autonomy. Autonomy allowed the PRG to make over 90% of its bank loans from state banks, go towards funding Grenadian industry, agriculture, and fisheries (Aberdeen, 1986: 27). The PRG also insisted on collaborating with the private sector for mutual benefits to be bestowed upon Grenada which would circumvent pushback from IFIs and Western governments, while also encouraging more robust (innovative) growth strategies in Grenada.

The PRG's belief in robust competition as a necessity for development in Grenada, is why they did not pursue outright nationalization. They were also

---

14   In 1985, a mere two years after the demise of the Grenadian revolution and five years after its initial pull out of Grenada, the Royal Bank of Canada would express interest in buying back its branch in the country.

concerned that nationalization would not bode well, given the broader economic crisis in the rest of the Caribbean region in the 1980s where capital flight was a huge concern. When the PRG came to power, "British and Canadian capital dominated banking and the import/export trade on the island" (Clark and Danns, 1997: 25). The overwhelming power of foreign entities and their potential capital flight were hard for the revolutionary government to ignore. Thus, purchasing the head offices of Canadian banks looking to divest from Grenada within the shareholder framework, versus nationalizing them, was less confrontational, thus more strategic, for the PRG. The PRG purchases of Canadian banks was viewed as transactional, and maybe even profit-saving from the view of the Canadian banks who sold to the state to exit the country. The PRG's estimations were correct, as the purchasing of CIBC and the Royal showed a willingness of the Grenadian Revolutionary Government to 'cooperate' with the international system.

Given the PRG's strategy of gradual public ownership in conjunction with strong private partnerships within Grenada, the PRG believed state institutions would grow to be competitive, and Grenada would be able to stick to its revolutionary path unscathed. The PRG recognized that it needed to transition away from traditional merchant forms of capital and trading that mostly benefited foreign capitalists in Britain and Canada. When the PRG came to power, the economic structure in Grenada was one that lent itself to a high import content of goods from Western states, that could be sourced locally, and uneven trade deals, that provided market access in Grenada to foreign corporations without extending the same access to Grenada in those corporation's home states. Local industries also received scant investments and loans. The PRG examined the problems facing the bigger (and more resource rich) independent English-speaking Caribbean countries (like Jamaica, Guyana, Trinidad and Tobago) which furthered its commitment to weaken the strength of dependent foreign economic relationships. The revolutionary government had to manage the problems of foreign ownership in a way that would also not directly attack foreign capital too quickly within their country. Thus, the PRG framed government investments within the Grenadian economy using the language of 'competition' and remaining competitive with private industry (Ambursley, 1985; Grenade, 2010; Coard, 2017).

When the state banks in Grenada were established, they did so with the intent to compete with foreign banks in Grenada that had previously dominated lending and investment decisions. To make banking in Grenada competitive, it was reasoned that the monopoly Canadian banks had within the Grenadian finance needed to be weakened. This, it was said, was to increase bank competition in Grenada to make these services better for everyone in the country. It was through walking this fine line of managing foreign imperial relations and its revolutionary mandate of development based on justice for the Grenadian people that made the PRG's policies successful. The PRG honored the financial loan obligations that Grenada had, which they had inherited from the government prior to the revolution. While the PRG did not have many Western allies, under their government the Grenadian economy did grow. This was because the PRG utilized the aid and loans it had received strategically to boost public employment opportunities. The PRG's commitment to walking the thin line between global financial capitalists and its own development proved successful. IFIs found the PRG government 'easier' to work with, given their competency over the pre-revolutionary government (Felix, 1998). As such, the IMF, and World Bank "disregarded the PRG's socialist orientation" and approved them for loans for infrastructure projects – however, these loans would be withdrawn given disapproval from the Reagan administration in the U.S. (Bartilow, 1997 quoted in Felix, 1998: 151).

Nonetheless, the PRG government was still able to utilize foreign investments that were already coming into Grenada in a way that would support local industries and new businesses. The PRG provided structured incentives for foreign investments in specific sectors of the economy to address the needs of Grenadians.[15] It provided incentives to investments that met "at least one of four specific objectives: (i) the creation of employment; (ii) the expansion of production; (iii) the preservation of the quality of the environment; [and] (iv) the generation of and/or the conservation of foreign exchange earnings" (Ambursley, 1985: 203–204). The main goal under the PRG was for foreign funds and investments to be invested back into the local economy, with "training of Grenadian nationals" a top priority (Ambursley, 1985). It was reckoned that overtime these structured incentives would help to develop a local economy within Grenada that was not only competitive, and environmentally friendly, but also less reliant on foreign investment. Given Grenada's good standing under the PRG, Canada obliged to fund local private sector initiatives in

---

15 Prior to the revolution, Grenadian unemployment stood a bit over 50% and more than 1/3rd of the employed were dependent on farming and farm labor. In spite of this, food consumption was based on imported food as the main agricultural products were exported to Britain, Canada, and the USA. Given the aforementioned, the livelihood of the majority of Grenadians was largely dependent on global price fluctuations. Additionally, of revenue accrued from farming, the land was owned by foreign businesses and Grenadian capitalists who "controlled the bulk of the processing and marketing firms" (Clarke and Danns, 1997: 23–24).

Grenada, including the provision of "economic assistance to Grenadian businessmen" (Ambursley, 1985: 204, 214).

The fine line walked by the PRG kept the Grenadian-Canadian relationship intact, even as the PRG "reserved the right to preclude private sector ownership and control" (Ambursley, 1985: 204). Essentially, the PRG played on Canada's commitment to providing aid to Caribbean states that had concluded remedial IFI programs (or made substantial payments on debts), and ones in which Canada had substantial interests in. Thus, it would be a mistake to think that the relationship between Canada and the PRG was one of 'goodwill.' One indicator of this being that the PRG restricted, and in some instances prohibited, the establishment of new businesses in sectors that Canadian companies utilized the region for (most profitably). That is: "banking, insurance, importing and wholesaleing, fishing (except artisanal fishing) and internal transportation" (Ambursley, 1985: 204). Otherwise, the traditional merchant forms of capital and trading alluded to earlier. While Canadian businesses remained skeptical of the PRG, the ones who remained in Grenada did so given that the PRG walked the fine line between foreign business and the state. For example, "the revolutionary government guaranteed the ownership rights of capitalists so long as they did not sabotage the economy or participate in illegal acts" (Clark, 1987: 26). The PRG also made it clear that the growth of "Grenada's productive forces" would take years to accomplish, especially in state sector industries like "banking, and trade" (Clark, 1987: 26–27). In other words, it was very clear that outright nationalization of whole sectors would not take place under the PRG. However, more immediate was the "adoption and enforcement of labor laws guaranteeing union rights and regulating the wages and job conditions of rural and urban workers" (Clark, 1987: 26–27).

Scotiabank, who throughout this entire period did not cease any of its Caribbean operations, remained in Grenada despite "the unease felt by the business community over the economic policies of the PRG" (Ambursley, 1985: 217). Plans to weaken bigger private monopolies overtime – via public ownership and competition – did not sit well with foreign industries and banks. Prior to the revolution, Canadian banks in Grenada heavily opposed worker unionization, and because Scotiabank remained in Grenada, its employees were now unionized after the revolution. According to a manager at the Bank of Nova Scotia during the revolutionary government's tenure, "Scotia had no plans to close, since, on account of the bank's professionalism and international contacts, it could compete successfully" with the now Grenadian run state banks (Ambursley, 1985: 217). The manager also noted that part of Scotia's recipe for success was that it had been doing business in Grenada, and in the region, for a such a long time that "most of the large companies prefer to stay with the private banks," especially due to their "mistrust of the PRG" (Ambursley, 1985: 217–218). Essentially, Scotiabank reckoned that it would remain a competitive bank in Grenada given that they were the preferred institution for bigger private, and foreign, companies. It also helped that Canadian aid to Grenada remained intact and Scotiabank did not feel immediately threatened by state competition.

Less pleased with the PRG's policies were the land-owning class in Grenada. Although overall the economic success of the PRG is notable, the post-revolution environment did witness an overall decline in foreign investment to Grenada during PRGs tenure. This even though aid to the state sector, from countries like Canada (other socialist and/or communist countries, NGOs, and oil-exporting countries), did result in an overall growth in the island's economy. The PRG's growth schemes were largely "at the expense of the comprador bourgeoisie" class, and even though this class had also seen an "increase [in their] profit margin[s]," it was not nearly "as well as was anticipated" due to the overall decrease of foreign investments (Ambursley, 1985: 222–223). Additionally, land reform and labor rights that were immediately championed by the PRG was also unpopular amongst this class – the majority of whom were local landlords and local capitalists tapped into Grenada's tourism industry (Clark, 1987; Ambursley, 1985). This local comprador class, along with the foreign business community in Grenada, supported political counterrevolution by way of conservative regional governments and U.S. intervention.

The PRG's project, while successful in drastically improving the social situation in Grenada and reviving what was, prior to the revolution, a stagnant Grenadian economy – even getting praises from the World Bank[16] – would come to an end during the latter half of 1983 with the assassination of PRG leaders. The U.S. invasion of Grenada would be supported by the classes within the private sector of Grenada tied to foreign interests, and other Western countries. Internally, these classes alone could not sustain or justify U.S. invasion. The invasion was unpopular within Grenada, which meant that the U.S. and its allies had to explicitly promote (through fliers, mailers, radio, and children's books) a series of anti-communist and anti-revolution propaganda (Bloomfield, 2020) – even going so far as to note that the beloved Prime Minister, Maurice Bishop, was himself a victim of communist forces acting in

---

16   The World Bank reported that while the PRG had "inherited a deteriorating economy," in three years they have made "Grenada … one of the few countries in the Western Hemisphere that continued to experience per capita growth during 1981" (Boodhoo, 1985: 20). Overall, the economy grew by 2.1% in 1979, 3% in 1980 and in 1981, and 5.5% in 1982 (World Bank quoted in Boodhoo, 1985: 20).

Grenada.[17] Externally, Western countries like Canada whose Prime Minister, Pierre Trudeau, publicly challenged the legitimacy of the U.S. invasion into Grenada, tacitly supported the move. This was most clearly demonstrated when Trudeau abstained from voting with other countries at the UN General Assembly calling for the immediate withdrawal of U.S. troops from Grenada (Posner, 1983: 2). Additionally, in Canada's House of Commons debates in October 1983 when the topic of the U.S. invasion came up, it was confessed that "The position of this [Trudeau] government was that we were concerned about the political orientation of Grenada under the late PM Bishop since the coup of 1979 which overthrew the unpopular government of Sir Eric Gairy" (Gerald Regan, Secretary of State for International Trade quoted in Swift and Tomlinson, 1991: 300). The next Canadian administration of Prime Minister Brian Mulroney in 1984, was much more vocal about giving the U.S. the benefit of the doubt for the invasion of Grenada (Noble, 2003; Nossal et al., 2015: 190).

The above follows a trend in Canadian politics, whereby Canada expresses an outward commitment to state sovereignty and human rights, but its official policy is to secure its economic advantages. In Grenada, by 1983 "approximately 45 percent of the banking industry was under state control," and Scotiabank and Barclays, the "two foreign-owned banks continued to function freely" (Boodhoo, 1985: 16). However, after the U.S. invasion "Canada substantially increased its aid" to Grenada with a focus on liberalizing, through increased privatizations, of the damaged post-invasion economy (Brown et al., 2014: 150). And foreign bankers applauded the increased deposits flowing into the banks "at a monthly rate that is the equivalent of what annual deposits were in the last three years of the revolutionary governments" (Treaster, 1985). It should be noted that in the aftermath of the invasion, Grenada became a hub for money-laundering, specifically in drugs (Chomsky, 1992); although I can find no statements from the Bank of Nova Scotia or its representatives regarding the post-invasion environment, which is only odd seeing as they were the only Canadian bank operating in the country at the time. Scotiabank was being investigated by U.S. authorities after the invasion, for accepting drug money and money laundering (Effros, 1992). Scotiabank refused to comply with the U.S. and Canada, with bank officials believing that its bank was being unjustly targeted.

Just as British imperialism linked Canada financially to the Caribbean region, U.S. hegemony provided Canada with justification for, and legitimacy

---

17   This strategy only worked, given that Bishop's assassination happened due to internal PRG infighting.

in, carrying out 'strategic' goals in the region to the benefit of Canadian investors and corporations. In the aftermath of the Cuban revolution in the 1950s, Canadian financiers were worried about potential spillover effects in the region – given the number of losses their financial institutions incurred from that revolution. While the U.S. focused on preventing ideologically opposed revolutions in its 'backyard,' Canada opposed progressive reforms – in what it deemed its 'sphere of interest' – that would pose challenges to its corporations operating in the hemisphere. As such, even prior to the Grenadian revolution, "Canada's policy in the Caribbean [was] closely linked with that of the United States," and the U.S. relied on Canada to "extend its influence into the former British West Indian colonies in the Caribbean" via defense and development (Momsen, 1992: 506). However, the relationship was fraught with tension, as U.S. geo-strategic and military aspirations, did not always align with Canada's purely economic ones (e.g., continuation of Canadian aid to states like Grenada after the revolution and the U.S. trying to isolate what it saw as Grenadian communism). Nonetheless, prior to the invasion of Grenada, Canadians "received permission [from the U.S.] to get their own people out the day before" (The New York Times 1983), but Canada was snubbed by the U.S. during the invasion and the U.S. embassy in Canada "cautioned Prime Minister [Trudeau] against meddling" (Fischer, 1994: 626).[18]

While the PRG sought to change the world system and carve out a new path for the independent English-speaking Caribbean region's integration into that system, ultimately, it would be (1) isolated from accessing finance from international institutions (the government would turn to economic aid from friendly and other developing country sources), (2) the PRG's leader would be assassinated along with other cabinet members and trade unionists, and (3) Grenada would be invaded by the U.S. military (under Reagan) in 1983 – backed by reformist-centrist governments in the independent English-speaking Caribbean region. There were overwhelming interests which felt threatened by a successful Grenada which flipped neoliberal development orthodoxy on its head. Testament to this is the fact that the U.S. utilized an air campaign and sent a total of 7,600 combined troops, against an unsuspecting army of

---

18   It seems that Reagan might have told Trudeau about the intentions to invade much sooner, had they not thought Trudeau was a socialist. In either event, Reagan believed that Trudeau would have been opposed to the Grenadian invasion, given that just two days prior Trudeau proposed a plan for East-West reconciliation, given the number of proxy wars during the 'Cold' war. American officials also did not allow Canadian press to Grenada and twice refused Canadian airlifts to extract Canadian nationals (Fischer, 1994: 626).

1,200 people. Unsurprisingly, reinserting a Caribbean state into a financial system that privileges foreign investors would help Canadian financiers – even as the Canadian government vocally expressed frustrations about the invasion. Given Canadian competitiveness in the region, and an overall alignment with U.S. foreign policy from Canada, the post-invasion environment in Grenada "generated Canadian financial and technical assistance to [Grenada] and witnessed a greater interest by Canada in the affairs of the smaller leeward and Windward islands" (Basdeo, 1992: 197).

5 Renewed Investment Consolidation by Canadian Banks in the Caribbean: Characteristics of New Investments and Neoliberal Development Strategies

By 1983, the Royal Bank ranked 4th in North America for largest bank, with the CIBC ranking 7th and Scotiabank ranking 10th (Kaufman, 1985). The greatest advantage that Canadian banks had was their history and concentration within Canada which associated these institutions with financial stability. That Canadian banks were seen as more stable, meaning that foreign banks entering the Canadian market during the 1980s, 1990s, and 2000s were restricted in their control and expansion within the Canadian banking financial industry.[19] In 1980, "no more than 25 percent of the assets of a major [Canadian] bank could be owned abroad, and total domestic assets held by subsidiaries of foreign banks were capped" to 8% of the market (Malminen, 1997: 80; Darroch, 1994: 279). This understanding afforded Canadian chartered banks greater room to diversify and expand the types of services and products that they offered both at home and abroad – as foreign banks within Canada were limited to a small segment of commercial lending (Darroch, 1994: 279). Effectively what was established within Canada via the Bank Act, was a formal a two-tiered system of banking.

This system provided Canadian chartered banks the ability to expand, concentrate, and consolidate into a wider array of financial services. As early as 1981, Canadian banks started looking for loopholes in the Bank Act which could help them convert "large amounts of debt into corporate equity," so that

---

19 New chartered status for all other banks that did not already exist in Canada would have been hard to come by, as chartered status could have only been gotten by an act of the Canadian parliament. Some of the restrictions were eased with the NAFTA agreement; however, deep benefits already had by the major Canadian banks within Canada, would continue to make competition against them harder.

they could have "substantial holdings in companies with billions of dollars of assets" for 'competition' sake (Kaufman, 1985: 62). The ability of Canadian chartered banks to expand into a wider array of financial services was enabled by the terms of the 1980s Bank Act. Prior to the 1980s, the boundaries between banks and other financial institutions within Canada were becoming blurred so that Canadian chartered banks would be the most effective financial competitors within Canada in relation to other Canadian financial institutions. Although after 1980 Canadian banks faced a more competitive environment due to these laws, they also had the ability to expand their profit-making activities by consolidating increased ownership over a wider range of financial services. By 1992, Canadian banks could offer "non-banking financial services such as trust or insurance [...] establish "networking" arrangements with other financial service providers [...] hold, manage, and develop land through their real property corporations and to own real estate brokerage firms" (Darroch, 1994: 280) as their competitors did elsewhere, even if they were restricted from doing so within Canada. The aim of these specific actions was to increase Canadian banks capacity for growth within their own domestic market, while remaining competitive given the changed international financial structure that provided opportunities for growth in international business.

6 Domestic Market Share of Canadian and Foreign Financial Institutions 2000

Canadian domestic policies helped the investment strategies of big Canadian multinational banks abroad, which made them largely profitable, but also better positioned to weather financial crisis during the 1980s that their international competitors could not. The developing world crisis was a "painful but salutary demonstration of the stability of Canadian banking" (McDowall, 1993: 417). This stability lent credence to Canadian financial structures and Canadian businessmen's ability for getting the indebted Caribbean region back onto its feet. Thus, throughout the second half of the 1980s and into the 1990s, Canadian banks focused on helping to privatize the economies of English-speaking Caribbean states and increasing their investments throughout the region (Table 6.3).

Additionally, the expanded sphere of financial activities for the banks in Canada also led to a growth and expansion of new financial products in the Caribbean region – most notably in digital banking and new linkages between insurance schemes and banks. Furthermore, the economic relationship between Canada and the English-speaking Caribbean remained concentrated

TABLE 6.3   Breakdown of Canadian and foreign bank revenue

	(%)
Canadian bank's revenue	94
Foreign bank's revenue	6
Total revenue	100
Canadian life and health insurers' premium income	71
Foreign life and health insurers' premium income	29
Total premium income	100
Canadian P&C insurers' premium income	34
Foreign P&C insurers' premium income	66
Total premium income	100

Note: The Canadian government has always protected its banks from foreign competition. This has included weakening other financial sectors within its own economy, by allowing banks to take customers away from those sectors and allowing banks to participate in the same services that the other financial sectors do. Therefore, Canadian bank revenue has remained Canadian (protected from undue foreign influence) and also high.
SOURCES: CONFERENCE BOARD OF CANADA, CANADIAN LIFE AND HEALTH INSURANCE ASSOCIATION, INSURANCE BUREAU OF CANADA: REPRINTED BY CANADIAN DEPARTMENT OF FINANCE 2002

in private sector growth and in the development of private sector capital. By 1989, Canadian private investment to the region "was approaching half a billion dollars in value and was concentrated in the utilities, communications, and financial sectors" (Mulroney quoted in Momsen, 1992: 510) in countries like the Bahamas, Jamaica, Trinidad and Tobago, and Antigua, given "favourable regulatory regime[s]" (Higgins quoted in Momsen, 1992: 510). Meanwhile, Canada's development assistance to the region during that same year was over $110 million, making the Caribbean the "highest per capita" recipient of "Canadian bilateral aid," accounting for over "half of the total for the Americas" (Momsen, 1992: 510).

As such, investment, aid, tourism, and 'technical assistance' underlined the relationship between Canada, Canadian financiers, and the English-speaking Caribbean from the 1990s onward. The expanded scope of Canadian banking activity in Canada also led to greater involvement by Canadian banks in helping to facilitate and broker new trade and investment deals in the Caribbean. Thus, even though natural resource trading and its associated investments declined in the late 1980s and 1990s, there were agreements and various business bodies created between Canada and Caribbean countries. One such agreement was CARIBCAN, which purported to increase Caribbean access to a Canadian market (Haar and Bryan, 1999: 4–5). However, CARIBCAN and other agreements like it have often "excluded certain items for which the [Caribbean] region is considered to have a comparative advantage" in, and the more successful agreements are ones that focused on "maintain[ing] a level of communication between Canada and the region" (Haar and Bryan, 1999: 5). Unsurprisingly, these types of communication agreements – like the Joint Trade and Economic Committee (JTEC) and the Canada-Caribbean Business Cooperation Office (CCBO) – have helped "to improve investment flows between Canada and the region" – indicating the amount of influence that Canada has in the region determining which sectors are worth investing in (Haar and Bryan, 1999: 5). These deals were extremely beneficial to Canadian banks and businesses in the Caribbean.

During the 1990s and 2000s, the Caribbean banking sector remained dominated by Canadian banks and their subsidiaries which continued to expand and merge throughout the region. It was predicted that the three big Canadian banks in the Caribbean would "continue their long-standing, stable, profit-earning operations. Although, some less-productive branches [would] be phased out," but even then, "the large network [would] be maintained and in a few cases[,] extended" (Kaufman, 1985: 74). An example of this was that by 1992 Scotiabank operated in 24 Caribbean markets with 172 locations. CIBC, though less ambitious than Scotiabank, also expanded taking advantage of new opportunities for merging and acquisitioning. Globally, Canadian banks were recognized as significant international players accruing 27% of their total net income abroad in the 1990s and increasing that amount to 45% by 2000 (Canadian Department of Finance, 2002). While increased interests in Latin America and Asia on behalf of Canadian banks received a lot of attention in the literature, the Caribbean region also accounted for a large portion of Canadian bank mergers.

In the English-speaking Caribbean, Canadian banks' lending and expansion, through incremental takeovers and mergers,[20] grew, even as regional trends included: (1) a decreased market share, of about 1–3% in different Caribbean states, overall, for foreign banks, and (2) an increase in market share for 'indigenous (or local) banks' in the region (Juan-Ramón et al., 2001). Whereas "from

---

20 Deregulation has a substantial impact on merger decisions.

1980 to 1989 there were only 83 mergers and acquisitions in the Caribbean ... in the 1990's there was a marked increase in activity, with 515 takeovers" (Wood and Wood, 2013: 38). Illustrative is the experience of Trinidad and Tobago, where from 1985 to 2009, 52% of the takeovers in that country resulted in foreign companies acquiring Trinidadian firms, "with the first of these acquisitions occurring in 1990" (Wood and Wood, 2013: 38). During this same period in Barbados, Canadian banks would come to control over 49% of the country's commercial bank assets (RBC 18.8%, Scotiabank 14%, and CIBC 16.5% respectively) – in large part due to an increase in credit demand, and their ability to provide (Clarke and Danns, 1997: 154, 160). What is interesting about Canadian renewed interest in the Caribbean region, is that the banks chose to remain there – even as they generally sought to expand into other countries experiencing their own periods of increased privatizations.[21] To echo a sentiment expressed by Baum in 1974: "the Commonwealth Caribbean is not the most important segment of [Canadian] bank's business. [However,] it is an area where they do business and happen to be dominant" (Baum, 1974: 77). This could perhaps explain their longevity in the region.

Another explanation offered by Létourneau and Heidrich (2010) for continued expansion by Canadian banks in the region is because the market in Canada was already saturated, and large-scale expansion, through merging was viewed negatively within Canada. For instance, in 1998 the Bank of Montreal (BOM) proposed a merger with the Royal Bank and CIBC proposed a merger with TD. If allowed, Canada would have had only three big banks. However, both proposals were rejected on the grounds that losses that would come due to branch closures would far outweigh the costs (Critchley, 2018). Since then and into the 2000s, both RBC and CIBC have sought to expand "their footprint by acquiring and consolidating assets respectively" in the Caribbean region (Létourneau and Heidrich, 2010: 15). Thus, in 2001 "First Caribbean" was created when CIBC merged with Barclays Bank, each receiving abut 47% of shares (Létourneau and Heidrich, 2010: 6). Limited prospects for expansion domestically within Canada was often allowed to be actualized abroad in the Caribbean, where Canadian banks' power was stronger and more concentrated. These Canadian banks were afforded a degree of security, given these countries dependence

---

21   Létourneau & Heidrich 2010, 6–20: Scotiabank, RBC, and CIBC positioned themselves strongly in Caribbean markets; Scotiabank into Mexico and Latin America as well. Scotiabank, RBC, and BMO are trying to break into Asian markets, specifically in China. Scotiabank wants to also extend its operations into Malaysia, Thailand, and India as well, going beyond China. Both TD and BMO have been more focused on North American markets, the U.S. in particular – with RBC, Scotiabank and CIBC also having U.S. operations.

on foreign/international capital and aid, as well as lax regulatory environment that the banks had helped to devise. This worked too, because there was "a sharp expansion of Canadian financial capital in the Western Hemisphere, growing from 15 percent of Canadian FDI in the early 1980s to close to half in the 2000s" of which the Caribbean region was the largest benefactor (Gordon and Weber, 2016: 16).

For Canadian banks reasserting their dominance in the English-speaking Caribbean region during the 2000s, what changed was the rise of local competition – especially from Trinidad and Tobago, which became a financial sector hub within the region. Trinidadian banks' acquisitions in multiple territories allowed them to compete with larger foreign owned banks, via the provision of services to regular Caribbean people. The most popular and identifiable of the regional banks during the 2000s, Republic Bank and RBTT Financial Holdings, were both based in Trinidad and Tobago, operating in multiple Caribbean states via the purchasing of smaller local banks within states. The bigger multinational and foreign-owned banks responded to the increased popularity and competition presented by regional banks via merging. Hence, the most popular merger of the early 2000s happened between UK based Barclays Bank and the CIBC – both of which merged to create 'First Caribbean International Bank' (FCIB) in 2002. FCIB placed its headquarters in Barbados, and quickly became the largest financial institution in the Caribbean. The merger left about 10% of remaining shares open for institutional and individual investors in the region (Caribbean Development and Cooperation, 2001). The merger and split shares allowed FCIB to remain competitive as both an international and regional bank, offering services to locals.

By 2000, the financial sector in the independent English-speaking Caribbean region accounted for 24% of total regional GDP (Ogawa et al., 2013). Growth in the financial sector was largely due to the dominance of foreign-owned banks and banking in general, which comprised 91% of financial sector growth (Ogawa et al., 2013). It should be noted that this estimation excludes offshore banks, because U.S. and European corporations dominate in independent English-speaking Caribbean in that sector. U.S. and European banking domination are concentrated in the Bahamas and Barbados due to offshore banking. If offshore banking were to be included in these figures, it would overemphasize Barbados and the Bahamas, as well as U.S. and European financial interests' asset wise, over that of Canadian banks. This is not to say that Canada is not involved in offshore banking. Deneault (2015) documented in detail how Canadian financiers played a decisive role in turning the English-speaking Caribbean region into tax and offshore havens. However, the inclusion of offshore banking would overemphasize the world's most capitalized banks in the world today, which are U.S. based.

Without this inclusion of tax and offshore havens, Canadian banks account for 60% of all banking system assets in the Caribbean, which is 6% higher than they were in 2000 – when Canadian banks collectively controlled 54.58% of the regions total banking sector. Although different sources provide different estimates – given that they're not all counting the same way – Canadian banks controlled anywhere between 6%–35% less of the Caribbean financial sector leading up to the 2008 financial crisis. Although 35% is a bit on the higher end, in regards to losing one's interest, part of the explanation includes the merger between CIBC and Barclays, which places Canadian total ownership below that of a majority shareholder.

7   Conclusion

The role of Canadian finance in the Caribbean region and the role of the Canadian government for maintaining the interest of Canadian financiers and investors in the Caribbean region is hardly discussed. Canadian banking investments in the region during the 1980s and 1990s match a longer documented history of Canadian banking investments in the English-speaking Caribbean, where broader state and global events have always challenged their power in their region or impacted Canadian investments there. As such, the resistance of the late 1970s in the region to Canadian power and finance would see immense pushback in the1980s as more states in the region gained independence, given the efforts of the U.S. and IFIs – often in direct consultation with Canadian banks – to re-assert Western foreign interests in the Caribbean through the creation of a new financial architecture. More aptly put, Canadian banks were tied into the politics of structural adjustment on states in the region, having been identified as already having high interests in the region given their history with states there.

Canadian banks were able to use the dynamics of the debt crisis to continue expanding throughout the Caribbean during the beginning half of the 1980s. Crucial to these banks' success was the increasing power of finance and the compatibility of corporate profit motives with IFI structural adjustment packages – which reinforced financial power and privatization over development. This change in the financial architecture, also helped Canadian banking investments in the region, as Canadian banks used their economic and political power to navigate Caribbean states integration into the U.S. and western-led capitalist system. Entering the 2000s, Canadian banking strength and dominance in the region is borne from this context of global (neoliberal) restructuring and the developing country crisis which preceded it. This chapter places emphasis on Canadian agency, versus Canada as a lapdog of imperialism, in the facilitation of Canadian expansion in the English-speaking Caribbean from the 20th century to the beginning of the 21st century.

If one were to do an updated analysis on Canadian banks in the Caribbean for the post-2008 period, one would witness a further decade of strength and growth given continued parasitic activities (mostly in the realm of online forms of banking and fees) in the aftermath of the Global Financial Crisis; and that from late 2018-early 2022, that Canadian banks have sought to decrease their interests in the Caribbean region – blindsiding many governments there, some who have stood up to these banks and not allowed them to sell off interests and simply leave – given declines in tourism, the COVID-19 crisis, and broader budgetary concerns where the IMF has been involved. The picture is one that includes the broader context of exploitation: global capital accumulation, economic stagnation, profit maximization, and structural adjustments.

References

Aberdeen, Michael (1986) *Grenada under the P.R.G: the Real Reason for the U.S. Military Invasion and Figures.* PPM.

Alleyne, Antonio, and Kimberly Waithe (2011) "Financial Development and Market Structure." In Conference Paper, 43rd Annual Monetary Studies Conferene on Financial Architecture and Economic Prospects Beyond the Crisis in the Caribbean. Bridgetown, Barbados: University of West Indies, Cavehill.

Ambursley, Fitzroy (1985) "The Grenadian Revolution, 1979–1983: the Political Economy of an Attempt at Revolutionary Transformation in a Caribbean Mini-State." *Doctor of Philosophy in Sociology*, West Midlands: University of Warwick. http://wrap.warwick.ac.uk/108795/1/WRAP_Theses_Ambursley_1985.pdf.

Basdeo, Sahadeo (1992) "Caribcan: a Continuum in Canada-CARICOM Economic Relations." *Institute of Caribbean Studies*, Caribbean Studies, 25 (3/4): 189–220.

Baum, Daniel (1974) *The Banks of Canada in the Commonwealth Caribbean, Economic Nationalism and Multinational Enterprises of a Medium Power.* iUniverse, Inc.

"Bishop Speech – In Nobody's Backyard." 1979. *Radio Free Grenada*. Radio Free Grenada. https://www.thegrenadarevolutiononline.com/bishnobodybkyd.html.

Bloomfield, Chelsy (2020) "Justifying the 1983 Invasion of Grenada With Comics for Kids?" *Bleeding Cool*, November 1, https://bleedingcool.com/comics/justifying-the-1983 invasion-of-grenada-with-comics-for-kids/.

Boodhoo, Ken I. (1985) "Revolutionary Grenada and the United States (Dialogue #48)," LACC Occasional Papers Series Dialogues (1980–1994), 1–69.

Brown, Stephen, Molly den Heyer, and David R. Black, eds. (2014) *Rethinking Canadian Aid*. Ontario: University of Ottawa Press.

Canadian Department of Finance (2002) "The Canadian Financial Services Sector." Department of Finance. www.fin.gc.ca.

Canterbury, Dennis (2016) "Neoliberal Financialization: the 'New' Imperial Monetary and Financial Arrangements in the Caribbean." *The CLR James Journal*, Clive Y. Thomas, 22 (1/2): 113–50.

Caribbean Development and Cooperation (2001) *"The Impact of Privatisation on the Banking Sector in the Caribbean." 2001*. Subregional Headquarters for the Caribbean: Economic Commission for Latin America and the Caribbean (ECLAC).

Chaitoo, Ramesh (2013) "Time to Rethink and Re-Energize Canada-CARICOM Relations." *Caribbean Journal of International Relations and Diplomacy* 1 (1): 39–67.

Chomsky, Noam (1992) "The Invasion of Panama: Excerpted from 'What Uncle Sam Really Wants.'" 1992. https://chomsky.info/unclesam06/.

Clark, Steve (1987) *The Second Assassination of Maurice Bishop*. New International, 6, 13–154.

Clarke, Laurence, and Donna Danns, eds. (1997) *The Financial Evolution of the Caribbean Community (1970–1996)*. University of the West Indies, St. Augustine Republic of Trinidad and Tobago: Caribbean Centre for Monetary Studies.

Coard, Bernard (2017) *The Grenada Revolution: what Really Happened?* Birmingham, UK: McDermott Publishing.

Critchley, Barry (2018) "Twenty Years of Bank Success Show Folly of Mega-Merger." *Financial Post*, January 23, https://business.financialpost.com/news/fp-street/twenty-years-of-bank-success-show-folly-of-mega-merger-pursuit.

Darroch, James (1994) "Appendix Two a Short History of the Bank Act and Related Events." In *Canadian Banks and Global Competitiveness*, 277–80. Montreal: McGill-Queen's University Press. https://www.jstor.org/stable/j.ctt81d4t.13.

Deneault, Alain (2015) *Canada: a New Tax Haven: How the Country That Shaped Caribbean Tax Havens Is Becoming One Itself*. Vancouver BC: Talonbooks.

Effros, Robert (1992) *Banking Secrecy: Coping with Money Laundering in the International Arena*. Washington, D.C.: International Monetary Fund. https://www.elibrary.imf.org/view/IMF071/01504-9781557751423/01504-9781557751423/ch12.xml?language=en&redirect=true.

Engler, Yves (2009) *The Black Book of Canadian Foreign Policy*. 1st ed. Halifax, NS: Fernwood Publishing Co.

Felix, David (1998) "Review of the Debt Dilemma: IMF Negotiations in Jamaica, Grenada, and Guyana, by Horace A. Bartilow." *Jounal of Interamerican Studies and World Affairs* 40 (3): 149–54.

Fischer, Beth A. (1994) "The Trudeau Peace Initiative and the End of the Cold War: Catalyst or Coincidence?" *International Journal* 49 (3): 613–34.

Forte, Maximilian C. (2013) "Thirty Years After the U.S. Invasion of Grenada, the First Neoliberal War." *Zero Anthropology*, October 28, 2013. zeroanthropology.net/2013/10/28/thirty-years-after-the-u-s-invasion-of-grenada-the-first-neoliberal-war/.

Francis, Carlene (1985) "The Offshore Banking Sector in the Bahamas." *Social and Economic Studies*, Memory of Dr. Adlith Brown. Coordinator, Regional Programme of Monetary Studies 1980–1984, 34 (4): 91–110.

Freedman, Charles (1998) "The Canadian Banking System*." In, 38. *The Jerome Levy Economics Institute of Bard College: Bank of Canada.*

Garrod, Joel Zackary (2018) *From the National to the Global; The Transformation of the Royal Bank of Canada, 1864–2014*. Dissertation, Ottawa, Ontario: Carleton University.

Gordon, Todd, and Jeffery Webber (2016) *Blood of Extraction Canadian Imperialism in Latin America*. Halifax, NS: Fernwood Publishing.

Grenade, Wendy C. (2010) "A View from Richmond Hill Prison: an Interview with Bernard Coard." *Journal of Eastern Caribbean Studies* 35 (3 & 4): 145–82.

Haar, Jerry, and Anthony Bryan, eds. (1999) *Canadian-Caribbean Relations in Transition: Trade, Sustainable Development and Security*. International Political Economy. New York: Macmillan Press LTD.

Hudson, Peter (2010) "Imperial Designs: the Royal Bank of Canada in the Caribbean." *Race and Class* 52: 33–48. https://doi.org/10.1177/0306396810371762.

Juan-Ramón, V. Hugo, Ruby Randall, and Oral Williams (2001) "A Statistical Analysis of Banking Performance in the Eastern Caribbean Currency Union in the 1990s." *IMF Working Papers*, 42, Washington, DC: IMF.

Kaufman, Michael (1985) "The Internationalization of Canadian Bank Capital (With a Look at Bank Activity in the Caribbean and Central America)." *Journal of Canadian Studies* 19 (4): 61–81.

Khan, Glenn A. (2001) *Caribbean Mergers and Acquisitions: Country Studies of the Financial Sectors of Guyana, Jamaica and Trinidad and Tobago*. St. Augustine, Trinidad: Caribbean Centre for Monetary Studies. https://cert-net.com/files/publications/monograph_book/CaribbeanMergersandAcquisitions.pdf.

King, Michael R. (2001) *Distributional Politics and Central Bank Independence: Monetary Reform in the United Kingdom, Canada, Australia and New Zealand*. Dissertation, London: University of London.

Kirton, Claremont D. (1989) "Development Planning in the Grenada Revolution: Applying AFROSIBER." *Social and Economic Studies* 38 (3): 1–52.

Klak, Thomas (1998) *Globalization and Neoliberalism: the Caribbean Context*. New York: Rowman & Littlefield International.

Létourneau, Hugues, and Pablo Heidrich (2010) "Canadian Banks Abroad: Expansion and Exposure to the 2008–2009 Finanial Crisis." Global Financial Markets and Regulations. Sunrise, Fl: The North-South Institute.

Malminen, Johannes (1997) "Canadian Policy Toward Foreign Direct Investment in an Age of Globalization." Master of Arts in Political Science, Vancouver, Canada: The University of British Columbia.

Maloney, S. M. (1988) "Maple Leaf Over the Caribbean: Gunboat Diplomacy Canadian Style?" In *Canadian Gunboat Diplomacy: The Canadian Navy and Foreign Policy*, 147–183. Centre for Foreign Policy Studies, Dalhousie University.

McDowall, Duncan (1993) *Quick to the Frontier: Canada's Royal Bank*. Toronto: McClelland & Stewart.

Melville, Juliet A. (2003) "The Impact of Structural Adjustment on the Poor." In *Eastern Caribbean Central Bank 7th Annual Development Conference Basseterre*, 1–12. Caribbean Development Bank.

Meyer, Stephen Paul (1995) "Canada's Multinationals: a Study in Outward Foreign Direct Investment." Dissertation, Ontario: The University of Western Ontario. https://ir.lib.uwo.ca/digitizedtheses/2478.

Momsen, Janet H. (1992) "Canada-Caribbean Relations: Wherein the Special Relationship?" *Political Geography* 11 (5): 501–13.

Moseley, Fred (1990) "The Decline of the Rate of Profit in the Postwar Economy: a Comment on Brenner." http://www.mtholyoke.edu/~fmoseley/HM.html.

Niddrie, David A., and Richard Tolson (2019) "Saint Vincent and the Grenadines." In *Encyclopædia Britannica*. Encyclopædia Britannica, inc.

Noble, John J. (2003) "Getting the Eagle's Attention without Tweaking Its Beak." In Policy Options Politiques: 40 Years of Shaping the Debate. https://policyoptions.irpp.org/magazines/canada-us-relations/getting-the-eagles-attention-without-tweaking-its-beak/.

Nossal, Kim Richard, Stéphane Roussel, and Stéphane Paquin (2015) *The Politics of Canadian Foreign Policy*. 4th ed. McGill-Queen's Press.

Ogawa, Sumiko, Joonkyu Park, Diva Singh, and Nita Thacker (2013) "Financial Interconnectedness and Financial Sector Reforms in the Caribbean." *IMF Working Papers* 13 (175): 1. https://doi.org/10.5089/9781484307830.001.

Owen, Barbara J., and Andrea W. Rhodin (1977) *Planning for Worldwide Economic Stability*. Washington, DC: IMF: 6–9.

Paxton, J. (2016) *The Stateman's Year-Book 1980–1981*. New York: Springer Press.

Phillips, Daphne (1993) "The IMF, Structural Adjustment and Health in the Caribbean: a Comparison with Brazil." In, 33. Kingston & Ocho Rios, Jamaica: The University of the West Indies. https://ufdcimages.uflib.ufl.edu/CA/00/40/01/44/00001/PDF.pdf.

Phillips, Dion (2002) "The Defunct Dominica Defense Force and Two Attempted Coups on the Nature Island." *Institute of Caribbean Studies, UPR, Rio Piedras*, Caribbean Studies, 30 (1): 52–81.

Posner, Michael (1983) "An Autopsy of an Invasion." *Macleans*, November 14, 1983. https://archive.macleans.ca/article/1983/11/14/an-autopsy-of-an-invasion

Ramsaran, Ramesh (1992) *The Challenge of Structural Adjustment in the Commonwealth Caribbean.* New York: Praeger.

Roos, Jerome (2019) *Why Not Default? the Political Economy of Sovereign Debt.* Princeton and Oxford: Princeton University Press.

Scott, Helen (2006) *Caribbean Women Writers and Globalization: Fictions of Independence.* Farnham, UK: Ashgate Publishing Limited.

Searle, Chris (1984) *Grenada: the Struggle Against Destabilization.* London: Writers and Readers Pub.

Simmonds, Keith (1987) "Political and Economic Factors Influencing the St. Kitts-Nevis Polity: an Historical Perspective." *Phylon: Clark Atlanta University* 48 (4): 277–86.

Stabroek News (2016) "Guyana Now Ranked below Haiti," 2016, *Stabroek News'* ongoing observances to mark its 30th Anniversary edition. www.stabroeknews.com/2016/features/30-years-of-stabroek-news/12/02/guyana-now-ranked-haiti/.

Swift, Jamie, and Brian Tomlinson (1991) "The Debt Crisis: a Case of Global Usary." In *Conflicts of Interest: Canada and the Third World.* Between the Lines. "The Canadian Financial Services Sector." 2002. Department of Finance. www.fin.gc.ca.

The New York Times (1983) "The International Scene Has Renewed Allure for Trudeau," November 6, 1983, sec. 4.

Treaster, Joseph B. (1985) "Grenadians Report Signs of an Economic Revival." *The New York Times*, March 27, sec. World. https://www.nytimes.com/1985/03/27/world/grenadians-report-signs-of-an-economic-revival.html.

Watson, Hilbourne A. (2016) "Democracy without Social Content and Capital Accumulation versus Development: Barbados in Crisis." In *Contradictory Existence: Neoliberalism and Democracy in the Caribbean*, ed. Dave Ramsaran, 35–67. Kingston, Jamaica: Ian Randle Publishers.

Williams, Marion (1989) "Regulation of Financial Institutions in the Caribbean: Implications for Growth and Development." *Social and Economic Studies* 38 (4): 181–99.

Wood, Anthony, and Trevor Wood (2013) "Emera's Takeover of Light and Power Holdings LTD: a Case Study in Corporate Governance and Takeovers in the Caribbean." *International Journal of Arts and Commerce* 2 (1): 27–48.

Worrell, Delisle (1997) "Bank Behaviour and Monetary Policy in Small Open Economies with Reference to the Caribbean." *Social and Economic Studies*, Special Monetary Studies Issue, 46 (2/3): 59–74.

Worrell, D., Cherebin, D., & Polius-Mounsey, T (2001). "Financial System Soundness in the Caribbean: An Initial Assessment." *International Monetary Fund*, IMF Working Papers, 37.

CHAPTER 7

Corporate Power and the Transition from Lomé to the CARIFORUM-EU EPA

Melissa Boissiere

1   Introduction[1]

A group of scholars has argued that the interests of transnational corporations (TNCs) have shaped the contents of preferential trade agreements in the era of neoliberal capitalism (1980-present). In this analysis, corporate power is thought to be deeply embedded in the structure, agenda and content of these agreements. This conceptualization of corporate power is often theorized as "transnational corporate power" where the accumulation of profits is enabled by the support, cooperation and assistance of those political and economic elites that derive benefits from trade and investment agreements ostensibly negotiated by nation-states. This perspective is often absent in state-centric analyses of preferential trade agreements in the neoliberal era, notwithstanding the centrality of state actors in the negotiation of these agreements.

Transnational corporate power has been the driving force behind neoliberal capitalism / capitalist globalization and has significantly influenced the progressive neoliberalization of Lomé era agreements between Europe and African, Caribbean and Pacific (ACP) states. It has also spurred the transition to a post-Lomé era of reciprocal neoliberal trade agreements. This chapter demonstrates the connection between corporate power and the neoliberalization of Lomé. In addition, it shows that the Cotonou Agreement of 2000 which marked the transition to a post-Lomé era, and the Economic Partnership Agreement (EPA) between the Caribbean Forum of ACP states (CARIFORUM) and the European Union (EU) of 2008, were both consistent with the pattern of transnational corporate pursuits. The investigation of these linkages in the context of EU-ACP and, even more specifically, EU-Caribbean relations, remains undertheorized. This study is also fundamental for understanding the role of corporate power, whether directly or structurally, in constraining the

---

1   This chapter is a revised and expanded version of Melissa Boissiere, "Transnational Corporate Power: From Lomé to the CARIFORUM-EU EPA," *Class, Race and Corporate Power*, Vol. 10 (1): Article 1.

already limited policy space in small, open, dependent, and vulnerable economies such as those in the Caribbean.

In the early postwar period, TNCs were primarily concerned with gaining access to foreign markets protected by high tariffs. Foreign Direct Investment (FDI) was an important strategy in achieving that objective. By the late 1960s, however, increasing international competition and rising wages led to declining corporate profits which provoked a change in the motivation for and nature of FDI. In response, production processes were internationalized – TNCs began to relocate simpler parts of production processes to low-wage developing countries. A defining feature of the latest phase of capitalist globalization from the 1980s had been the fundamental restructuring of these processes into ever smaller segments, with the location of various stages across multiple countries, creating cross-border production networks or global value chains. A marked increase in cross-border mergers and acquisitions allowed firms to reduce competition and control costs, and consolidated corporate market and economic power. Neoliberal trade and economic policies, advocated by TNCs in collaboration with political and other actors in dominant states, facilitated this era of capitalist expansion and profit.

The Lomé conventions – Lomé I (1975–1980), Lomé II (1980–1985), Lomé III (1985–1990) and Lomé IV (1990–2000, including Lomé IV bis from 1995–2000) – constituted the framework for trade and economic relations between the European Economic Community (EEC)[2] and ACP states. These agreements, based on preferential trade and accompanied by European aid, allowed for products originating in ACP states – mainly agricultural products, as well as manufactures and semi-manufactures – to enter the EEC market without the imposition of customs duties and quantitative restrictions. ACP goods that competed with those protected by the EEC's Common Agricultural Policy (CAP) were given more favorable treatment than that accorded to other states exporting the same products. Under the Lomé arrangement, there was no requirement for reciprocal preferential treatment for EEC members.

In parallel with developments within Europe and at the global level, later Lomé agreements increasingly contained provisions that reflected neoliberal trade and economic policies advocated by transnational corporations in collaboration with political and other actors in dominant states. Lomé-era agreements, however, stopped short of the dramatic shift that occurred at the turn of the twenty-first century with the transition to a post-Lomé framework

---

2 In Lomé IV bis, contracting parties that were Western European were referenced collectively as the European Community as opposed to the European Economic Community which was the terminology contained in earlier iterations of the Convention.

for engagement between the EU and ACP states. To explain the evolution of Lomé and its contrast with the post-Lomé era, I first outline below the main elements of the Lomé accords. Second, I discuss the rise of transnational corporate power in Europe and the link between the latter and the progressive neoliberalization of Lomé. Lastly, I analyze the connection between transnational corporate power and the post-Lomé framework for EU-ACP / EU-Caribbean engagement, specifically the Cotonou Agreement of 2000 and the CARIFORUM-EU EPA of 2008.

2 The Lomé Conventions

Some of the most salient features of the Lomé agreements were the special commodity protocols on sugar, bananas, rum, and beef/veal, and the compensation mechanisms established with the aim of stabilizing the export earnings of ACP states dependent on certain agricultural and mineral exports. The commodity protocols secured the EEC's purchase of certain quantities of these products at guaranteed prices that were usually above world market prices. Taking into account ACP dependence on the export of mainly primary commodities and their vulnerability to fluctuations in earnings due to world market price volatility or shortfalls in quantities available for export, Lomé also established systems to provide for compensation in this regard.

The system commonly referred to as STABEX, established in Lomé I, guaranteed "the stabilization of earnings from exports by ACP states to the Community of certain products on which their countries [were] dependent and which [were] affected by fluctuations in price and/or quantity" (Article 16). The products covered by this scheme were mainly agricultural with the exception of one mineral product – iron ore. Similarly, Lomé II, under a separate and new title, established a system to assist ACP states dependent on mining sectors to "cope with a decline in their capacity to export mining products to the Community and the corresponding decline in their export earnings" in order to "remedy the harmful effects on their income of serious disruptions affecting those mining sectors and beyond the control of the ACP states concerned" (Article 49).

Nine mineral products in total were eligible for compensation under this scheme. This "special financing facility" for mining products was assigned the acronym SYSMIN in Lomé III and is also referred to by some as MINEX. In addition, the Lomé conventions provided for industrial cooperation as well as cooperation in other sectors, such as transport and communication, energy and agriculture, with the aim of facilitating ACP development. ACP states were also treated as one unit with regard to defining the origin of an export product (Dolan 1978, 373). Moreover, in every iteration of the Convention, the European Development Fund (EDF) made available certain quantities of aid for the purpose of supporting social and economic development in ACP states, including projects aimed at economic diversification, as well as to finance the systems for the stabilization of export earnings.

The literature on the Lomé conventions is extensive and includes a range of views. The perspectives on the first Lomé Convention, in particular, "have varied from extremes of approbation to extremes of condemnation" (Parfitt 1981, 89). Lomé I was hailed by some as revolutionary, as representative of the New International Economic Order (NIEO),[3] and as a model for North-South relations (Dolan 1978, 369). By Lomé II, however, which did not differ greatly from Lomé I, "the flaws of the existing regime had become obvious" resulting in "much greater consensus among observers that Lomé 2 had fallen short of expectations than there had been over Lomé 1" (Parfitt 1981, 92).

A closer and critical examination of Lomé revealed that certain provisions such as those on trade "initially seemed more generous than they actually were" (Parfitt 1981, 92). Michael Dolan (1978) explains that laudatory views of Lomé I were understandable if comparing the latter to previous agreements such as the Yaoundé Conventions of 1963 and 1969 and the Arusha Convention of 1969 (371). In this light, the Lomé Convention appeared to have addressed the major criticisms of those previous agreements, and to have met many of the demands of ACP states (Dolan 1978, 371).

Several significant shortcomings became apparent, however, upon deeper examination (Dolan 1978, 369). These were particularly evident in the provisions on trade and aid which provoked many critical scholars to view the Convention as an instrument that institutionalized the traditional capitalist division of labor and the underdevelopment and dependency of ACP states. Timothy Shaw (1979), for example, contends that Lomé's primary purpose was to facilitate trade and other economic exchanges between the EEC and ACP states, but that "because of the international division of labour that the

---

3   As described by the United Nations Economic and Social Commission for Western Asia (UNESCWA) (2020), the New International Economic Order (NIEO) "was a set of proposals put forward during the 1970s by some developing countries through the United Nations Conference on Trade and Development to promote their interests by improving their terms of trade, increasing development assistance, developed-country tariff reductions, and other means. It was meant to be a revision of the international economic system in favour of Third World countries, replacing the Bretton Woods system, which had benefited the leading states that had created it – especially the United States".

states and corporations of Europe designed and established during the colonial period any increase in exchange [meant] more of Africa's raw materials being traded for more of Europe's manufactured goods" (142). Although Shaw's analysis focused on Lomé as it related to African states, this assessment was also quite applicable to the Caribbean.

Kojo Yelpaala (1981) explains, additionally, that the possibilities for trade expansion were relatively small for a few reasons, and that the preferential treatment of agricultural products was of little benefit to ACP states.[4] Yelpaala clarifies that due to the characteristics of ACP products (a substantial portion being agricultural raw materials), as well as a higher market demand concentration, the EEC import demand schedule was relatively inelastic. This meant that any fall in prices would not result in a considerable increase in the quantities purchased. Furthermore, transnational corporations with substantial market power likely manipulated both the prices of these products and the quantities purchased. United Nations studies also found that transnational corporations were working to reduce their dependency on ACP raw materials as well as to diversify their operations (830–831).

Yelpaala (1981) argues further that the already "meagre trade expansion effects" and preferential treatment of agricultural products in the form of duty-free entry were even more greatly reduced by the increase in the number of beneficiaries of the Lomé Convention compared to previous Yaoundé agreements. Under Lomé, ACP countries that produced and sold similar products came into competition within the same preferential regime, limiting the possibilities for capturing greater market shares. Similar products from non-ACP states also enjoyed preferential access to EEC markets under the latter's Generalised Scheme of Preferences (GSP), and some benefits of Lomé were duplicated under the latter, as well as by the GATT's Most-Favored-Nation (MFN) arrangement. Both the GSP and the MFN arrangement allowed some products included in Lomé to enter the EEC duty-free. Given that an estimated 75% of ACP exports were raw materials, they could enter the EEC duty-free under MFN treatment. Correspondingly, approximately 95% of ACP manufactures could enter the EEC duty free under either the GSP or MFN treatment.

---

4 Most Caribbean ACP states at the time, however, were heavily dependent on the benefits of the special commodity protocols such as those on bananas and sugar, given Europe's purchase of guaranteed quotas at fixed prices usually above world market prices. These agricultural products were longstanding traditional Caribbean exports to Europe, the industries, consequently, being important sources of employment, contributors to GDP and earners of foreign exchange (Ahmed 2001, Richardson-Ngwenya 2010).

Yelpaala consequently concludes that the net product coverage under Lomé, as well as the benefits, were less than they appeared to be (831–832).

Additional factors also reduced the ability of ACP states to benefit from the preferential treatment of their manufactures. These included the characteristics of ACP manufacturing sectors, as well as limitations of the rules of origin provisions and the safeguard clause in the Lomé agreement. Nearly all ACP states in which there were manufacturing sectors were at an early stage of industrialization, a sizeable portion of their industry involving the assembly and packaging of component parts from developed countries (Asante 1981, 665; Dolan 1978, 373). The rules of origin provisions which specified a minimum of 50% value to be added in ACP states to qualify for duty-free entry to EEC markets, disqualified most ACP manufactures from benefiting from this opportunity given that they were usually unable to meet this requirement (Asante 1981, 665–667).

While ACP manufactures did not significantly benefit from Lomé provisions, the rules of origin, as well as the classification of the ACP group of states as a single customs unit, *did* benefit EEC multinationals wishing to establish industries in ACP states. This was particularly so if component parts were obtained from EEC states, given that materials from both the Community and ACP states were considered to be originating products (Asante 1981, 665).

The schemes created to stabilize export earnings of ACP states in the event of shortfalls in earnings from agricultural and mineral exports, STABEX and SYSMIN, respectively, also came under criticism. Funding allocated for each, for example, was considered to be greatly insufficient for their purposes, making it unlikely that the resources available could adequately respond to shortfalls in the earnings of ACP states due to fluctuations in the prices or quantities of ACP primary commodity exports. Each was also criticized for their limited product coverage, which some scholars viewed as discriminatory against countries that did not export the commodities covered by the schemes (Asante 1981, 667).

In the case of SYSMIN, for instance, ACP states were only eligible for compensation if earnings fell short of the specified average with respect to the 9 minerals covered by the scheme. Notably, these 9 minerals were of utmost important to the EEC. The ACP's demand that the list of products covered by SYSMIN include 8 additional minerals of great significance to their own economies, was rejected. The list could be extended but this decision was entirely up to the EEC. Moreover, SYSMIN would not benefit countries that did not export to EEC markets the minerals covered by it (Rajana 1980, 94–95).

STABEX and SYSMIN, moreover, were seen to disincentivize export expansion and diversification. In this context, Lynn Mytelka (1977) explains that STABEX did not attempt to stabilize the price of commodities, but rather merely compensated for shortfalls in export earnings of the listed commodities (cited in Asante 1981, 668). As Dolan (1978) notes, by providing "a minimum, and almost static, price support level", the terms of STABEX implied that "the EEC support[ed] the present levels of agricultural exports, but ... will not support ACP growth in the agricultural sector" (375).

In addition, ACP states eligible for financial transfers may be denied compensation if the European Commission ruled that the reduction in export earnings was the result of a policy that discriminated against the EEC, such as a trade policy that increased domestic processing of commodities and decreased the quantity available for export in its raw state. This circumstance led various scholars to conclude that "STABEX in effect penalize[d] efficiency", and that by "penalizing domestic production, STABEX tend[ed] to support the ACP states' function of supplying raw materials, hindering policies which would lead towards increased industrialization and development" (Dolan 1978, 376). Similarly, Asante (1981) contends that these limitations of STABEX disincentivized diversification of ACP export markets, as well as diversification away from specific exports, which discouraged domestic industry and consumption (668).

The safeguard clause in the Lomé agreements, furthermore, reinforced the circumstances identified above. The safeguard allowed for the prohibition of duty-free access to European markets if imports receiving preferential treatment threatened to disturb a sector of the European economy. A commonly referenced example was the EEC's expression of intent to use the clause to limit textile imports from ACP states in accordance with the Multifibre Arrangement. In this connection, Parfitt (1981) expresses the view that the actions of the EEC violated the "spirit of trade liberalization in which the Convention [was] supposed to have been concluded" and "put a brake on the expansion of one the ACP's few dynamic export-oriented industries" (90).

In addition to the critiques identified above, aid accompanying the Lomé regime was often viewed as insufficient to respond to the most urgent needs of ACP states and slow to be disbursed. Funds were disbursed on the basis of decisions made solely by the EEC and not necessarily in partnership with ACP states as the Convention purported to promote. In addition, commitments were concentrated on capital-intensive industries aimed at the export of raw materials. Aid thus also appeared to facilitate a continuity in the conceptualization of financial and technical corporation, leaving ACP states no less vulnerable to unstable market prices (Asante 1981, 667).

The rhetoric of the Lomé agreements generally promoted equality, partnership, and cooperation between the two blocs that were parties to them, as well as the development needs of ACP states. Other provisions of the same agreements, however, undermined and inhibited the achievement of exactly these principles and objectives. There was some disconnect between the rhetoric of the Lomé conventions and the reality of their contribution to advancing ACP development. While the Lomé regime indeed accorded non-reciprocal preferential treatment to ACP states and provided aid for various projects through the EDF, the circumstances of ACP states remained largely unchanged throughout its duration. In fact, the terms of trade between the EEC and the ACP steadily declined over the course of the 25 years of Lomé.

Some scholars have expressed the view that the terms of trade between the EEC and ACP states may have been worse without the preferential treatment afforded to the latter under the Lomé regime, that EDF aid provided necessary funding to various ACP states for a range of purposes, and that there were successes in which some non-traditional ACP exports benefited from the Lomé agreements. The non-traditional exports that experienced some successes were mainly cases in which ACP states enjoyed a preferential advantage in the EEC linked to the CAP, or due to other restrictions on competing exports from non-ACP developing states (Cosgrove 1994, 228–229).

Nevertheless, there was a general consensus that the circumstances of ACP states did not meaningfully improve in spite of the Lomé regime. The terms of trade between the EEC and the ACP had, on the contrary, steadily declined. Later assessments of the Lomé regime essentially confirmed this conclusion made by numerous earlier analyses. Many of the critiques were, for example, confirmed in Carol Cosgrove's (1994)[5] examination of the record of ACP exports to the European Community, and the problems associated with ACP trade performance in that market.

More recent data referred to in Cosgrove's (1994) piece, showed that the value of duty-free access to the EEC market was still not of great significance to ACP states almost twenty years later, since approximately two-thirds of ACP exports could enter the EEC market duty-free in any event under the GSP or MFN arrangement. Cosgrove (1994) also demonstrates that the ACP share of

---

5   The data presented in Cosgrove's (1994) analysis is widely referenced and useful in so far as it allows for an important comparison of the implications of Lomé from 1975 to the early 1990s. A number of her comments, as well as her final conclusion that ACP states should help themselves instead of seeking assistance externally, were however, contradictory to the evidence she presents in her piece. Her assessment of the opportunities available to ACP states and recommendations regarding action that they should take disregard the external factors that have prevented their ability to pursue policies that could have advanced their development, including those mentioned by scholars that have critiqued the Lomé agreements. There is no doubt that ACP states must be responsible for their advancement, but those efforts must also be supported by a facilitative international environment.

the EEC import market "declined fairly steadily" since 1975 in comparison to exports from other developing countries and that, in the 1990s, ACP exports were still dominated by a small group of primary commodity exports which accounted for 54% of ACP exports in 1992 (225).[6] Furthermore, although 27% of ACP exports in the same year were classified as processed or manufactured, this represented an increase of only 7% from 1976 to 1992 (Cosgrove 1994, 227).

In addition to several new factors such as the constraints of Structural Adjustment Programs (SAPs), a 1993 report confirmed that the Lomé rules of origin and the CAP prevented ACP states from most effectively utilizing the latest iteration of Lomé's trade provisions, contained in Lomé IV (Cosgrove 1994, 237). Moreover, Cosgrove's (1994) examination of the problems associated with ACP export performance revealed that various objectives of the Lomé regime aimed at building the capacity of ACP states to expand or diversify their export sectors, industrialize, acquire appropriate technology, develop or improve products, and enhance transportation, communication, distribution or competitiveness, were generally not successfully achieved.

3   Transnational Corporate Power in Europe, the Uruguay Round, and Lomé

Lomé agreements evolved against the backdrop of capitalist globalization, increasing transnational corporate power, the influence of the latter in propelling the shift to a neoliberal economic order, a debt crisis that adversely affected the global south, and the decreasing importance of ACP states for Europe, notwithstanding European interest in deeper liberalization of ACP markets in keeping with the contemporary movements in this direction. A closer examination of successive Lomé agreements revealed evidence of the impact of these factors on their evolving provisions. It is first, however, important to understand the rise of transnational corporate power in Europe given its central role in the continued deepening of European integration and the EU's promotion of economic globalization, in order to appreciate the transformation of Europe-ACP relations.

The European Round Table of Industrialists (ERT) (now called the European Round Table for Industry, abbreviated identically), created in 1983, is one demonstrative manifestation of the rise of transnational corporate power in

---

6   Cosgrove (1994) identified 7 primary commodities that dominated ACP exports: crude petroleum, uncut diamonds, cocoa beans, wood, coffee beans, copper, and fruit (especially bananas) (227).

Europe and its influence on the progressive neoliberalization of policy therein. Corporate lobbying and a commingling of economic and political interests, underpinned by the increasing predominance of neoliberal ideology, began in individual states such as the U.S. in the 1970s. Even within Europe by the late 1970s, British Prime Minister Margaret Thatcher is hailed alongside U.S. President Ronald Reagan, as leading the shift at the political level from a Keynesian approach to economic policy to a new neoliberal economic order.

By the early 1980s, the inability of policymakers to respond to the high inflation, growing unemployment and declining growth which characterized Europe in the 1970s, prompted the then CEO of Swedish car manufacturer Volvo, to embark on a campaign to encourage growth as well as the development of industry and infrastructure in Europe. Supported by the CEOs of other large European corporations and the then European Commissioner of Industry, the ERT was formed, modeled on the Business Roundtable established a decade earlier in the United States. In the beginning, the ERT was split between corporations favoring protectionist policies and those favoring free trade globally. Ultimately, the interests of the latter became the ERT's unanimous objective (Balanyá et al., 2003, 20, 21, 24). Comprising 17 members at its outset, the ERT today "includes CEOs and Chairs from around 60 of Europe's largest companies in the industrial and technological sector" (European Round Table for Industry 2023).

Since the 1980s, several factors facilitated the increasing power and influence of transnational corporations in Europe. These included economic and political alliances between big business and the European Commission, the organization of European decision-making, an explosion of mergers and acquisitions that resulted in a concentration of corporate power, and the growing establishment of corporate lobbies and corporate-funded think-tanks. The latter became instrumental in propelling developments within and outside of Europe that aligned with transnational corporate interests. The relationship between the European Commission and big business, for example, changed from a more critical approach in the 1970s to one that steadily morphed into "the current virtual symbiosis between the EU's key political and economic actors" (Balanyá et al. 2003, 4).

Specifically, in the 1980s, the Commission began to actively engage industry and encouraged the involvement of large corporations in Brussels. Links between business and politics, of course, weren't new and were already well-established at national levels. A critical element in the ERT's lobbying success, however, was its "access to the Brussels bureaucracy". In this period, it was also the European Commission that enthusiastically encouraged the wave of corporate mergers that resulted in corporate concentration. These further facilitated the "disproportionate bargaining powers held by TNCs, and thereby their corporate dominance in political decision-making" (Balanyá et al. 2003, 4, 7, 8, 10, 20).

Post-war recovery in major economies resulted in increasing global competition, enabled by unprecedented technological advancements that facilitated the globalization of production processes. These also occurred alongside various crises and declining economic growth, as well as declining profits for large corporations. Efforts to cut costs and maximize profits in the context of being globally competitive became the focus of large corporations, and united big business and politics in various core economies, including several in Europe, as well as at the regional level in Brussels.

While the "explicit goal" of the European Commission's industrial policy of the 1980s was to ensure that large European firms could become "European champions" that could easily contend with U.S. and Japanese competitors, increasing "European industrial competitiveness within the global economy ha[d] always been the ERT's main objective". In this context, the ERT was created with "the express intention of reviving the unification process and shaping it to the preferences of European corporations". Joined in their objectives, the ERT played a major "agenda-setting role" at the regional level in Brussels, "pushing for deregulation, liberalization and other measures to increase the international competitiveness of European industry". These policies were beneficial to transnational corporations as they gained from economies of scale which allowed them to "centralise and automate production, and relocate to regions with lower wages and more relaxed regulations" (Balanyá et al. 2003, 5, 9, 20, 26).

The ERT's distinctive role in the shift in European policy direction to favor big business and economic globalization was most visible in the late 1980s and early 1990s. The ERT, for example, strongly supported the creation of the Single European Market, Trans-European Networks (TENS) for improved inter-European transport, and the 1992 Maastricht Treaty which established the foundation for European Monetary Union. Following the achievement of these objectives, the ERT "focused on the mainstreaming of complementary policies encouraging competitiveness, public policy benchmarking", and "its new buzzword" at the time, "innovation". With the end of the Cold War, the ERT also launched a vigorous lobby in support of EU enlargement into Central and Eastern Europe given the attractiveness of these new markets for neoliberal capitalist expansion (Balanyá et al. 2003, 19, 26).

The process behind the creation of the Single European Act (SEA) in 1986, which formed the legal basis for the Single European Market, provides a more detailed example of the ERT's central influence. It also demonstrates the monopoly held by transnational corporate interests in the direction of policy in Europe. Research uncovered that although the European Commission sought to further efforts to remove trade barriers within the Community with proposals it put forward since 1984, "pressure from industrial leaders for the unification of European markets" was a decisive factor in pushing forward the process. Jacques Delors, then President of the European Commission, and Lord Cockfield, then European Commissioner, were two of the personalities credited with the coming into being of the SEA. Delors revealed in a 1993 television interview, however, that the ERT was one of the main forces behind the creation of the Single Market. Lord Cockfield "eventually admitted" that the White Paper he prepared, considered to be the basis of the SEA, "was influenced by the ERT's action plan" (Balanyá et al. 2003, 21–22).

ERT Chairman at the time, Wisse Dekker, of Philips, had released an ambitious proposal in 1985 which outlined a five-year plan "to remove barriers, harmonise regulations and abolish fiscal frontiers". A speech encouraging same made by Jacques Delors and Lord Cockfield's White Paper both bore strong resemblance to Dekker's plan. The latter was also accompanied by an intensive ERT campaign to lobby governments not initially enthusiastic about such a progressive proposal for deeper integration. The Commission, furthermore, was said to have disregarded other voices in deciding on the SEA, "including critical reports from among their own ranks", such as the conclusions of the Task Force Report that the Commission itself had ordered, given the Report's "ominous inventory of possible negative effects" of the SEA. The result was that "the ERT got its free trade zone with 340 million consumers and the Commission saw the relaunch of European integration that it desired". Once concluded, the ERT's focus became the "speedy implementation" of the agreement (Balanyá et al. 2003, 22).

The rise of transnational corporate power in Europe and the objectives their lobbies aggressively sought to accomplish mirrored the broader trend in this regard. Mergers and acquisitions, including cross-border processes, facilitated by neoliberal policies, have concentrated power in the most globally competitive firms (Balanyá et al. 2003, 7). As seen in Europe, and as was the case elsewhere, the shift to a neoliberal economic order was achieved through the actively close collaboration between big business and politics at all levels – national, regional and, as I will shortly examine more closely, international.

Large corporations, having consolidated considerable market, economic and political power, played a central role in the restructuring of the global economy since the 1970s, utilizing their influence to actively propel the shift to a neoliberal economic order characterized by the deregulation of financial markets, the privatization of public services, greater concentrations of wealth, the easing of business regulations and, consequently, reduced protections for workers and the poor. The interests of the corporations that became dominant in the neoliberal era – those in the financial and information technology sectors – were those which shaped the rules of international trade and directed the content of intergovernmental trade and investment agreements (Cox 2019, 19).

The restructuring of the global economy was supported by political and economic alliances including core capitalist states such as the U.S., those in the EU, and Japan; "transnational corporations with vested interests in expanding production and financial operations at lower costs; and elites within developing countries with close ties to transnational capital" (Cox 2019, 5). Ronald Cox (2019) has labelled these collaborative networks of actors – transnational interest blocs (10, 28).

Economic and political alliances between transnational corporations and states, as well as the active involvement of corporate lobbies in advocating the adoption of neoliberal policies, were also evident at the international level. Their close collaboration worked in a similar fashion, for example, in the Uruguay Round of GATT negotiations, which began in 1986 and concluded in 1994 with the establishment of the World Trade Organization (WTO).

Seen at the regional level in Europe, there was also a significant imbalance between the representation of transnational corporate interests and other interests, including those of civil society, at the international level. Evident during the Uruguay Round of GATT negotiations and in the subsequent operation of the WTO, big business and their lobbies benefited from unparalleled access to high-ranking political decision-makers in this setting, were selected to chair various committees charged with policy-making, and possessed unmatched resources that easily funded their vigorous lobbies as well as think tanks.

Just as TNCs played a decisive role in the direction of policy in Europe since the 1980s, the Uruguay Round embodied "many of the demands of transnational capital", and the "WTO and its international trade regime" thus represented "the most obvious international advocate and agent of the neoliberal international order" (Tabb 2004, 294, 289). William Tabb (2004) explains, for example, that "the redoubled U.S. efforts" for the Uruguay Round to begin "were the result of strenuous lobbying by U.S.-based TNCs, especially in the area of trade in services". In addition, during this Round of trade talks, "representatives from TNCs chaired and staffed all of the fifteen advisory groups set up by the U.S. administration to develop U.S. negotiating positions". For these reasons, it was not surprising "that the GATT and WTO favored transnational over national capital interests" resulting in the bias that formed the basis of the system (305, 306).

Similarly in Europe, the European Round Table of Industrialists which consisted of leading European-based TNCs such as Philips, Nestle, Bayer and Unilever, among others, also had access to the highest levels of government and their technical staff. There was, moreover, coordination of the business agenda by governments at the international level such as at more formal meetings of the World Economic Forum, as well as at gatherings such as the Transatlantic Business Dialogue. Like other main organizations, the membership of the latter comprised CEOs of the largest transnational companies (Tabb 2004, 306).

Tabb explains further that while the WTO considered civil society to be important partners and welcomed their contributions, the majority of accredited civil society organizations were business interests. One reason given for the massive street demonstrations at WTO meetings was the exclusion of trade unions and NGOs from those discussions, while business associations and individual firms were "routinely major influences in global governance". For example, at WTO Ministerial meetings in Geneva, Singapore and Seattle, the "most influential non-governmental actors were corporate lobbyist – advisers", whereas grassroots organizations that opposed the neoliberal agenda "had no direct entry to the WTO" (Tabb 2004, 305–306).

Major international financial institutions essentially forced the adoption of structural adjustment measures throughout the developing world since the debt crisis in the 1980s and 1990s, which led to the widespread implementation of free market policies. The World Trade Organization, however, "extended and standardized the neoliberal system across the global south in one fell swoop" (Hickel 2018, 177). The WTO expanded the definition of trade from the exchange of goods to include several new areas, principally the trade in services, intellectual property rights and investment measures. Additionally, it instituted a more stringent dispute resolution mechanism. These developments resulted in a strong imbalance in the new rules of international trade in favor of the most powerful transnational corporate interests tied to core capitalist states.

With the establishment of the WTO, developing countries lost much of the special treatment they succeeded in obtaining under the GATT, as well as the flexibility that the latter facilitated. Developing countries really had no choice but to accept the agreement even though such a decision was technically optional. After more than a decade of structural adjustment, their economies were even more dependent on Western markets for survival. Countries of the global south consequently subscribed, notwithstanding the fact that it represented the opposite of what they needed for meaningful and sustainable development (Hickel 2018, 177).

The impact of major factors such as capitalist globalization, increased transnational corporate power, the shift to a neoliberal economic order, and the debt crisis was seen in the evolution of the Lomé conventions. Lomé I was essentially concluded at a time in which neoliberal ideology began to come into direct conflict with Keynesian socio-economic theories. Although the global economy had been transforming in parallel, the early 1970s was characterized by the continuation of decolonization efforts, the concern of colonial powers about future relations with their colonies and former colonies, and increasing solidarity among developing countries as well as their desire to have their concerns addressed.

The year 1961, for example, saw the creation of the Non-Aligned Movement (NAM) whose members supported self-determination and, thus, were opposed to colonialism and imperialism. In 1964, the United Nations Conference on Trade and Development (UNCTAD) was established, as well as the Group of 77 (G77) at the end of UNCTAD's first session. UNCTAD became a forum utilized by the G77 to advocate a New International Economic Order that addressed the gross inequity in the contemporary system (Tabb 2004, 293).

In 1971, under the GATT, a Generalized System of Preferences (GSP) was instituted which allowed preferential treatment for goods from developing countries, thereby according special and differential treatment to developing countries within the world trading system (Tabb 2004, 293). In addition, ACP states were still important sources of primary commodities for Europe, as well as markets for European manufactured goods. The oil crisis was credited with creating the fear that the same fate could befall other commodities of importance to Europe such as sugar, uranium, coffee, and cocoa (Montana 2003, 72, 84). A combination of these factors gave ACP states the strongest bargaining position they seemed to have ever had in negotiating with Europe, notwithstanding that the final agreement was not as generous as it appeared to be.

The Lomé regime was rooted in the long history of relations between Europe and ACP states although it officially began at the end of the period of formal colonization in which certain colonial powers, such as France and later Britain, wished to maintain their imperial economic system in the post-war era (Murray-Evans 2019, 42). It was, additionally, based on an understanding of development that acknowledged that developing countries required special treatment to facilitate their advancement.

Lomé I (1975) (Publications Office of the European Union, 1975) and Lomé II (1980) (Publications Office of the European Union, 1980), which were largely similar, included some elements that were consistent with the ascendancy of neoliberal ideology. A more pronounced shift, however, was seen in later Lomé conventions. Earlier agreements, for example, did include references to liberalizing capital flows to allow foreign investments to move capital into markets with fewer restrictions (Lomé I), and to facilitating the conditions necessary to deregulate local economies in order to incentivize the profitable relocation of foreign capital (Lomé II). These initial iterations of the agreement, nonetheless, still largely reflected the understanding of international trade in the earlier postwar period which entailed the exchange of goods, securing greater market access for the latter, and reducing trade barriers such as tariffs and restrictions on quotas.

As developments progressed globally (increased capitalist competition, the globalization of production and the rise of transnational corporate power), within Europe (the rise of transnational corporate power in Europe and deepening European integration) and internationally (the Uruguay Round, and the use of the debt crisis by IFIs to enforce structural adjustment policies throughout the global south), the focus in later Lomé conventions expanded from a concentration on trade in goods (primary commodities/raw materials, and manufactured products) to a wider range of activities, including services and investment promotion and protection. The agreements, then, already began to shift from trade to trade and investment-type treaties before the post-Lomé era of drastic change. In addition, the disbursement of aid became more conditional, signaling a change in European priorities and in their approach to development (assistance).

With specific regard to services, for example, while there was a subtle change in Lomé II which makes the reference more ambiguous (Title IX), provisions on services in these earlier conventions were generally in the context of cooperation. They largely referred to remuneration for various types of professional services, and to non-discrimination against nationals, companies or firms of parties to the agreements in the provision of same. Lomé III (1985) (Publications Office of the European Union, 1985), significantly, began to prioritize the development of services in cooperation between the two parties, included services not previously mentioned such as shipping, as well as included more detailed provisions on specific services such as those related to tourism.

By Lomé IV (1990) (Publications Office of the European Union, 1992), there was an unambiguous expansion of the definition of trade to include services, linking sectors not so explicitly tied to trade in earlier conventions such as transportation, communications, and tourism. This occurred, then, even before the conclusion of the Uruguay Round. The evolution of Lomé corresponded with broader contemporary trends at the global level that sought to expand trade into new areas for capital accumulation, primarily areas of importance to transnational corporate interests.

In later Lomé conventions, there were also several additional developments that coincided with those taking place globally. For example, by Lomé III, there was emphasis on private investment (mentioned only briefly in Lomé II and not at all in Lomé I), developing the private sector (mentioned once in Lomé II and not at all in Lomé I), investment protection (not explicitly mentioned in earlier conventions at all), the market, and policies that promoted market freedom and financialization. There was, in addition, stronger language on subcontracting arrangements that facilitated the incorporation of ACP states into global value chains, even though the references reflected an early stage in the promotion of same.

By Lomé IV, moreover, aid became more conditional, just when developing countries were in the midst of a debt crisis. For example, there was an entirely new section on 'Debt and Structural Adjustment Support' reflecting European endorsement of the move by international financial institutions to attach financial assistance to the adoption of policies that supported neoliberal objectives throughout the global south. These provisions appeared alongside references to respecting the right of ACP states to determine their own development strategies and priorities. This rhetoric, which feigned respect for ACP sovereignty became almost, if not entirely, meaningless, when juxtaposed with measures to support structural adjustment since this very approach removed that right by prescribing a set of policies that must be followed in exchange for financial relief and support, usually to the detriment of sustainable development in ACP states.

There was evidence, then, of the progressive neoliberalization of Lomé-era agreements between Europe and ACP states between 1975 and 1995. These reflected developments occurring within Europe and globally that supported the interests of transnational capital such as greater liberalization and trade expansion, deregulation, privatization, and investment protection. Although there was movement in this direction, however, the Lomé conventions stopped short of the dramatic changes that occurred in the post-Lomé framework for engagement between Europe and ACP states.

4 Corporate Power and the Post-Lomé Framework for Europe-ACP Engagement

The post-Lomé framework for engagement enshrined in the Cotonou Agreement of 2000 and in the CARIFORUM-EU EPA of 2008 was consistent with the pattern of transnational corporate pursuits within Europe and globally.[7] This new era followed a period of corporate power consolidation, a transition to a TNC-influenced neoliberal economic order as the dominant paradigm globally, the debt crisis in the global south and the use of same by international financial institutions to enforce the adoption of neoliberal policies throughout the developing world, the continued deepening of EU integration and expansion, including following the end of the Cold War, and Europe's changing priorities in line with those of transnational corporate interests – primarily a focus on competitiveness, accumulation and facilitative policies in this regard.

So, how did these factors influence the post-Lomé framework for engagement? The literature on the subject of Europe-ACP relations converged on two direct triggers that, against the backdrop of all of the above, propelled the dismantling of Lomé-era terms of engagement in favor of a relationship in which neoliberal policies formed the rigid base – evolving policy norms within the EU, and the wider trajectory of the international trade regime towards ever deepening trade liberalization, and in which rules became more enforceable (Murray-Evans 2019, 9).

Murray-Evans (2019) explains in useful detail how the parallel evolution of the long history of relations between Western Europe and ACP states, and international trade rules, particularly those on special and differential treatment (SDT) and dispute resolution, as enshrined in the GATT and subsequently the WTO, influenced the movement toward and the outcome of the Cotonou Agreement of 2000. This author argues that these factors provided the institutional context that facilitated the possibility of reforming the Lomé regime which began in the 1990s. Until that point, the relationship between Europe and ACP countries evolved alongside GATT rules on SDT, at times responding to similar pressures to accommodate the needs of developing states, but "driven by divergent priorities and imperatives", which brought these two components of the existing trade regime into conflict before their later alignment (Murray-Evans 2019, 40).

In 1993, the European Union launched its Single Market. In addition to facilitating the free movement of people, goods, services, and money within Europe (European Union, n.d.), the completion of the Single Market resulted in the establishment of a single set of EU import rules. The latter, in combination with "the increased legislation and enforceability of multilateral trade

---

7 In this last section of this chapter, it should be noted that when I speak of the EPA, I will speak mainly to the CARIFORUM-EU EPA given that it is the focus of this study. The same conclusions may not apply in the cases of EPAs concluded with other ACP regions or subregions. For a detailed discussion on this, see Murray-Evans (2019).

rules on SDT as a result of the launch of the WTO in 1995", created a situation in which the special relationship between Europe and ACP states based on non-reciprocal preferential treatment was finally challenged, specifically, the EU's banana regime and "by extension the unilateral preferences that it provided to ACP countries under Lomé" (Murray Evans 2019, 40).

These challenges in the WTO directly prompted the reform of the Lomé-era relationship between Europe and ACP states. They also presented European policymakers already weary of Lomé-era trade policies with a timely and convenient opportunity to advocate changes that would open ACP markets. In this regard, these actors argued emphatically that committing to reciprocal trade liberalization was the only way to maintain the relationship while respecting international trade rules. This argument was based on a "strict and legalistic interpretation of GATT/WTO rules that were, in reality, a great deal more ambiguous than EU policymakers claimed". Nonetheless, that same ambiguity made it difficult for those opposing the European Commission's approach (including various EU Member States and the European Parliament) to put forward concrete counterproposals that appeared to be similarly supported by international law (Murray-Evans 2019, 40, 41, 58).

Approaches to development prior to the establishment of the WTO, whether bilaterally between Europe and ACP states or in the context of the GATT, reflected the thinking advocated via UNCTAD by newly independent developing countries in the 1960s and 1970s – that due to their disadvantaged position in international trade, they were not obliged to provide reciprocal preferences to advanced economies. In addition, developing countries were eligible to receive special and differential treatment (SDT) under GATT in the form of exemptions from GATT rules, such as to facilitate the protection of their infant industries. While this was a more informal, non-binding undertaking since 1971, special and differential treatment was enshrined in the GATT in 1979 (Montoute and Virk 2017, 15–16; Murray Evans 2019, 48–49).

Lomé conventions, especially earlier agreements, reflected this 'structuralist' understanding of development and various elements of the New International Economic Order that underpinned them. The preamble of Lomé I, for example, acknowledged the existence of structural barriers to development and pledged to work on establishing a new archetype for relations between developed and developing countries that addressed the imbalances in the existing economic order. In this context, many developing countries were able to pursue their own industrialization policies with little to no encroachment on their policy space. With the growing emphasis on neoliberalism since the 1980s, however, there was a shift away from this structuralist understanding to a rejection of same. Skepticism grew with regard to the ability of SDT in the form of non-reciprocity and preferences to facilitate development. Instead, the idea that development failures were an endogenous problem caused by inefficiencies at national levels emerged as the dominant perspective (Murray-Evans 2019, 45, 49–50).

It should be noted that the European approach to development as enshrined in Lomé-era conventions always appeared to be in contravention of GATT rules, specifically GATT Article XXIV and the 1979 Enabling Clause. Article XXIV provided an exemption to the principle of non-discrimination permitting countries to form customs unions or free trade areas in which substantially all trade was liberalized and in which parties to the agreement received preferential treatment. The 1979 Enabling Clause allowed for more favorable treatment to be provided to developing countries universally, the only sub-category among them eligible for more special treatment being Least Developed Countries (LDCs). Having provided non-reciprocal preferential treatment to a sub-group of developing countries that were not all LDCs, the Lomé Conventions were not in conformity with these criteria. Despite a GATT ruling in the early 1990s that recognized this, "the permissive nature of the GATT legal system meant that the latter went unchallenged for an extended period" (Murray-Evans 2019, 47).

The establishment of the WTO cemented a shift away from the structuralist understanding of development and SDT which permitted non-reciprocity in favor of developing countries, to a neoliberal approach which emphasized non-discriminatory liberalization for everyone. Under the WTO, developing countries were made to follow the same rules as advanced economies. SDT under the WTO now involved "technical assistance and transition periods designed to facilitate the gradual integration of developing countries into the global economy rather than allowing them to avoid integration altogether" (Murray-Evan 2019, 50). Furthermore, while the Lomé conventions legally codified an approach to development that reflected a structuralist perspective, SDT provisions as reformed in the context of the WTO, (just as under the GATT pre-WTO), "are largely non-binding, and the nature and extent of the concession to be made are at the discretion of the industrialised countries" (Montoute and Virk 2017, 16).

The new Dispute Settlement Understanding (DSU) which came into effect under the WTO strengthened the dispute settlement process and made blocking legal challenges much more difficult. Practices that developed under GATT's ambiguous rules, including "schemes like Lomé", were now significantly more likely to be successfully challenged based on WTO rules (Heron 2013 cited in Murray-Evans 2019, 50). The challenge to the EU's Single Market banana regime within the WTO by states that claimed that it violated the principle of non-discrimination, which resulted in the infamous 'banana wars',[8] however, ultimately coincided with an alignment between the EU's interests and the direction of multilateral trade.

While there had been a disconnect between EEC trade and development policy and multilateral trade rules in the era of Lomé, from the 1990s, "any remaining commitment within the European Commission to the ideas that had underpinned Lomé was disappearing". These Conventions also increasingly came into conflict with other areas of EU foreign policy. During the 1990s, "EU's primary external trade policy was the pursuit of further multilateral trade liberalization, particularly with regard to new generation trade issues such as competition, investment, intellectual property rights and technical barriers to trade" as it sought to "build a multilateral trade system based on the set of trade and trade-related rules that governed Europe itself, and with the EU at its center". A re-thinking of the Lomé-era approach to its relationship with ACP states therefore began before the end of the Uruguay Round and any challenges that arose within the WTO (Murray Evans 2019, 50–51).[9]

Although states are at the forefront of international affairs, state-centric analyses of neoliberalism, European integration, the WTO, the proliferation of preferential trade agreements and Europe-ACP relations obscure the dominant influence of transnational corporations that collaborate closely with state and non-state representatives. The previous section established the deepening ties between transnational corporate interests and the European Commission since the 1980s, and their unmistakable and assertive presence at national and regional levels in Europe, and at the international level such as at the Uruguay

---

8 Following the creation of the WTO, Lomé-era privileges were severely threatened, particularly the mainstay of four Windward Islands in the Caribbean – bananas. In 1996, the U.S., together with 4 Latin American countries filed a complaint with the WTO that Lomé's Banana Protocol unfairly discriminated against Latin American banana producers (which included U.S. MNCs), and should be discontinued. Although the regime was amended as a result, it was still deemed unacceptable by both the U.S. and the WTO in 1999, and led to further amendments by the EU in order to conform to WTO rules. The liberalization of trade in agricultural products was a severe threat to Caribbean economies at the time given their heavy dependence on the export of traditional agricultural commodities such as bananas and sugar, and on the preferential treatment of the latter under Lomé's special protocols. (Ahmed 2001, 2–3). Following challenges to Lomé-era preferences extended by the EU to ACP states with regard to both bananas and sugar, as well as the evolution of EU policies on agriculture, the EU liberalized the trade in bananas in 2006, and sugar and rice in 2009 (for further information, in addition to Ahmed 2001, see Clegg 2005, ECDPM 2003, Girvan and Montoute in Montoute and Virk 2017, La Force 2013 and Richardson-Ngwenya 2010).
9 Murray-Evans (2019) has cited a number of different authors in connection with these points, namely Woolcock (1999), Elsig (2007), Evenett (2007) and Barker (2012).

Round and the WTO. Transnational corporate interests have also been central to the negotiation of preferential trade agreements (PTAs). The negotiation of PTAs has, additionally, reflected the operation of transnational interest blocs.

Since the creation of the WTO, bilateral and regional trade agreements have evolved to incorporate provisions in new areas that encroach on the domestic policies of formally sovereign states. Dani Rodrik (2018) explains that with regard to bilateral and regional trade agreements, "[b]usiness is rarely far from the actual negotiation" and that it is in fact "commonplace for business lobbyists to wait just outside the negotiation room and influence the outcome in real time" (84). Rodrik (2018) explains further that their significant influence in the expansion of trade into new areas within these agreements is "rarely exercised through the naked application of power", but rather by persuading policymakers and the wider public that their goals advance public interests (85).

Business interests influence negotiation processes as members of various trade advisory groups that are established for the purpose of negotiations, and business lobbies sometimes form a larger part of national delegations than official government representatives. Governments also come to rely on the knowledge and expertise of business lobbies to negotiate these "complex regulatory changes", as the latter help to define various issues as well as garner additional support from other transnationally oriented business groups. This accordingly results in the formation of close partnerships between business lobbies and governments in the negotiation of bilateral and regional trade agreements. In addition to exchanging votes and providing funding to lobby against regulations, firms "offer expertise and political support in exchange for access to the elaboration of specific stakes" (Woll and Artigas 2007, cited in Rodrik 2018, 86).

The widely cited negotiation of the North American Free Trade Agreement (NAFTA) involving the United States, Canada and Mexico provides an illustrative example. Membership of the U.S. Business Roundtable overlapped with the membership of the U.S. Trade and Advisory Committee which was responsible for negotiating the specifics of the agreement. The corporate sectors most engaged in the restructuring of production on a global scale, such as those tied to "industrial and consumer electronics, telecommunications, pharmaceuticals, computers, agribusiness, auto manufacturers and the most globally competitive textile and apparel manufactures" were most disproportionately represented in the negotiation process (Cox 2019, 32). Although trade advisory committees in principle included a broad range of stakeholders, in reality "business representatives and trade associations [were] by far the dominant group" (Rodrik 2018, 87).

The EPAs can be understood as part of this broader trend towards the turn of the century "in which major trade powers such as the U.S. and EU increasingly sought deep and comprehensive trade liberalization via PTAs, often with developing countries". As the Doha Development Agenda suffered numerous setbacks and the pursuit of deeper liberalization stalled in the multilateral arena, developed countries increasingly pursued these objectives via the negotiation of PTAs (Murray-Evans 2019, 15).

The U.S., for example, "pursued such agreements from as early as 2000 as part of a strategy of 'competitive liberalisation'... aimed" at using "a combination of bilateral, regional and multilateral negotiations to induce the opening of foreign markets to U.S. exports and the external adoption of U.S.-style economic regulations" (Evenett and Meier 2008, cited in Murray-Evans 2019, 18). The EU, on the other hand, issued a moratorium on the conclusion of new PTAs during the initial phase of the Doha Development Round. Given the deadlock that obtained at the international level, however, "the EU abandoned this strategy and from 2006 adopted a policy dubbed 'Global Europe', under which it sought PTAs" with several countries and regions, following which it also concluded the CARIFORUM-EU EPA (Murray-Evans 2019, 18).

The Cotonou Agreement signed in Cotonou in 2000, which replaced Lomé as the new basis for relations between the EU and ACP states reflected "to a large extent the agenda set out by the European Commission in a series of papers and negotiating mandates in the lead up to 2000" (Murray-Evans 2019, 40). The radical changes occurring within the EU and globally discussed in greater detail earlier in this chapter prompted an assessment of the EU-ACP relationship in the context of Lomé carried out by the European Commission and contained in a widely referenced 1996 European Green Paper "on the relations between the European Union and the ACP Countries on the eve of the 21st century, Challenges and opportunities for a new partnership". The Green Paper indicated the inevitability of embarking on a new course in keeping with redefined interests within Europe as well as the international environment at that time, if an EU-ACP relationship were to be maintained, and presented several options in that regard which formed the subject of consultations on the way forward (European Commission 1996).

The European Commission, subsequently, in 1997, produced a document containing "Guidelines for the negotiation of new cooperation agreements with the African, Caribbean and Pacific (ACP) countries" following the conclusion of consultations held on the basis of the 1996 Green Paper. The European Commission held the view that the "intense", "fruitful", and "interactive" process "revealed the foundations for a new relationship able to cope with international and regional change" (European Commission 1997, 3).

The Cotonou Agreement of 2000 (EUR-Lex 2000) institutionalized the framework for post-Lomé cooperation and was generally consistent with the five major policy guidelines identified in the 1997 European Commission document, namely, "giving the new partnership a stronger political dimension", adjusting "Commission policy to make poverty alleviation the cornerstone of the new partnership", "opening up cooperation to economic partnership", completely overhauling the "practical procedures for managing financial and technical cooperation", and preserving "the ACP as a group while introducing considerable geographic differentiation".

The post-Lomé framework, therefore, was markedly distinct from the Lomé era of trade and development cooperation in several ways. Notably, the Cotonou Agreement of 2000 established the goals, principles, and scope for the negotiation of Economic Partnership Agreements between the EU and various ACP regions (Bernal 2013, 20). Although the Cotonou Agreement rolled over for the last time Lomé-era non-reciprocal preferential trading arrangements, this was covered by a WTO-waiver which expired on December 31, 2007, by which time Economic Partnership Agreements were to be in place.

EPAs were essentially conceived as preferential trade agreements requiring that ACP states open their markets to exports from the EU. Moreover, "EPAs were originally proposed as 'comprehensive' trade agreements that would apply the reciprocity principle not only to goods but also to services and a range of trade-related regulatory issues including investment, competition, public procurement, and intellectual property" (Murray-Evans 2019, 1).[10]

Negotiating EPAs with ACP regions and sub-regions reflected the EU's "growing focus on interregional relations with developing countries and on its own role as a model" for both cooperation and regional integration (Murray-Evans 2019, 54). While support for ACP regional cooperation was always part of the Europe-ACP framework for engagement, the strengthened emphasis also represented a movement away from the idea of "closed" to "open" regionalism, that is, the replacement of protectionist trade policies with regional integration schemes that "could serve as building blocks for an open, liberal, multilateral trading system" under the WTO, that would be "open" meaning "non-discriminatory to outsiders and based on the liberalisation of 'substantially all trade'" (Montoute and Virk 2017, 14).

---

10 EPAs were ultimately concluded between the EU and various ACP *countries* and regions. The current focus regarding EPAs is on implementation of signed and ratified agreements. Attention is also centered on extending the scope of agreements that have not been far-reaching to "upgrade them to modern and comprehensive trade agreements" that include issues such as services, investment, trade and sustainable development (European Commission a, n.d.).

Another update widened the scope of participation in EU-ACP engagement. In addition to central governments, participation was opened to non-state actors such as local and regional authorities, civil society, and the private sector. According to Regina Gerrick's (2004) assessment, the private sector, however, appeared to receive the most attention within the expanded group of actors (140).

Fundamental, moreover, was the institutionalization of differentiation which featured with regard to the EU's approach to development cooperation, including in respect of the availability of aid which was, in principle, previously available to all ACP states. The EU's approach to cooperation under the new arrangement, in contrast, took into account the levels of development, needs, performance and long-term development strategies of ACP states as outlined in Article 2 of the Cotonou Agreement (Arts 2003, 99–100). Under these terms, the EU chose to be much more selective in its use of resources in ACP states (Gerrick 2004, 140).

Differentiation also involved distinguishing between developing countries more broadly and Least Developed Countries (LDC S). While developing countries were generally entitled to special and differential treatment, international trade rules allowed for more special treatment to be accorded to LDCs. With this distinction, incorporated into EU development policy and instituted in the post-Lomé framework, EU-ACP cooperation no longer contravened the GATT 1979 Enabling Clause.

With respect to the above, among CARIFORUM states, only Haiti was classified as an internationally recognized LDC. Accordingly, only Haiti was entitled to more favorable treatment outside of an EPA framework.[11] Although the post-Lomé framework also "took into account the vulnerability" of landlocked and island ACP states with respect to the provision of special treatment (Cotonou Agreement, Article 2), it was necessary for other CARIFORUM states to conclude an EPA in an attempt to secure preferential treatment more favorable than that provided under the EU GSP. The latter was the alternative offered by the EU upon expiration on December 31, 2007, of the WTO waiver that covered

---

11 In 2001, the EU unilaterally introduced the Everything But Arms (EBA) initiative which granted "duty-free access to all products, except for arms, from LDCs without quota restrictions" (ECDPM 2003, 17). This applied to all LDCs, whether ACP states or not. The division of ACP states into sub-regional groups by the EU, as well as the treatment extended only to LDCs shortly after the conclusion of the Cotonou Agreement of 2000, and even before the start of preparations for any EPA negotiations, resulted in tensions in the subsequent negotiation of the EPAs given that LDCs were included in each sub-regional group required to conclude an EPA with the EU, while at the same time allowed to continue to engage in non-reciprocal preferential trade (Flint 2009, 87).

the extension of Lomé-era non-reciprocal preferential treatment under the Cotonou Agreement of 2000.

The CARIFORUM-EU EPA was a 'comprehensive' agreement which went beyond the coverage of trade in goods and agricultural products to include "commitments on trade in services, investment, trade-related issues such as competition policy, government procurement, intellectual property rights, as well as sustainable development aspects" (European Commission b, n.d.). The Agreement also brought preferential trade between the EU and the Caribbean into compliance with GATT Article XXIV given its basis on (asymmetrical) reciprocal market access commitments occurring within the framework of a free trade area in which "substantially all trade" between the parties was liberalized. Asymmetrical liberalization commitments allowed for longer liberalization periods for CARIFORUM states. Development cooperation continued within this context in the form of technical assistance and support for adjustment and implementation.

The CARIFORUM-EU EPA replaced Part II of the Cotonou Agreement of 2000, "namely, the provisional trade arrangements applicable during the EPA negotiations", which ended on December 31, 2007. Although the "Cotonou trading regime [was] no longer available to ACP countries after that date", the Cotonou Agreement "remain[ed] the sole legal document governing the delivery of EU development cooperation", that is, while the CARIFORUM-EU EPA also "incorporate[d] provisions on EU development cooperation", the "Cotonou Agreement remain[ed] the relevant legal instrument to deliver" the EPA's commitments (Lodge 2011, 29).[12]

5   Conclusion

Transnational corporate power has shaped trade and economic policy at national, regional, and international levels in the era of neoliberal capitalism, including in the context of preferential trade agreements. This chapter investigated its influence on the transition from Lomé to the post-Lomé framework for EU-ACP cooperation, specifically in the context of the Cotonou Agreement of 2000 and the CARIFORUM-EU EPA of 2008. The influence of

---

12   The Cotonou Agreement of 2000 was set to expire in 2020. A new agreement, referred to as the "Post-Cotonou Agreement" was initialed "by chief negotiators on" April 15, 2021. The application of the Cotonou Agreement is being extended until June 30, 2023, however, "unless the new Agreement enters into force or is provisionally applied before that date" (European Commission c, n.d.).

transnational corporate power was evident in the progressive neoliberalization of Lomé and in the transition to the Cotonou Agreement of 2000, as well as the CARIFORUM-EU EPA of 2008. Its influence was found to be fundamentally structural given its instrumental role in shaping the direction of policy in Europe, in the crafting of the new rules of international trade instituted with the establishment of the WTO, and in the pursuit of bilateral and regional preferential trade agreements in the quest for deeper liberalization commitments than those that were possible at the multilateral level.

The Cotonou Agreement of 2000 and the CARIFORUM-EU EPA of 2008 represented a dramatic shift from the Lomé-era of non-reciprocal preferential trade and development cooperation between the EU and ACP states. The agreements introduced reciprocal trade liberalization, albeit asymmetrical, and expanded trade cooperation beyond goods to services and all areas related to trade. They also emphasized support for regional integration as well as the integration of ACP states into the global economy. The agreements were ultimately consistent with evolved EU policy as well as the rules of international trade as instituted with the establishment of the WTO. Although the framework retained an explicit development dimension, commitments were largely related to support for adjustment and implementation. The Cotonou Agreement of 2000 and the CARIFORUM-EU EPA of 2008 also reflected ACP and CARIFORUM priorities, respectively. The extent to which they did, however, constitutes the subject of other studies in the existing literature on EU-ACP engagement and on the CARIFORUM-EU EPA.

References

Ahmed, Belal (2001) "The Impact of Globalisation on the Caribbean Sugar and Banana Industries." *The Society for Caribbean Studies Annual Papers* 2: ISSN 1471-2024.

Arts, Karin (2003) "ACP-EU Relations in a New Era: the Cotonou Agreement." *Common Market Law Review* 40: 95–116.

Asante, S.K.B. (1981) "The Lomé Convention: Towards Perpetuation of Dependence or Promotion of Interdependence?". *Third World Quarterly* 3, no. 4 (October): 658–672. https://www.jstor.org/stable/3991039.

Balanyá, Belén, Ann Doherty, Olivier Hoedeman, Adam Ma'anit, and Erik Wesselius (2003) *Europe Inc.: Regional and Global Restructuring and the Rise of Corporate Power*. London: Pluto Press.

Bernal, Richard (2013) *Globalization, Trade, and Economic Development: the CARIFORUM-EU Economic Partnership Agreement*. New York: Palgrave MacMillan.

Clegg, Peter (2005) "Banana Splits and Policy Challenges: the ACP Caribbean and the Fragmentation of Interest Coalitions." *European Review of Latin American and Caribbean Studies* no. 79 (October): 27–45. JSTOR.

Cosgrove, Carol (1994) "Has the Lomé Convention Failed the ACP Trade?" *Journal of International Affairs* 48, no. 1 (Summer): 223–249. www.jstor.org/stable/24357341.

Cox, Ronald W. (2019) *Corporate Power, Class Conflict, and the Crisis of the New Globalization*. Maryland: Lexington Books.

Dolan, Michael B. (1978) "The Lomé Convention and Europe's Relationship with the Third World: a Critical Analysis." *Journal of European Integration* 1, no. 3 (December): 369–394. Routledge. DOI: 10.1080/07036337808428707

ECDPM (2003) "A User's Guide for Non-state Actors." https://ecdpm.org/work/the-cotonou-agreement-a-users-guide-for-non-state-actors.

EUR-Lex (2000) "Cotonou Agreement". *Official Journal of the European Communities*. https://eur-lex.europa.eu/resource.html?uri=cellar:eebc0bbc-f137-4565-952d-3e1ce81ee890.0004.04/DOC_2&format=PDF.

European Commission (1996) "Green Paper on Relations between the European Union and the ACP Countries on the Eve of the 21st Century, Challenges and Opportunities for a New Partnership". https://op.europa.eu/en/publication-detail/-/publication/fd0026af-3614-4e2d-9330-73b2078bb9b1.

European Commission (1997) "Guidelines for the Negotiation of New Cooperation Agreements with the African, Caribbean and Pacific (ACP) Countries." COM (97) 537 final, 29 October.

European Commission c. n.d. "International Partnerships." Accessed March 2023. https://international-partnerships.ec.europa.eu/policies/european-development-policy/acp-eu-partnership_en.

European Commission b. n.d. "Access2Markets." Accessed March 2023. https://trade.ec.europa.eu/access-to-markets/en/content/eu-cariforum-economic-partnership-agreement.

European Commission a. n.d. "Trade." Accessed March 2023. https://policy.trade.ec.europa.eu/development-and-sustainability/economic-partnerships_en.

European Round Table for Industry (2023) "About ERT." https://ert.eu/about/.

European Union. n.d. "Single Market." Accessed March 2023. https://european-union.europa.eu/priorities-and-actions/actions-topic/single-market_en.

Evenett, Simon J., and Michael Meier. 2008. "An Interim Assessment of the U.S. Trade Policy of 'Competitive Liberalization'". *The World Economy* 31, no.1 (January): 31–66. https://doi.org/10.1111/j.1467-9701.2007.01081.x

Flint, Adrian (2009) "The End of a 'Special Relationship'? The New EU-ACP Economic Partnership Agreements." *Review of African Political Economy* 36, no. 119 (March): 79–92. Taylor & Francis, Ltd. JSTOR.

Gerrick, Regina (2004) "The Cotonou Agreement: Will It Successfully Improve the Small Island Economies of the Caribbean?" *Boston College of International and Comparative Law Review* 27, no. 1: 131–146. HeinOnline.

Heron, Tony (2013) *Pathways from Preferential Trade: the Politics of Trade Adjustment in Africa, the Caribbean and Pacific.* London: Palgrave Macmillan.

Hickel, Jason (2018) *The Divide: Global Inequality from Conquest to Free Markets.* New York: W.W. Norton and Company.

La Force, Vanessa Constant (2013) "A comparison between the Cotonou Agreement and the EU Generalized System of Preferences, the case of sugar." *Journal of International Trade Law and Policy* 2, no. 1: 42–67.

Lodge, Junior (2011) "A Trade Partnership for Sustainable Development." In *The CARIFORUM-EU Economic Partnership Agreement, a Practitioners' Analysis*, edited by Americo Beviglia Zampetti and Junior Lodge, 19–42. The Netherlands: Kluwer Law International.

Montana, Ismael Musah (2003) "The Lomé Convention from Inception to the Dynamics of the Post-Cold War, 1957–1990s." *Africana and Asian Studies* 2, no. 1: 63–97.

Montoute, Annita and Kudrat Virk eds. (2017) *The ACP Group and the EU Development Partnership: Beyond the North-South Debate.* Cham: Palgrave Macmillan.

Murray-Evans, Peg (2019) *Power in North-South Trade Negotiations: Making the European Union's Economic Partnership Agreements.* Abingdon: Routledge.

Mytelka, Lynn (1977) "The Lomé Convention and a New International Division of Labour." *Journal of European Integration* 1, no. 1: 63–76, Cited in S.K.B. Asante, "The Lomé Convention: Towards Perpetuation of Dependence or Promotion of Interdependence?" *Third World Quarterly* 3, no. 4 (October 1981): 658–672. JSTOR.

Parfitt, T.W. (1981) "The Lomé Convention and the New International Economic Order." *Review of African Political Economy* no. 22 (October – December): 85–95, https://www.jstor.org/stable/3998142.

Publications Office of the European Union (1975) "ACP-EEC Convention of Lomé signed on 28 February 1975 and related documents." https://op.europa.eu/en/publication-detail/-/publication/c973175b-9e22-4909-b109-b0ebf1c26328.

Publications Office of the European Union (1981) "The Second ACP-EEC Convention signed at Lomé on 31 October 1979 and related documents." https://op.europa.eu/en/publication-detail/-/publication/f06ebd58-a3d7-4b11-966d-02548c8cb918/language-en/format-PDF/source-search.

Publications Office of the European Union (1985) "Third ACP-EEC Convention Signed at Lomé on 8 December 1984 and related documents." https://op.europa.eu/en/publication-detail/-/publication/851e7cf4-1d67-4c13-9d1a-abb8a220feef/language-en/format-PDF/source-search.

Publications Office of the European Union (1992) "Fourth ACP-EEC Convention signed at Lomé on 15 December 1989." https://op.europa.eu/en/publication-detail/-/publication/ea62466c-93ce-40ca-87f3-66e196a987ab/language-en/format-PDF/source-search.

Rajana, Cecil (1980) "Lomé II and ACP – EEC Relations: a Preliminary Assessment." *Africa Development* 5, no. 3 (July – September): 91–111.

Richardson-Ngwenya, Pamela (2010) "The EU sugar reform and the responses of Caribbean sugar producers." *Geography* 95, no. 2 (Summer): 70–79.

Rodrik, Dani (2018) "What Do Trade Agreements Really Do?" *Journal of Economic Perspectives* 32, no. 2 (Spring): 73–90.

Shaw, Timothy (1979) "EEC-ACP Interactions and Images as Redefinitions of Euroafrica: exemplary, exclusive and/or exploitative?" *Journal of Common Market Studies* 18: 135–158.

Tabb, William (2004) *Economic Governance in the Age of Globalization*. New York: Columbia University Press.

United Nations Social and Economic Commission for Western Asia (2020) "New International Economic Order." https://archive.unescwa.org/new-international-economic-order.

Woll, Cornelia and Alvaro Artigas (2007) "When Trade Liberalization Turns in to Regulatory Reform: the Impact of Business-Government Relations in International Trade Politics." *Arizona State Law Journal* 49, (Special Issue): 821–66, Cited in "What Do Trade Agreements Really Do?" by Dani Rodrik. 2018. *Journal of Economic Perspectives* 32, no. 2 (Spring): 73–90.

Yelpaala, Kojo (1981) "The Lomé Conventions and the Political Economy of the African-Caribbean-Pacific Countries: a Critical Analysis of the Trade Provisions." *N.Y.U Journal of International Law and Politics* 13, no. 807: 807–880.

CHAPTER 8

The Necessity of Poverty in the High-Income Countries

Jamie A. Gough and Aram Eisenschitz

1   **Introduction**[1]

Poverty has been present in all the advanced capitalist countries since the dawn of industrial capitalism in the late 18C, and remains so to this day. A large proportion of the working class, sometimes the majority, have long hours of grinding work both paid and unpaid, unhealthy living and working conditions, slum housing, food of low quality and quantity, inadequate or non-existent health care. In consequence, they have short life expectancy relative to the upper and middle classes ('absolute poverty'). Moreover, part of the working class has incomes well below the national median ('relative poverty'), and are consequently excluded from normal living conditions and cultural norms. The persistence of poverty in the rich countries requires explanation. In this chapter we present a Marxist explanation, which understands poverty not as an anomaly but as an inherent feature of the most advanced capitalism.

To understand the persistence of poverty in high-income countries (HICs), the mainstream academic and policy literature does not get us very far. There are innumerable studies of poverty in particular countries at particular times. But these present explanations, rather than being merely descriptive, tend to focus on national peculiarities (economic or political) and particular periods of the country's history. In contrast, a thorough explanation of poverty in a given country and period needs to start from the more abstract processes which underlie the creation of poverty. The specific forms and causes of poverty in a

---

1   This chapter is a revised and expanded version of Jamie A. Gough and Aram Eisenschitz, "Poverty in High-Income Countries: a Marxist Alternative to Mainstream Ideologies," *Class, Race and Corporate Power*, Vol. 9 (2). We avoid the common term 'More Developed Countries' because of its uncritical implication that capitalist 'development' is a unilinear, equitable and wholly-beneficial process. We do not use the term 'imperialist countries' in this chapter, despite believing that imperialism is a real and important set of processes, because of lack of space to distinguish between the many different Marxist theories of imperialism, and because some imperialist countries such as China have low average income by international standards.

particular country and period are, to be sure, important in developing struggles against it; but these need to be understood as dialectical developments – more concrete forms – of the historically- and spatially-abstract causes. This epistemological point leads to a political one: struggles against poverty need to see themselves as transnational and as anti-capitalist, rather than simply addressing some 'problems' particular to a specific country and time.

Since the work of Booth and Rowntree in the late 19C, there have been innumerable empirical investigations into the extent and forms of poverty in particular countries. Some have described correlations of income poverty with poor housing, diet, health, family life, crime and so on. Many studies have described the spatial distribution of poverty between regions, within regions, and between neighbourhoods within cities (for example Dorling, 2015). Other research describes the overall distribution of income within a country, sometimes comparing countries. A large literature discusses definitions of poverty (Townsend, 1970). But these studies remain descriptive, abstaining from explanation.

There is a large literature on poverty framed as an issue of 'social policy', focused on certain impacts *of the state* on poverty (for example, Alcock, 1997). This literature typically has detailed accounts of state transfer payments and targeted 'anti-poverty' policies in a particular country. But this literature is far too narrowly focused to constitute a theory of poverty: its consideration of economy and social life in the creation of poverty is sketchy at best.

There have also been theorisations of poverty in the HICs. These are highly political. Four political strands may be distinguished. First, (neo-) liberal authors have argued that poverty is a result of 'political' blockages in labour markets – trade unions, national industrial bargaining, minimum wages, excessive state transfers to the unemployed. If these were removed, labour markets would clear, and employment and wages would rise (Mankiw, 2001). But this neo-classical economics has been shown to be thoroughly unscientific (Green and Nore, 1977). Second, organic conservatives argue that poverty is due to the culture of the poor: lack of stable nuclear heterosexual families disrupts domestic reproduction, participation in wage labour and the socialisation and education of children; 'welfare dependency' saps initiative and self-esteem; pervasive crime provides an alternative to waged employment while disrupting social reproduction (Lewis, 1979; Murray, 1984). In some versions, the poor are inherently biologically and psychologically inferior. The organic conservative view often pictures the poor as a 'residuum' or 'underclass', a group qualitatively distinct from the rest of the population. By locating the causes of poverty within poor neighbourhoods, this view entirely misses (and politically obscures) the role of the capitalist labour market. Third, social democratic thought during the post-war boom argued that poverty was the result, variously, of insufficient regulation of the labour market and housing markets, insufficient counter-cyclical policies, and insufficient funding of public services and benefits. Thus, intensified state action could eliminate poverty in the rich countries. But this view vastly overestimates both the autonomy and influence of the state *vis à vis* capital. Finally, social democratic thought since the 1980s has shifted towards associationalist and community-development explanations of poverty, which argue that the poor lack 'social capital' and effective social networks; this lack causes weak community ties for social reproduction and community organisation, and barriers to upward mobility, resulting in 'social exclusion' (Cabinet Office, 2002; Social Exclusion Unit, 2001). This repeats the error of organic conservatism of a narrow focus on poor neighbourhoods (for a critique, see Das et al., 2023).[2]

There has been surprisingly little Marxist theorisation of poverty in the HICs. An exception is the work of Tony Novak and Chris Jones (Jones and Novak, 1999; Novak, 1995, 1996). Novak (1995) argues that poverty cannot be understood in isolation from the exploitation and oppression of the whole working class, defined as those dependent on wages of themselves or their family members as their main income over the life span. The material and psychological misery of the poor rests on the class relation between labour and capital, and on the oppressions of gender and racism which are internally related to class. The emergence of wage labour as the only means of survival for the majority of the population in the early modern period imposed on them a chronic state of insecurity and struggle for survival. In the late 18C and the first half of the 19C, this condition of the working class was understood as poverty; the whole working class was poor. In the second half of the 19C in Britain, the bourgeoisie became interested in poverty, partly due to fear of rebellion and partly because of concern that an adequate labour force was not being reproduced for certain industries and occupations and for the army. Bourgeois ideology started to picture 'the poor' as a problem group distinct from the rest of the working class. This group was surveyed, its conditions of life measured, a 'poverty line' drawn to demarcate it, and policies formulated to either improve or repress. In this process, the roots of poverty in wage labour as such were forgotten. Novak argued that it is precisely this connection that needs to be re-established. The poor are those who experience the sharpest forms of the disempowerment experienced by the whole working class.

---

2 For critiques of these four approaches, see Gough and Eisenschitz, 2006: Part III.

This crucial insight is the starting point for this chapter. We develop Novak's insight by exploring in detail how poverty is produced by structures which span the whole society – economy, social life, the state – and which involve the whole working class. We show that differentiation in the material circumstances of workers, far from being an 'imperfection', is produced systematically within each of these spheres.

In the dialectical Marxist approach which we use, capitalist society is a totality, within which the parts are *internally* related (Gough and Das, 2017; Ollman, 1993). Thus poverty, a particular aspect of society, needs to be understood as part of the totality, as Novak pointed out. Moreover, economy, social life and 'politics'/the state are internally related moments in the construction of poverty: they do not merely interact with but rather constitute each other. In contrast, the mainstream explanations of poverty just considered concentrate their attention on just one realm of economy, social life or politics, with the other two considered, at most, as 'context'. In this chapter, we will present the determinants of poverty in the waged economy, the state and social life in turn, while showing how each of these is mediated by the others.

Contemporary poverty in the HICs is often attributed to neoliberalism. Since the 1970s the neoliberal strategy of capital and the state has indeed widened and deepened poverty. Wages have been reduced, labour has been intensified, employment contracts have been made more flexible for capital, and unemployment has increased. Taxation has been switched from capital to labour, public services have deteriorated, and state benefits have been reduced and made more restrictive. Housing has become increasingly subject to capitalist logics. Social life has become increasingly individualised and dominated by commodity consumption, and networks of support for the poor have been eroded (Gough and Eisenschitz, 2006: Part II). But this should not hide that poverty is produced by capitalism even in 'normal' times. The essence of neoliberalism is to strengthen the rule of capital over labour; this necessarily deepens capital's production of poverty – exactly the opposite of the claim of neoliberal ideologues.

We focus on the HICs, within which the great majority of the population are directly or indirectly dependent on wage labour, where an independent peasantry, urban petty-trading and artisanal production are only a small part of the economy, where there are substantial public or socially-insured services, and where there are some state transfer payments to those on low incomes. The analysis here concerns roughly the last 120 years, the period within which the state has played a major role in both economy and public services. To our knowledge, this is the first account of the creation of poverty in the HICs at this level of historical and spatial abstraction.

2   Poverty and the Waged Economy

Two central proximate causes of poverty and economic insecurity are unemployment and what we will call 'poor jobs'. The latter are jobs which pay low wages per hour, per week, or per year, have disciplinary management of the labour process, have high intensity of work, and are insecure; they may also be part time, have hours varied daily by the employer, or anti-social shifts; they often lack benefits such as pensions, sick pay or parental leave. Poor jobs not only give poor incomes but also disempower and devalue workers within the production process, with negative impacts on their autonomy, personal development and self-esteem. Moreover, the capital-labour relation causes competition between workers for jobs, particularly at the lower end of the labour market, and thus social and political atomisation. Both poor jobs and unemployment are created by the fundamental dynamics of capitalism.

2.1   *Employment*

For a capitalist economy to function continuously, wages cannot for long periods rise above a level which leaves business with an inadequate rate of profit on capital invested. If the rate of profit is too low, investment will fall because of lack of funds and lack of incentive to invest. There is therefore a permanent downward pressure on wages and a disciplinary pressure on workers: if workers do not work sufficiently hard and/or do not accept low enough wages to make their employer's business profitable, they risk losing their jobs. This pressure acts on workers in each industry and firm. It also acts on the unemployed, requiring them to accept jobs at a wage level that will ensure their prospective employer's profitability. This endemic competition means that other employees are competitors for jobs and promotion, and employees of other firms are rivals. Industries where the workers have 'privileged' conditions are put under pressure to lower them to the average; and workers in each locality or nation can easily come to perceive those in other territories as 'thieves' of their jobs (Gough, 1992; Gough, 2003: Ch.13).

These processes put constant downward pressure on employment conditions. But wages, employment benefits, security of employment and managerial control are highly differentiated between industries, types of work and territories. Thus, territorial industries with high levels of fixed investment often obtain higher than average profit rates. High levels of innovation in products or processes enable technical or design rents to be reaped by industries and firms. High profit rates permit workers to bargain for higher-than-average wages and for relatively secure employment and good conditions of work. Conversely, territorial industries or firms with low profitability tend to compensate by depressing wages and conditions and imposing 'numerical flexibility' (variations in hours, times of work and number of jobs) on their workforces. Job skill also affects employment conditions. Workers in low skill jobs where management can directly dictate the form of tasks and the pace at which they are performed are in a weak bargaining position. They can be replaced easily. A cooperative attitude and commitment from the worker is of small importance; the firm can therefore offer poor wages and conditions with impunity (Friedman, 1977). Indeed, where workers are strongly organised employers often seek to develop technologies that supplant human skills (Braverman, 1974; Noble, 1984).

These processes, then, systematically produce inequalities in jobs. The universal discipline of labour by capital is intensified in particular sectors and sites. The outcome is a large 'secondary' sector of poor jobs. These not only offer low and insecure incomes, but belittle the workers, fail to develop their skills, and are often unhealthy. The workers are denied even a limited degree of autonomy and responsibility.

These problems are compounded in irregular forms of work such as self-employment, the informal economy and crime. Low-skilled self-employment, or where the required skills are widespread, is typically not only insecure but also low paid. In the modern economy much 'self-employment' is *de facto* employment by a firm, which thereby avoids regulatory obligations. The firm can even make 'self-employed' workers responsible for their own costs for working or pay a fee to the firm for the right to work for it. Self-employed status, far from giving autonomy, is particularly strong subordination to capital. Other large categories of 'self-employment', particularly for women and migrant workers, are domestic service and home work (piecework performed at home). Their spatial and social isolation, often compounded by immigration status, subordinate the worker brutally to her employer.

High rates of unemployment or the availability of only poor jobs force people to seek their income from the unregistered (or 'informal') economy. Informal status is usually found in sectors with intense price and cost competition, where many firms survive by avoidance of tax and regulation of wages, work conditions and layoffs. Workers, like the self-employed, may choose an informal job status to avoid tax, but thereby lose legal rights and future state benefits. These jobs are particularly poor as both a cause *and* consequence of their informal status.

Criminal work has always and everywhere been major survival strategy for the poor. The two most important contemporary sectors are sex work (mostly women), and the supply of criminalised drugs (mostly men). The criminalisation of sex work ensures that the work is controlled by pimps and gangs, and that international trafficking leads to *de facto* slavery. Drug dealing is organised by partly non-capitalist rules: competition between gangs proceeds through violence. But production and distribution are organised by pseudo-capitalist firms. They are class-divided: to make a high income usually requires one to be a crime boss; for the criminal proletariat incomes are low and unpredictable (Davis, 1992: Ch.5). Thus, the contemporary illegal-drugs industry "has involved 'deskilling' and the growth of the 'mass labour market'. The mass labourers ... may be as disadvantaged in this as in any other form of employment" (Croall, 1998: 266). The majority of burglars are young men with few skills, who face high risks of detection and reap low rewards (*op.cit.*: 229). Theft by women is mainly shoplifting, with even lower returns.

Thus, the majority of self-employment, informal and criminal work may be regarded as the extreme end of a continuum of poor jobs which begins in the formal sector. Whilst breaking certain capitalist rules, these forms of work are reproduced systematically by capitalism: workers are forced into them through lack of decent formal jobs, and cost-cutting sectors are *informalised* to cut costs further. These parts of the economy should not, then, be regarded as outside the logic of capitalism.

2.2 *Unemployment*

Capitalism offers no guarantee or right to employment. Unemployment is not an 'imperfection' of capitalism but is systemically produced and essential for capital accumulation. Unemployment is created by four processes, each intrinsic to capitalism:

(i) Intensification of work (absolute surplus value) and investment in new technologies of production (relative surplus value) constantly displace labour. These are propelled by management's wish to gain greater control over its workforce, and by competitive pressure to increase productivity (Marx, 1970).

(ii) Particular territorial economies (national, regional, local) can become uncompetitive as a result of insufficient investment in fixed capital, R&D and training, because labour has become too strong, insufficient investment in social and physical infrastructures, or due to inflation in land prices. Capital then shifts to other territories and unemployment rises. This spatial uneven development is, again, intrinsic to capitalism (Das, 2017).

(iii) The capitalist business cycle of 6 – 10 years results in regular recessions in which workers are laid off and new workers cannot find jobs. In the upswing of the cycle firms invest without coordination and wages tend to rise. This eventually results in excess capacity, falling final prices and decreasing profits or rising losses, resulting in cuts to investment, capacity and output; unemployment rises and wages fall (Gough, 2003: Ch.12; Hahnel and Sherman, 1982).

(iv) Capitalism generates long waves in which investment rate and increases in output are strong for 20–30 years and periods of 20–50 years when they are weak. Over the latter periods unemployment is much higher than the former. These long waves, too, are generated by fundamental dynamics of capitalism (Mandel, 1978; Roberts, 2016).

These processes have particular impact on poverty. Unemployment enables employers to create and recreate the poor jobs described above, by recruiting the unemployed and threatening existing workers with replacement. High levels of unemployment can enable employers to effect qualitative change in employment practices. Moreover, the least skilled workers are most likely to suffer unemployment, since employers, even for poor jobs, select workers with better skills and work experience; a long period of unemployment thus worsens the chances of obtaining a job.

2.3 Social Differentiation of Employment and Unemployment

Jobs and unemployment are also affected by the oppressions of gender, ethnicity and age. Social life produces different status, imputed need for a (good) job, and different access to skills demanded in waged work. Employers providing poor jobs may prefer women, certain racialised groups or young people as cheap or malleable labour; these groups then may have relatively low rates of unemployment but low rates of pay. But in some localities oppressed groups have high rates of unemployment because of their low skill levels or lack of continuity of employment, inability to access jobs because of care commitments, discrimination by employers, or hostility from other workers. In either case, poverty of these groups is reproduced. This then reinforces their oppression within social life: poor jobs reproduce social oppressions and social oppressions reproduce poor jobs. The competition between workers for jobs which is a fundamental feature of capitalism then leads native-born workers to resent immigrants for undercutting wages and taking 'their' jobs. Thus, the ethnic/racial division of labour politically divides the poor more than it does better-off workers (Gough, 2017).

This analysis suggests that class and social oppressions should not be regarded as distinct sets of social relations which merely interact or 'intersect' with each other externally, but rather are *internally* related processes which construct each other (McNally, 2015).

2.4 Spatial Differentiation

We have seen that investment and output are spatially uneven. Alongside such quantitative differences, qualitative differences are systematically produced, so that particular types of poor jobs are concentrated in particular areas. Industries with high productivity and innovation tend to be spatially agglomerated into particular 'core' localities and regions. Agglomeration enables the reproduction of a workforce with the skills and attitudes desired by employers, and helps to foster cooperative relations between firms and their employees. It facilitates networking, collaboration and changing divisions of labour between firms for flows of goods, services, information and personnel. These virtuous circles of agglomeration tend to be strongest in the production of complex goods and services which require strong knowledge generation and application and which use relatively skilled labour (Storper and Walker, 1989).

The high value-added can then be partly appropriated by workers as good wages and conditions. In contrast, in industries or stages of production which produce standardised goods or services, where little new knowledge is generated, and where tasks are relatively low skilled, production tends to be located in 'peripheral' low-cost locations. Many of these jobs have been split off from higher-level work in the same firm or production chain precisely in order to separate them spatially and socially (Massey, 1984). Since low costs can be found in many regions of the developed countries and in most of the HICs, this production is footloose, moving in search of yet lower wages, more pliant workers, or new state subsidies.

Core and peripheral areas create poverty in distinct ways. In the peripheral areas the majority of jobs are poor. Substantial levels of unemployment are chronic. It is hard for unions to recruit. The informal and criminal economies usually form a large proportion of economic activity. When this situation persists over decades, expectations regarding wages, conditions, skill and career are low, and people's self-confidence as economic agents is minimal.

But the core areas also create poverty. Consumer service jobs, whether in the private or public sector or in domestic service, are as poor in these areas as in others: low skilled and 'numerically flexible', offering low wages and poor conditions and security (Bryson et al., 2004). But land and housing, dominated by core production activities and core workers, are expensive, so that those in poor jobs are even worse off in core regions than in peripheral ones (Sassen, 1991). Low aggregate unemployment rate across a core region disguises high rates of unemployment and underemployment for those with a poor work history, for ethnic minorities, and for people living in stigmatised neighbourhoods.

Immigrants naturally try to settle mainly in core regions. The work of these migrant communities is typically in the consumer service sectors, in the informal economy, or in businesses owned by people of their own ethnicity; in the latter, bonds of ethnicity are used to subordinate workers and jobs are typically very poor (Kakios and van der Velden, 1984). 'Illegal' immigrants working in sweatshops, domestic service or sex work are subject to the very worst conditions, violence, and often de facto slavery. Where members of migrant communities are employed in large numbers by a local industry in order to worsen wages and conditions, this creates resentment and xenophobia on the part of people born in the area.

Whereas in weak regions poverty can be the majority culture, a widely shared experience represented in dominant discourses, in core regions the socially-oppressed and the poor appear as anomalous because they have somehow failed to share in the 'general' prosperity; the cultures of the poor tend to be more suppressed, and indeed seen as threatening, within the region's dominant discourses (Stedman Jones, 1971; Davis, 1992). Whereas in the weak regions, capital mobility undermines collective organisation, in the core regions divisions *within* labour undermine collective organisation (Gough, 2003).

We see, then, that poor jobs and low incomes from work are constructed systematically by patterns of capital accumulation and internally-related capitalist wage relations. Since the late 19C these processes have been increasingly strongly mediated by the state, to which we now turn.

3   Poverty and the State

In the view of the Right, the state is a major creator of poverty since it blocks the 'free markets' which can price the poor into work. This view neglects the enormous positive role of the state in capital accumulation and in the production of labour power needed by capital. In the social democratic view, the state is an institution which can intervene into the economy 'from the outside' in the interests of 'the public good', thus potentially eliminating poverty. But this greatly exaggerates the autonomy of the state from capitalist dynamics. In the Marxist approach taken here, the state arises from the contradictions and failures of capital accumulation and the reproduction of labour power, and is a site of the conflict between capital and labour (Clarke, 1991). State policies can therefore either benefit or disbenefit the poor, depending on class struggle and how the reproduction of the poor articulates with capital accumulation. We examine four areas of state intervention directly impacting poverty: policies for the waged economy to benefit the poor, taxation, public services, and state benefits.[3]

3.1   State Intervention into the Waged Economy

Since 1945, states have intervened strongly into the waged economy. Some policies have ostensibly been directed at reducing poverty; they are, however, always also aimed at strengthening capital accumulation, and their success is conditional on achieving the latter. Five types of policy are important here.

First, states have used fiscal and monetary policy to counter the business cycle, and thus lessen the rise of unemployment in recessions. When profit rates on capital are moderate or high, these interventions can stimulate investment and expansion of output. However, if long term profit rates are low, fiscal or monetary stimulus instead results in inflation in the price of goods and services (1960s – 1970s) or in financial assets (since the 1980s). This illustrates the limited effectiveness of the state on the dynamics of capital (Clarke, 1988; de Brunhof, 1978).

Second, the state has attempted to stimulate investment in regions, localities and parts of cities with high unemployment. This has been done partly by national government investing in physical infrastructures and giving subsidies for capital investment. It has been done by regional or local states either attempting to attract inward investment, or by stimulating investment by locally-based industries and firms (Eisenschitz and Gough, 1993). Interregional redistribution of investment has had some success in increasing manufacturing investments in poor regions (Rhodes, 1995). But the great majority of this has been low skill, standardised production, which was spontaneously locating to these regions (Massey, 1979; Peet, 1987). Policy largely failed to increase higher value-added production. Moreover, firms often move elsewhere after five or ten years when re-equipment is needed. Some regional and local initiatives have attempted to root production more strongly in the area by organising relations between firms and institutions and linking investment to training and reproduction of labour power (Gough and Eisenschitz, 1996; Gough, 2002). But this strategy has often been too weak to change the cost cutting and labour-disciplinary strategies of firms, or to counter national and global flows of commodities, information and capital (Eisenschitz and Gough, 1996). Regional and local economic strategy has thus generally failed radically to improve the quantity and quality of jobs in poor areas.

Third, during depressions governments may consider the classic Keynesian policy of directly creating jobs wholly funded by state spending, through physical infrastructure building or social service provision; the classic case was the U.S. New Deal in the 1930s. But this approach has been little used, and the New Deal itself was very limited in scale. In a depression capital is particularly resistant to increased state spending. Moreover, this type of state intervention is dangerously politicising, in showing the socialist potential of state-funded jobs for all the unemployed; this danger underlay the refusal of Roosevelt to carry out the New Deal in cities, confining it to rural areas where organised labour was weaker.

Fourth, training funded and organised by the state has sometimes been targeted on disadvantaged workers, including the long term unemployed, those with redundant skills, poor education or work experience, and women and BME people, ostensibly to improve their position in the labour market. This usually involves training in basic numeracy, literacy and work habits, plus low-level manual or clerical skills. In localities with low unemployment these programmes can have positive effects. But where unemployment is substantial, training does not lead into a job; rather, by increasing the supply of low-skilled labour power, the schemes tend to exacerbate competition between workers and enable employers to further reduce wages (Martin, Nativel and Sunley, 2003). To be successful such schemes would need to be tied to effective local job creation. As so often, a 'common sense' policy targeting a particular problem on its own terrain fails, or is actually counter-productive, because it is not joined up with other policies (Gough, 2002).

Fifth, the state may attempt to improve wages and health and safety of poor jobs by regulation of employers to meet minimum standards. However, in countries with liberal traditions, resources for policing these standards are usually wholly inadequate and penalties for violations derisory.[3] Moreover, if a firm is closed down by regulators, it often starts up under another name. Effective regulation usually requires strong industry or community-based trade unions.

Sixth, since the 1970s states have sponsored entrepreneurship for the poor, whereby the poor 'create their own jobs'; this has been a favourite policy in many HICs since the 1970s. Conventional firms and not-for-profit enterprises have been subsidised in various ways and management training, targeted particularly on the unemployed, women and BME people (Eisenschitz and Gough, 1993: 88–99). But despite the subsidies, these enterprises are drastically under-capitalised and lack innovative or distinctive products. They are generally in sectors with low barriers to entry, where start-ups simply add to over-production, exacerbate intense price competition, and thus put further downward pressure on prices and wages and leads to more failures (Eisenschitz and Gough, 1993: 172–9). This is true of cooperative social enterprises as well as

---

[3] Policing of the poor has major impacts, mostly negative. These are not discussed here due to lack of space; see Gough and Eisenschitz, 2006: 122–125, 203. Where policing has the greatest negative impact on the poor is, however, the repression and sabotage of the trade unions, social movements and struggles of the *whole* working class.

private firms (Eisenschitz and Gough, 2011). The new private firms tend to have very low wages and poor conditions; BME-owned enterprises employing workers of the same ethnicity typically use community ties to super-exploit them (Kakios and van der Velden, 1984). Overall, state encouragement of entrepreneurship of the poor thus results in many losing their meagre savings, and in further downward pressure on wages and conditions in small-firm, low capitalisation sectors.

We see, then, that state economic interventions in the interests of the poor often fail because they cut across patterns of capital accumulation, are too weak, or are insufficiently coordinated with other policies. But for the state to be bolder and more holistic would risk politicisation and encourage demands which challenge capital (Eisenschitz and Gough, 1996).

3.2   Taxation of the Poor

The enormous growth of state spending in the last 100 years has required a corresponding increase in taxation. The majority of tax revenue comes from the population rather than business. Workers pay tax in four main forms: income tax, purchase taxes, social insurance contributions, and local taxes on house value. Income tax is progressive (a higher rate the higher the income) from low incomes to the upper middle class, but middle-income earners often have tax breaks, and the rich pay little income tax by using international tax evasion. Purchase taxes are broadly neutral. Taxes on housing value are regressive. The result is that the poor can pay tax at a rate similar to, or even more than, the average. This problem has been exacerbated by neoliberalism: taxes on corporations have been cut; purchase taxes have increased relative to income tax; income tax has become less progressive, and evasion of it by the rich easier. Taxation is thus a very substantial contributor to poverty. Accordingly, middle and low earners often fiercely resist increases in taxation (British poll tax uprising in 1989, French *gilets jaunes* in 2019).

3.3   Social Services

From the late 19C until the 1980s there was qualitative and quantitative growth of universal public services funded by the state or by compulsory social insurance; particularly relevant to the poor are education, nurseries, health care, and social services. These forms of care were provided inadequately or not all at by working-class households, which lacked the time and skills to provide them internally and the money to buy them externally. Their hundred-year growth was powered both by working class demands, and by the wish of some sections of capital for a more skilled, and healthy, workforce (I. Gough, 1982).

Women, particularly, benefited from these services as they socialised some aspects of care work regarded as women's responsibility (Wilson, 1977).

These services have undoubtedly benefited the poor, and to some extent compensated for low household incomes. But the promise of universal services that they would give equal benefit to all, irrespective of income, has not been met. First, public services often have inadequate funding. Even in times of prosperity there is resistance to increases in taxation from parts of business and the population. Social provision transgresses the capitalist belief that the individual is responsible for their own reproduction. Public services are labour intensive and increases in productivity are hard to make without sacrificing quality, so that their cost tends to increase as a proportion of GDP. Where public services are funded substantially from local taxation (something which varies enormously between countries), poorer localities are forced to have lower spending.

Second, public services have tended to prioritise their function for business, to reproduce useful labour power. Thus, services for the elderly, the disabled and the mentally ill tend to be poorly funded. The quality of care varies enormously as a function of the political pressure from the working class; where this is weak, the services can be drastically underfunded, disciplinary, cruel, and sometimes lethal. School education has been strongly influenced by the aim of feeding young people into the labour market. The education of future professional workers (mainly middle-class children) has been separated from that of manual and clerical workers (working class children) in different schools or streams. A large part of the real curriculum has been to teach children to be quiet, sit still, postpone gratification, and accept the teacher's authority (Bowles and Gintis, 1976; Illich, 1983). This obedience is a crucial quality required by all employers (Braverman, 1974), and this is the *only* quality required in poor, routine jobs.

Third, the working class, and the poor particularly, tend to get less out of given public services than middle class people. Service delivery often favours the 'respectable' working class over the poor, men over women, white people over black. The poor, lacking daily experience of performing with middle class people, tend to negotiate less well with teachers, doctors, housing managers and social workers. The poor often *need more* from the service – more intensive teaching due to lack of cultural knowledge, more health care due to poorer health, more help from social workers due to material deprivation and consequent family tensions (Carrier and Kendall, 1998; Tudor Hart, 1971). Poor children often have low attention span at school due to hunger or to a highly processed diet, and have no quiet space at home to do homework (Millar, 2004). Many poor children reject the class-disciplinary aspect of education, as they often do not see the kind of knowledge imparted by schools as relevant to their situation. School therefore becomes a game of wills, in which misbehaviour provides the only sense of power and enjoyment (Willis, 1977).

The failures of public services for the poor are, then, embedded in, and subordinate to, society-wide structures of exploitation and oppression: the services to a large extent serve and reproduce individuals' places within the dominant social relations, especially of class, and individuals bring to the services their past conditioning by those relations.

3.4 State Benefits

The wages of the poor often do not allow the most basic social reproduction (Section 2). In consequence, over the last century the state has been drawn increasingly into providing incomes and money-benefits (I. Gough, 1982). Sections of business sometimes support unemployment benefits in order to reproduce a workforce of sufficient quality and in the right place. In contrast, state incomes for those who can never work and the retired have been the result of pressure from the working class.

State-funded transfer incomes are, however, severely constrained by capitalist social relations. Because of the extent of the failure of wage incomes, their aggregate cost to the state is enormous: in Britain in 2005, for example, it was 11% of GDP and a third of all state spending (Millar, 2003). Moreover, state incomes for people of working age must be low enough not to deter them from seeking the lowest wage employment, while being high enough to avoid destitution. This contradiction results in the 'poverty trap' (from the point of view of workers) and disincentives to work (from the point of view of employers). This contradiction underlies, and disrupts, three alternative forms for delivering benefits:

(i)   Social insurance and contributory benefits

These incomes for sickness, unemployment and retirement are funded by contributions from waged workers, and sometimes also from employers and the state. The form fits capitalist norms in that individuals fund their own benefits, and benefits may increase with contributions. A disadvantage for workers is that the benefits are limited to those with a (sufficient) work record, excluding many. Moreover, because they are not tied to needs, benefits may not meet the costs of subsistence for a particular household and place.

(ii)   Non-contributory benefits

These contradictions of social insurance have led to the development of non-contributory benefits. These purport to address unmet need, and are *selective* with respect to social group, existing income and savings, household form, and living costs. Members of specific groups such as children or the retired may get a 'categorical benefit' irrespective of their household income; but benefits to (potential) workers and their households are means tested. Non-contributory benefits can also pay towards the cost of items regarded as essential such as housing, school meals, heating of pensions' homes, basic durables, and local taxes, thus taking account of variable living costs.

The variable and targeted nature of such benefits and their lack of relation to the labour market cause problems for both state and recipient. First, these benefits are more likely than social insurance to lead to the 'poverty trap' since they are designed to meet basic subsistence but no more, cutting off if a slightly higher wage income is obtained. This then produces pressure to extend the benefits to those on higher incomes. Second, whereas social insurance provides benefits to individuals, mean-tested benefits are tailored to *households*, tending to reinforce the financial dependence of women on men (McKay and van Every, 2000). Third, the state has to employ investigators to check the income, expenditures and household composition of claimants. This policing conflicts with the fundamental capitalist ideology of the privacy of the home. Fourth, many fail to apply for means-tested benefits, because of resentment of the invasion of privacy, ignorance of their rights, the complicated and slow administration involved (Dean and Taylor-Gooby, 1992: 72). Fifth, landlords of benefit claimants tend to raise their rents knowing that they will still be paid. Six, unlike contributory benefits, the state may make receiving non-contributory benefits conditional on 'searching for work', that is, taking any job however unsuitable, low paid or remote ('workfare'). This is not only bad for the individual, but in aggregate fuels the expansion of poor jobs (Jones and Novak, 1999).

(iii) Tax credits

One way in which states have attempted to deal with the contradictions of benefits is to reduce income tax on low wage-income. The possibility and the need for this policy arise from the substantial income tax paid on low wages (see *Taxation* above). The effective benefit paid is still means tested, but the poverty trap is reduced since tax reduction continues to apply as claimants take up waged employment. Tax credits avoid one of the problems of non-contributory benefits by appearing as retained earnings rather than 'a handout'.

However, if tax credits are to reflect household composition or costs, administration is still intrusive. Moreover, tax credits for low-waged workers, in the long term and in aggregate, enable employers in low-age sectors to reduce wages. The state expenditure then flows as subsidy to employers, with little net benefit to the employees, just as housing benefits end up as subsidies to landlords with little benefit to tenants.

There are, then, important material and ideological differences between these three forms of state benefit. But none of them escapes from the tension between the capitalist wage relation and the meeting of need by the state. The problems of state benefit are not simply technical or administrative, as they are portrayed in most the social policy literature, but are expressions of contradictions of the wage relation.

In these ways, the state fails to overcome poverty (economic policy, public services), or actually intensifies poverty (taxation, benefits).

4 Social Reproduction and Poverty

The self-reproduction of people within households and neighbourhoods is closely entwined with poverty. Social life is a bulwark against poverty, but it also involves many particular material deprivations, and tends to deepen wage inequality. We consider here some interconnected threads: households and gender difference, neighbourhood survival strategies, housing, neighbourhood poverty, and consumption of commodities. All of these are deeply connected to the economic and state relations discussed in previous sections.

4.1 *Household, Caring Work and Gender*

In capitalism, the core site of the reproduction of people is the household, which uses wage and state-benefit income to purchase goods and services, including housing, and use them to carry out domestic and caring work, the majority of which is carried out by women. Poor housing and inadequate durables and non-durables mean the poor have to perform more domestic work than the better-off. This is compounded by lack of income to buy services: nurseries and child minders, care homes for elderly relatives, repairs to the house and durables, ready-cooked meals. The results are a massive burden of domestic work falling mainly on women, the 'triple working day' (Little et al., 1988), and also a tendency for the poor to be inadequately cared for materially and sometimes emotionally.

Since the earliest industrial capitalism, the burden of domestic work has been particularly onerous because both women and men in poor heterosexual-families have had, or sought, waged employment. From the late nineteenth century better-paid working-class men demanded, and sometimes obtained, a 'family wage' so that their wives could be full-time carers. Since the 1960s, however, women with male partners have increasingly taken up waged employment. Women have sought the financial and social independence of a job. But a new *norm* of a dual wage household has also enabled capital to hold wage rises for both men and women below increases in productivity while still meeting household consumption norms. In consequence, the two-wage couple has become the norm, as it has always been for the poor. This development has the *potential* for greater gender equality; but the reality has largely been for women to continue to do the lion's share of domestic work, so that the net result is an intensification of their working day. Moreover, the new social *norm* of two wages means that working class couples with one or no wage are much poorer relative to the average household than trends in individual wage distribution suggest (Leira, 2002).

In the nineteenth and early twentieth centuries, extended poor families living within a neighbourhood enabled much caring work to be shared between generations of women (Young and Willmott, 1957). But since the Second World War the family has tended to shrink to parents and their biological children. This shift has been underpinned by rising real wages, lightening of some domestic tasks, the state pension, smaller numbers of children, and by more frequent moves to obtain jobs. The result, however, is that working class careers are now more isolated, and thus have greater difficulty in taking up waged employment.

4.2 The Decline of Neighbourhood Survival Strategies of the Poor

This tendency has been exacerbated by decline of support from non-kin neighbours. The poor have traditionally survived through the material and moral support of their neighbourhood. Neighbours supplied help with domestic work, and constituted mini-welfare systems that helped to solve problems in family relations, finance and housing. Childcare and repairs were available on a reciprocal basis (Pahl and Wallace, 1985). Children could play safely in the streets because watched over by neighbours (and the absence of cars). What this lacked was privacy or room for unconventional social behaviour (Hoggart, 1957). Kin and neighbourhood also provided access to jobs. Better jobs, especially, required someone to 'speak for' you (McKibbin, 1998: 120). Moreover, communities facilitated 'ducking and diving' – the entrepreneurship of the poor (Ross, 1983; Tebbutt, 1983). Cheap illegally acquired goods were available. These means of survival were legitimated by the local culture, which consequently tended to be hostile to policing of the neighbourhood.

But this system has been eroded. During the 20C networks in poor neighbourhoods were weakened by the increase in women's time spent in wage work, increasing commoditisation of consumption, growing state services, and suburbanisation. All of these were associated with increases in living standards for the majority, and, to some extent, for the poor. Yet their paradoxical effect has been to weaken the social structures through which the poor survived, and to reduce their control over their lives and ability to recover from setbacks. Greater dependence on commodities has eroded practical skills for work and creativity in the home. Expanding public services have individualised their users rather than developed community cooperation. Slum clearance dispersed longstanding communities by failing to re-house them *in situ*. Indeed, this was often an aim of planners who sought to break up what they saw as a negative 'culture of poverty' (Burns, 1963; Davies, 1972). Social housing opportunities for young adults often located them far from their neighbourhood support networks (Speak and Graham, 2000).

These changes have had the effect of isolating poor individuals and households (Li et al., 2003). Help with caring work, moral support in crises and job networking have been weakened. Many consequently suffer from isolation, sometimes reinforced by depression and low self-esteem. Moreover, weakening of neighbourly ties has made it more difficult to deal with bad neighbours by reducing the collective pressure and actions that kept noise, rubbish dumping, public violence and vandalism in limits, so that these have become major problems of many poor areas.

This is not to argue that mutuality and community solidarity have disappeared among the poor. Indeed, community networks may be strongest in the poorest working-class neighbourhoods (Forrest and Kearns, 2001). The strength of community ties varies strongly between neighbourhoods, depending partly on the degree of population stability (Cattell and Evans, 1999; Johnston et al., 2000). The diagnosis of complete social fragmentation is an ideological one: it deflects attention from external conditions creating poverty and legitimates the capacity building approach to poverty alleviation. Nevertheless, social-spatial modernisation *has* eroded many of the traditional survival mechanisms.

4.3   *Housing*

Since the dawn of industrial capitalism, housing of the poor has been overcrowded, cold and unhealthy; this continues to the present day. There are large differences between HICs in their mixes of housing tenures, historically produced by class struggles and forms of urbanisation. But certain features of capitalist housing are universal. First, houses are expensive to build relative to working class incomes, and *a fortiori* incomes of the poor. The cost of new build, or purchase of existing houses, is met by borrowing (by whatever agent) from banks or savings/loan institutions; repayments or rent on this debt are large relative to working class incomes, particularly if interest rates are high. Moreover, the production of housing and its repair is labour intensive and hard to mechanise; the production cost of housing therefore tends to rise in the long term relative to the costs of manufactures and some services, that is, it rises in real terms.

Second, in capitalism land is a commodity. Since it is not produced, its price depends on the ground rent, the locationally-specific portion of profit realisable on the site (commercial land), or on the house price premium payable for the location of the site (housing land) (Edel, 1976); to the extent that commercial and housing uses respectively can be exchanged, these prices tend to converge. The price for a house site in cities and towns can therefore be high, sometimes many times the production cost of the house itself. Land price is thus a tribute paid by the poor to landowners. The housing land price is highest in the cities where jobs are plentiful and well-paid, and lowest in cities and rural areas where unemployment is high and wage low. Workers thus face a geographical trade-off between job availability and housing price. In particular, the poor in poor areas usually cannot afford to move to growth locations to work. At a smaller scale, land in distant suburbs can be cheap, particularly in countries with low-density cities (North America, Australia); but this has the severe penalty of dependence on the car for all journeys for all members of the household.

These problems are mediated by tenure (Conference of Socialist Economists, 1975). The poor generally cannot get mortgages because they lack secure long-term income. Where the poor do obtain a mortgage, they become vulnerable to any rise in interest rates and then face losing everything, as with 'sub-prime' mortgages in the U.S. in 2007. In many countries the poor in cities have no option but to rent from private landlords. The latter have an effective class monopoly, and can charge high rents for cramped accommodation in poor repair, with no security of occupation (Harvey, 1973). This causes continual disruption to the lives of poor households, including children's schooling. The only way that rents become affordable, tenancies become secure, and repairs get done is through strong state regulation, which always requires working class struggle. By far the best housing for the poor is state-owned or cooperative. These, too, require state regulation and loan guarantees. Expansion of social housing is sometimes supported by sections of capital which see low rent housing as a way to moderate wages, but its expansion always relies on working class pressure.

4.4 Poor Neighbourhoods

Since the 18C, capitalist towns and cities separate different income groups by area. People who have the money seek to live in the 'best' neighbourhood they can afford in terms of house quality, amenities and physical environment, and for social-cultural reasons seek neighbours of the same (or higher) income.

House and land price in these neighbourhoods rise. These prices then exclude people of lower income. The outcome over time is that the whole city acquires a structure of *single-income* neighbourhoods, and thus neighbourhoods which have only poor residents.

In British and U.S. cities the pattern has been of outward movement of the better-off to newly-built suburbs: the middle class from the early nineteenth century, the better-off working class from the late 19C through to the 1950s. Social democratic reformers saw the leafy suburb as a solution not just to the housing problems of the poor but to poverty in all its forms (Howard, 1902). But the poor could not afford housing costs of the suburbs nor the costs and time of commuting, and thus largely remained in their old areas. In consequence, by the 1960s inner city areas were largely poor. In Britain, as elsewhere in Western Europe, public housing has been built either in old working-class areas or on peripheral green field sites. The majority of public housing has thus been in lower income neighbourhoods, *mirroring* market patterning (Wadhams, 2002).

Spatial concentration of the poor is deepened for BME groups by racism. Due to low income and racist exclusion from many suburbs, BMEs locate in existing areas of poor, cheap housing. This pattern then develops cumulatively, due to the wish of ethnic minorities to live with others of the same ethnicity to obtain jobs and for social support and shared cultural facilities, as well as to minimise racist attacks.

Spatial segregation by income has led to vicious circles of privilege at one pole and deprivation at the other. Higher-income neighbourhoods tend to have better private services, better exam grades in schools, more open space, and fresher air, which strongly shape life chances and class position. The housing market enables the better off to capture these 'public goods' and capitalise them. The *logical counterpart* to these processes is the worsening of conditions of the poor through their ghettoisation. Public services, retailing, financial services and transport are often of poor quality. Industrial and vehicle air pollution are often high. The area then becomes stigmatised. Residents are stereotyped by employers as illiterate and innumerate, unreliable or dishonest (Mee, 1994). Mortgage providers often 'red line' these areas, which leads to cumulative under-investment in housing (Harvey, 1973).

These problems then cause households that can move out to do so, draining the neighbourhood of economic and political resources (Byrne, 1999; Power, 2000). This has led some poor neighbourhoods in low-growth cities to become seriously depopulated; streets become emptied and rapidly vandalised; the physical environment becomes atrocious (Harvey, 2000).

Spatial changes in capitalist investment in employment and consumer services across cities have further disadvantaged the poor. As cars have become the norm, retail has become increasingly concentrated in giant malls, and neighbourhood shops close. Health services have tended to concentrate. New office, warehouse and (remaining) factory investment is located in large sites, on city peripheries or further out. For poor people without cars – or without the *use* of the household car as is often the case for women and young people – these services and jobs become inaccessible or require very long (and expensive) journeys by bus.

We should, however, note that spatial concentration of the poor is a potential resource for political mobilisation. Collective action tends to be easiest to organise on the basis of shared problems. Local organisation is easier in terms of time and money. Social networks provide a starting point for organising. Moreover, collective organisation depends on trust of its leaders; in a neighbourhood the latter are known personally, and subject to collective will (Beitel, 2013). However, neighbourhood mobilisation of the poor is limited by the heavy, often racist, policing of poor neighbourhoods.

A different type of problem for poor neighbourhoods is their eviction by uses with higher ground rent. In cities at the top of the business-service hierarchy, professional employment has increased steadily since the 1960s. Some of these professionals wish to live in inner city locations, because of the easy access to the CBD, the historic architecture, or, iteratively, the 'vibrant' social atmosphere. Up until the 1980s this was largely achieved by the individual professional household buying single houses from owner occupiers or landlords; the former could then move out to the suburbs. Since the 1980s, however, gentrification has been accelerated, and carried out in more 'difficult' neighbourhoods, by local governments in association with large property companies; the existing residents are evicted together, the housing demolished, and rebuilt, often at higher density, for middle class use. The evicted residents may be offered small compensation, or offered cheap low quality housing in remote locations (Lees et al., 2008). In both 'classical' and state-led gentrification, the working class lose their social and kin networks, and access to their jobs in the inner and central city. Less well-recognised are the problems for the rural poor created by the move of middle-class commuters and retirees into pretty villages and the purchase of second homes there. This has severely depleted the housing stock available to working class people and forced young people to leave their communities (Cloke et al., 2002). Once again, the life-world of the poor is disrupted by capitalist land and housing markets.

4.5 Damaged by Commodities

Long-term growth in the productivity of consumer commodity sectors tends to increase the volume and types of commodities (goods and services) which constitute normal consumption. While some of these commodities can be useful for the poor, they can also damage them. First, many common commodities do physical or psychological harm. Unhealthy foods and fast food, dangerous chemicals used in thousands of household products, the video games and social media which decrease children's attention span – these are part of the consumption of the whole society. But they are a particular problem for the poor, since they have the least choice in what they buy and are most deprived of information on these products. The capitalist production of information and entertainment means that the poor consume newspapers, TV, music and games which often convey reactionary assumptions on gender, 'race' *and* class, and thus contribute to their low self-esteem and disempowerment.

Second, new products become necessities: the car (by its reconfiguration of the urban fabric), the internet (to be in touch with the contemporary world), the mobile phone (for young people to have a social life), and so on. Culturally-loaded commodities (clothes, music, leisure spaces) become important for the formation of personal identities. These commodities are then not freely chosen but are coercive. But the poor often cannot afford these commodities, or have to sacrifice essentials in order to buy them. This leads to the poor being excluded from mainstream social and cultural life.

Third, the poor sometimes consume luxuries, again at the expense of essentials. They may buy expensive versions of simple commodities. Poor youth aspire to luxury brands of clothing, luggage, jewellery, drinks and perfume. Expensive school proms and lavish nights out on the town are popular, as are stag and hen weekends in distant cities. Luxuries have long been promoted by advertising, life-style magazines and TV, and now by the social media. But the main push is from people's own lives: luxuries offer compensation for disempowering jobs and conflictual social life, and enable a brief moment out of poverty.

Taking all these aspects of social life together, we can see that households and neighbourhoods enable the poor to survive and to make life in some ways tolerable. But the atomised and antagonistic relations of social life and its material deprivation mean that the poor are not able adequately to reproduce themselves nor their labour power. Moreover, by further weakening their position in the labour market, their social life worsens their income deprivation.

5 Conclusion: the Poor and the Working Class as a Whole

We can conclude from this analysis that poverty in the HICs is not due to 'market imperfections', nor to internal features of poor neighbourhoods which can be remedied by limited reforms targeted on the poor themselves. Rather, it is systematically produced by the basic structures and processes of these societies. The sphere of capitalist waged employment systematically produces poor jobs and unemployment. Reciprocally, the poor play a crucial role in capital accumulation. State economic and industrial policies fail substantially to improve employment for the poor because constrained by lack of control over capital and reluctance to politicise the economy; some policies actually worsen poverty. Public services provide inferior outcomes for the poor. State transfer incomes are inadequate because of their subordination to the capitalist wage relation. Households and social life and the relations of kin and neighbourhood are a vital support to the poor. But the effects of low and uncertain income are exacerbated by materially-deprived caring and domestic work, inadequate public and private services, and cramped and unhealthy housing. Moreover, these undermine the poor's reproduction of their own labour power and thus deepen the employment causes of poverty. Gender and racism intertwine with class to reinforce poverty as well as to differentiate it. Poverty is thus created and perpetuated by the internally-related economy, state and social life of capitalism.

This theorisation shows the vacuity of conceiving the poor as an 'underclass'. This views the poor as radically different from the rest of the population in their capacities, attitudes and habits. But to the extent that the poor differ from the non-poor, this is a way of coping with poverty, not its cause. The 'underclass' is typically portrayed as completely outside the normal waged economy. This is true of some individuals and households for certain periods, but it is not generally true: many are employed in poor jobs; and the breaks in that employment are an intrinsic feature of those jobs, not of the workers who fill them (Gans, 1990). Moreover, as we have seen, at a deep level the lives of all the poor are dominated by the wage relation, capitalist accumulation, and their mediation by the state; they are in no sense outside these relations.[4]

In social-democratic thought, which dominates academic writing on poverty, the suffering of the poor is presented as distinct, as qualitatively different, from the condition of the rest of the population. It is certainly materially and

---

[4] The analytical Marxist E.O. Wright incorporated an 'underclass' into his theorisation of class structure (1995). He sees this underclass as wholly outside the wage relation, though 'economically oppressed'. For a critique see Novak (1996).

psychologically worse. But all forms of exploitation, oppression, exclusion and suffering of the poor are found also in the lives of the whole working population, that is, in the 90%, the working class in the Marxist sense. The poor experience *a condensation* of these oppressions, often in extreme forms, which moreover compound each other. But the qualitative forms of these oppressions operate across the whole population.

This internal relation between the poor and the not-poor also operates in the reverse direction: the existence of the poor weighs down the lives of the whole working class (Novak, 1995: 70–71; Jones and Novak, 1999: 18–24). Poor jobs put chronic downward pressure on the wages and conditions of all workers. The particular difficulties for workers in poor jobs to organise weaken the trade unions. The unemployed and those in poor jobs are a reserve army which employers in some sectors can use to undermine their employees' wages and conditions. Perhaps most importantly, workers in the non-poor economy accept the discipline of their employers, and remain in tyrannous jobs, through fear of losing their job and falling into the condition of the poor. Ideologically, the constant campaign of denigration by the media and politicians against the poor portrays the whole working class (in the conventional sense) as lazy, feckless and stupid, thus justifying their exploitation and the forms of discipline directed against all working class people (O. Jones, 2011).

If poverty is produced by the totality of society, then measures which target particular sites or aspects of poverty are doomed to failure: it cannot be solved outside of an end to capitalism. Since poverty is a condensation of oppressions which are experienced by the whole population, it can only be addressed by struggles against all forms of economic exploitation and social oppression, including within, through and against the state. These struggles benefit the whole population, not just the poor. The collective organisations of the whole working class in both the production and reproduction spheres and within the state are thus crucial for addressing both the immediate needs and long-term interests of the poor.

References

Alcock, Pete (1997) *Understanding Poverty*, 2nd ed. Basingstoke: Macmillan.
Beitel, Karl (2013) *Local Protest, Global Movements*. Philadelphia: Temple University Press.
Bowles, Samuel and Herbert Gintis (1976) *Schooling in Capitalist America*. New York: Basic Books.

Braverman, Harry (1974) *Labour and Monopoly Capitalism*. New York: Monthly Review Press.
Bryson, John, Peter Daniels, and Barney Warf (2004) *Service Worlds*. London: Routledge.
Burns, Wildred (1963) *New Towns for Old*, London: Leonard Hill.
Byrne, David (1999) *Social Exclusion and the City*. Milton Keynes: Open University Press.
Cabinet Office (2002) *Social Capital: a Discussion Paper*. London: Performance and Innovation Unit.
Carrier, John and Ian Kendall (1998) *Health and the NHS*. London: Athlone Press.
Cattell, Vicky and Melvyn Evans (1999) *Neighbourhood Images in East London*. York: Joseph Rowntree Foundation.
Clarke, Simon (1988) *Keynesianism, Monetarism and the Crisis of the State*. Aldershot: Elgar.
Clarke, Simon (1991) State, class struggle, and the reproduction of capital. In Simon Clarke (ed.) *The State Debate*. Basingstoke: Macmillan.
Cloke, Paul, Paul Milbourne, and Rebekah Widdowfield (2002) *Rural Homelessness*. Bristol: Policy Press.
Conference of Socialist Economists (ed.) (1975) *Political Economy and the Housing Question*. London: CSE.
Croall, Hazel (1998) *Crime and Society in Britain*. Harlow: Longman.
Das, Raju (2017) "David Harvey's Theory of Uneven Geographical Development: a Marxist Critique." *Capital and Class* 41 (3): 511–36.
Das, Raju, Aram Eisenchitz and Jamie Gough (2023) *The Challenges of the New Social Democracy: Social Capital and Civic Association or Class Struggle?* Leiden: Brill.
Davies, Jon (1972) *The Evangelistic Bureaucrat*. London: Tavistock.
Davis, M. (1992) *City of Quartz*. London: Verso
Dean, Hartley and Peter Taylor-Gooby (1992) *Dependency Culture: the Explosion of a Myth*. Hemel Hempstead: Harvester Wheatsheaf.
De Brunhof, Suzanne (1978) *The State, Capital and Economic Policy*. London: Pluto Press.
Dorling, Danny (2015) *Injustice: Why Social Inequality Persists*. Bristol: Policy Press.
Edel, Matthew (1976) "Marx's Theory of Rent: Urban Applications." In Conference of Socialist Economists (ed) *Housing and Class in Britain*. London: CSE.
Eisenschitz, Aram and Jamie Gough (1993) *The Politics of Local Economic Policy*. Basingstoke: Macmillan.
Eisenschitz, Aram and Jamie Gough (1996) "The Contradictions of Neo-Keynesian Local Economic Strategy," *Review of International Political Economics* 3 (3): 434–58.
Eisenschitz, Aram and Jamie Gough (2011) Socialism and the 'Social Economy'. *Human Geography* 4 (2): 1–15.
Forrest, Ray and Abe Kearns (2001) "Social Cohesion, Social Capital and the Neighbourhood." *Urban Studies* 38 (12): 2125–43.
Friedman, A. (1977) *Industry and Labour*, Basingstoke: Macmillan

Gans, Herbert (1990) "Deconstructing the Underclass: the Term's Dangers as a Planning Concept." *Journal of the American Planning Association* 56 (3): 271–277.
Gough, Ian (1982) *The Political Economy of the Welfare State*. London: Macmillan.
Gough, Jamie (1992) "Workers' Competition, Class Relations and Space". *Environment and Planning D: Society and Space* 10: 265–86.
Gough, Jamie (2002) "Neoliberalism and Socialisation in the Contemporary City: Opposites, Complements and Instabilities." *Antipode* 34 (3): 405–26.
Gough, Jamie (2003) *Work, Locality and the Rhythms of Capital*. London: Continuum/Routledge.
Gough, Jamie (2017) "Brexit, Xenophobia, and Left Strategy Now". *Capital and Class* 41 (2): 366–372.
Gough, Jamie and R Das (2017) "Introduction to Special Issue: Marxist Geography." *Human Geography* 9 (3): 1–9.
Gough, Jamie and Aram Eisenschitz (1996): "The Construction of Mainstream Local Economic Initiatives: Mobility, Socialisation and Class Relations." *Economic Geography* 76 (2): 178–95.Gough, J. and Eisenschitz, A. with McCulloch, A. (2006) *Spaces of Social Exclusion*, Abingdon: Routledge
Green, Francis and Peter Nore (eds) (1977) *Economics: an Anti-Text*. London: Macmillan.
Hahnel, Robin and Howard Sherman (1982) "The Rate of Profit Over the Business Cycle." *Cambridge Journal of Economics* 6: 185–94.
Hart, Julian Tudor (1971) "The Inverse Care Law." *Lancet* i: 405–12.
Harvey, David (1973) *Social Justice and the City*. London: Edward Arnold.
Harvey, David (2000) *Spaces of Hope*. Edinburgh: Edinburgh University Press.
Hoggar, Richard (1957) *The Uses of Literacy: Aspects of Working Class Life*. London: Chatto and Windus.
Howard, Ebenezer (1902) *Garden Cities of Tomorrow*. London: Swan Sonnenschein.
Illich, Ivan (1983) *Disabling Professions*. London: Marion Boyars.
Johnston, Les, Robert MacDonald and Paul Mason, Ridley R and Webster C (2000), *Snakes and Ladders: Young People, Transitions and Social Exclusion*. York: Policy Press.
Jones, Gareth Stedman (1971) *Outcast London*. Oxford: Oxford University Press.
Jones, Owen (2011) *Chavs: the demonization of the working class*. London: Verso.
Jones, Chris and Tony Novak (1999) *Poverty, Welfare and the Disciplinary State*. London: Routledge.
Kakios, Michael and John Van der Velden (1984) "Migrant Communities and Class Politics: the Greek Community in Australia." In G. Bottomley and M. de Lepervanche (eds) *Ethnicity, Class and Gender in Australia*. Sydney: George Allen and Unwin.
Lees, Loretta, Tom Slater and Evan Wyly (2008) *Gentrification*. London: Routledge.
Leira, Arnlaug (2002) *Working Parents and the Welfare State*. Cambridge: Cambridge University Press.
Lewis, Oscar (1979) *The Children of Sanchez*. London: Vintage Books.

Li, Yaojun, Mike Savage and Andrew Pickles A (2003) "Social Capital and Social Exclusion in England and Wales." *British Journal of Sociology* 54 (4): 497–562.

Little, Jo, Linda Peake and Patricia S. Richardson (1988) *Women in Cities*. London: Macmillan.

Mandel, Ernest (1978) *Late Capitalism*. London: Verso.

Mankiw, Greg (2001) *Principles of Economics,* 2nd ed. Fort Worth: Harcourt College.

Marx, Karl (1970) *Capital, Volume 1*. London: Lawrence and Wishart.

Massey, Doreen (1979) "In What Sense a Regional Problem?" *Regional Studies* 3 (2): 233–44.

Massey, Doreen (1984) *Spatial Divisions of Labour*. Basingstoke: Macmillan.

McKay, Ailsa and Jo Van Every (2000) "Gender, Family and Income Maintenance: a Feminist Case for Citizens' Basic Income." *Social Politics* 7 (2): 266–84.

McKibbin, Ross (1998) *Classes and Cultures: England 1918–1951*. Oxford: Oxford University Press.

McNally David (2015) "The Dialectics of Unity and Difference in the Constitution of Wage-labour: On Internal Relations and Working-class Formation." *Capital and Class* 39 (1): 131–146.

Martin, R., Nativel, C. and Sunley, P. (2003) 'The local impact of the New Deal: does geography make a difference?' In R. Martin, and P. Morrison (eds) *Geographies of Labour Market Inequality,* London: Routledge.

Mee, Kathleen (1994) "Dressing Up the Suburbs: Representations of Western Sydney." In Katherine Gibson and Sophie Watson (eds.) *Metropolis Now*. London: Pluto.

Millar, Fiona (2004) "The Links between Housing and Educational Outcomes Cannot be Ignored any Longer." *The Guardian*, 18 January.

Millar, Jane (2003) "From Wage Replacement to Wage Supplement: Benefits and Tax Credits." In Jane Millar (ed.) *Understanding Social Security*. Bristol: Polity Press.

Murray, Charles (1984) *Losing ground: American Social Policy: 1950–1980*. New York: Basic Books.

Noble, David F. (1984) *Forces of Production: a Social History of Industrial Automation*. Oxford: Oxford University Press.

Novak, Tony (1995) "Rethinking Poverty." *Critical Social Policy* 15 (44–45): 58–74.

Novak, Tony (1996) "A Class Analysis of Poverty: a Response to Erik Olin Wright." *International Journal of Health Services* 26 (1): 187–195.

Ollman, Bertell (1993) *Dialectical Investigations*. New York: Routledge.

Pahl, Ray and Claire D. Wallace (1985) "Forms of Work and Privatisation on the Isle of Sheppey." In Roberts B, Finnegan R and Gallie D (eds), *New Approaches to Economic Life*. Manchester: Manchester University Press.

Peet, Richard (1987) "The Geography of Class Struggle and the Relocation of U.S. Manufacturing Industry." In Richard Peet (ed) *International Capitalism and Industrial Restructuring*. Winchester, Mass.: Allen and Unwin.

Power, Anne (2000) Poor Areas and Social Exclusion. In Power A and Wilson W (eds) *Social Exclusion and the Future of Cities*, CASE Paper 35. London: Centre for Analysis of Social Exclusion.
Rhodes, M (ed) (1995) *The Regions and the New Europe*. Manchester: Manchester University Press.
Roberts, Martin (2016) *The Long Depression*. Chicago: Haymarket Books.
Ross, Ellen (1983) "Survival Networks: Women's Neighbourhood Sharing in London Before World War 1." *History Workshop* 15: 4–28.
Sassen, Saskia (1991) *The Global City*. Princeton: Princeton University Press.
Social Exclusion Unit (2001) *Preventing Social Exclusion*. London: SEU.
Speak, Suzanne and Steve Graham (2000) *Service Not Included: Social Implications of Private Sector Services Restructuring in Marginalised Neighbourhoods*. Bristol: Policy Press.
Stedman Jones, G. (1971) *Outcast London*. Oxford: Oxford University Press
Storper, Michael and Richard Walker (1989) *The Capitalist Imperative*. Oxford: Blackwell.
Tebbutt, Melanie (1983) *Making Ends Meet: Pawnbroking and Working Class Credit*. Leicester: Leicester University Press.
Townsend, Peter (ed) (1970) *The Concept of Poverty*. London: Heinemann.
Wadhams, Clarke (2002) *Neighbourhoods: a Guide to Neighbourhood Management for Registered Social Landlords*. London: Harding Housing Association.
Willis, Paul (1977) *Learning to Labour: How Working Class Kids Get Working Class Jobs*. London: Saxon House.
Wilson, Elizabeth (1977) *Women and the Welfare State*. London: Tavistock.
Wright, Erik Olin (1995) "A Class Analysis of Poverty." *International Journal of Health Services* 25 (1): 85–100.
Young, Michael and Peter Willmott (1957) *Family and Kinship in East London*. London: Routledge.

CHAPTER 9

The Limits of the Concept of Neoliberalism in Action

Bryant William Sculos

1   What's New in Neoliberalism?[1]

The argument here will not be that any particular theory or historical categorization of neoliberalism is wrong. In fact, most, if not all, of the scholars who have offered theoretical and/or historical descriptions of neoliberalism have produced not only excellent academic work, but are politically righteous as justifiable opponents of what they call "neoliberalism" (Biebricher, 2018: 1). Neither should it be inferred from what follows here that the majority of theorists of neoliberalism view neoliberalism as something completely distinct or separate from capitalism more generally. Many of these scholars argue precisely the opposite, that there is an important relationship between capitalism and neoliberalism and/or that neoliberalism is a particular iteration of capitalism—but still that there is something uniquely "neoliberal" that is worth describing. Many of these scholars are also critics of capitalism more generally. However, it is precisely the space for one to be a critic of neoliberalism but not necessarily a critic of capitalism that will be the primary focus of this chapter. Put more directly, by emphasizing the uniqueness of neoliberalism (even where conceptualized more specifically as "neoliberal capitalism"), the structural and theoretical continuity between the capitalist system and the enduring neoliberal age can fade into the background—or, at worst, disappear completely.[2] While the theoretical strengths and limitations will be covered

---

1   This chapter is a revised and updated version of Bryant William Sculos, "It's Capitalism, Stupid: The Theoretical and Political Limitations of the Concept of Neoliberalism," *Class, Race and Corporate Power*, Vol. 7 (2): Article 7.

2   There are several recent exceptions. These are books that deal with the substance of what is typically referred to as neoliberalism, but treat it as a manifestation of longer, deeper trends of capitalism and also do not give pride of place to the concept or term "neoliberalism" or "neoliberal capitalism." Though there are others, three important exemplars include: *The New Spirit of Capitalism* by Luc Boltanski and Eve Chiapello (trans. Gregory Elliot) (Verso, 2005); *Zombie Capitalism* by Chris Harman (Haymarket, 2010); *Buying Time* by Wolfgang Streeck (Verso, 2014); *Profitable Ideas* by Micheal O'Flynn (Haymarket, 2012); *The Long Depression*

generally here, the focus will be on the problematic political implications of the use of the concept of neoliberalism.

This chapter offers three interrelated contributions around the aforementioned argument: First, I provide a brief discussion of how neoliberalism has been theorized by critics of neoliberalism (critics of the reality of neoliberalism, not the cluster of ideas and claims that comprise the concept). Second, the essay emphasizes the specifically political limitations of the use of the concept of neoliberalism. The examples of healthcare and climate change are used here to briefly elucidate these limitations. Next are brief discussions of neoliberalism in relation to the COVID-19 pandemic and recent arguments about neoliberal authoritarianism. Finally, given that this chapter is motivated by a particular political position and goal—the achievement of a democratic, egalitarian world beyond capitalism—the relationship between the psycho-social dimensions of political economy and the politics of achieving a just, democratic and egalitarian transition to a broadly socialist form of postcapitalism plays an important, if still underdeveloped, role in the argument here.

It is a perverse and deeply ingrained ideological irony that one of the results of the focus on neoliberalism from within neoliberal capitalism, is that neoliberalism is reified. In other words, we can forget that neoliberalism is neoliberal capitalism, which is simply a specific historical and structural iteration of capitalism, and further that neoliberal capitalism still bears all of the problematic hallmarks of historical capitalism (e.g., exploitation, oppression, anti-democracy, and alienation, among others). There is thus a verifiable risk that by merely criticizing and opposing neoliberalism, the possibility, and indeed even the desirability, of maintaining a less aggressive and destructive form of capitalism remains pragmatically actionable and therefore this opportunistic avenue retains an excessive degree of political gravity. In turn, we can end up focusing our energies on resisting only the very worst excesses of the

---

by Michael Roberts (Haymarket, 2016); and *Portfolio Society* by Ivan Ascher (Zone Books, 2016). Additionally, one book that deals with neoliberalism that is difficult to categorize is Ray Kiely's excellent *Clash of Globalisations* (Haymarket, 2009), which describes the roots of globalization and neoliberalism in the capitalist mode of production, but then proceeds to focus nearly exclusively on the connection between the Third Way and neoliberalism, without much return to the deeper connection to capitalism. If one reads back through the book, the connection to capitalism is clearly discussed, but as one reads forward through the book, the connection back to capitalism progressively fades. The result is that the need to move beyond capitalism completely is only vaguely argued for. Regardless, *Clash of Globalisations* is useful as an introduction to debates about globalization, the Third Way, neoliberalism, cosmopolitanism, and left resistance strategy—while also offering original treatments of the same.

development of global capitalism, undoubtedly exacerbated by the sheer magnitude of thinking and organizing against the deeper, broader, and far more ideologically durable system of capitalism.

Before getting too far into things, it is useful to appreciate how it is that neoliberalism came to bear this apparently confounding label. The answer is represented by the treatment of thinkers like Milton Friedman, Friedrich Hayek, and Von Mises variously as libertarians, conservatives, and (neo)liberals. Neoliberalism represents an intersection of political-economic ideologies that makes the concept difficult to treat in any simplistic manner. Over the course of the twentieth century, liberalism took on a more social democratic flavor, from its early progression in the late work of John Stuart Mill and his *Chapters on Socialism* (late nineteenth century), to John Dewey's social liberalism in various works like *The Public and its Problems*, through the political agendas of liberals such as FDR, up through the works of John Rawls and his academic progeny. This trajectory—along with the material political-economic contradictions of capitalism (embodied in both the "defeat" of supply-side approaches and the limits of post-WWII Keynesianism)[3] leading to the need for the capitalist class and supportive governments to pursue the privatization and deregulation policies associated with neoliberalism—overdetermined the rebranding of hyper-capitalist (now viewed as "conservative") policies as a return to the foundational principles of classical liberalism in Locke and Smith (despite Locke's and Smith's more or less clear opposition to the kinds of politics based on justifying pure profit-seeking that neoliberals have deployed their names and theories to justify). Put even more simply, "neoliberalism" is the result of an ideological battle over two increasingly divergent trends of liberalism, in the context of the on-going material instabilities of capitalism, which all forms of liberalism have been continuously unable to deal with consistently or satisfactorily.

To capture the relationship between the diversity of treatments of the concept of neoliberalism, it is helpful to categorize approaches to neoliberalism in three general ways: 1. As a period of certain privatization and deregulation policies in the 1970s, 80s and beyond; 2. A political project pursued by certain capitalist ideologues, politicians, and representatives of the interests of capital(ism); 3. A governing, and increasingly dominant, rationality or mode of

---

3 These contradictions can be articulated by under-consumptionist, over-productionist, or more orthodox surplus-value/declining rate of profit theories, discussed in detail in Michael Robert's *The Long Depression* (though Roberts offers a strong defense of the last approach).

thinking and being that is associated with the neoliberal period mentioned in point one.[4]

Theories that prioritize one of these approaches over others also tend to mention the others' arguments or claims, simply with less emphasis (that is, the best theories of neoliberalism treat it as a political-economic project serving the interests of capitalism during this late twentieth and early twenty-first century and has become a kind of governing rationality or dominant social-psychology). While there are plenty of disagreements among proponents of one emphasis over others, this chapter is primarily focused on theories of neoliberalism that in some way engage with all three categories (and for the most part, though with some exceptions, this chapter treats them generally). Even insofar as we can discretely categorize theories of neoliberalism for the sake of argument, representatives of each approach still vary significantly (sometimes even within their own individual presentations) on whether neoliberalism is primarily political or economic, as well as the role of agency in (re)producing neoliberalism. These distinctions are important but are not the focus of this chapter.

What this chapter focuses on are theories of neoliberalism (and neoliberal capitalism) that either by explicit argumentation or by the sheer fact of being written, assert the theoretical and political value of the concept of neoliberalism (again, primarily as an object of critique). Though there are plenty of excellent contributions to the theorization of neoliberalism that are left out here, mainly for a matter of space, some of the strongest, enduring, and recent books that meet the criteria, and serve as a generalized basis of analysis for this chapter include: David Harvey's *A Brief History of Neoliberalism*, David Kotz's *The Rise and Fall of Neoliberal Capitalism*, Pierre Dardot and Christian Laval's *The New Way of the World*, Wendy Brown's *Undoing the Demos*, Philip Mirowski's *Never Let a Serious Crisis Go to Waste*, William Davies *The Limits of Neoliberalism*, and Thomas Biebricher's *The Political Theory of Neoliberalism*.[5]

---

4 Though it does not fit neatly into this category, Adam Kotsko's *Neoliberalism's Demons: On the Political Theology of Late Capital* (Stanford University Press, 2018) most closely resembles the kinds of arguments typical in this category.

5 While Harvey and Kotz are included here in the general treatment, it is important to keep in mind that both do highlight the capitalistic qualities of neoliberalism (as neoliberal capitalism). William I. Robinson's various works on the theory of global capitalism (moving beyond the interpretation of capitalism as a world-system) also deals with neoliberalism within the context of the history of capitalism and as capitalism—and is probably not even best categorized as a theorist of neoliberalism at all. These thinkers are careful to not reify neoliberalism as something wholly or even primarily novel in the history of capitalism. Coming from more or less neo-Marxist perspectives, these authors explore and describe neoliberalism as capitalism, but, still, in my judgment, lend themselves to less radical interpretations by, however

Capitalism is hard enough for the average person to define with any degree of rigor, and understandably so. Ask the average person what neoliberalism is and the political problem with the concept is made manifest. Surely it qualifies as jargon, which, however frustrating that reality may be, is not reason enough to cast it aside. The question of the value of the concept of neoliberalism is dually how accurately it describes a unique phenomenon, and, precisely because of the deeply harmful policies and practices that scholars are calling "neoliberalism," whether the concept is politically useful. The task remains for scholars, activists, and organizers offering both a critique of capitalism and neoliberalism to distinguish more clearly between capitalism and neoliberalism—or, absent important or relevant distinctions, to ditch the critique of neoliberalism altogether and focus their critical work on capitalism itself.

To put my argument here more directly, if neoliberalism is, as some scholars like Harvey (2007) have suggested, the political ideology of late capitalism, it is more useful to focus on the particularly capitalistic aspects of neoliberalism and to emphasize the continuity of these aspects with historical capitalism, as opposed to being some unique political-economic ideology and/or system. Further, we can understand that capitalism itself has always been a political project, and how the increasing academic focus on the particularities of neoliberalism is more distraction than praxis.[6] If capitalism is, as is widely accepted on the left, a political-economic system (with broader social and cultural dimensions) rooted in generalized commodity production and the extraction of surplus value through wage labor (based on various forms of gendered, racialized unpaid social-reproductive labor and unaccounted for ecological destruction), with the role of the state to manage the overall health

---

unintentionally or against their actual political perspectives, fail to come down strongly against the idea that resistance to neoliberalism is best, or only possibly successful, in the context of a deeper and broader resistance to the fundamental aspects of capitalism, including its unpaid social reproductive and extractivist dimensions. Although it is difficult and always problematic to make such a generalization, the purpose of doing so here is to develop a strong critical position, partly in the hopes of pushing readers to more deeply explore the treatment and political efficacy of focusing on or using the concept of neoliberalism. While there is admittedly some degree of reductionism and effacement of nuance in this analysis, the goal of this chapter is a *politicized* political theorization of the issues with the prevailing treatments of neoliberalism over the past couple decades. There is more to value in this body of literature than this chapter shows. For example, the concept of "neoliberalization" discussed later in this essay shows a positive theoretical, and effective political, use of neoliberalism, was influenced by Harvey's use of the same concept.

6 Praxis here meant in the classical Marxist sense of the interpenetration and co-constitutiveness of theory and practice (theory produced in and through practice and practice informed by and rooted in theory).

and stability of the system in the interests of the ruling class, what is novel about neoliberalism? What is new about neoliberalism besides the reality that what we are calling neoliberalism is merely the reality of the ruling capitalist class succeeding in the further expansion and instantiation, horizontally and vertically, of capitalism under dynamic global conditions?

While this last characterization could be interpreted as a kind of answer to the question of what is actually new about neoliberalism (namely, changing capitalist conditions tied to changes in forms of class struggle, state formation, and ideology), there is a political cost in implying that these developments are importantly discontinuous, historically or theoretically, with the admittedly diverse character of the capitalist mode of production, distribution, and consumption—including is social reproductive elements. Placing the emphasis on neoliberalism shifts the psycho-social focus and aim of political activity away from truly systemic transformation (from capitalism to some kind of socialism or democratic egalitarian post-capitalism with whatever label) and more in the direction of milquetoast reformism (from neoliberalism "back" to regulated capitalism).

Returning to the question of the state, even some of the most discursively and ideologically-focused scholarship on neoliberalism (e.g., Brown's *Undoing the Demos*, Mirowski's *Never Let a Serious Crisis Go to Waste*, Han's *Psychopolitics*, Koning's *The Emotional Logic of Capitalism*, etc.) acknowledge that the state, despite the ideological claims of the proponents of the policies, practices, discourses, and ideas that are collectively referred to as "neoliberalism," played and plays an important role in the production of neoliberalism. There is far too much debate within the Marxist tradition (most notably between Miliband and Poulantzas) to claim, as Dardot and Laval (2013) do most explicitly, that Marxism is too reductive in its treatment of the juridical and political realm to the economy to properly or fully understand the developments that are captured in the concept of "neoliberalism." There is even a diversity of perspectives presented in Marx's work regarding the content of what we today refer to as the base-superstructure metaphor, so much so that it would be justifiable to conclude that it is actually Dardot and Laval who are guilty of reductionism—reducing all Marxism to economism.

2 The Critique of the Critique of Neoliberalism: Theory and Politics

One could reasonably argue that given the historical consequences of the Cold War, especially in the OECD world (global North), it might be politically easier to convince more people of the idea that neoliberalism needs to go than the idea that capitalism, as a whole, needs to go. The thinking goes, since people like the idea of capitalism, in whatever abstract way people think about that word, and neoliberalism stimulates less ideological intransigence, we should take the path of least resistance and first delegitimize and turn back the clock on the developments of neoliberalism. Once accomplished (or in the process of opposing neoliberalism without success), the enduring contradictions of capitalism will remain as limitations on the achievement of the kind of world that a rigorous opposition to neoliberalism would necessarily be rooted in, a more robust, explicit opposition to capitalism can be organized and enacted.

I cannot say *for sure* that that perspective is wrong—but the goal of this polemic is to convince you that there are very good reasons to believe it is indeed wrong. While the critique and abolition of whatever is captured in the concept of neoliberalism may well be a necessary step in the historical process of delegitimizing capitalism and building a serious alternative from within capitalism in order to move beyond capitalism—that is, before the planet becomes uninhabitable for all but the very richest among us (whom at that point will have undoubtedly developed protections from the worst aspects of global climate change and thus will no longer be "among us"), the question remains whether targeting neoliberalism is *more* politically useful than targeting capitalism. Spoiler alert: there's very little evidence that it is—but I still do my best here to show the use of the concept of neoliberalism at its strongest and most useful, particularly in the context of understanding various left positions on healthcare and the environment.

Before proceeding to the political limitations of the concept of neoliberalism, it is fair to consider the strengths of the concept, both theoretically and politically. Politically, one of the important contributions is that it avoids controversies around capitalism versus socialism. One can oppose neoliberalism, or so it is assumed, and not necessarily be opposed to capitalism as such. Certainly, or so it is assumed, one can oppose neoliberalism but not be any kind of socialist (or perhaps one is merely required to be a "*democratic* socialist"[7]).

The other suggested political advantage is that neoliberalism, whether understood as a distinct political project from the broader political project of

---

7 "Democratic socialist" here meaning either a social democrat or welfare state liberal, though there are many people who use this label to refer to a wide array of non-revolutionary socialists as well. The first part of the "democratic socialist" label is also historically meant to distinguish between the twentieth century state communist projects and conceptions of socialism that are critical of these totalitarian perversions and even of Marxism as such, despite the historical and contemporary reality of innumerable Marxist socialists, including Marx himself, who are imminently democratic in their conceptions of socialism/communism.

capitalism (or neoliberalism as the political project of capitalism in the late twentieth and early twenty-first century), it is useful to both consider the particular iteration of capitalism, including its distinct ideological political project, at the current historical moment and that by emphasizing the political dimension of the (contemporary) political project of capitalism, through the use of the label neoliberalism, *repoliticizes* debates and struggles over capitalist political-economic practices.

Whereas for many non-academics, non-activists, and non-organizers, capitalism may be viewed strictly as an economic system that proceeds, more or less, of its own accord. This depoliticized conception of capitalism, as described in somewhat different terms by J.K. Gibson-Graham (1996), makes political resistance or alteration to the capitalist economy seem to be non-starter, either because it is inherently not susceptible to political control (rooted in a rigid liberal distinction between political and economic spheres, or public and private realms) or that such attempts are futile because the power of capitalism in practice, even if theoretically susceptible to political control, makes such attempts to actually gain control over the capitalist system ineffective. By using the concept neoliberalism as a kind of discursive alternative, capitalism's political project is in actuality brought to the forefront from the outset. If one is talking about neoliberalism, one is automatically talking about more political-economic phenomena, implemented through intentional policies by particular factions of the ruling class in the service of the whole of capitalist class. Or so this line or argument generally goes.

Put a bit differently, the ostensible theoretical or historical value of the concept of neoliberalism is that neoliberalism refers to a specific set of policies, goals, and ideological assumptions and conclusions that pertain to a particular historical period of capitalism that differ in crucial ways from the previous history (or theorizations) of capitalism—and therefore in order to develop appropriate political strategies to deal with contemporary (neoliberal) capitalism, we must have a proper theory of neoliberalism.

Even if neoliberalism is *just* capitalism during a historical period with some, even if mainly superficially, novel political and economic traits (but still basically capitalism), as I am more or less arguing here (as others cited above have before me), understanding those novel traits and their distinctive manifestations and effects in our contemporary world, especially as they affect how effective resistance and transformation can be pursued, insofar as the concept of neoliberalism/neoliberal capitalism draws productive attention to these characteristics, it has genuine political value. The assumption here is (one that will only be determined accurate or inaccurate over time and with self-reflection): the distinctiveness of neoliberalism/neoliberal capitalism necessitates making different strategic and tactical choices by those interested in systemic change. This is especially true when one gives increased attention to the psycho-social dimensions of neoliberalism/neoliberal capitalism.

Indeed, one of the noteworthy emphases in many theories of neoliberalism and neoliberal capitalism is the production of certain collection of psycho-social dispositions, or a mentality, that is distinct from previous periods of capitalism, and may even, as Dardot and Laval argue, signal a reconfiguration of the relationship between the economic base and the ideological superstructure (especially in terms of the law) that is, perhaps with exaggerated rigidity, attributed to the Marxist tradition. Even with the ferocity of their criticisms of the Marxist approach to neoliberalism, even Dardot and Laval (2013: 11) say "we must refer to *neo-liberal society*, and not merely a neo-liberal *policy* or neo-liberal *economics*. While unquestionably a capitalist society, *this* society pertains to a unique form of capitalism that must be analyzed as such in its irreducible specificity." So, while these authors are certainly well-within the camp of asserting the uniqueness of neoliberalism, even for them neoliberalism is still a kind of capitalism, and it is capitalism that must eventually be overcome.[8]

However, one need not rely on more recent poststructural theories of neoliberalism, such as Dardot and Laval's and Brown's (2015), to understand and appreciate the importance of the psycho-social conditions of capitalism—even how they may evolve over time. Not only is some of this work pre-figured in the early Marx, Lev Vygotsky, Theodor Adorno, Max Horkheimer, Erich Fromm, and Herbert Marcuse each made similar arguments, connecting the political economy of capitalism to the social-psychological realm (including discussing how this shapes or should shape approaches to revolutionary socialist transformation).

Fromm's (1955; 1994) work is crucial here. Throughout his career Fromm presented a historically-nuanced presentation of the evolution of the psycho-social character of capitalism (privileging more cautious, restrained psychologies in its earliest period to the hyper-marketing character that became dominant through the emergence of consumer society in the global North),

---

8 Beyond the contribution of Dardot and Laval, the idea of neoliberalism as a kind of socially-penetrating and increasingly hegemonic affective discourse or governing rationality is also a central element of some of the most innovative treatments of neoliberalism, such as (excluding ones previously mentioned): William Davies' *The Happiness Industry* (Verso, 2015); Martijn Koning's *The Emotional Logic of Capitalism* (Stanford University Press, 2015); and Byung-Chul Han's *Psychopolitics: Neoliberalism and New Technologies of Power* (trans. Erik Butler)(Verso, 2017).

while leaving open the possibility that capitalism could even evolve further in terms of what social-psychological traits are best suited to the endurance of capitalism.

There are correlative dangers in the neoliberal theorists' assumption about the value of emphasizing the uniqueness of the conditions of neoliberalism—one that Fromm's work highlights retroactively. In reality, it is Fromm's theorizing of the marketing social character and the psycho-social harms of the alienating, hyper-individualizing effects of capitalism in the early twentieth century that speaks to the intimate connection between what is described as neoliberalism and the fundamental psycho-social traits of capitalism in general. Neither for Marx, as far back as his early work in the *Economic and Philosophic Manuscripts of 1844*, nor for the Frankfurt School Critical Theorists, Fromm being just one example, was capitalism ever merely an economic system. It was always also a political project with social-psychological and cultural dimensions and implications. The novelty with which theorists of neoliberalism treat these aspects of neoliberalism, plus the intersection of politics and socioeconomics (with the former used to allow the latter to overtake the former), is itself surprising—and fundamentally unoriginal (if not outrightly incorrect, if attributed to neoliberalism exclusively and not shown to be produced, at least in part, through all forms of historical capitalism).

Having read thousands of pages of work on neoliberalism at this point, I remain highly skeptical that this "neoliberalism" is really categorically new. Maybe it is not categorically new, but the specifics are new. Well, of course they are. Things are never the same all the time. No one would ever expect them to be. The question then becomes not just one of *how novel* the various traits typically attributed to neoliberalism are, but *how politically useful* highlighting them specifically as elements of neoliberalism versus attributing them to capitalism is (or, put a bit differently, not more generally the result of the historical victories of capitalism is).

3 The Political Trap of (Critiques of) Neoliberalism

One can look at capitalism without homogenizing its history, but one can look at neoliberalism and forget that what is really being talked about is capitalism. The concept of "neoliberal capitalism" contains less of this potential, given that it maintains the capitalist component. However, "neoliberal capitalism" still contains a danger. If I say I am a critic of neoliberal capitalism, can you be sure which of the parts I am a critic of? Am I a critic of neoliberal capitalism and capitalism as a whole, or am I simply a critic of the particular manifestation of capitalism in the neoliberal period (or a critic of the neoliberal project—depending on where one is on the spectrum of views on the intentionality of neoliberalism as a political project or as an agent-less historical period or process)?

In practice, the problem can be represented by the figure of Bernie Sanders (though we will get to how Barack Obama fits in this conversation as well shortly). Bernie Sanders can rightly be viewed as a critic of neoliberalism and neoliberal capitalism. While one might conclude, based on reading Sanders's (2015) memoir, that he holds genuinely anti-capitalist views, his policies and campaign rhetoric are certainly not anti-capitalist, despite his "liberal" (in both senses of the word) use of the label "democratic socialist." This, along with a lot of historical development in the use of labels, also produces (or at least relates to) the complicated situation where Bernie Sanders can be both a (democratic) socialist and a supporter of capitalism (so long as it isn't neoliberal capitalism). While scholars and politicians may have a similar interest in avoiding the grotesque and intellectually immature red-baiting that making overtly anti-capitalist arguments incurs, the result is an intellectual and political confusion that undermines basically all of the possible political advantages of the concept of neoliberalism, perhaps with the exception of not scaring off progressive liberals who are not quite ready for the full-on anti-capitalist critique that comes from a genuinely socialist perspective. Sanders certainly pushes the limits of acceptable politics in the U.S. by being an ardent critic of neoliberal capitalism and using the label "democratic socialist," there is a lot of curb-appeal, especially among young people, for a less onerous conception of socialism and for mitigating the very worst elements of (neoliberal) capitalism—but this is a vision of "socialism" that deliberately eschews genuine systemic transformation.

While it would be hasty to dismiss the possible benefit of this strategy completely for all time, it is unclear from history just how effective it has been for socialists to prioritize concerns for not alienating near-left liberals (By this I mean it is unclear whether any benefit has ever been produced by being concerned about alienating politically-engaged ideological liberals.). Tactful, persuasive engagement is still vital for any socialist movement with hopes of earning mass support, but the question here is whether it is useful to attempt to enlist the support of progressive anti-neoliberal (but not anti-capitalist) liberals by focusing our critiques and organizing energies against neoliberalism or neoliberal capitalism, as opposed to capitalism as such, in all of its historical forms. Persuading well-meaning progressive liberals of the need to be anti-capitalist seems likely to be more (and at least not less) likely to be effective towards building a broad-based socialist movement than playing strategic word-games around neoliberalism would be (and has been).

To elaborate further on the political and theoretical value of the concept of neoliberalism (and the corollary limitations), it is useful to think through an argument made by Jeffrey Goldfarb in *Public Seminar* in 2017. Goldfarb (2017) explores the problems of the term and concept of neoliberalism, specifically its inconsistent application by those on the left. He claims that neoliberalism is used to describe a wide range of policy positions from public-private ventures up to the complete deregulation of private industry or "market fundamentalism." Goldfarb also argues that "neoliberalism" is a kind of "elite-speak," incomprehensible to anyone outside of a narrow coterie of left-leaning academics. Despite these cogent observations, I contend that neoliberalism as a concept is both more coherent and more problematic than Goldfarb's analysis suggests.

My response to Goldfarb, a version of which was published with *Public Seminar* as well, connects most closely to the last example of political and theoretical usefulness just mentioned above (not alienating those who aren't quite ready for the full anti-capitalist plunge), while also again pointing to "neoliberalism's" limitations (Sculos, 2017a). First, taking neoliberalism as proceeding in degrees, we could understand politicians as diverse as Paul Ryan and Barack Obama as neoliberals, without the concept losing complete coherence and/or instrumental-critical value. Second, there is a countervailing limitation to the value of any critique of neoliberalism if such a critique, as they typically do, too easily maintain belief in the false possibility of the fundamental reformation of capitalism. If neoliberalism is perceived as the central problem, our critique of capitalism is weakened. The critique of neoliberalism, often regarded as a unique political perversion of a nicer, more humane capitalism, too easily moves the goal posts of radical and progressive change.

In this context, in order to retain the coherence of neoliberalism as a concept, we need to distinguish between the ideal-typical political ideology of "neoliberalism," represented in the work of thinkers like Friedrich Hayek and Milton Friedman, and the process of "neoliberalization." Neoliberalism, as an ideal-type, is best understood as a government-driven[9] market-based political economy, which places the private property rights and profits of corporations above the democratic control and interests of the people. Again, how this differs fundamentally from capitalism is unclear, but, regardless, neoliberalization then

---

9 Despite neoliberal thinkers' insistence that neoliberalism is foundationally antithetical to government intervention (a belief that has been too often accepted by those on the left), this is a mythology that has been debunked by many critics of neoliberalism. Thus, this component is included here.

would be any policy, process, or movement that in some form advances neoliberal interests or ends. Neoliberalization, as the process of moving towards the "normative horizon" (or cliff) of neoliberalism, thus typically involves the erosion of public-democratic services, spaces, and even "the public" itself. When most academics refer to something as neoliberal, what they really mean is that it contributes to neoliberalization, not that it represents some pure ideal-type. This is likely the source of Goldfarb's and many others' quite justifiable confusion, which is itself relevant to the broader argument of this chapter regarding the limitations of the concept of neoliberalism: beyond shifting the goal posts, if people are so excessively confused about what a term means, it is difficult to build a coherent and effective struggle against it.

4   Healthy Profits, Unhealthy People

That neoliberalism, at its most conceptually-valuable, is a matter of degree can be understood by looking at the on-going debate over health care in the U.S. (though the logic can be applied in any context). There are three policies, which are each, to varying degrees, part of a neoliberalization process.

This is where neoliberalism can connect to the problematic discussions and categorizations of someone like Barack Obama. We have the Affordable Care Act, or "Obamacare," wherein the government mandates that individual citizens buy health care from private companies. This individual mandate leaves the roots of the American healthcare system in the market, and even forces citizens into that market to the benefit of private insurance companies. On the other hand, the ACA also expanded the government's role in providing health insurance by offering citizens subsidies and offering states increased funding to expand Medicaid coverage. Thus, the ACA contains elements that contribute to neoliberalization and others that hedge against full-scale neoliberalism.

Compare the ACA to the Ryan-Trump plan that was eventually withdrawn from a planned floor vote in the House of Representatives (Lawder and Holland, 2017). This bill was a more aggressive form of neoliberalization than the ACA in that it removed the individual mandate (the penalty for violation being paid to the federal government) and replaced it with a rule allowing private insurers to charge up to 30% more for people who lacked health insurance for more than 63 days in the previous calendar year. There is still a government-allowed penalty for failing to buy insurance, but in the case of the Ryan-Trump plan the penalty money is paid directly to private companies. Additionally, while the plan retained subsidies, they were substantially more regressive than with the ACA.

Another alternative bill proposed by the so-called "Freedom Caucus" of the House GOP, called for the complete repeal (without replacement) of the ACA. No subsidies to help people buy insurance. No individual mandate in any form. Insurance companies would be able to charge more or less whatever they wanted to anyone. They could discriminate based on age, gender, and pre-existing conditions. This bill is much closer to—if not fully representing—neoliberalism in its ideal form.

Privatization can take many forms, but when we think about the drift towards neoliberalism, it is fundamentally a matter of degree, with few policies ever likely to fully meet the ideal-typical definition of neoliberalism sketched out above. This is where the concept of neoliberalism has value; it allows us to understand how policies as diverse as the ACA and the Freedom Caucus proposal each embody neoliberal values in distinct ways and why all degrees of neoliberalization need to be resisted.

One can also put the ACA against various proposed versions of Medicare-for-All. In his earliest comments on Medicare-for-All, Bernie Sanders, considered the political father of this proposal in the popular imaginary, simply stated that Medicare-for-All means dropping the age limitation from the existing Medicare statute. However, while the existing Medicare statute is an example of a kind of single-payer (though still with co-pays and premiums, depending on the plan and the procedure), it is primarily processed through private, for-profit insurance companies, which the ability to profit off of is increasingly difficult for the public to find information about (but obviously happens or these for-profit companies wouldn't provide Medicare plans at all). If Medicare-for-All were to proceed under the current conditions of Medicare, it would be a regression of neoliberalism and neoliberalization, without removing us from the overall structure of a capitalist political economy. If the prescription drugs are still produced and distributed within a for-profit model, if medical devices are still produced and distributed within a for-profit model, if nurses and doctors and medical workers of all kinds still produce surplus-value for for-profit health care companies, Medicare-for-All is still progress, but it does not represent moving outside of neoliberalism or neoliberalization, at least not completely, but it is certainly moving in the right direction. In other words, Medicare-for-All, in its various interactions, is a challenge to neoliberalism as neoliberalization, but it is not automatically a fundamental challenge to capitalism. Certainly, if one views Medicare-for-All as a last-ditch effort to maintain the legitimacy of for-profit health care, even through its single-payer model, it fits contradictorily within the ideological and structural-historical parameters of capitalism—and may even serve some of the forces of neoliberalization, even as it is obviously less neoliberal than the Freedom Caucus plan or the ACA.

Conversely, there are other versions of Medicare-for-All that are more aggressively progressive and anti-neoliberal (though still not necessarily anti-capitalist). Sanders's newest (2019) iteration of his Medicare-for-All plan represents the strongest left position on offer at the moment, but even this improved proposal fails to address some important aspects of the broader systemic context (Kim, 2019; Pramuk, 2019). If Medicare-for-All was provided through a publicly-controlled and managed system, without using private insurers as middlemen, and if Medicare-for-All includes negotiated prices for tests, treatments, prescription drugs, and devices, under more fully-democratic political conditions, this would appropriately be considered outside of neoliberalism and neoliberalization. It would be a complete rejection of privatization, and even some of the fundamental aspects of capitalism; health care would be less commodified and provided based on need—and while surplus-value extraction would still be a systemic component of even this expansive version of Medicare-for-All, surplus-value would be more equitably redistributed based on need and not profit-seeking. While Sanders's new approach meets many of these criteria, it would need to be accomplished without compromise, and would likely demand deeper structural transformation in regard to how democracy works in the U.S. (including in relation to the rest of the planet's population). This speaks to the importance of critical engagement with campaigns such as Sanders's in the U.S., and other more socialistic ones around the world, without sowing confusion or delusions in the ability of capitalism to be substantially reformed or that we can merely turn back the clock on the neoliberalization occurring within the global capitalist system without opposing capitalism (and thus neoliberalization) wholesale. These distinctions can be observed in other single-payer health care systems around the world and their distinct funding methods and degrees of privatization for different aspects of their respective health care systems.[10]

---

10 For example, Canada, with a single-payer system, still has nominally private providers (though plenty more publicly-controlled providers as well), but it also has anti-profiteering regulations in place, such as price controls, especially for hospitals. The United Kingdom on the other hand, despite decades of austerity, still maintains not only a single-payer system of sorts, but there are very few providers that are not under the umbrella of the National Health Service (NHS). Even the education and training of doctors and nurses is largely done under the auspices of the NHS. While neither are fully outside the influence of neoliberalization, each maintains different distant relationships to neoliberalism (and both are quite obviously superior to the current U.S. system or even the most Medicare-for-All plans currently proposed, though the plan proposed recently by Sanders is quite similar to Canada's system in most important respects).

5 Verdant Capitalism, Decrepit Planet

Similar to the preceding discussion about heath care, neoliberalism, and the critique of capitalism, we can see the problems with a "mere" critique of neoliberalism (even understood as neoliberalization) in the context of debates around climate change, neoliberalism, and capitalism. There are three general positions on climate change that are prevalent in various specific iterations: 1. Green capitalism, 2. Against green neoliberalism, and 3. Ecosocialism (or ecological anti-capitalism more broadly). These categories can be best represented by major figures in these debates: 1. Thomas Friedman (2008), 2. Naomi Klein (2015), and 3. John Bellamy Foster (2009; 2010), Chris Williams (2010; 2017), Paul Burkett (2014), Jason Moore (2015), and Andreas Malm (2016; 2018).[11]

Friedman's position is the most laughable, and yet is probably the one taken most seriously by politicians and centrist-liberal and moderate conservatives who accept the mainstream scientific evidence on climate change. While there are many distinct theories of green capitalism, ranging from neoclassical, supply-side, and demand-side approaches, they all more or less share important elements. The first element, fundamental to Friedman's position, is that capitalism is not viewed as the fundamental problem at the heart of climate change. Similar to, and building on, the Third Way complicity with neoliberalism in the mid-to-late 1990s and early 2000s, according to supporters of the green capitalism position, capitalist markets are viewed as not just *a* path towards defeating climate change, but capitalist markets (with some help from targeted, narrow government policies and encouraged partnerships, including tax breaks for "green" technology and "green" corporations) is the *only* viable solution to climate change. Friedman is specifically well-known for advocating public-private partnerships and the need to ensure that the price of goods in the marketplace take into account their environmental costs (but the suggestion is actually merely to subsidize "green" products—for which there is no actual definition and could include products made and sold using polluting and GHG (greenhouse gases) releasing production and distribution processes just so long as they are *less* polluting and *less* carbon-intensive—and making

---

11 There isn't a single major figure that captures the range of ecological anti-capitalist (socialist, Marxist, and/or post-Marxist) positions, and there is a range of theoretical and political differences around the boundaries of the different positions within this diverse camp, but what ties them all together is the position that climate change and ecological destruction are integral to capitalism and capitalism cannot exist without its ecologically harmful elements (and therefore the reverse is true, that any serious approach to climate change must be anti-capitalist).

"dirtier" products more expensive) thus that "green" technologies and products can gain market dominance. This is a kind of neoliberalization of climate change (non-)solutions.

The deep flaws and dangers of thinking in terms of green capitalism, a perverse kind of dystopian magical thinking, is well-articulated by thinkers in the next two categories. While critical of Friedman, touching the limits of a mere critique of neoliberalism (after all, she even mentions capitalism in the title of her book on the subject of climate change and in the book itself), is best represented by Naomi Klein and her work *This Changes Everything: Capitalism vs. the Climate*.[12] Despite Klein's (and others' who may fit in this category) broaching the issues of capitalism, much of the critical energy is directed against privatization and deregulation associated with neoliberalism and neoliberalization. The suggestions offered by those in this category include: building social movements against corporations and politicians who don't have aggressive climate change mitigation plans; calling for regulation and taxation of carbon intensive production and distribution; and demanding the use of taxation to ensure that those most responsible for climate change bear the disproportionate cost of dealing with mitigation. Despite their attempt to point to these issues as elements of contemporary capitalism—of neoliberal capitalism—there is nothing in the suggestions that thinkers and activists in this category offer that gets at the *systemic* heart of the connection between ecocidal climate change and capitalism. This category of climate change thinkers would have us believe that the commodification of the environment and our alienation from nature were extreme products of the new age of neoliberalism or neoliberal capitalism.[13] It

---

12 George Monbiot's (2017) work would also fit into this category of getting so close to moving beyond a mere critique of neoliberalism, especially in the context of climate change, yet fails to bring the critique specifically to the fundamental elements of capitalism. Additionally, Adrian Parr's (2013) *The Wrath of Capital: Neoliberalism and Climate Change Politics* explicates the connection between capitalism and various elements of climate change, also fails—despite the title of the book—to bring the critical tools offered by the tradition of critical theory to bear on the connection between capitalism, as such, to climate change. The frustration produced by Parr's work is that it is fundamentally a critique of capitalism—but it is one that is characterized by the author as a critique of neoliberalism. The hard core of the whole of this second category is clear good intention and excellent scholarly work, but it is also a category of political shortsightedness and ongoing and eventual failure.

13 For a spectacular theorization of contemporary (and future!) climate change politics, particularly the limits of the first two categories here: green neoliberalism and green neo-Keynesianism, see Mann and Wainwright's (2018) *Climate Leviathan: A Political Theory of Our Planetary Future*. This book served as an inspiration for elements of the argument in this chapter, particularly in thinking about the important theoretical and political differences between these three approaches, especially between categories two and three.

would perhaps surprise them to find out that the commodification of nature and the corollary alienation from nature were theorized by Marx as far back as 1844.

This is where the thinkers in the third category come in, focusing on the problems with approaches in the first two categories, affirming directly that ecocidal climate change cannot be mitigated by or within any form of capitalism precisely because capitalism is a root cause of the environmental destruction that we are only just beginning to experience the consequences of. For the theorists and activists in this category is it a fundamental truth that capitalism cannot function without the exploitation of wage workers, without the unpaid racialized, gendered labor involved in social reproduction, and it certainly cannot exist without the devaluations of extraction and pollution that are inherent aspects of capitalist production, distribution, and consumption. The only "green" that capitalism cares about is money—and how the devaluation of nature, workers, and reproductive and care work enable an increasing transnational capitalist class to make more "green."

Accepting much of Klein's analysis of the exacerbating relationship between neoliberalism/neoliberal capitalism, this last position, the anti-capitalist position, sees the issues that Klein points out, as well as others, as fundamentally rooted in capitalism as such, not a particular iteration of capitalism. This ecosocialist position is one that challenges both the neoliberalization characteristic of the current period of capitalism, but more deeply articulates various positions on how ecocidal climate change is rooted in the metabolic rift that the inherently extractive character of all forms of capitalism create between humanity and nature (even where some scholars in this category may not buy this specific conceptualization of the problem, [see Jason Moore's world-ecology approach]).[14] Capitalism inherently produces this metabolic rift,[15]

---

14 For Moore (2015), capitalism discursively and materially creates particular conceptions of nature that are suited to exploitation by and through capitalism (and more specifically criticizing Foster's and others', that the dualist conception of society and nature or capitalism and nature is a kind of thinking that could lend itself to capitalist exploitation of nature as well—or at least misses the way that conceptions of nature are co-produced through the development of capitalism). Instead, Moore argues for a fundamentally monist approach, which aims to highlight the co-constitutedness of society, capitalism, and (particular ideas about, and policies toward) nature. Both of these sub-positions, despite their theoretical differences, view capitalism as the fundamental horizon that must be superseded in order for a genuinely habitable planet to be maintained for all people.
15 Metabolic rift, as theorized by John Bellamy Foster and other ecological Marxists, to put it overly simply, refers to this imbalance that capitalism produces between humanity and nature; capitalism incentivizes the production of this imbalance by underappreciating

and therefore capitalism must be overcome and replaced by an ecosocialist alternative in order to produce any semblance of an ecological equilibrium between humankind and the planet's various ecosystems and biospheres.

When we keep either climate change politics and/or health care policy within the murderous confines of capitalism—not merely neoliberalism, itself a product of historical and contemporary failures to overcome capitalism—people suffer needlessly from preventable causes and die prematurely. Revolutionary movements should not separate these issue areas from one another, nor should they separate them from workers' rights, racism, cisheterosexism, or endless imperial war, but climate change is a truly catastrophic horizon.[16] It can longer be avoided; the question will be in what context climate change occurs and precisely how many people suffer and die prematurely, living horribly degraded lives? Health care policy is part of this, but unless climate change is approached with a sternly anti-capitalist perspective, our future capacities to maintain any semblance of a universal health care system (or a world without, or with decreased, cisheterosexism, racism, and war) will be seriously undermined. Rearranging the deck chairs on the Titanic was never a good use of time, but perhaps people didn't and continue to not see that that is what they were and are doing. However, it is imperative that we gain clearer perspective: when it comes to the critique of neoliberalism in the context of climate change, the political—and indeed planetary—stakes could not be more immensely pressing.

6   Capitalism Is the Pandemic

Rob Wallace (2020) and Mike Davis (2020) have long argued that epidemics and pandemics represent the intersection of imperialist capitalist political

---

the "value" of nature and the limits of its largely non-renewable capacity to be exploited, while placing near-exclusive emphasis on the possible production of exchange value, surplus value, and profit.

16   While not explicitly anti-capitalist, in the summer of 2019, shipyard workers in Belfast seized control of one of the oldest and most iconic shipyards in the country after it was announced that it would be closing. Not only were the workers demanding that the shipyard be nationalized and kept open, but also that the shipyard be retrofitted to build renewable energy infrastructure (Gurley, 2019). In terms of the relationship between working class and oppressed peoples' struggles against climate change, this is just the tip of the iceberg (no pun intended, but this shipyard is the very same one that built the Titanic—which fittingly enough has a similar relationship to icebergs as an ecologically-vibrant planet has with capitalism).

economy, insufficient for-profit public health and health care regimes, and ecologically damaging industries and practices ("agribusiness"). The COVID-19 pandemic is a kind of culmination of this intersection over time. While the extremity of neoliberalized capitalism has exacerbated the harms, there is nothing unique about neoliberalism that has produced a susceptibility to mass harm from novel viruses, bacteria, and fungi.

While the capitalist countries and their corporate siblings, primarily in the global North/Western Europe and North America produced effective vaccines for COVID-19—with market and research and development risk mitigation through guaranteed profits provided by these governments—there were also at least three counties that developed safe and effective vaccines: Russia, China, and Cuba (and Cuba achieved their vaccine under the illegal embargo that prevented Cuban researchers from getting access to necessary supplies needed to develop and test their vaccines; especially problematic was the shortage of syringes). These countries are not considered neoliberal by most standards, but all are fundamentally capitalist in their internal and external economic practices, albeit with a much larger and overt role for the government than is typical of neoliberal capitalist countries (although their governments also play a significant role in their economies).

During the first half of the pandemic, we witnessed a huge increase in the use of the category "essential workers" to describe a range of typically underappreciated jobs that apparently for the first time the general public was realizing were central to keeping society—and more importantly, the economy—running. "Essential workers" includes delivery people, postal workers, nurses and doctors, teachers, kitchen staff in restaurants, etc. These workers were essential because they held the capitalist economy together just enough to provide enough people with their basic needs during sporadic and unpredictable lockdowns, through various closures and shortages. But with the exception of certain regions, provinces, and states in certain countries for short periods of time, the global economy was never really shutdown. Remote work increased exponentially. Zoom stock skyrocketed. And, in due course, essential workers began demanding raises and better treatment in general. These were heroes insofar as they did their jobs without complaint and without asking for proper remuneration, apparently. The essential worker discourse disappeared just as soon as it ceased being an emotional cudgel effective at keeping these "essential workers" working at great risk to themselves and their families for the same disgracefully low pay they had before.

Capitalism didn't take a vacation. It was omnipresent. It found its way deeper into our homes. And yet we also saw some incredibly surprising policies emerge, most notably in the United States. In the U.S. we saw rent and mortgage payment freezes, student loan payment (and interest) freezes, eviction moratoriums, multiple sizeable direct cash payments to middle and lower income people, and eventually vaccinations that were free at the point of care.

We also saw a lot of confused people, at least somewhat aware of the authoritarian impulses of contemporary government and the power of large corporations in the pharmaceutical approval processes, who renewed their membership in what amounts to a death cult. They protested the public health-based temporary closure of businesses. They opposed the requirement (or even voluntary!) wearing of facemasks, a simple measure that can significantly reduce the spread of the virus (and something that people around the world have done regularly for years). Even people within communities of color in the U.S. were skeptical about what a government that has never shown much care for their well-being was telling them, now begging for their trust. While it was never a guarantee, with mountains of reasons for anyone to be skeptical: safe and effective COVID-19 vaccines were produced relatively quickly. Before the vaccines emerged, even among people who believed the virus was real and deadly, there were calls, like the one from Texas Lt. Governor Dan Patrick, to keep the economy fully open—that our grandparents and immunocompromised neighbors should be (and actually are!) willing to sacrifice themselves for the good of the economy (Knodel, 2020).

While some countries like China and South Korea put a lot of effort into testing and contact-tracing from the early months of the pandemic, most countries like the U.S., refused to spend sufficiently on these crucial mechanisms that could limit the spread of the virus without blanket shutdowns. So, to whatever degree the overall economy was "shut down," it was the combination of the economic drive and lack of willingness to do the cheap things (e.g., masking) and not spending enough on the more expensive things (e.g., mass testing and contact-tracing) that reinforced the death-for-the-economy narrative. The irony however is that people like Dan Patrick, whose rhetoric is hardly an anomaly, are always willing to sacrifice other people for the economy. The entire conception of capitalist economics he espouses is always rooted in the sacrifice of the many for the good of the few, pandemic or not.

It was also during the COVID-19 pandemic that one of the longest active strikes in U.S. history happened. Nurses at St. Vincent hospital in Worcester, MA went on strike demanding not only better pay, but more relevantly for the patients, safer patient limits and increased staffing. From the perspective of these nurses, the pandemic was creating major issues in work conditions for the nurses that was actually causing harm to patients—harm that could be prevented even within the context of a pandemic. The executives of this privately-owned hospital refused to accede to the nurses' demands. It took nearly a year and there wasn't much experimentation with more aggressive labor struggle tactics, but the nurses won some key concessions from Tenet Healthcare, the parent company of St. Vincent.[17] There were smaller actions with similar motivations around the U.S. and around the world.

While COVID-19 was not an escape from neoliberalism and certainly was not an escape from capitalism, just like the history of capitalism has always been, it was a confusing period with a range of contradictory and/or inconsistent policies. Consciousness among the working class and elites reflected the contradictions in the material reality we all experienced. Defenders of the value of the concept of neoliberalism (as something distinct from a visceral defense of the fundamentals of capitalism itself) must be able to account for continuity of the rationalizations of capitalism that have accompanied it since the conceptual formulation of capitalism as such (at least as far back as the 19th century).

One issue that has here been left unaddressed, and during which during the pandemic was treated in an arguably unique way, is that of nation-state borders. If there is a particular approach to borders associated with neoliberalism, it would have to be open borders (at least for capital). While there is not space left in this chapter to address it, the way that borders were closed during the peak of the pandemic (and many as of the writing of this remain basically closed, including the U.S.) is a significant complication that deserves further research. However, given that the variable (and highly contested) degree of openness of borders has been a significant component of the history of capitalism, it is unlikely that such research would significantly alter the thrust of the argument here. Nonetheless, it is fair to consider this something of an open question and definitely deserving of further exploration. The issue of border policy is one of the key aspects of the argument for the apparently novel conceptualization of "authoritarian neoliberalism" (or, alternatively, "neoliberal authoritarianism"). Without exploring the concept of borders specifically, the following section takes up the argument for the idea that not only is neoliberalism an accurate and useful conceptual label, but that we have entered a new phase in the supposed history of neoliberalism, an authoritarian phase.

---

17 The author's experience participating in solidarity on the picket lines with the nurses is the primary source for these observations.

7 Authoritarian Capitalism

Of the recent theorizations of neoliberalism, the attempt to theorize so-called "neoliberal authoritarianism" is the most prominent—what Dardot and Laval (2019) have bluntly labeled "the new neoliberalism." What follows is an attempt to show that what is being referred to as "neoliberal authoritarianism" or "authoritarian neoliberalism" is, consistent with what has been argued above, an otherwise uninterrupted goal of capitalist political economy and not at all inconsistent with the history of neoliberalism, according to the major theorists of neoliberalism. Dardot and Laval (2019) define new neoliberalism as the same basic neoliberal rationality they theorized in their earlier work (Dardot and Laval, 2013) turned into an overt war against the population. However, if we look at the prevalence of war, massive increases in surveillance, policing, torture, prisons, and broader curtailments of civil and political rights over the past several decades we can see that new neoliberalism is more continuity than deviation. Capitalism, no less than neoliberalism, is always already a war against the vast majority of the population. This isn't to say that *nothing* has changed. What is called neoliberalism has certainly won this period of history; capitalism has won this round (and many before), and the continued development of authoritarian, anti-population policies have been are the core of neoliberalism—and capitalism—from the beginning, but most notably, for a critique of the "new neoliberalism" thesis, is this former claim that neoliberalism has always been, and aspired to be more, authoritarian. The forms of oppressive have evolved unevenly, new countries have been taken over by these "logics" and practices, but the idea that there was a time where neoliberalism as an approach, when implemented, was not already a war on the population is simply unsupported by historical evidence. And while it is not the main purpose of this chapter, the history of capitalism itself is a history of different periods of war on the populations of the world (and it is a history of resistance to those wars as well). As Dardot and Laval admit themselves, "[b]asically the new neoliberalism is the continuation of the old for the worse" (2019; xxix).

While the project of neoliberalism emerged a bit earlier, the most frequent reference point for the historical instantiation(s) of neoliberalism is Reagan (in the U.S.), Thatcher (in the UK), and then Pinochet (in Chile). In all three cases, these respective "leaders" ushered in expansions of their respective countries' national security regimes and engaged in overt belligerence. Reagan not only expanded the U.S. military (and intelligence) budgets to unprecedented levels (lacking a congressional declaration of war) and engaged in active aggressive military violence, most notably with the invasion of Grenada. Thatcher, not to be dissuaded by her femininity (something liberal identitarians in the U.S., and around the world, should keep in mind), also built out the powers of the executive bureaucracy in the UK, which were they expanded by Tony Blair, David Cameron, and others in the post-9/11 context. While they may have had authoritarian dispositions and built a foundation for further expansions of the authoritarian aspects of their capitalist societies, but it would be something of an exaggeration to say that they fully achieved a kind of order best labelled as "authoritarian neoliberalism"—but their governments were a kind of proof of concept for the synergy between authoritarianism and neoliberalism. Augusto Pinochet's regime in Chile in the 1970s and 1980s is the original evidence for the authoritarianism latent in neoliberalism. Pinochet, with the support of the "Chicago Boys," oversaw the development of a truly authoritarian government that operated with a neoliberal capitalist political economy. There is little debate about this, and so the recent interested in the theorization of neoliberal authoritarianism is likely more reflective of the spread of the already-present but perhaps latent or underdeveloped authoritarian elements within neoliberal capitalism. A more persuasive theorization is that the failures (or successes depending on your perspective) of neoliberal capitalism have led to the rise of neofascism in supposedly democratic countries (India, Hungary, Brazil, Israel, and the U.S., for example) (Cox and Skidmore-Hess, 2022).

COVID-19 pandemic responses have complicated matters further. While many regimes around the world took advantage of legitimate public health guidance to close borders, discriminate against immigrants and asylum seekers, and increasingly surveil their populations in general, we also saw a lot of increase in transfer payments, including enhanced unemployment, supplemental food programs, and direct cash payments to individuals in need, but also rent and eviction moratoriums (something that would have been politically inconceivable just a few months prior). In the U.S. in particular, there were also fundamentally unregulated giveaways to businesses with little oversight to ensure compliance with program requirements. Although the investigations are unlikely to recover much in terms of money, the U.S. government is at least superficially looking into PPP loan abuse. Other countries approaches were similarly chaotic. Most countries were more successful than the U.S. is avoiding mass death for much of the pandemic, but other countries' economics didn't fare as well or recover as quickly as the U.S.—but no countries were entirely spared harms to their people nor their economies (and the harms to the economies were and remain primarily felt by those poor and working class people least able to withstand them, as is so often the case).

We have authoritarian measures mixed with corporate giveaways mixed with non-market poverty reduction programs that were some of the most expansive in history for many of these countries—countries that would have up until that point been labeled "neoliberal." Allowing COVID-19 related protections to expire and undercutting organizing worker in the U.S. at least suggests that the deviation from neoliberal capitalism business-as-usual was an aberration, but it is entirely understandable when we view the reactions to the global pandemic as attempts to salvage global capitalism. As has always been the case within capitalism, neoliberalism being no exception, the government has played an important role in mitigating the worst harms of the exploitative, violent capitalist system. Understanding the complexities and ostensible contradictions in the COVID-19 responses is best understood under the umbrella of capitalism as opposed to neoliberalism. What is typically referred to as neoliberalism it is claimed thrives through crisis (Dardot and Laval, 2019; xii), it important to never forget this is always also capitalism thriving (or at least adapting and surviving) during crises—almost always crises of its own creation whether strictly economic, economically-conditioned political and military conflict, and/or ecological and biological crises.

8 It's (Still) a Trap!

The question lingers still: does the concept of neoliberalism, even understood as neoliberalization, offer a better theoretical understanding than a perhaps more reductionist move to think in terms of capitalism? While the answer to that question may be a tentative yes, this still does not necessarily mean that the political costs are worth the academic nuance, at least insofar as left movements are concerned. Neoliberalism (even understood as neoliberalization) is still a flawed concept, but less for analytical reasons than for the political-strategic reasons discussed earlier. While there is an analytical coherence to the concept, especially when thought of as a spectrum in relation to an ideal-type, Goldfarb is right to point to the conceptual drift that occurs too often with the concept of neoliberalism. This looseness that Goldfarb, discussed above, identifies is closely tied to, though not solely caused by, the academic left's general desire to avoid directly criticizing the capitalist system. If you criticize capitalism, you "become" a socialist or Marxist, tough identities to maintain within the academy. Being a critic of neoliberalism quite simply does not hold that same stigma.

When the Left aims its criticism against neoliberalization (e.g., austerity) however helpful it may be to avoid ostracization and motivate movements in the short-term, it too easily allows activists and critical scholars to lose sight of the broader oppressive horizon of global capitalism. Yes, welfare-state capitalism is better than pure neoliberal capitalism, but both have, historically, been actively criticized by the Left. Now it seems like the Left's goal is "less neoliberalism," not "no capitalism." The political trap here is that one builds a movement against "neoliberalism" that never becomes what it needs to be in order to be truly effective: anti-capitalist; that it never sets its sights properly or practically against the deeper systemic elements that produce the phenomena typically referred to as neoliberalism, but which are better understood as the historical "victories" of capitalism.

As I argued in *New Politics* in 2017, when those on the left focus on resisting specific manifestations, periods, or trends of capitalism, the system as a whole, even with all its diversity and "non-capitalistic" elements, is no longer thought of as the enemy (Sculos, 2017b). This is not to suggest that radical reforms or transitional demands (positions that push capitalism to and beyond its limits of adaptability while also improving the lives of people in the short-term) aren't important. Radical politics should never make the perfect the enemy of the good, but it is vital to avoid excessively reformist and vapid opportunistic impulses. It is through the struggle for more expansive revolutionary achievements that builds the subjectivities and consciousness necessary to produce emancipatory political movement(s) suited to overthrowing capitalism and building an egalitarian, democratic postcapitalist (i.e., socialist) alternative. It is not "making the perfect the enemy of the good" to suggest that what many well-meaning people consider "good" isn't really good at all. To paraphrase Malcolm X, stabbing someone and pulling the knife out part of the way isn't "good." It's not only not good *enough*, it isn't relevant progress at all.

To the left of the center-left, the focus on neoliberalism is not as analytically problematic as Goldfarb suggests, but on the other hand, it is far more politically problematic than merely being elitist. Even if the general public knew what neoliberalism was (conceptually—as they certainly know what it means materially in their everyday lives already), focusing on resisting that would be a far cry from resisting capitalism in its entirety. Goldfarb is right that "democratic intellectuals" need to be cognizant that people may misunderstand the term neoliberalism. We are talking about privatization. We are talking about a kind of extreme capitalism, of "market fundamentalism." We should be clear about this, and this means exploring how policies like the ACA and even possibly Medicare-for-All, depending on the particular proposal one is looking at, still, in various ways reinforce neoliberalism and resist genuine democratic socialization of the fundamental spheres of life—the achievement of which is necessary for a just, egalitarian, and humane society. Neoliberalism is a perverse escalation of an already-perverse political-economic capitalist system, and that is what we should focus our energies convincing people of.

9 Conclusion: Rethinking Relevance through the Critique of (the Concept of) Neoliberalism

Throughout, I have attempted to show that neoliberalism, as a concept, is useful in some important ways. As a concept it can help scholars and activists develop a better understanding of specificities of the contemporary moment and its recent past, which a simplistic treatment of capitalism would not as easily accomplish. Particularly when neoliberalism is understood as a multi-faceted process combining privatization, deregulation, and tax cuts, it can be easier to intellectually digest than the practical meaning of something like "the expansion or recession of capitalism" would be for those without graduate degrees or years of self-study on the subject of political economy. Beyond that, the deeply thoughtful and strenuously researched historical and analytical work that has been produced around the concept of neoliberalism is largely excellent, even, and perhaps especially, where the scholars and activists disagree with one another about various premises and conclusions. So then why dedicate an entire chapter to criticism of the concept of neoliberalism?

Part of the reason is to perform a provocation, to challenge those working on and utilizing the concept of neoliberalism to consider how theoretically informative and politically useful the concept actually is, especially compared to the broader, more politically-controversial (and perhaps still more salient) term "capitalism." Scholars who are uninterested in the political value of their work will likely be unmoved by the arguments made here, especially regarding political usefulness as a standard. However, given the variable prominence of "relevance" in many fields and subfields of the academic disciplines of Political Science and International Relations/Global Politics, such as Security Studies and Foreign Policy, where relevance is often interpreted to mean "how can we develop better concepts and frameworks of analysis to defend or enhance the positions of governments, corporations, and the capitalist class more generally" (though they are rarely honest or aware enough to be so explicit about this meaning of "relevance"), left scholars, which most critics of "neoliberalism" are, should adopt a similar, but countervailing, conception of relevance—while refusing to apologize for meeting an equivalent standard of political engagement that is acceptable for more conventionally liberal, centrist, and conservative scholars. Avoiding overtly political work has been a way for those on the left to find something of a comfortable home in academia, but when one has to pretend to not be a leftist one can, over time, cease to be a leftist. This is the perversion of the "critic of neoliberalism." As Vonnegut (2009) wrote in *Mother Night*, "we are what we pretend to be so we must be careful what we pretend to be."

While there is certainly possible political value in building a united front against neoliberal austerity (for the sake of argument, here understood as different from building a movement against capitalism or in favor of genuine socialism), the question that remains to be asked (and answered) is whether it is actually possible or efficient to merely resist neoliberalism. There is a real possibility that resisting neoliberalism is like resisting the gun or sword of an opponent. Does one attack the weapon or the person wielding the weapon? If they put the gun or sword away or drop it, does one stop fighting?

Lastly, critics of neoliberalism and neoliberal capitalism must be intimately aware of the question: what comes next? What is the alternative to neoliberalism? If it is possible—or perceived to be reasonable—to answer this question with some answer that would fail to meet the general parameters of a democratic, egalitarian post-capitalism (socialism), we have at least begun to see the consequences of the left "critique of neoliberalism" compared to the left critique of capitalism. This is not to exclude the possibility of a right nationalist critique of neoliberalism, which should also be a concern (as it allows people to see strong similarities between political leaders as different as Bernie Sanders and Donald Trump)—whether or not the Trump presidency actually represented anything other than the continuation of the authoritarian tendencies of capitalism or neoliberalism is still an open question, though this chapter has suggested an answer).This comment is not meant to exclude a more conventional conservative opposition to capitalism either (Kolozi, 2017), but given the role that capitalism plays in maintaining historical systems of oppression (white supremacy, cisheteropatriarchy, etc.) and the increased popularity of "capitalism" among conservatives, a critique of capitalism is less likely to be abused by conservatives and nationalists, even if such an appropriation would still be possible (especially given the history of conservative criticism of capitalism).

When considering what comes after neoliberalism or neoliberal capitalism, without an emphasis on the capitalistic qualities of neoliberalism, it will be exceptionally difficult to build towards a genuine alternative that is not merely a superficially different form of capitalism. Additionally, because of the deep psycho-social infestation of the collective psyche of those in capitalist societies, this predominance of the capitalistic mentality, unless the specifically capitalistic dimensions of the "neoliberal" subject are resolved, capitalism will live on in the minds—and more importantly, in the material everyday practices—of the living, beyond whatever death neoliberalism can have that is not also the death of capitalism.

References

Biebricher, Thomas (2018) *The Political Theory of Neoliberalism*. Stanford, CA: Stanford University Press.

Brown, Wendy (2015) *Undoing the Demos: Neoliberalism's Stealth Revolution*. Brooklyn, NY: Zone Books.

Burkett, Paul (2014) *Marx and Nature: a Red and Green Perspective*. Chicago: Haymarket.

Cox, Ronald W. and Skidmore-Hess, Daniel (2022) "How Neofascism Emerges from Neoliberal Capitalism." *New Political Science*, Vol. 44 (2).

Dardot, Pierre and Laval, Christian (2013 [2017]) *The New Way of the World: on Neoliberal Society*. New York: Verso.

Dardot, Pierre and Laval, Christian (2019) *Never-Ending Nightmare: the Neoliberal Assault on Democracy*. Trans. G. Elliot. New York: Verso.

Davis, Mike (2020) *The Monster Enters: COVID-19, Avian Flu and the Plagues of Capitalism*. New York: OR Books.

Foster, John Bellamy (2009) *The Ecological Revolution: Making Peace with the Planet*. New York: Monthly Review Press.

Foster, John Bellamy, et al. (2010) *The Ecological Rift: Capitalism's War on the Earth*. New York: Monthly Review Press.

Friedman, Thomas (2008) *Hot, Flat, and Crowded: Why We Need a Green Revolution—and How It Can Renew America*. New York: Farrar, Straus, and Giroux.

Fromm, Erich (1994 [1941]) *Escape from Freedom*. New York: Holt.

Fromm, Erich (1955) *The Sane Society*. New York: Holt.

Gibson-Graham, J.K. (1996) *The End of Capitalism (as we knew it): a Feminist Critique of Political Economy*. Cambridge, MA: Blackwell.

Goldfarb, Jeffrey C. (2017) "What Do You Mean When You Use the Term Neoliberalism?: a Question to My American Friends, Colleagues, Students and Comrades on the Academic Left." *Public Seminar*, April 7.

Gurley, Lauren (2019) "Workers Seize the Shipyard That Built the Titanic, Plan to Make Renewable Energy There." *Motherboard by Vice*, August 14.

Harvey, David (2007) *A Brief History of Neoliberalism*. Oxford, UK: Oxford University Press.

Kim, Catherine (2019) "Read Bernie Sanders's 2019 Medicare-for-all plan." *Vox*, April 10.

Klein, Naomi (2015) *This Changes Everything: Capitalism vs. the Climate*. New York: Simon & Schuster.

Knodel, Jamie (2020) "Texas Lt. Gov. Dan Patrick suggests he, other Seniors Willing to die to get Economy Going again." *NBC News*, Mar. 24.

Kolozi, Peter (2017) *Conservatives Against Capitalism: from the Industrial Revolution to Globalization*. New York: Columbia University Press.

Lawder, David and Holland, Steve (2017) "Trump Tastes Failure as U.S. House Healthcare Bill Collapses." *Reuters*, March 24.

Malm, Andreas (2016) *Fossil Capital: the Rise of Steam Power and the Roots of Global Warming*. New York: Verso.

Malm, Andreas (2018) *The Progress of this Storm: Nature and Society in a Warming World*. New York: Verso.

Mann, Geoff and Wainwright, Joel (2018) *Climate Leviathan: a Political Theory of Our Planetary Future*. New York: Verso.

Monbiot, George (2017) *Out of the Wreckage: a New Politics for an Age of Crisis*. New York: Verso.

Moore, Jason (2015) *Capitalism in the Web of Life: Ecology and the Accumulation of Capital*. New York: Verso.

Parr, Adrian (2013) *The Wrath of Capital: Neoliberalism and Climate Change Politics*. New York: Columbia University Press.

Pramuk, Jacob (2019) "Bernie Sanders introduces new 'Medicare for All' bill as he tries to set 2020 Health-care Agenda." *CNBC*, April 10.

Sanders, Bernie (with Huck Gutman) (2015) *Outsider in the White House*. New York: Verso.

Sculos, Bryant William (2017a) "On Theorizing Neoliberalism: the Problems and Politics of a Critique." *Public Seminar*, April 20.

Sculos, Bryant William (2017b) "The Capitalistic Mentality and the Politics of Radical Reform: a (Mostly) Friendly Reply to Michael J. Thompson." *New Politics*, Vol. XVI No. 2, Whole Number 62.

Vonnegut, Kurt (2009 [1961]) *Mother Night*. New York: Dial Press Trade.

Wallace, Rob (2020) *Dead Epidemiologists: On the Origins of COVID-19*. New York: Monthly Review Press.

Williams, Chris (2010) *Ecology and Socialism*. Chicago: Haymarket.

Williams, Chris and Magdoff, Fred (2017) *Creating the Ecological Society: Toward a Revolutionary Transformation*. New York: Monthly Review Press.

CHAPTER 10

Corporate Power and Praxis in Critical Scholarship

Ronald W. Cox

1   Introduction

This volume is intended to challenge scholars and activists to think systematically and critically about the implications of corporate power. The authors included here develop a rich analysis of the relationship of capitalism and the state that involves centering the instrumental and structural power of corporate interests. This centering of corporate power goes against the trends of both mainstream and critical scholarship across the past several decades. Mainstream scholarship in the U.S., and increasingly much of the world, pivots around traditions that separate states from "markets" and in the process mystify power relationships. As I have documented elsewhere, there has been a decades-long retreat from Marxism in the academy that tracks closely the corporatization of universities (Cox, 2019a). As scholars have been encouraged to perpetually re-invent themselves to quality for tenure and promotion, scholarship has been less engaged with big picture questions of power and agenda-setting in political economy, continuing to minimize or ignore corporate power even as corporations have expanded the scope, scale and impact of their market and political power within states and around the world. The relegation of corporate power to the margins has been facilitated by the dominant traditions within international relations scholarship: realism and liberalism.

Realist scholars in international relations prioritize the state as the primary unit of analysis, thereby ignoring the embeddedness of corporate power within the state. Contrary to realist assumptions, corporate power is not just an adjunct that is used by state elites to pursue "national interests." Instead, corporate power intersects and informs how state officials frame the "national interests." The intersection of capitalist power with state power, well-documented in this volume, gets erased by realist theory, arguably the most dominant scholarly tradition in international relations. Similarly, liberals who separate "markets" from states commit two errors. The first is in the definition of "markets" as largely competitive and driven by supply and demand factors. This definition ignores and minimizes how corporate power is used in markets to concentrate wealth, check competition, and produce outcomes based on strategic rivalry between large-scale capitalist interests. The "market" is less about unfettered competition and more about how corporations use market power to strategically advance their interests against other large-scale competitors. The second is an artificial separation of corporate power from the state. Neoliberalism, in liberal scholarship and even some critical scholarship, is defined as reduced state intervention in favor of greater market autonomy. These accounts of neoliberalism omit how corporate power has shaped a very interventionist state that is much more embedded in corporate power networks across the policy-making spectrum (Hathaway, 2020).

The dominance of realist and liberal scholarship within international relations and political science does not mean that critical scholarship has vanished. Quite the contrary, there are outlets for critical perspectives on capitalist power. However, what often emerges, even among some of the best critical perspectives, is a partial and incomplete analysis of corporate power that often minimizes the reach of corporate influence within states and throughout the global economy. One reason for the gaps in critical scholarship is a retreat from Marxist traditions in favor of identity, culture and ideological approaches to agency and power. For several decades, Marxist studies of political economy have been sidelined in favor of agency-centered or culture-centered narratives that seek to better understand how the exploited and oppressed experience their own subjugation. At one level, that is a worthy goal, but often one that has replaced class analysis with identity perspectives that decenters power relationships in favor of localized and culturally specific narrative accounts, without locating these narratives within a broader structure of who profits from immiseration and how ideology serves as a conduit to maintaining an unjust status quo that benefits the top sections of the ruling class the most. Post-structuralism has celebrated a move away from "top-down" structural analysis of corporate and class-centered political economy toward a variegated understanding of power that is often reduced to individual agency, ideology, and culture absent historical-structural analysis of corporate or class power (Sullivan, 2020). Postcolonial theorists have criticized Marxism for what they consider its Eurocentric biases and its inapplicability to post-colonial societies, in the process often discarding or minimizing class analysis (Chibber, 2013). Likewise, even the best critical constructivists who discuss the importance of materialist power structures, give overwhelming emphasis to ideological and cultural construction of belief systems over time, as opposed to interrogating how class power has shaped such belief systems (Teschke and Heine, 2002).

In contrast, critical scholars who focus on a transnational capitalist class (TCC) have contributed greatly to our understanding of the extent to which the most concentrated and powerful blocs of transnational capitalists are organizing their collective interests on a global scale. This research paradigm is vast and is to be applauded (Sklair, 2000; Robinson, 2019; Harris, 2016). However, this TCC approach operates at such a high-level analytical framework that it often misses the complexity of how variegated patterns of corporate and class power are articulated in different regions, states, and societies. A midrange Marxist or elite power framework, epitomized by many of the chapters included here, allows for a more concrete analysis of capitalist fractions of political and economic power whose influence is mediated, contested, and challenged by other capitalist interests, depending on factors specific to locational, historical, and societal circumstances.

I have long advanced a transnational interest bloc approach to better understand how dominant transnational corporate interests have worked nationally, regionally, and globally to advance their profit-making interests in a world increasingly dominated by transnational production (Cox, 2012). My framework starts from the premise that transnational capitalists in the dominant locations of the U.S., Western Europe, Japan, and China have pursued political and economic relationships with investors in developing countries to lower the costs of production through the creation of global value chains. I have written extensively about this process in my 2019 book, which documents the role of a transnational bloc of capitalists from the global North using their political and market power to construct favorable outcomes in trade and investment agreements. This has created transnational investment blocs of competing political and economic interests linked globally around profits extracted from global value chains. This bloc includes transnational corporate elites at the top of the global value chains, who extract the most profits from these value chains, the middle-range investors who profit from managing and coordinating these global value chains, and thousands of global production networks that compete to produce goods and services for these value chains. Corporate power within the market and within the state has structured these value chains, with power relationships negotiated and mediated by actors within these transnational interest blocs, which include corporations, political elites, and junior partners within these investment blocs integrated across a North-South exploitative dynamic. I discuss in my book the extent to which these global value chains are in crisis, with neoliberalism in retreat, due to the complexity of managing the political and economic relationships in the context of declining profit rates, global economic and climate crises, and a dramatic rise of global inequality and exploitation that have fractured societies and produced political instability around the world (Cox, 2019b).

Academics who value equality, democracy and social justice need to study the specificities of the current crisis of neoliberalism by centering corporate and class power the way that authors in this volume have done. This means a commitment to interrogating the power structures of the ownership class within the constellation of political and economic history of state-societies, institutions, and regional and global linkages to transnational corporate power structures. This approach is what I have referenced as a mid-level Marxism that is sensitive to how class power is articulated within different locations. The purpose is to be able to engage more productively with activists and organizers who are risking their lives around the world to challenge and replace these capitalist power structures with systems that are accountable to working class people and the poor, whose political and economic agency has declined during the past four decades of neoliberal capitalism, but who also were never in power in any meaningful way throughout capitalist history. In order to outline the key lessons for scholars interested in pursuing this kind of work, I have devoted the rest of this conclusion to specifying the direction such scholarship should take and what type of society is worth fighting for.

2   The Structural, Instrumental and Contextual Power of Capital

The first lesson for scholars of critical political economy is to appreciate the scope and scale of capitalist power. Capitalist agency, whether it be lobbying or campaign contributions or direct ties to policymakers through policy planning organizations or crony capitalism, is only one aspect of capitalist power. The large-scale concentration of wealth hoarded by capitalist firms, often shielded from governments in tax havens, operates as a multipurpose instrument of structural power. Capitalists can and will withhold this wealth from direct investment in order to attempt to extract the maximum profits from future investments, but also to strategically deploy this wealth to maximize market power against competitors, to financialize this wealth in currency markets and speculation, to pressure contractors and subcontractors to undertake cost-cutting measures in exchange for accessing such wealth, and to delay investing in markets without assurances that tax and regulatory policies are acceptable for assuring expected profit margins. Politicians, regardless of party and/or ideological label, gravitate toward satisfying the conditions necessary to reassure capitalists with disproportionate market power—especially those that politicians depend on to grow the economy and/or to finance the operations of government through purchasing debt and issuing loans. This structural power of capital has been accentuated throughout the past four decades of global capitalist accumulation, as the world economy has become more interconnected through webs of financial investment ties that bind transnational investors across a range of countries and regions, creating layers of structural power for corporate investors that limit the extent to which policymakers can depart from the orthodoxy of financial markets without paying a steep price (Young, Banerjee and Schwartz, 2020; Christophers, 2023).

Often governments that label themselves socialist, or take seemingly counter-hegemonic stances, accommodate the interests of powerful transnational capitalist actors or to the dominant socioeconomic classes at home that disproportionately profit from existing power structures (Molyneux, 2021). Those of us undertaking systemic critiques of corporate and class power need to avoid looking at what political leaders say, or the labels they use, and instead focus on analyzing their relationship to capitalist power structures: domestically, regionally, and globally. Whose interests are being served by political actors? What are the mechanisms for government financing? Where are profits being accumulated in society and how widely are they disbursed and distributed? These questions help us interrogate the dimensions of class struggle, the structure of political and economic power, and the opportunities for shifting the balance of power from the ruling class to the working class.

3 The Importance of Organic Intellectuals

Over the past four decades in the United States and to varying degrees across the capitalist world system, there has been a corporatization of the universities that has involved significant reductions in public sector funding, a greater reliance on corporate donors and tuition increases, dramatic increases in high-paying administrative positions, and a hollowing out of full-time tenure track faculty in favor of waves of adjunct hiring at super-exploitative rates of pay without benefits (Bostock, 1999; Newfield, 2011; Cox, 2013). Faculty who define themselves as critics of this corporatization need to understand the way that this process of attacks on higher education is tethered to broader attacks on the provision of public goods and public institutions within capitalism. Therefore, as academics, we should not see ourselves as neutral observers of these ruling class attacks. We should position ourselves as organic intellectuals committed to allying with working class people who are fighting against the same trends in both the public and private sectors. This means helping to build alliances with fellow teachers in the K-12 system in the U.S. to fight against privatization, attacks on unions and attacks on the rights of educators to teach the truth about the conditions of the exploited and oppressed. Alliances between organic intellectuals and the broader working class are essential in fighting for democratic and grassroots control over educational institutions by teachers themselves, as well as supporting the fight among workers for living wages, unionization and class solidarity campaigns that target those corporations and politicians that have led decades of reactionary attacks against workers (Burgis, 2023).

As part of the role of academics as organic intellectuals, we need to see our classrooms as spaces for articulating a critical pedagogy, a pedagogy of the oppressed, which places no limits on engagement with systemic critiques of capitalist power structures and institutions (Freire, 2000)). This means pushing students to think critically, to envision how societies might be constructed to operate as radical democracies within both the economic and political spheres. We should invite speaker organizers and activists into our classrooms to learn about existing class struggles as well as struggles on behalf of groups at the margins of U.S. and global societies, whom are often the first targets of reactionary and neo-fascist political movements (Cox and Skidmore-Hess, 2022).

4 Building Class Power for Systemic Transformation

The critiques of corporate power advanced in this book are examples of the kind of research that is intended to have universal appeal for the overwhelming majority of the world's population. Those without power and those within the working class are clearly in the majority in every society and they have the power to change the capitalist system through collective action. Of course, ruling classes everywhere have used their power to build alliances well beyond their numbers in an effort to protect their wealth and check opposition to their class-based political and economic hegemony (Robinson, 2022). There has been a burgeoning literature on the left that has tried to make sense of the fact that ruling class interests are better at understanding collective interests and uniting to develop strategies to maintain and expand their wealth. The "left," on the other hand, barely exists in the U.S. and much of the world as a coherent and powerful force for class solidarity and organizing capable of fighting for systemic change. Instead of building a left around universal working class demands, the contemporary "left" remains fractured around an issue-based organizing logic that almost never centers corporate power, let alone capitalism, as the starting point for building a working-class movement that can unite the largest numbers of people in a way that would maximize their power, though there has emerged a worldwide set of movements in which leftism has been redefined away from the working class in favor of "the people," away from organizations and parties to "networks" and "movements" (Therborn, 2022). This volume outlines the urgency of building a large-scale working-class movement that can more effectively fight the corporate plunder produced by the capitalist system.

This move toward a universal, class-based movement has to grapple with the urgency of supporting, unequivocally and without reservation, the struggles of the most oppressed and most exploited groups in society. Therefore, any effective universalism must be anti-racist, anti-sexist and pro-LGBTQ rights—these fights should be considered part and parcel of building a universal working-class movement that is defined by class interests but also recognizes that oppression of minorities is thoroughly and systemically part of the capitalist power structure that we are trying to change. Instead of a "class-only" politics, I am advocating a class politics that fights for and with the most marginalized sectors of the working class as essential to building a large-scale movement of the working class (Post, 2019; Cox, 2020).

5 Self-Emancipation of the Working Class

What kind of society should we fight for in the struggle to go beyond capitalism? That too has been the subject of much recent discussion, debate, and reflection on the left. As a starting point, if we are fighting for socialism, then the self-emancipation and self-empowerment of the working class is the only meaningful definition of having achieved our goals. This has never been achieved (in my view). Instead, what has passed for "actually existing socialism" has been some combination of state capitalism and bureaucratic collectivism that has simply replaced one set of exploiters with another, relying on exploitation of workers and excluding workers from any real power within the political and economic system. We on the socialist left need to be thoughtful, creative, and flexible about envisioning the kind of societies we want to construct. At a minimum, it should involve an abolition of capitalist profits—a prohibition of an ownership class who extracts surplus value from workers, communities, and societies—the forms of corporate power that we have dissected in this book. This capitalist system needs to be replaced by a socialist system that guarantees everyone housing, health care, education, and a basic income necessary to survive. That means a centralized state that operates to ensure these basic provisions are realized, and is accountable to workers, communities, and stakeholders within society through a public financing mechanism and a public banking system whereby the democratic majority pay their taxes to support universal public goods.

However, we have to go beyond the conception of a centralized state to include mechanisms of checks and balances within society to ensure that the centralized state does not emerge as a parasitic or unaccountable bureaucracy, the fate of too many top-down experiments in past self-descriptions of "socialist" societies. One way to check the centralized state is by constructing a set of civil rights foundational principles that protects a wide range of individual rights, including speech, religion, assembly, protest, and political affiliation. These freedoms would coexist with fundamental organizing societal principles led by a prohibition of capitalist ownership and profits, guarantees for a broad social wage that includes housing, health care and education as fundamental rights. However, there would still be markets and enterprises at the local, regional, and national levels, embedded within structures of democratic participation, debate and community governance. The enterprises that existed within the market would range from worker-owned businesses, non-profit cooperatives, community owned businesses, and local and regional public banking systems that would operate on principles of money being invested by these businesses, communities and individuals and returned to the communities that provided the money. There would be a taxation system that would transfer money to cities, counties, and regional bodies in addition to the central federal state, monies which would all be reinvested nationally and within this diversified system of regions, counties, and cities. In that way, a myriad of institutional arrangements could flourish within such a socialist system (Gindin, 2018).

Of course, this is a utopian construct with the recognition that any attempt to construct this would be met with counterattacks and resistance. The issues of internationalism and solidarity with immigrant workers, including acknowledging the right for immigrants to be a part of this socialist system, would need to be established and fought for. There would also need to be solidarity with other foreign struggles led by working class organizations who were trying (or perhaps had achieved) such a system in their own countries. This is provided as a very brief and undoubtedly highly simplified template of basic characteristics and principles.

6   Conclusion

This chapter reflects my own views and not necessarily the views of all of the contributors to this volume. I wrote this in the spirit of suggesting direction for future critical scholarship that involves critiques of corporate power, support for working class struggles, and building large-scale anti-capitalist organizing with messaging that unites working class people who share a material interest in fighting for systemic change, whether or not they are currently constituted as a "class for themselves." The ruling class has been effective in advancing their interests as a class. Now those of us committed to emancipation of workers and oppressed people have to develop the capacity to begin to challenge these powerful structures of corporate and capitalist power. This book is simply a very small tool, however incomplete, that is offered to help these efforts.

References

Bostock, William W. (1999) "The Global Corporatization of Universities," *AntePodium*, Vol. 3, online.

Burgis, Ben (2023) "A Workers Triumph at Rutgers," *Compact*, May 6 online.

Chibber, Vivek (2013) *Postcolonial Theory and the Specter of Capital*. New York: Verso Press.

Christophers, Brett (2023) *Our Lives in their Portfolios: Why Asset Managers Rule the World*. New York: Verso.

Cox, Ronald W., ed. (2012) *Corporate Power and Globalization in U.S. Foreign Policy*. New York: Routledge.

Cox, Ronald W. (2020) "A Left Critique of Class Reductionism," *Class, Race and Corporate Power*, Volume 8 (2): Article 4.

Cox, Ronald W. (2019a) "Marxism and IPE," in *Teaching Marx and Critical Theory in the 21st Century*, edited by Bryant William Sculos and Mary Caputi, 48–65, Leiden, The Netherlands: Brill.

Cox, Ronald W. (2019b) *Corporate Power, Class Conflict and the Crisis of the New Globalization*. Blue Ridge Summit, PA: Lexington Books.

Cox, Ronald W. (2013) "The Corporatization of Higher Education," *Class, Race and Corporate Power*, Vol 1 (1): Article 8.

Cox, Ronald W. and Daniel Skidmore-Hess (2022) "How Neofascism Emerges from Neoliberalism," *New Political Science*, Vol. 44 (4): 590–606.

Freire, Paulo (2000) *Pedagogy of the Oppressed: 30th Anniversary Edition*. New York: Continuium International Publishing Group.

Gindin, Sam (2018) "Socialism for Realists," *Catalyst*, Vol. 2 (3), Fall.

Harris, Jerry (2016) *Global Capitalism and the Crisis of Democracy*. Atlanta, GA: Clarity Press.

Hathaway, Terry (2020) "Neoliberalism as Corporate Power," *Competition and Change*, Vol. 24, (3–4): 315–337.

Molyneux (2021) "State Capitalism Today," *Irish Marxist Review*, Vol. 10, No. 31: 67–69.

Newfield, Christopher (2011) *Unmaking the Public University: the Forty Year Assault on the Middle Class*. Boston: Harvard University Press.

Post, Charlie (2019) "Marxism and the Race Problem," *Marxist Sociology Blog*, Jan. 2.

Robinson, William (2022) *Global Civil War: Capitalism Post-Pandemic*. San Francisco: PM Press.

Robinson, William (2019) *Into the Tempest: Essays in the New Global Capitalism*. Chicago: Haymarket Books.

Sklair, Leslie (2000) *The Transnational Capitalist Class*. Hoboken, NJ: Wiley Blackwell.

Sullivan, Tony (2020) "Post-Structuralism: a Marxist Alternative," *Marxist Left Review*, Mar. 8.

Teschke, Bruno and Heine, Christian (2002) "The Dialectic of Globalization," in *Historical Materialism and Globalization*, edited by Mark Rupert and Hazel Smith. London: Routledge.

Therborn, Goran (2022) "The World and the Left," *New Left Review*, Vol. 137, Sep-Oct.

Young, Kevin A.; Banerjee, Tarun; and Schwartz, Michael (2020) *Levers of Power: How the 1% Rules and What the 99% Can Do About It*. New York: Verso.

Index

Abu Dhabi 85
acp (African, Caribbean, Pacific) states 177–183, 191–200, 203
Adam Smith Institute (U.K.) 113
Adams & Associates 85
Adorno, Theodor 244
Aecom 101
Affordable Care Act 248, 249, 261
Afghanistan
　Soviet invasion 17, 24
　U.S. at war in 15, 21, 22, 28, 31
　U.S. counterinsurgency in 27, 28, 29
　U.S. withdrawal 29, 30, 31
Air Product & Chemicals 101
Airbnb 58
Al-Assad family 125, 126, 127, 128
Al-Benyan, Yousef 92
Al-Qaeda 18, 21, 22, 25, 123, 124
Alcoa mining 101
Allende, Salvador 126
AlliedSignal Aerospace 85
Amazon (*See also* Bezos, Jeff) 55, 57, 59
　Amazon Web Services 67
　in India and Mexico 58
　labor exploitation 68
"Amber and the Amberines", *See* Grenada, U.S. invasion
anc (S. Africa) 118, 119, 120, 121
Antigua 154, 167
Apple 55, 57
　in China 58
　iPhone 59, 60, 66
　labor exploitation 68
Arab Bankers Association of North America 84, 85
Arab Spring, the 5, 108, 117
aramco, *See under* Saudi Aramco
Archer Daniels Midland 63
Archimedes Group 112
artificial intelligence (ai) 57, 66
Arusha Convention (1969) 180
at&t 85
Atomic Energy Agency (iaea) 15
automobile firms, financialization of 63
"axis of evil", *See* rogue states

Babylon Media 129
bae Systems (*See also* Bell Pottinger) 117, 125, 127, 128
Bahamas 153, 154, 155, 167, 170
Bahrain 85, 102
Bank of America 96–97, 99
Bank of Montreal 169
Bank of Nova Scotia, *See* Scotiabank
Barbados 140, 147, 151, 155, 169
　as offshore hub 153, 170
Barclays 144, 156, 163, 169, 170, 171
Bayer 63, 190
Bechtel 85, 86, 87, 100, 101
Belize 146, 154
Bell Pottinger 4
　and A. Lukashenko 112, 125, 126, 127, 128
　and A. Pinochet 112, 125, 126, 127, 128
　and Al-Assad family 125, 126, 127, 128
　and bae Systems 117, 125, 127
　and Iraq 4, 5, 112, 122–125, 128
　and Kirchner family 125, 127
　and South Africa 4, 5, 112, 116, 117–121, 125–130
　and T. Shinawatra 125, 127, 128
　and Thatcher government 4, 5, 108, 111, 112
　and U.S. Defense Department 5, 122
　and Venezuela 127
　collapses 5, 129
　develops political contracts 111–112
　origins 108, 112, 116
　pioneers social media disinformation 5, 128
　Tim Bell 108, 112, 115, 126
Bezos, Jeff (*See also* Amazon) 47, 57, 71
Biden Administration 29, 30, 32, 35
Biebricher, Thomas 239
billionaire class/wealth 2, 3, 43, 46, 72
Bin Salman, Mohammed 89, 99
Bin Talal, Alwaleed 98
Bishop, Maurice 135, 155, 156, 162, 163, 164
Black River Asset Management 65
Blackrock 98
Blackstone 99
Blair, Tony 127, 259

Bloomberg, Michael 47
Boeing 13, 20, 85, 86, 87, 94, 97
Booth, Charles 208
Booz Allen & Hamilton 85
Boston 55
Bretton Woods system 137
Brookings Institute 81
Brown, Wendy 239, 240, 244
Bryan Cave llp 85
Buchi, Hernan 126
Burdeshaw Associates 21
Bureau of Investigative Journalism 129
Burkett, Paul 251
Bush, George H.W. 19
Bush, George W. 21
Bush Administration (G.H.W.) 18, 19, 23, 32
Bush Administration (G.W.) 20, 21, 22, 23, 24, 25
business conflict theory 12
Business Roundtable 16, 198

Cambridge Analytica 111, 112, 128, 129
Cameron, David 259
Canada, oil sales to U.S. 90
Canada-Caribbean Business Cooperation Office 152, 168
Canadian Bank Act 142, 165, 166
Canadian Bankers Association 137
Canadian Council for International Cooperation 145
Canadian Imperial Bank of Commerce (CIBC) 142, 143, 149, 151, 156, 157, 165–171
Canadian International Development Agency 151
Cargill Corporation 62, 63, 65, 67
Cargill family 61, 71
Caribbean (English-speaking)
    British imperialism in 5, 164
    Canadian imperialism in 5, 6, 136, 145, 146
    Commonwealth Caribbean 136, 154
    economic crises in 135
    states gain independence 153, 154, 155
    structural adjustments (SAPs) in 133, 134, 135, 139, 143–146, 151, 152, 153
caribcan agreement 168
caricom (Caribbean Community) 152

cariforum 177, 201, 202
cariforum-eu Economic Partnership Agreement (2008) 6, 7, 179, 193, 199, 201, 202, 203
Carter Administration 81
Census Bureau 48, 49, 56, 61
    Herfindahl-Hirschman Index 48, 49, 50, 54, 60
Center for Security Policy 20, 25
Center for Strategic and International Studies 18
    Reagan report (1988) 18
Centre for Policy Studies 113
    M. Thatcher, president 114
Chavez, Hugo 127
Chevron 87
Chicago, University of 23
Chicago Boys 259
Chime Communications (See also Bell Pottinger) 108
China 89, 92, 255, 256, 268
    foreign investment in 146
    military expansion by 37
    perceived threat from 2, 13–16, 21, 29–37, 123
    sanctions against 35
    tech development by 65
    trade wars with 63
chips and Science Act (2022) 35, 59
CIA (Central Intelligence Agency) 123
Citigroup 86, 96, 98, 99
climate change (See also "green capitalism") 9, 242, 251, 253, 254
Clinton Administration 19, 22, 27, 32
Coard, Bernard 158
Cockfield, Lord 188
Cohen, William 83
Cold War 2, 12, 14, 23, 30, 38, 125
    post-war period 2, 12–26, 30, 31, 32, 187, 194, 241
Commission on Integrated Long-Term Strategy 18
Committee for Economic Development 16
Committee for the Liberation of Iraq 24
Committee on the Present Danger 17, 23, 24
Congo, Democratic Republic of 58
Congress 13, 32, 35, 36, 62, 80, 93, 94, 95, 102
Conservative Party (U.K.) 112, 113, 115, 116, 117

INDEX 279

Containment Doctrine 17
Cooperative Defense Initiative 83
CorpWatch 122
Cotonou Agreement (2000) 177, 179, 193, 194, 199–203
Council on Foreign Relations 17, 81, 82, 84
covidpandemic 35, 37, 47, 57, 60, 61, 63, 172, 237
    essential workers 255
    resultant policies 255–256, 259, 260
    strike, St. Vincent hospital (MA) 256–257
    vaccine production 255, 256
"crony capitalism" 3, 45, 52, 61, 70–71, 72
csFirst Boston 98
Cuadrilla 127
Cuba 18, 134, 151, 164, 255

Daesh, *See* Islamic State
Dardot, Pierre 239, 241, 244, 258, 260
Davies, William 239
Defense Health Programs funding 27
Defense Security Assistance Agency 95
Dekker, Wisse 188
Delores, Jack 188
Department of Agriculture 63
    Farm Service Agency 67
Department of Commerce 83, 86, 89
Department of Defense 11, 13, 14, 19, 22, 29, 31, 37, 38, 83
    Advanced Research Projects Agency Network 59
    aid/development spending 26, 59
    employs Bell Pottinger 5, 122
    Joint Chiefs of Staff 18
    spending 15, 20
Department of Energy 13
Department of Homeland Security 13
Department of Justice 61
Department of State 26, 83, 86
Dewey, John 238
Dimon, Jamie 51
Disney 97
Doha Development Agenda 199
Doha Development Round 199
Dole, Bob 24
Dominica 154
    Defense Force 136, 154
drug dealing 212, 213

dual wage households 223, 224
Duerte, Rodrigo 129

Eastern Caribbean Community (ECC) 147
Eisenhower, Dwight 31
Eisenhower Administration 15
Eli Lilly & Company 85
elite power theory (*See also* Mills, C. Wright) 11, 12, 268
Ellison, Larry 47
Emergency Economic Stabilization Act (2008) 52
Environmental Working Group (U.S.) 63
eurodollars 4, 88
European Commission 183, 186, 187, 188, 195, 197, 199
European Economic Community (EEC)
    Caribbean market access to 7
    Common Agricultural Policy 178, 184, 185
    Generalised Scheme of Preferences 181, 184, 201
    trade agreements (*See also*acp states; gatt; Lomé Conventions) 6, 178, 180, 182, 184
European Green Paper (1996) 199
European Monetary Union 187
European Organization for Nuclear Research (CERN) 59
European Parliament 195
European Roundtable of Industrialists (ERT) 7, 185, 186, 187, 188, 190
European Union (EU) 7
    expansion of 32, 187
Exxon 82, 85
    Exxon Chemical 88
    ExxonMobil 86, 87, 90, 91, 92

Facebook (*See also* Zuckerberg, Mark) 5, 55, 57, 59, 66, 97, 128, 129
Federal Home Loan Mortgage Corporation 53
Federal National Mortgage Association 53
Federal Reserve 43, 52
    Bank 46
Feed the Truth 62
finance sector (U.S.) 3, 46
    concentration in 49–50
    state subsidization 52–54, 66

First Caribbean   169, 170, 171
First Chicago   98
"Fix the Debt" coalition   39
Flint Hills   91
Fluor Corporation   85, 100
fmc Corporation   85
Fontenrose, Kirsten   124
food/beverage sector (U.S.)   3, 46, 47, 65
   and gdp   48
   concentration in   60–61
   income distribution in   61–62
   state subsidization   62–64
Forbes Magazine   46, 47
   Forbes 400 wealth list   63
Ford, Gerald   94
Ford Administration   93
Foreign Service Institute (U.S.)   84
Fortune 500 firms   109
Foster, John Bellamy   251
Foster Wheeler Corporation   85
Foxconn   58
Frankfurt School critical theorists   245
Freedom Caucus (GOP)   249
Friedman, Milton   238, 247
Friedman, Thomas   251
Frito-Lay   60
Fromm, Erich   244, 245

Gairy, Eric   134, 157, 163
Garces, Joan   126
Gates, Bill   47
   as landowner   63
Gates, Robert   26
gatt (General Agreement on Tariffs and Trade)   89, 190, 194
   Article XXIV   196, 202
   Enabling Clause (1979)   196, 201
   Most Favored Nation arrangement   181, 184
   Uruguay Round   189, 192, 197
gdp, U.S. (Gross Domestic Product)   15, 43, 46
General Dynamics   13, 20, 85, 89
General Electric   85, 86, 89, 99
Generalized System of Preferences (U.S)   191
Georgetown University   97, 98
Germany   109
gig economies   57

Global North   2, 241, 244, 255, 268
Global South   2, 68, 134, 136, 185, 190, 193, 194
Global Warming Policy Foundation   114
Goldfarb, Jeffrey   247, 248, 260
Goldman Sachs   51, 98, 99
Google   55, 57, 59, 66
   labor exploitation   68
Great Depression   30, 109
"green capitalism" (*See also* climate change)   9, 251
Grenada   6, 134
   anti-Canada protests   145
   Canadian banks in   156, 157, 161, 162, 163
   money-laundering in   163
   People's Revolutionary Government   135, 156–164
   Royal Bank of Canada and   138, 156, 158
   state banks   157, 158, 159
   U.S. invasion   135, 136, 154, 155, 162–165, 258
Grenada United Labour Party   155, 156, 157
Group of   77, 191
Growth Employment and Redistribution policy (S. Africa)   121
Gulf War, *See under* Iraq
Gupta family   121, 129
Guyana   6, 134, 140, 145, 159
   bank privatizations   150
   borrows from imf   144
   foreign banking law   141
   Royal Bank of Canada leaves   138, 144, 151
   Scotiabank in   149

Hadley, Stephen   24
Haiti   144, 201
Han, Byung-Chul   241
Harvard University   98
Harvey, David   239, 240
Hayek, Friedrich   238, 247
Heritage Foundation (U.S.)   17
Hoechst-Celanese   89
Horkheimer, Max   244
Housing and Economic Recovery Act (U.S., 2008)   53
hsbc bank   99
Hughes Aircraft   89
Hussein, Saddam   24

INDEX　　　　　　　　　　　　　　　　　　　　　　　　　　　　　　281

Icahn, Carl　51
Ignatieff, Michael　122
Impact DataSource　92
information technology sector
　　(U.S.)　3, 35, 46
　　and gdp　47
Inkatha Freedom Party (S. Africa)　118, 120
Institute of Economic Affairs (U.K.)　113, 114
Intel　55
intelligence, privatization of　26
International Monetary Fund (IMF)　6, 134–146, 152, 160, 172
Investopedia　46, 47
Iran　18, 81
　　Shah of　92
　　U.S. foreign policy on　79
Iranian Revolution　17, 92
Iraq　18, 21, 24
　　invasion of Kuwait　18, 19
　　U.S.-backed government　4, 5, 122
　　U.S. cost of war in　29
　　U.S. counterinsurgency in　27, 28
　　U.S.-led war in (Gulf War 1990–1)　4, 15, 19, 22
　　U.S.-led war in (2003–11)　4, 15, 22, 28, 31, 122, 129
　　U.S. occupation　4, 24, 28, 29, 117, 122
　　U.S. withdrawal　28, 30, 31
Iraqi Dream　129
Islamic State of Iraq and the Levant (IS/ISIS/Daesh)　28, 29

Jackman, Frank　145
Jackson, Bruce　24
Jacobs Engineering Group　100
Jamaica　134, 140, 146, 159, 167
　　bank privatizations　150
　　Royal Bank of Canada leaves　138, 149, 151
　　Scotiabank in　149
Jamaica Mutual Life Assurance　146
Japan　81, 109, 187, 189, 268
Jazan (S. Arabia)　99
Johns Hopkins University　98
Joint Trade and Economic Committee　168
Joseph, Keith　113
J.P. Morgan bank　51, 98, 99
Jubail project　100

Kaidanow, Tina　93
Kalanick, Travis (*See also* Uber)　57
Kalicki, Jan H.　82
kbrInc.　100
Kemya joint venture　91
Keynesian economics　12, 16, 109, 186, 191, 217, 238
Khashoggi, Jamal　94
Kirchner family　125, 127, 128
Kissinger, Henry　94
Klein, Naomi　122, 251, 252, 253
Klerk, F.W. de　116, 117, 118, 119, 121
Korean War　15, 23, 24
Kotz, David　239
Kupperman, Charles　25
Kuwait　85

labor
　　devaluation of　44, 68
　　displacement of　44, 68
　　ethnic/racial division of　214
　　exploitation of　3, 7, 8, 52, 67–69, 72
Labour Party (U.K.)　113, 116
Laval, Christian　239, 241, 244, 258, 260
Lawson, Nigel　114
Leonie Industries　125, 129
LexisNexis database　36
Libya　18
Lincoln Group　123, 125, 129
lobbying　45, 70
　　"Arab Lobby"　95
Locke, John　238
Lockheed Martin　13, 20, 24, 25, 85, 87, 89, 94
　　foreign payments　95
Lomé Conventions (1975–2000)　6, 7, 194, 196, 197, 199, 200, 202
　　and aid　183
　　Lomé I (1975–80)　178, 179, 180, 191, 193, 195
　　Lomé II (1980–5)　178, 179, 180, 191, 193
　　Lomé III (1985–90)　178, 179, 193
　　Lomé IV & IV bis (1990–2000)　178, 185, 192, 193
　　neoliberalization of　177, 178
　　rhetoric of　183, 184, 193
　　stabex　179, 182, 183
　　sysmin/minex　179, 182
London, City of, finance hub　46, 113

Lowe Bell (*See also* Bell Pottinger)   108, 116
Lucent Technologies   85
Lucid   96
Lugar, Richard   26
Lukashenko, Aleksandr   125, 126, 127, 128
Lyft   96, 98

Ma'aden mining   86, 101
Maastricht Treaty (1992)   187
MacGuigan, Mark   152
Magic Leap   96
Major, John   127
Malm, Andreas   251
Manchester City Football Club   127
Mandela, Nelson   117, 118, 119, 120
Manley, Michael   134
Marcuse, Herbert   244
market concentration   3, 43
  in finance   49–50
Marxism   12, 207–210, 216, 241, 244, 245, 253, 260, 266, 268, 269
  Eurocentrism of   267
Massachusetts Institute of Technology   98
McDonalds   62
McDonnell Douglas   89, 94, 95
McNamara, Robert   17
Medicaid   248
Medicare   39, 249
Medicare-for-All   249, 250, 261
Merill Lynch   98
Microsoft   57, 59
Miliband, Ralph   241
Mill, John Stuart   238
Mills, C. Wright   11, 12, 20
Ministerial Committee for Privatization and Deregulation (S. Africa)   118
Mirowski, Philip   239, 240
Missile Defense Agency   27
Mitsubishi   89
Mobil   82, 85, 88
Moelis   99
Moore, Jason   251
Morgan Stanley   86, 98, 99
Mosaic Company   101
Motiva   91
Mulroney, Brian   152, 163
Multifibre Arrangement   183
Murdoch, Rupert   113

News Corp   114
  9/11 terror attacks (*See also* Terror, War on)   16–24, 27, 30, 31
  9/11 Commission   25
  post-9/11 period   2, 12, 13, 14, 15, 29, 259
  response to (Bush Doctrine)   22, 24, 25
nafta (North American Free Trade Agreement)   146, 147, 198
nasa (National Aeronautics and Space Administration)   13, 15
National City Bank   144
National Council on U.S.-Arab Relations   82, 83, 85
  B.P. Bacheller, chair   82
  J. Anthony, ceo   82, 83, 85–86
National Defense Industrial Association   38
National Income and Products account   15
National Institute for Public Policy   20, 24, 25
National Intelligence Estimate (G.W. Bush)   25
National Party (S. Africa)   117, 118, 119, 120, 121
National Press Club (U.S.)   83
National Restaurant Association (U.S.)   62
National Security Council (U.S.)   83, 123
  Arms Transfer Initiative   93
National Security Strategy (U.S.)   21
  reports   31
nato (North Atlantic Treaty Organization)
  expansion   24, 32, 33
Neille, Diana   120
neofascism, rise of   259
neoliberal capitalism   2, 3, 43
  conceptual limitations   237, 240
  difficulty in defining   8
  origins   110
  theories of   239
  Third Way and   251
neom project   99, 101
Nestle   190
New Deal (1930s)   217, 218
New Democratic Party (Canada)   138
New Jewel Movement (Grenada)   155, 156
Nicaragua   18
Nimir Petroleum   92
Nixon Administration   88
Non-Aligned Movement (1961)   191
North Korea   18

INDEX

Northrop Grumman   13, 20, 21, 85, 89, 94, 95
nsc-68 (National Security Council paper)   23
Nuclear Posture Review   25
nuclear weapons industry   24
    "low-yield" weapons   25
Nunn, Sam   19

Oakes, Nigel   111
Obama, Barack   246, 247, 248
Obama Administration   28, 31, 34, 102
Obamacare, *See* Affordable Care Act
Occidental Petroleum   98
Office of Munitions Control   95
Office of Security Assistance and Sales   95
Office of the Assist. Sec. of Defense for International Security Affairs   95
offshore finance (*See also* tax)   15, 153, 170
oil price rises (1973)   4
Olayan, Hutham S.   84
Olayan Group   98
opec (Organization of the Petroleum Exporting Countries)   4
Oxfam   62

Parson Corporation   85
patents   59, 60
Patrick, Dan   256
Paulson, John   51, 71
pedagogy of the oppressed   271
pension
    funds   53, 54, 66
    Kentucky Public Pension Authority   67
    state   224
Pepsi   62
Persian Gulf   22, 23, 24, 84
    Bell Pottinger in   5
    Gulf Coast Growth Ventures   91
    Gulf Cooperation Council (gcc)   78, 80
    U.S. access to oil reserves   3
    U.S. militarism in   3, 4, 78, 93, 101–102
    U.S. policies in   78, 79, 80, 82, 101
    U.S. political/economic alliances in   3
    u.s.-gcc Business Initiative   80, 84, 87
    u.s.-gcc Corporate Cooperation Committee   80, 82, 83, 84, 85
Petraeus, David   123
petrodollars   81, 84, 88, 94–99, 142

Petromin   90
Phalippou, Ludovic   53
Philips   190, 191
Pinochet, Augusto   117, 125, 126, 127, 128, 258, 259
Pinochet Foundation   126
Port Arthur (tx) refinery   91
Poulantzas, Nicos   241
Powell, Colin   19
Predix   100
Princeton University   98
Project for the New American Century (pnac)   20, 23, 24
Project on Defense Alternatives   27
Project on Government Oversight   37
Project on Transitional Democracies   24
Putin, Vladimir   33

Qiddiya project   101
Qualcomm   60, 66
Quorum database   36

Rawls, John   238
Raytheon   13, 20, 85, 89, 94, 95
rbtt Financial Holdings   170
Reagan, Ronald   18, 110, 111, 186, 258
Reagan Administration   17, 18, 80, 160, 164
Real Player   124
Reconstruction and Development Plan (S. Africa)   121
Red Sea Development Project   101
'rentierism'   3, 43, 59, 63, 66–67, 72, 112
Republic Bank   170
Riegle-Neal Act (banking)   50
Rogue Doctrine   17, 18, 19, 22, 27
    rogue states   17, 18, 21, 22, 23, 31
Roosevelt, Franklin D.   218, 238
Rowntree, Seebohm   208
Royal Bank of Canada   144, 165
    Caribbean operations   142, 145, 150, 151, 156, 169
    Caribbean pull-outs   138, 143, 149, 151
    Latin American pull-outs   138
Russell 1000 Index   54
Russia   255
    perceived threat from   2, 13–16, 21, 29, 30, 31, 34, 35, 37
Ryan, Paul   247, 248

S&P 500 index   54
Saatchi & Saatchi   108
   Conservative Party contract   112, 115
   "Labour isn't Working" campaign   112, 115, 116
   Maurice Saatchi   115
saicinformation tech   85
St. Kitts and Nevis   154
St. Lucia   154
St. Vincent   138
St. Vincent and the Grenadines   154, 155
San Diego   55
San Francisco   55
San Jose (CA)   55
Sanders, Bernie   246, 249, 250, 263
Sandinista National Liberation Front (Nicaragua)   17
Saudi Arabia   87, 88, 92, 93, 95
   National Guard   94
   Planning Commission   82
   Saudi-U.S. investment/investors   4, 90, 93, 96
   social media investment by   97
   sovereign wealth (Public Investment) fund   79, 89, 90, 96, 97, 98, 101
   U.S. debt creditor   96
   U.S. military sales to   94, 101
   U.S. policies on   78, 79, 80, 81, 101
   U.S.-Saudi Arabia Business Council   80, 84, 86, 87
   U.S.-Saudi Joint Commission on Economic Cooperation   81, 82, 86
Saudi Aramco   79, 86, 87, 90, 91, 92, 99, 100
   Arabian American Oil Company (ARAMCO)   81, 82, 87, 89
   Saudi Aramco Mobil Refinery   91
Saudi Basic Industries Corporation   86, 88, 90, 91
Saudi Electric Company   100
Saudi Refining   91
Saudi Yanbu Petrochemical   91
Scotiabank   142, 151, 156, 161–169
   Caribbean expansion   143, 149
Seaga, Edward   134
Seattle   55
sex work   212–213
shareholder culture   44, 69–70, 72
Shell   88, 90, 91, 96

Shinawatra, Thaksin   125, 127, 128
Silicon Valley   57, 90, 96
Simon, William   88
Single European Act   187, 188
Single European Market   187, 188, 194, 196
Sinopec   92
Sisco Systems   96
Six Flags   101
Slack   96
Smith, Adam   238
Smucker, J.M.   60
Snap   97, 98
SoftBank Corp   96
South Korea   256
Southern California, University of   97, 98
Soviet Union (USSR)   16, 18, 19, 23, 27, 30, 38, 134, 154
   collapse of   32, 123, 146
   invasion of Afghanistan   17, 24
Special Forces (U.S.)   4
stagflation   109, 113
Standard Oil of California   82
Star   91
state benefits   210, 211, 212, 216, 223, 272
   contributory   221
   non-contributory   221–222
Stiglitz, Joseph   67
Stockholm International Peace Research Institute   92–93
structural adjustment policies (SAPS)   133–146, 151, 152, 153, 185
Syria   29, 102

Taiwan   35, 37
Taliban   29
tax   216, 273
   and climate change   252
   avoidance   212, 219
   credits   8, 222
   havens   170
   incentives   49
   local   219, 222
   loopholes   45, 71
   onlabor and the poor   8, 210, 219, 223
   policies   45, 71, 72
   reductions   5, 219, 251
   revenue (U.S.)   15
Taylor, Allan   146

INDEX

tech sector (U.S.)   65
   childlabor in   58
   concentration in   54–56
   income distribution in   56–58
   state subsidization   58–60
Texaco   82, 91
Texas, University of   98
Texas Eastern   89
Thatcher, Margaret   4, 111, 114, 116, 127, 186, 258, 259
   and Bell Pottinger   5, 108
   and Saatchi & Saatchi   112
   and South Africa   118
   government   5, 114
   neoliberal policies   110
Thermo Electron   98
Third World   144
   debt   88
   loans   142
Thompson, Scott   57
threat construction/definition   13, 14, 16, 21, 26–31, 38, 80
Trade and Advisory Committee (U.S.)   198
trade unions   109, 116, 157, 190, 208, 218, 271
Trafigura   127
Trans-European Networks   187
Transamerica   98
Transatlantic Business Dialogue   190
Treasury (U.S.)   52, 83, 96
   bonds   81, 88
Trilateral Commision   81
Trilateral program   90
Trinidad and Tobago   140, 146, 151, 155, 159, 167, 169, 170
   Bank of   138
   revolution (1970)   141
   Royal Bank of Canada in   145, 149
Tronox Limited   101
Troubled Asset Relief Program (TARP)   52
Trudeau, Pierre   163, 164
Trump, Donald   35, 94, 102, 248, 263
Trump Administration   31, 34
trwaerospace   85, 89
Twitter   97, 98, 129

Uber (*See also* Kalanick, Travis)   55, 66, 96
   in Bangladesh and Uganda   58
   labor exploitation   68
Ukraine, Russian invasion of   32, 34

U.S. engagement   33
U.N. Conference on Trade and Development (1964)   191, 195
U.N. General Assembly   163
Unilever   190
United Arab Emirates (UAE)   89, 102
   U.S.-uaeBusiness Council   86
United Technologies   89
universities, corporatization of   270
U.S. Foreign Military Construction Sales agreements   92
U.S. Mideast Policymakers Conference   85
U.S. military spending   11–19, 24–30, 35
U.S.-Qatar Business Council   86

Venezuela   81, 127
Vieques (Puerto Rico)   135
Vietnam War   15, 30
Villiers, Wim de   118
Vinnell Corporation   94, 95
Virginia, intelligence firms in   26
Vision 2030 conference   98, 99
Vogue magazine   126
Von Mises, Ludwig   238
Vonnegut, Kurt   262, 263
Vygotsky, Lev   244

Wall Street, finance hub   46, 65, 99
"War on Terror" (*See also* 9/11)   2, 12, 14, 21, 25–35, 38, 117, 122, 123
   costs of   28
Warren, Elizabeth   36
Washington D.C.   82
welfare state (U.K.)   113, 114, 116
Wells, Martin   123, 124
WeWork   96
Williams, Chris   251
Wilshire 5000 index   54
Windward Islands (Grenada)   154
Wohlstetter, Albert   18, 23
Wolfowitz, Paul   23
World Affairs Council   83
World Bank   6, 117, 134, 140, 160, 162
World Economic Forum   190
World Investment Report (1997)   88
World Trade Organization   34, 89, 189, 194–201, 203
   Dispute Settlement Understanding   196
   lobby access   190

World War II 11
    post-war period 19, 30, 36, 109, 134, 224

Xenel Group 86

Yanpet joint venture 91
Yaoundé Conventions (1963/69) 180, 181

Yemen 102
Yugoslavia (former) 32

Zamil Group 86
Zoom 255
Zuckerberg, Mark 47
Zuma, Jacob 121

www.ingramcontent.com/pod-product-compliance
Lightning Source LLC
Chambersburg PA
CBHW070613030426
42337CB00020B/3778